Equilibrium is a key concept across the natural and the social sciences, both in various precise senses and in its more 'poetic expression'. Valeria Mosini's *Equilibrium in Economics: Scope and Limits* is a rich study by scholars with backgrounds from chemistry to economics to history and philosophy, and there is a great deal to be learned from it – not only about the concept of equilibrium and its history in various sites but also about transfers of ideas and techniques across the sciences, about the relation of theory to evidence and about what makes a research programme progressive.

Nancy Cartwright, Philosophy, London School of Economics

The concept of equilibrium has been central to economics ever since the discipline was established in its modern form. It has been central also to the formulation of fundamental theories in natural sciences: in physics, in the first place, but also in chemistry, biology or ecology. This book is a very accurate historical reconstruction and an excellent presentation of the differences and similarities that characterise the use of the concept of equilibrium in economics and in the natural sciences. It is an important contribution to the present debate on the foundations of scientific knowledge.

Marcello Cini, Physics, Università La Sapienza, Rome

Everyone knows that equilibrium is a bedrock idea in economics, whether in economic theories dealing with economic behaviour (partial equilibrium versus general equilibrium) or in the analysis of financial markets (fundamentals versus ordinary stock market prices). To an economist, economic reasoning without equilibrium is not just heretical; it is impossible. But the natural sciences too deal with equilibrium concepts, which turn out to be quite different in meaning and application from economic equilibria. This book explores these two worlds, asking what we can learn about one world by studying the other.

Mark Blaug, Economics, University of Amsterdam

I have read *Equilibrium in Economics: Scope and Limits* with interest. Although not an economist myself, I have come across these ideas in their physics context and I found them well discussed here. Valeria Mosini's book should be of use and of interest not just to economists, but to scientists as well.

Peter T. Landsberg, Mathematics, University of Southampton

Equilibrium in Economics

Around the 1860s, with the introduction of the neoclassical paradigm, the concept of equilibrium acquired almost as prominent a role in economics as it had already gained in the natural sciences. General Equilibrium Theory (GET), which dominated, by and large, the scene after the Second World War, is founded on the postulated existence, uniqueness and stability of equilibrium in all economic processes. Despite sustained criticism of the emphasis on equilibrium by Austrian economists, Marxists and critical realists, among others, in the main, economists are still reasoning in terms of equilibrium.

A host of international experts in the field come together in this volume to critically evaluate equilibrium both historically and philosophically. They consider whether similarities exist between equilibrium in economics and in the natural sciences, highlight current notions of equilibrium in economics, and examine the links between economic theory and economic reality.

Valeria Mosini is at the London School of Economics and at the University 'La Sapienza' in Rome.

Routledge frontiers of political economy

1 **Equilibrium versus Understanding**
Towards the rehumanization of economics within social theory
Mark Addleson

2 **Evolution, Order and Complexity**
Edited by Elias L. Khalil and Kenneth E. Boulding

3 **Interactions in Political Economy**
Malvern after ten years
Edited by Steven Pressman

4 **The End of Economics**
Michael Perelman

5 **Probability in Economics**
Omar F. Hamouda and Robin Rowley

6 **Capital Controversy, Post-Keynesian Economics and the History of Economics**
Essays in honour of Geoff Harcourt, volume one
Edited by Philip Arestis, Gabriel Palma and Malcolm Sawyer

7 **Markets, Unemployment and Economic Policy**
Essays in honour of Geoff Harcourt, volume two
Edited by Philip Arestis, Gabriel Palma and Malcolm Sawyer

8 **Social Economy**
The logic of capitalist development
Clark Everling

9 **New Keynesian Economics/Post Keynesian Alternatives**
Edited by Roy J. Rotheim

10 **The Representative Agent in Macroeconomics**
James E. Hartley

11 **Borderlands of Economics**
Essays in honour of Daniel R. Fusfeld
Edited by Nahid Aslanbeigui and Young Back Choi

12 **Value, Distribution and Capital**
Essays in honour of Pierangelo Garegnani
Edited by Gary Mongiovi and Fabio Petri

13 **The Economics of Science**
Methodology and epistemology as if economics really mattered
James R. Wible

14 **Competitiveness, Localised Learning and Regional Development**
Specialisation and prosperity in small open economies
Peter Maskell, Heikki Eskelinen, Ingjaldur Hannibalsson, Anders Malmberg and Eirik Vatne

15 **Labour Market Theory**
A constructive reassessment
Ben J. Fine

16 **Women and European Employment**
Jill Rubery, Mark Smith, Colette Fagan and Damian Grimshaw

17 **Explorations in Economic Methodology**
From Lakatos to empirical philosophy of science
Roger Backhouse

18 **Subjectivity in Political Economy**
Essays on wanting and choosing
David P. Levine

19 **The Political Economy of Middle East Peace**
The impact of competing trade agendas
Edited by J. W. Wright, Jnr

20 **The Active Consumer**
Novelty and surprise in consumer choice
Edited by Marina Bianchi

21 **Subjectivism and Economic Analysis**
Essays in memory of Ludwig Lachmann
Edited by Roger Koppl and Gary Mongiovi

22 **Themes in Post-Keynesian Economics**
Essays in honour of Geoff Harcourt, volume three
Edited by Claudio Sardoni and Peter Kriesler

23 **The Dynamics of Technological Knowledge**
Cristiano Antonelli

24 **The Political Economy of Diet, Health and Food Policy**
Ben J. Fine

25 **The End of Finance**
Capital market inflation, financial derivatives and pension fund capitalism
Jan Toporowski

26 **Political Economy and the New Capitalism**
Edited by Jan Toporowski

27 **Growth Theory**
A philosophical perspective
Patricia Northover

28 **The Political Economy of the Small Firm**
Edited by Charlie Dannreuther

29 **Hahn and Economic Methodology**
Edited by Thomas Boylan and Paschal F. O'Gorman

30 **Gender, Growth and Trade**
The miracle economies of the post-war years
David Kucera

31 **Normative Political Economy**
Subjective freedom, the market and the State
David Levine

32 **Economist with a Public Purpose**
Essays in honour of John Kenneth Galbraith
Edited by Michael Keaney

33 **Involuntary Unemployment**
The elusive quest for a theory
Michel De Vroey

34 **The Fundamental Institutions of Capitalism**
Ernesto Screpanti

35 **Transcending Transaction**
The search for self-generating markets
Alan Shipman

36 **Power in Business and the State**
An historical analysis of its concentration
Frank Bealey

37 **Editing Economics**
Essays in honour of Mark Perlman
Hank Lim, Ungsuh K. Park and Geoff Harcourt

38 **Money, Macroeconomics and Keynes**
Essays in honour of Victoria Chick, volume one
Philip Arestis, Meghnad Desai and Sheila Dow

39 **Methodology, Microeconomics and Keynes**
Essays in honour of Victoria Chick, volume two
Philip Arestis, Meghnad Desai and Sheila Dow

40 **Market Drive and Governance**
Reexamining the rules for economic and commercial contest
Ralf Boscheck

41 **The Value of Marx**
Political economy for contemporary capitalism
Alfredo Saad-Filho

42 **Issues in Positive Political Economy**
S. Mansoob Murshed

43 **The Enigma of Globalisation**
A journey to a new stage of capitalism
Robert Went

44 **The Market**
Equilibrium, stability, mythology
S. N. Afriat

45 **The Political Economy of Rule Evasion and Policy Reform**
Jim Leitzel

46 **Unpaid Work and the Economy**
Edited by Antonella Picchio

47 Distributional Justice
Theory and measurement
Hilde Bojer

48 Cognitive Developments in Economics
Edited by Salvatore Rizzello

49 Social Foundations of Markets, Money and Credit
Costas Lapavitsas

50 Rethinking Capitalist Development
Essays on the economics of Josef Steindl
Edited by Tracy Mott and Nina Shapiro

51 An Evolutionary Approach to Social Welfare
Christian Sartorius

52 Kalecki's Economics Today
Edited by Zdzislaw L. Sadowski and Adam Szeworski

53 Fiscal Policy from Reagan to Blair
The left veers right
Ravi K. Roy and Arthur T. Denzau

54 The Cognitive Mechanics of Economic Development and Institutional Change
Bertin Martens

55 Individualism and the Social Order
The social element in liberal thought
Charles R. McCann Jnr

56 Affirmative Action in the United States and India
A comparative perspective
Thomas E. Weisskopf

57 Global Political Economy and the Wealth of Nations
Performance, institutions, problems and policies
Edited by Phillip Anthony O'Hara

58 Structural Economics
Thijs ten Raa

59 Macroeconomic Theory and Economic Policy
Essays in honour of Jean-Paul Fitoussi
Edited by K. Vela Velupillai

60 The Struggle Over Work
The 'end of work' and employment alternatives in post-industrial societies
Shaun Wilson

61 The Political Economy of Global Sporting Organisations
John Forster and Nigel Pope

62 The Flawed Foundations of General Equilibrium Theory
Critical essays on economic theory
Frank Ackerman and Alejandro Nadal

63 Uncertainty in Economic Theory
Essays in honor of David Schmeidler's sixty-fifth birthday
Edited by Itzhak Gilboa

64 The New Institutional Economics of Corruption
Edited by Johann Graf Lambsdorff, Markus Taube and Matthias Schramm

65 The Price Index and its Extension
A chapter in economic measurement
S. N. Afriat

66 Reduction, Rationality and Game Theory in Marxian Economics
Bruce Philp

67 Culture and Politics in Economic Development
Volker Bornschier

68 Modern Applications of Austrian Thought
Edited by Jürgen G. Backhaus

69 Ordinary Choices
Individuals, incommensurability, and democracy
Robert Urquhart

70 Labour Theory of Value
Peter C. Dooley

71 Capitalism
Victor D. Lippit

72 Macroeconomic Foundations of Macroeconomics
Alvaro Cencini

73 Marx for the Twenty-first Century
Edited by Hiroshi Uchida

74 Growth and Development in the Global Political Economy
Social structures of accumulation and modes of regulation
Phillip Anthony O'Hara

75 The New Economy and Macroeconomic Stability
A neo-modern perspective drawing on the complexity approach and Keynesian economics
Teodoro Dario Togati

76 The Future of Social Security Policy
Women, work and a citizen's basic income
Ailsa McKay

77 Clinton and Blair
The political economy of the third way
Flavio Romano

78 Marxian Reproduction Schema
Money and aggregate demand in a capitalist economy
A. B. Trigg

79 The Core Theory in Economics
Problems and solutions
Lester G. Telser

80 Economics, Ethics and the Market
Introduction and applications
Johan J. Graafland

81 Social Costs and Public Action in Modern Capitalism
Essays inspired by Karl William Kapp's *Theory of Social Costs*
Edited by Wolfram Elsner, Pietro Frigato and Paolo Ramazzotti

82 **Globalization and the Myths of Free Trade**
History, theory and empirical evidence
Edited by Anwar Shaikh

83 **Equilibrium in Economics**
Scope and limits
Edited by Valeria Mosini

Equilibrium in Economics

Scope and Limits

Edited by Valeria Mosini

Routledge
Taylor & Francis Group
LONDON AND NEW YORK

First published 2007
by Routledge
2 Park Square, Milton Park, Abingdon, Oxon OX14 4RN

Simultaneously published in the USA and Canada
by Routledge
270 Madison Ave, New York, NY 10016

Routledge is an imprint of the Taylor & Francis Group, an informa business

Typeset in Times by Wearset Ltd, Boldon, Tyne and Wear
Printed and bound in Great Britain by MPG Books Ltd, Bodmin

British Library Cataloguing in Publication Data
A catalogue record for this book is available from the British Library

Library of Congress Cataloging in Publication Data
A catalog record for this book has been requested

ISBN10: 0-415-39137-7 (hbk)
ISBN10: 0-203-08668-6 (ebk)

ISBN13: 978-0-415-39137-5 (hbk)
ISBN13: 978-0-203-08668-1 (ebk)

To the memory of my grandmother Ida,
for teaching me what matters in life, and what doesn't

Contents

Illustrations

Contributors

Roger E. Backhouse is Professor of the History and Philosophy of Economics at the University of Birmingham. He is author or editor of several books on the history of economics and economic methodology, including *The Penguin History of Economics/The Ordinary Business of Life* (2002) and (as editor, with Bradley W. Bateman) *The Cambridge Companion to Keynes* (2006). He has been review editor of the *Economic Journal*, one of the editors of the *Journal of Economic Methodology*, and is an associate editor of the *Journal of the History of Economic Thought.*

Bernadette Bensaude-Vincent, Doctor in Philosophy (Paris–Sorbonne, 1981), is Professor of History and Philosophy of Science in the Department of Philosophy of the University of Paris X (France). Her research interests are the history and philosophy of chemistry and the science/public issue. Among other titles she is the author of *Lavoisier, mémoires d'une révolution* (1993), *A History of Chemistry* (with Isabelle Stengers, 1996), *Eloge du mixte. Matériaux nouveaux et philosophie ancienne* (1998), *La science et l'opinion. Histoire d'un divorce* (2000), *Se libérer de la matière? Fantasmes autour des nouvelles technologies* (2004) and *Faut-il avoir peur de la chimie?* (2005).

Victoria Chick is Emeritus Professor of Economics at University College London. She writes on monetary theory and policy, on the economics of Keynes and on methodological issues in monetary theory and macroeconomics. Recent work includes 'On open systems', *Brazilian Journal of Political Economy* 24 (2004), 'Theory, method and mode of thought in Keynes's *General Theory*', *Journal of Economic Methodology* 10 (2003) and 'Lost and found: some history of endogenous money in the twentieth century', in G. Fontana and R. Realfonzo (eds), *The Monetary Theory of Production* (2005).

Andy Denis is Senior Lecturer in Political Economy in the Department of Economics, City University, London, and currently Research Associate at the Centre for Philosophy of Natural and Social Science, LSE. His research interests are in the history and philosophy of economics and in heterodox economics. He has published papers on Smith, Hayek, Keynes and the methodology of economics.

William Dixon teaches macroeconomics, history of economic thought and political economy in the Department of Economics, Finance and International Business at London Metropolitan University. He researches and writes on issues relating to the economic discipline considered within a social context.

Alan Freeman is a visiting fellow of the University of Greenwich and an economist at the Greater London Authority. He is co-editor, with Boris Kagarlitsky, of *The Politics of Empire. The End of Globalisation* (2004). He wrote *The Benn Heresy* (1982), a biography of Tony Benn, and has co-edited three books on value theory with Ernest Mandel, Guglielmo Carchedi, Andrew Kliman and Julian Wells.

Ivor Grattan-Guinness is holder of both the doctorate (Ph.D.) and higher doctorate (D.Sc.) in the history of science at the University of London, he is Emeritus Professor of the History of Mathematics and Logic at Middlesex University, London. From 1986 to 1988 he was the President of the British Society for the History of Mathematics. Editor of the history of science journal *Annals of Science* from 1974 to 1981, in 1979 he also founded the journal *History and Philosophy of Logic*, editing it until 1992. He is an effective member of the Académie Internationale d'Histoire des Sciences. He edited a substantial *Companion Encyclopedia of the History and Philosophy of the Mathematical Sciences* (two volumes, 1994). His individual books include *Convolutions in French Mathematics, 1800–1840* (three volumes, 1990), *The Fontana and Norton History of the Mathematical Sciences: The Rainbow of Mathematics* (1997) and *The Search for Mathematical Roots, 1870–1940: Logics, Set Theories and the Foundations of Mathematics from Cantor through Russell to Gödel* (2000). He was the associate editor for mathematicians and statisticians for the *Oxford Dictionary of National Biography* (2004). He edited a large collection of essays on *Landmark Writings in Western Mathematics, 1640–1940* (2005).

Louise Jarvis is a final-year PhD student in the department of Science and Technology Studies at University College London. She trained as an evolutionary biologist (University of Exeter 1995–98) but adopted a historical approach to the study of evolutionary biology through the Master's programme in the Philosophy of Science, Technology and Medicine at Imperial College London (1999–2000). She studies the history of the Darwinism versus Lamarckism debate of the late twentieth century, with particular attention to the social study of controversy as it relates to this case study.

Tony Lawson is Reader in Economics in the Faculty of Economics at the University of Cambridge. He edits the Routledge Series 'Economics as Social theory'. Amongst his various publications are the books *Economics and Reality* (1997) and *Reorienting Economics* (2003).

Valeria Mosini has a tenure position at the Science Faculty of 'La Sapienza' in Rome; she is also Associate of the Centre for the Philosophy of Natural and

Social Sciences of the London School of Economics, where, from the academic year 2003–04, she has been seminar leader for 'Dissent in Science'. She has published widely in chemistry and, more recently, in history and philosophy of science.

Warren J. Samuels is Professor Emeritus of Economics at Michigan State University (East Lansing). His principal fields are the history of economic thought, methodology, and the economic role of government. He is co-editor of *Research in the History of Economic Thought and Methodology*, an annual. His most recent book is *Essays on the History of Economics*. His principal current work is on the use of the concept of the invisible hand.

Jim Thomas is Emeritus Reader in Economics at the London School of Economics. Having carried out research on informal economic activity, in particular on the urban informal sector and urban poverty in Latin American and on the history of econometrics, he is writing a book on the history of economics at LSE.

Richard van den Berg is Principal Lecturer at the Business School of Kingston University, Kingston on Thames. He teaches statistics and managerial economics. His primary area of research is the social and economic thought of the French Enlightenment.

François Vatin holds a doctorate in economics and in sociology. He is professor at the University of Paris X and the director of the postgraduate programme in social science and sociology. He is also researcher in the IDHE-CNRS Laboratory (Institutions et dynamiques historiques de l'économie, Centre National de la Recherche Scientifique) and co-Director of the CNRS network Economics and Sociology. He has written many works on industrial sociology, economic sociology and the history of technical, economic and social thought in nineteenth-century France.

David Wilson is senior lecturer in the Department of Economics, Finance and International Business at London Metropolitan University. His main area of work is in the historical and conceptual foundations of modern economics. Recent publications include papers on the communications-theoretic basis of Adam Smith's economics and the critique of games theory, and a forthcoming book on the value theory of Karl Marx.

Foreword

Frank Ackerman

There is an essential strangeness about modern economic theory, an inescapable sense of mistaken or misstated identity. Economics is the study of activities that occur only in human societies; one might think that it was securely located in the social sciences. Yet economics bears little resemblance to other social sciences, except in so far as other fields have recently begun to emulate economics. Description and analysis of society exist within mainstream economics only in ever narrower, more mathematical forms.

What economic theory looks like, at first glance, is a natural science. The mathematical apparatus, deductive approach and dense professional jargon seem like something that might be at home in the physics department. But a second look reveals important differences. The physical sciences, despite their abstract theorising, ultimately refer back to experiments whose results are decisive for the acceptance or rejection of theories. In contrast, 'experimental economics' is a very recent and subsidiary part of the discipline of economics; most of the interesting questions in the field are not susceptible to controlled experiments. The biological sciences, with their focus on organisms, ecosystems and evolution, seem like more promising models, but they have had surprisingly little influence on economists.

Some American bookstores have resolved the identity puzzle by classifying economics books neither with social sciences nor with natural sciences but rather with business literature (an unfortunate decision for those of us who write non-business-oriented economics). At least it seems clear that economics is not part of the humanities. And, with any luck, it remains in the non-fiction section.

The identity puzzle results in no small part from economists' adoption of mathematical models and techniques from physics. As the chapters of this volume demonstrate, conscious borrowing from physics stretches back to the late nineteenth-century writings of Leon Walras, and perhaps even earlier. The trend only intensified throughout the twentieth century, as more and more advanced mathematical techniques were imported into economic theory. Understanding what works and what doesn't work, in the apparatus borrowed from physics, is one of the central challenges for economics today, and one to which this book makes an excellent contribution.

My personal suspicion is that the success of quantum mechanics set an overpowering example, from which economists learned all the wrong lessons. Quantum mechanics begins with bizarrely counter-intuitive assumptions; continues with incredibly difficult mathematical analysis; and arrives at astonishingly accurate empirical predictions. As a result of all that impenetrable mathematics, some physical constants are predicted to nine significant figures. In economics it is exactly the same – all except for the predictions. There are certainly no economic constants that are reliably predicted to two significant figures; arguably, there are no economic constants that are predicted at all by abstract economic theory. It is far from clear what would count as a sufficiently accurate empirical prediction to validate the avant-garde developments in economics today. Milton Friedman's famous essay on positive economics, often cited in defence of intricate mathematical analyses, explicitly endorses the use of counter-intuitive or implausible assumptions, so long as they lead to valuable results (Friedman 1953). This is undoubtedly reasonable in the abstract; the more controversial question is, how often is it applicable to economics today? How often are the results valuable in any broad sense? On this point the authors represented here, like economists more generally, continue to disagree.

The concept of equilibrium, the subject of this book, is one of the central pillars of the Great Borrowing from physics. Reasoning about equilibrium pervades economic theory: in the basic story of general equilibrium, voluntary exchange matches up buyers and sellers, prices float until everyone is content, and all markets clear. The similarity to the ideal gas law of physics is not at all accidental, as Paul Samuelson, who did so much to formalise the economic theory, relied on and sought to incorporate the insights of nineteenth-century thermodynamics.

The first part of this book demonstrates that the concept of equilibrium in the natural sciences is much subtler and more complex than one would guess from its reflections in economics. Physics, chemistry and biology all have multiple understandings of equilibrium – and there is more to thermodynamics, even in its classical form, than Samuelson understood. The second part recalls the multifaceted thoughts, on issues related to equilibrium, of Adam Smith and other forefathers of economics (back then they were all men). These chapters convey an interest in moral and philosophical questions that suggests the early economists could have felt at home in the humanities section of the bookstore.

The final part of the book returns to the present, with rival perspectives on the use of equilibrium in economics today. Why does this relatively technical topic generate so much interest and debate? The answer leads back to the question of the uniqueness of social sciences – for economics is, undeniably, a social science. It has been clear at least since the work of Max Weber that social sciences are different, because their 'elementary particles' are autonomous actors who can understand, argue, influence and act on each other in ways that cannot entirely be predicted. The failure of the physical science analogies turns on this, among other points, as I suggested in my contribution to the debate (Ackerman 2002).

In addition, because the subject matter is society, findings in social science have a directly ideological meaning that is muted or mediated in the natural sciences. The question of equilibrium, or its absence, is politically loaded: in informal discussion it blends into a judgement about whether the economy is working well or needs fundamental change.

Imagine a group of aeronautical engineers, of varying political perspectives, working on the design of a new aeroplane. They will have the same criteria, and the same interest in getting the answer right, when addressing the problem of whether air currents will flow smoothly or turbulently around the plane. Turbulence is much farther from physical equilibrium than smooth airflow, but conservative engineers and their left-wing colleagues will apply the same standards in understanding and dealing with turbulence.

Now imagine a group of economic advisers, of varying political perspectives, working on the design of a new public sector employment programme. Is it possible to believe that they will have the same standards for judging labour market equilibrium, the same interpretations of 'turbulence' in the market? Different interpretations of market outcomes and economic equilibrium go to the heart of why some are politically on the left and some on the right.

In short, social sciences are not only less predictable, because of human agency and behaviour, but also more ideological, because of their implications for human welfare. A notion from the biological sciences, such as Stephen Jay Gould's image of 'punctuated equilibrium' in evolution (equilibrium as the normal state of affairs, punctuated by occasional bursts of rapid change), might seem like a promising analogy for economics. But it also might sound reminiscent of sophisticated forms of Marxism, leaving conservatives happy that Gould stuck to writing about biology and baseball.

The uses and abuses of equilibrium in economics are guaranteed to remain important, and controversial, for the foreseeable future. Congratulations to the authors and editor for producing a valuable book that advances our understanding of the question.

References

Ackerman, F. (2002), 'Still dead after all these years: interpreting the failure of general equilibrium theory', *Journal of Economic Methodology*, 9(2), 119–39.

Friedman, M. ed. (1953), 'The methodology of positive economics', *Essays in Positive Economics*, Chicago: University of Chicago Press.

Preface

Most, if not all, the chapters in this book are written versions of talks given in the academic year 2003–04 and in the Michaelmas term of 2004–05 at the Centre for the Philosophy of the Natural and Social Sciences of the London School of Economics. The talks were part of the activities of the seminar series 'Dissent in Science' that I had created a year earlier.

The idea to discuss economic equilibrium, however, originated in another seminar series, aimed to critically discuss mainstream economics, that Giorgio Di Maio and I had organised in 2001 at the Science Faculty of 'La Sapienza' in Rome. The speakers, Giorgio Rodano, Domenico Tosato, Roberto Ciccone and Giorgio Israel, did not mention the concept of economic equilibrium more than in passing, and concentrated on other issues.

After listening carefully to the talks, I (a chemist with a long-standing interest in history and philosophy of science) was struck by the fact that, although equilibrium seemed more a postulate of economic theorising than a feature of actual economic systems, and although its meaning was far from being clearly defined, there seemed to be little appetite among the speakers (and the audience, for that matter) to challenge the use of the concept of equilibrium in economics. I persevered in thinking that economic equilibrium deserved discussing and, with a bit of luck, managed to convince a few colleagues that this was so. The rest is in this book.

Valeria Mosini

Acknowledgements

Among the contributors in this book, I wish to thank in particular Roger Backhouse and Ivor Grattan-Guinness for editorial advice, and Tony Lawson for generous encouragement and friendly support.

I am deeply grateful to Nancy Cartwright, Director of CPNSS, and to the Leverhulme Foundation for the three-year grant awarded in January 2005 to fund the activities of the seminar series 'Dissent in Science'.

Without Robin Judd's (IT, LSE) help, it would have taken very long for this book to see the light of day.

I also wish to thank some of my colleagues at La Sapienza, in particular Giuseppe D'Ascenzo and Aldo Laganà (Chemistry) for allowing me the intellectual freedom required to embark on the interdisciplinary 'adventure' represented by this book. I am also grateful (in alphabetical order), to Marcello Cini (Physics), Giorgio Di Maio (Chemistry), Giorgio Rodano, Michele Tucci and Domenico Tosato (Economics). Carlo Sperilli and Giuliano Gervasoni lent a generous hand with technical problems when I was working on the book from Rome. Silvio Bergia (Physics, Bologna) and Mark Blaug (Economics, Amsterdam) read and commented on a draft of the introduction.

My loved ones helped me a lot, and they know it, and so did my friends.

V.M.

Introduction

Three ways of looking at economic equilibrium

Valeria Mosini

The concept of equilibrium has been central to economic theorising ever since the discipline was established in its modern form. For Adam Smith, one of the founders of classical political economics in the eighteenth century, equilibrium represented the harmonious outcome of the behaviour of selfish individuals achieving co-ordination as if under the influence of an 'invisible hand'. Smith's concept of equilibrium resulted from a qualitative analysis of economic affairs heavily influenced by considerations of a political, social, and moral nature.

By contrast, Léon Walras, and the other founders of neoclassical economics in the late nineteenth century, endowed the concept of equilibrium with a 'scientific' character largely associated with the mathematisation of the discipline, which was assumed to have put economics in the same basket as the natural sciences. These, physics, in particular, had been extensively mathematicised in the first decades of the nineteenth century, as a result of the spreading of Newton's philosophy and methodology of science (see, for instance, Fox 1974).

The mathematisation of economics turned equilibrium into a 'magnitude' that could be indirectly measured, as it were, through the values of the system's parameters just as it is in the natural sciences. However, most economists, rather then concerning themselves with checking the validity of the equilibrium assumption of the neoclassical school, accepted it as a fact, and debated whether economic equilibrium was partial, in its obtaining in a single market (see, for instance, Marshall 1890), or general, in its relating to the supplies and demands of all commodities (see, for instance, Hicks 1939). John Maynard Keynes gave a uniquely important contribution by aiming to construct a theory that might have an equilibrium among other results while enabling the determination of disequilibrium positions as well.

The formulation by Kenneth Arrow and Gérard Debreu in 1954 of a model that 'proved' the general character of economic equilibrium[1] glorified (or pushed one step too far, depending on opinion) the mathematical interpretation of the concept. Arrow and Debreu's model met with serious difficulties, principally of a conceptual nature (as in the case of the question of the uniqueness of equilibrium), but also related to finding data from real economies that would corroborate the model and ways of accounting for the dynamic processes leading to the

1 See also McKenzie (1954).

convergence to the equilibrium point. Perceptive critiques of the concept of economic equilibrium developed, most notably in Cambridge in the 1970s, inspired and led by as prominent economists as Joan Robinson and Nicholas Kaldor.

Alternative schemes of accounting for economic events, such as those based on game theory, evolutionary thinking, non-linear dynamics, emerged, and disequilibrium economics developed.[2] Yet the belief in an equilibrium theory has survived and still provides the dominating paradigm in economics, unrivalled both in the academic *milieu* (with consequences on the teaching of the discipline) and in discussion of policy strategies and related action. If anything, the recent emphasis on the part of economists, politicians and the media on the allegedly unquestionably positive impact of globalisation – which heavily relies on general equilibrium – shows the persistent influence of the equilibrium paradigm in the face of the several failed (sometimes disastrously) abrupt exportations of the open economy model into developing countries,[3] or those of the ex-socialist bloc.

This state of affairs notwithstanding, the need to re-discuss economic equilibrium has been felt of late in some quarters, leading to important works such as Addleson's (1995), Mandler's (1999), and Ackerman and Nadal's (2004) books. *Equilibrium in Economics: Scope and Limits* is a further contribution to that discussion. It addresses the question of economic equilibrium along three main lines, and is, therefore, divided in three parts.

Part I – which represents a novelty with respect to the discussion in the literature thus far – provides an overview of the way in which equilibrium is treated in the natural sciences that will prove useful in taking a fresh look at the ways in which the notion of equilibrium has been deployed in economics. This is all the more true given that the founders of neoclassical economics had defended their assigning a central role to equilibrium by claiming that various analogies existed between economics and the natural science, which made it credible that, just as there is equilibrium in the natural world, so there is in the economic world.

Part II addresses the question of the meaning invariance over time of the concept of economic equilibrium: surely, a requisite for a concept endowed with such a central role. In particular, the chapters in Part II discuss whether the connotations and meaning attributed to economic equilibrium by A. Smith, the crucial figure of classical political economics, and by A.N. Isnard and A.A. Cournot, who are often represented as French precursors of neoclassical economics, are compatible with the connotations and meaning attributed to economic equilibrium by L. Walras.

Part III presents seven different ways of looking at the concept of equilibrium from the point of view of contemporary economics.

Part I requires the definition of some basic concepts from the natural sciences, while the other two parts are introduced in a rather straightforward manner.

2 For a recent reassessment of disequilibrium economics, see De Vroey (2002).

3 See Nadal (2004a).

The three parts

My starting point in Part I is the *fact* that there is a great deal of equilibrium in the world we live in: so much so that, whenever equilibrium is lost, whether in the body (or in the mind) or in the environment, the consequences are always serious, sometimes tragic. Equilibrium was a precondition for the establishment of life on Earth, and remains an essential ingredient for maintaining life; accordingly, equilibrium is a key concept in the theoretical body of the natural sciences. (I return to this point later, when I discuss the interplay between theory and evidence, respectively, in the natural sciences, and in economics.) Recall, for instance, that one of the first realisations of modern science was that rectilinear, uniform, motion represents a state of equilibrium, and that Newton's second law – which describes the effect of a force on a system at rest or in uniform motion – could be formulated only against the background of the aforementioned realisation.

Equilibrium, and its various conditions, form the subject-matter of as large a sub-discipline as statics, one of the three branches of mechanics, together with dynamics and kinematics. Thermal equilibrium was the starting point for the discovery, stated in the first law of thermodynamics, that heat is a form of energy, which, together with mechanical energy, is conserved.[4] Electrodynamics was established through equilibrium experiments with which, in 1820, André Marie Ampère tested his genial intuition, prompted by Christian Oersted's experiments, that electricity and magnetism interact and interconvert, something that was ruled out at the time.[5]

The list of examples of the crucial role of the concept of equilibrium in the natural sciences may be long; the ones just given suffice to prepare the ground for a few definitions of equilibrium taken from the basic lexicon of physics.

A system is said to be in equilibrium in a given domain when the values of the system's parameters that are relevant to that domain are constant over time. The number of relevant parameters varies from domain to domain. If thermal equilibrium is considered, temperature is the only relevant parameter: thermal equilibrium is the state in which all parts of the system are at the same temperature, and this is the same as that of the environment. If mechanical equilibrium is considered, a distinction needs drawing between static and dynamic equilibrium. The former corresponds to the system being at rest (with respect to translation and rotation) and the position of the system is the only relevant parameter; the latter corresponds, for instance, to a pendulum oscillating with constant period in a vacuum, with the position of the system and its velocity (or period, in the pendulum case) as the relevant parameters.

4 The discovery of the conservation of energy was made, around the same time, by several scientists – Mayer, Joule, Helmholtz – a fact that led Kuhn (1957) to speak of it as a 'simultaneous discovery'.

5 For Ampère's insistence on the stumbling-block effect exerted by the unproven hypothesis that electricity and magnetism were altogether different kinds of imponderables, which could not influence each other in any way, see Ampère's letter to his friend Roux-Bordier discussed in Mosini (2002).

Notably, dynamical equilibrium is not confined to mechanics; in thermodynamics, for instance, the equilibrium distribution of a given substance between two phases, say, liquid and gas, exemplifies dynamic equilibrium in that it corresponds to the same number of molecules evaporating and condensing per second. The relevant parameters in a phase distribution are pressure and temperature.[6] Other kinds of equilibria depend on more than just two parameters.[7]

Equilibrium, whether static or dynamic, is also defined as stable, unstable and neutral, and these definitions are given with respect to the energy of the system, be it mechanical, thermodynamic or other. A system is said to be in stable equilibrium when its total energy is at a minimum, in unstable equilibrium when its total energy is at a maximum and in neutral equilibrium when its total energy is constant. Slight changes in one or more parameter of the system, which produce slight changes in the system's total energy, have different effects depending on the system being in stable or unstable equilibrium, and no effect at all on a system in neutral equilibrium. In the case of stable equilibrium, the system reacts against the change, balancing it, and reverting to the initial equilibrium. In the case of unstable equilibrium, the system follows the change to completion, reaching a different energy state, which, more often than not, is one of stable equilibrium. (These definitions will be useful in reading the chapters by Grattan-Guinness and by Bensaude-Vincent and Mosini.)

An important element in comparing the way in which equilibrium is treated in the natural sciences with economics relates to the relation between evidence and theory in the two domains. In the natural sciences, the relation in question is one of mutual, incessant, interplay, with evidence providing either the observation that suggests, or the experimentation that tests to corroborate or reject, a given theoretical account. Equilibrium is no exception: the various concepts of equilibrium employed in the natural sciences represent, no question about it, idealisations of the states of affairs they stand for. But these idealisations, and the models they give rise to, have been severely tested against evidence for their empirical adequacy prior to being accepted into the conceptual body of science.

The same cannot be said of economic equilibrium, which became the central concept of the discipline prior to being ascertained that there *is* enough equilibrium in *actual* economic processes to justify the concept acquiring so central a

6 The concept of dynamical equilibrium, whether in mechanics or in thermodynamics, stands in stark contrast with the concept of dynamical equilibrium in economics, which refers either to a process leading to equilibrium in the short or in the long run (Marshall 1890: book 5, chapter 1), or to the succession of instantaneous *equilibria* in time. (For discussion of stationary and dynamic concepts of economic equilibrium see Donzelli (1986).

7 Thermodynamic equilibrium, for instance, corresponds to the system being in mechanical equilibrium (with no unbalanced force inside it or between it and the surroundings), as well as in thermal and chemical equilibrium. Since chemical equilibrium, in turn, is defined as the state in which the chemical potential is the same for all the system's components, and since the chemical potential of each chemical species is defined as the first derivative of the total energy of that species, which depends on the entropy, volume and number of particles (Gibbs 1875–78; Duhem 1886), these parameters are all relevant to chemical equilibrium, and, through this, to thermodynamic equilibrium.

role. Although several influential economists insist that the concept of equilibrium applies to theoretical models, not to actual economies (see, for instance, Dorfman *et al.* 1958; Weintraub 1983), accepting this position would create a gulf with the natural sciences, which, ever since Galileo's time, have required the corroboration of theories by data.[8]

The fact that evidence and theory interplay differently in the natural sciences and in economics is suggested, for example – and in a wider context than that of equilibrium – by Machlup's definition of an 'operational theory', which he described as one having 'links with the practical domain, with data of observation' (Machlup 1963, p. 66), rating those links as sufficient 'if they allow us . . . to subject the theoretical system to *occasional* verification against empirical evidence' (Machlup 1963, p. 66, my emphasis). Machlup was speaking within the context of economics; by contrast, in physics, where operationalism was originally formulated (Bridgman 1927), it required that scientific concepts be *always* defined in terms of the set of operations involved in the measuring procedures of the entities they refer to. Although the term 'operationalism' has acquired over time slightly different connotations, to reflect specific measurement problems in the different contexts, it always takes measurability, whether direct or indirect, as a mandatory requirement for scientific concepts to be meaningfully defined.

The different ways in which evidence and theory interplay, respectively, in the natural sciences and in economics should be taken into account in evaluating the analogies that the neoclassical economists invoked between their theories and the physical sciences, mechanics in particular.[9] Stanley Jevons, for instance, claimed that the trading ratios of the marginal utilities of two goods followed the same mathematical expression as that stated by the law of the lever (Jevons 1879), and Walras that the laws through which the market determines prices are similar in all respect to those ruling the motions of the celestial bodies (Walras 1909). Fisher claimed that the laws of fluid dynamics are appropriate in describing economic equilibrium (Fisher 1892). Marshall preferred to draw analogies with biology, but in rather vague terms, when he claimed, for instance, that, as economies progress, demand and supply go from being represented by a mechanical equilibrium to being represented by an equilibrium between organic forces (Marshall 1890).

The question of the different ways in which evidence and theory interplay in the natural sciences and in economics has a bearing also on critical analyses of neoclassical theories that identified inspirational links between these and

8 A requirement that became the core of Bacon's (1620) and Newton's (1687) inductive methodologies, and which led Karl Popper (1963) to make testability against data the criterion on which he built the demarcation line between science and 'non-science'. (For an evaluation of Bacon's and Newton's inductive methodologies *vis-à-vis* Descartes's deductive one (1637), see Mosini 2002 and 2005.)

9 In one case the analogy drawn was plain wrong: Edgeworth (1881) identified 'maximum energy' and the 'maximum principle' as key concepts of 'moral and physical science', while, in fact, natural systems tend to minimise energy, individuals to maximise profits.

various branches of physics, notably, mechanics (Ingrao and Israel 1990; Donzelli 1997) and thermodynamics (Mirowski 1989). The analogies invoked by the neoclassical economists and the inspirational links identified by the historians are not, in themselves, sufficient to claim that tight links exist between the natural sciences and economics, which might have justified the importation of such a key concept as that of equilibrium from one domain to another. This is because, to claim that tight links exist between two domains, the analogies between those domains should be firmed through the same consistency checks employed to claim analogies within each of the two domains. In the natural sciences, such consistency checks require satisfying a formal and an empirical requirement.[10] The formal requirement is that the relevant parameters of the system satisfy the same relations in the two domains, the empirical requirement that the match between the theoretical and observational values of the systems' parameters should be equally good in the two domains.

Neither requirement has been satisfied with respect to any of the analogies invoked or identified between economics and the natural sciences. To be more precise, the very idea of consistency checks amounting to satisfying the aforementioned requirements has never entered discussion on the analogies claimed between economics and the natural sciences.

So, for instance, Walras's point – in a letter to his pupil Albert Aupetit – that 'a perfect similarity' holds 'between our equations of general equilibrium with the equations of universal gravity' (Walras 1873, III, p. 339) was simply stated. The analogies often identified between economics and biology, particularly with respect to evolutionary theory, have been argued for on several grounds (see, for instance, Hodgson 1993), among which the fact that both theories attribute competition a major role in bringing about equilibrium. However, the analogies so far identified resulted from biology and evolutionary theory exerting a mutual influence on one another, which often led to the validation of a theoretical concept in one discipline on the basis of its being used in the other, prior to being the concept validated in either discipline (see Jarvis and Mosini's chapter on this point).

The chapters in Part I discuss some alleged analogies between economics and, respectively, mechanics, chemistry, biology.

Part II deals with the question of the different connotations, and, therefore, of the different meanings, attributed to economic equilibrium, which cause the concept to be multi-faceted. This aspect of economic equilibrium is widely

10 The first example of such proof being given that springs to mind refers to mechanical and thermodynamic systems; it paved the way to the 'reduction' of thermodynamics to statistical mechanics. The proof, given by Boltzmann in 1884 for monocyclic systems of finite period (pendulum) and for two classes of 'orthodic' microscopic systems that he called 'ergode' and 'holode' (later to be called 'microcanonical' and 'canonical ensemble' (Gibbs 1902), consisted in showing that those systems, like thermodynamic ones, satisfy the heat theorem: $du = T\,ds - P\,dv$, with u = specific energy, T = temperature, s = entropy, P = pressure, v = specific volume (see Gallavotti 1999 and references therein).

acknowledged among the practitioners of the discipline, to the point that Weintraub has claimed that

> as 'equilibrium' is dependent for its meaning on the context in which it is found, the meaning of 'equilibrium' changes over time as the texts change. No meaning has a privileged status ... 'Equilibrium' is associated with a Wittgensteinian language game, and the meaning of the word is dependent on the players of the game and the rules that they decide to play by at a particular moment in the history of economic thought.
>
> (Weintraub 1991, p. 108)

Yet the multi-faceted character of economic equilibrium causes a problem, which refers to the extent to which its different meanings are compatible with one another, so that the concept can still be regarded as *one*. (Surely, this is desirable for a concept endowed with such central status in the discipline!).[11] The question of the degree of mutual compatibility between the different meanings attributed to economic equilibrium is often overlooked in the literature, as if it had been settled to everyone's satisfaction. A remarkable example is to be found in Arrow and Hahn's well known claim that:

> there are two basic, incompletely separable, aspects of the notion of general equilibrium as it has been used in economics: the simple notion of determinateness, that the relations describing the economic system must be sufficiently complete to determine the values of its variables, and the more specific notion that each relation represents a balance of forces ... almost any attempt to give a theory of the whole economic system implies the acceptance of the first part of the equilibrium notion; and Adam Smith's 'invisible hand' is a poetic expression of the most fundamental of economic balance relations, the equalization of rates of return.
>
> (Arrow and Hahn 1971, p. 1)

The view that the two aspects of economic equilibrium can – and do – coexist, that the balance of forces responsible for equilibrium is susceptible of mathematical treatment that admits of analytical solutions, is important inasmuch as it implies affirming the mutual compatibility of the two aspects of economic equilibrium, thereby preserving a central role for the concept. Weintraub has forcefully opposed this view by claiming that Arrow and Debreu's linking an equilibrium price vector with a Nash equilibrium represents

> A fundamental shift in the imagery of equilibrium ... from a balance between market forces to a price that, once established by the desires of the agents, would not be modified as long as the desires of the agents remained

11 For discussion along similar lines of one of the most important concepts of the natural science, the gene, see, for instance, Weber (2004).

> unchanged . . . the ordinary language of economic analysis was, in this case, at least, modified by the metaphors associated with a mathematical theorem.
> (Weintraub 1991, p. 108)

The question of the mutual compatibility of the various aspects attributed to scientific concepts relates to their meaning invariance, either over time or over different theoretical frameworks. This is part of the wider question of the cumulative/non-cumulative character of knowledge, which originated with Kuhn in the context of physics (1962), spread to all areas of science, and found solution in none.[12] The prevailing view in economics claims continuity in the discipline (see, for instance, Bowley 1973; Blaug 1978), although neoclassical theory has also been seen as an abrupt conceptual change of revolutionary import (see, for instance, Schumpeter 1910, 1954; Mirowski 1989), and discontinuity between Walras's and Debreu's models of equilibrium has been argued (Clower and Leijonhulfvud 1975).

Part II discusses the question of the meaning invariance of the concept of economic equilibrium by means of three case studies. These refer to A. Smith, the founder of modern economics, A.N. Isnard, and A.A. Cournot, who are widely regarded as precursors of neoclassical economics. The three chapters consider the entire production of the authors in question rather than just a section, as often done in the past. The aim of this part is to evaluate whether any crucial element was lost in the transition from Smith's, Isnard's and Cournot's qualitative concepts of economic equilibrium to Walras's quantitative one. The conclusion, common to all three chapters in this part, is that the balance of forces to which Smith's, Cournot's and Isnard's concepts of equilibrium referred to does not lend itself to mathematical description, as neoclassical economics (whether in Walras's version or in any development of it) requires. Hence the concept of economic equilibrium shows meaning variance even in the first stages of its formulation (a conclusion that would reinforce Weintraub's position against Arrow and Hahn's).

Part III aims to give a brief overview of how the concept of economic equilibrium is understood, deployed and/or criticised, in current economic discourse. The part has no other aim than the one just stated: no thesis is defended, no conclusion drawn. One fact, however, emerges from it, which Samuels's chapter fully captures: that the discussion on economic equilibrium becomes all the more interesting, and fruitful, when it is framed within a well defined philosophical context, as in Lawson's and Backhouse's chapters, which deal, respectively, with realism and instrumentalism. Thomas's evaluation of the role of economics equilibrium for econometricians is also connected with a philosophical question, that of the empirical adequacy of scientific theories. The last three chapters explore various aspects of the question of the different meanings attributed to economic equilibrium.

12 For extensive discussion of Kuhn's theses and related consequences see, for instance, Horwick (1993) and Hoyningen-Huene (1993).

Presentation of the chapters

A critical evaluation of the influence of mechanics on economics from the 1860s to the 1920s is the topic that Ivor Grattan-Guinness addresses in Chapter 1, 'Equilibrium in mechanics and then in economics, 1860–1920: a good source for analogies?'. After reviewing the three traditions that had come to dominate mechanics by the time indicated, Grattan-Guinness lists a few cases of connections between mechanical and economical principles – the efficiency of machines, linear programming and locational equilibrium – which failed to be rapidly and fully developed. He then turns to economics proper, in particular, to the so-called 'neoclassical' tradition, as pursued by Jevons, Walras and Pareto, challenging these authors' appeals to mechanics as their source of inspiration. Grattan-Guinness's point is that a thorough philosophical analysis of the attempts at comparing and/or contrasting economics with mechanics requires discussing, for instance, the testability and generality of the theories in question, their approximating to the phenomena under study, and the status of the types of equilibria within each discipline. Another important point raised in this chapter is the need to spell out the manner in which a given analogy between two disciplines is put forward; Grattan-Guinness suggests that four such manners are available: reduction, emulation, corroboration, instantiation.

The question of the influence of chemistry on economics (and vice versa) with respect to the concept of equilibrium is the focus of Chapter 2, 'Between economics and chemistry: Lavoisier's and Le Chatelier's notions of equilibrium'. In it, Bernadette Bensaude-Vincent and Valeria Mosini introduce the two concepts of equilibrium deployed in chemistry, one static, the other dynamic. The first one (also historically speaking) is associated with Lavoisier, the founding father of modern chemistry. It was the use of the scale, and the consequent introduction of quantitative methods in chemistry, which enabled Lavoisier to challenge (and defeat) the widely accepted – at the time – phlogiston theory, to give a definition of chemical elements that is still in use, and, finally and importantly, to extricate chemistry from the Aristotelian framework, bringing it under the influence of the Enlightenment philosophy. The second way in which the concept of equilibrium is deployed in chemistry is linked with the name of H. Le Chatelier; it was framed within the context of a late, *fin de siècle*, nineteenth-century positivism, which emphasised to the utmost the role of observation and experimentation. Bensaude-Vincent and Mosini discuss P.A. Samuelson's suggestion to adopt the Le Chatelier principle and apply it in economics, and show the suggestion ill founded on account of being based on a misapprehension of what the concepts of stable and unstable equilibrium, defined in the natural sciences, mean.

Chapter 3, 'The ubiquity of the concept of equilibrium in biology, and its relation with equilibrium in economics' by Louise Jarvis and Valeria Mosini, emphasises a difference between two cases of deployment of the concept of equilibrium in biology that is relevant to economics. One case relates to the phenomenon of homeostasis, the mechanism whereby living organisms keep their physiologically relevant parameters quasi-constant. Homeostasis, which instantiates dynamic equilibrium as described in the Le Chatelier principle, was discovered through observation and experimentation. The other case of the concept of equilibrium being deployed in biology considered in this chapter relates to the costs–benefits analyses of late nineteenth century Darwinian evolutionism. The balance of costs–benefits analyses exemplifies a static concept of equilibrium; furthermore, it is a theoretical concept, imported from economics. The history of mutual influences between biology and economics is long; an interesting aspect of it is that concepts often travelled across the disciplines, and received indirect corroboration in one by being applied in the other, before being validated in either one.

In Chapter 4, '"Sympathy", "character" and economic equilibrium', William Dixon and David Wilson point out a contradiction that runs through most of post-Walrasian equilibrium theorising. This concerns the appropriation by the post-Walrasian tradition of Smith's metaphor of the invisible hand, accompanied by the endorsement of Hobbes's theory of human behaviour. This is a curious fact, since it was as an alternative to Hobbes's theory that Smith had developed the concept of 'sympathy' as the key element that would achieve the happy co-ordination to which the metaphor of the invisible hand refers.[13] Dixon and Wilson emphasise that the *Theory of Moral Sentiments*, in which Smith spelled out his characterisation of human co-ordination, should be read as a necessary compendium to the *Wealth of Nations*. They show that, on Smith's account, sympathy would not be imposed on individuals, but would, in fact, originate from *within* the individuals themselves, and claim that Smith's notion of sympathy may be seen as a precursor of Chalmers's notion of 'character', the disposition to take into account the feelings and expectations of others before embarking on a given course of action. Notably, Chalmers, like Smith, assumed that character would develop from *within* the individuals. After showing that remnants of Smith's and Chalmers's views on human motivation and co-ordination may be traced in some leading twentieth century economists, Dixon and Wilson present and discuss the work of social psychologist G.H. Mead, suggesting that it provides a way out of the sterile debate on egoism versus moral considerations, and that the picture it provides is in line with Smith's and Chalmers's.

In Chapter 5, 'Economic equilibrium in the French Enlightenment: the case of A.N. Isnard', Richard van den Berg recalls that Isnard is often considered a precursor of neoclassical economics on account of his first-rate contributions to mathematical economics, but that he is denied even a fraction of the recognition awarded to Walras for understanding the intricacies behind economic phenomena. By examining, together with the mathematically oriented *Traité des richesses*, Isnard's other books, in particular, the *Cathéchisme social*, van den Berg shows that, contrary to common opinion, Isnard conceived a sophisticated economic system, which was not based on utility maximising but harmonised

13 For a similar point, see Nadal's (2004b) paper entitled 'Freedom and submission'.

the profit seeking of individual entrepreneurs with wider considerations concerning the well-being of all individuals in the society. Hence, for Isnard, the establishment of a 'natural' economic order regulated by an equilibrium would depend on more than just self-interest. He thought that considerations of wider import, framed in Condillac's sensualist philosophy, and co-ordinated by reflection and judgement, would be responsible for bringing about the 'considered' interests that would result in equilibrium. Van den Berg shows that Isnard described the process of developing those 'considered' interests as akin to the acquisition of good habits. Hence, at variance with Smith, Isnard assumed that the force that would bring about economic equilibrium by taming greed and selfishness was not innate, while denying that it was imposed on individuals from outside. The acquisition of considered interests would come about through an act of free will, based on the advantages that considered interests had delivered in the past.

In Chapter 6, 'Influences on the economic theory of A.A. Cournot: mechanics, physics and biology', Francois Vatin develops two interconnected theses. One is that the widespread interpretation of Cournot as an equilibrium theorist of mechanistic inspiration – and, therefore, as a precursor of neoclassical economics – is wrong in that Cournot's main source of philosophical inspiration was Leibniz's energeticism. Cournot's use of the term 'equilibrium' well exemplifies Vatin's thesis: against what should be expected of an equilibrium theorist, the term appeared very seldom (only twice) in the (1838) *Recherches*, and not much more often in the (1863) *Principes*. Vatin's second thesis is that there is no need to assume an abrupt shift in Cournot's views to realise the fact that he was *not* an equilibrium theorist: Leibniz's energeticism provides the common thread between the various periods that can be identified in Cournot's entire production. Vatin's analysis explains why Cournot considered it inappropriate to describe human behaviour other than as between individuals that are part of a society, and why he regarded societies as biological organisms in their initial stages, and as mechanisms in their later ones.[14] Interestingly, in his mature works, Cournot denied that the societies of his time had reached the state of mechanisms, and could, therefore, be subjected to mathematical description as he had done in his 1838 book, putting on hold, if not denouncing in retrospect, the mathematical treatment of economics of his early work. Cournot's late formulation of economic equilibrium was not susceptible of being expressed in mathematical terms, and was, in fact, a qualitative concept linked with the complexity of the metaphors from evolutionary theory and thermodynamics that Cournot had come to choose to describe economic phenomena.

Chapter 7, 'Tensions in modern economics: the case of equilibrium analysis' by Tony Lawson, brings the discussion on economic equilibrium under the spotlight of contemporary, critical, thinking. Lawson's staring point is that there is a

14 Recall, by way of contrast, Marshall's later use of mechanical and biological metaphors, which he applied in the reverse temporal order. He thought that, in the earlier stages of economies, demand and supply may be seen as tending towards a mechanical equilibrium, while, in the later stages, economic equilibrium resembles that between organic forces (Marshall 1890).

connection between the role attributed to equilibrium in economic theorising and the predominant attitude within the profession of mainly – if not exclusively – encouraging ever more sophisticated mathematical treatments of economic phenomena, with little concern for the empirical adequacy of the conclusions so reached. Lawson notes that the variety of meanings attributed to economic equilibrium result in the concept being intrinsically ambiguous, its use – and abuse – bringing about incoherences, and generating a vertical split in the profession between advocates and its critics. The lack of clarity in the discussion is well exemplified by the fact that even the critics of economic equilibrium, such as, for instance, institutionalists, post-Keynesians and feminists, have emphasised the inadequacy of one or other assumption underlying the concept while still taking it, as a whole, at face value. This is due to a confusion between the epistemic and the ontic aspects of the concept, between claims about models (and their properties) and claims about the phenomena the models aim to represent. This confusion has led to evading the question of properly criticising mainstream economics for inventing a reality that it can address, instead of striving to find the appropriate means to describe the existing one. Hence discussion on equilibrium thus far has not helped economics recover from what Lawson calls an 'unhealthy state'.

Chapter 8, 'Equilibrium and problem solving in economics' by Roger Backhouse, frames the discussion of the concept of economic equilibrium within the philosophical context of instrumentalism, thereby creating a fruitful contrast with Lawson's realist stance. Backhouse regards economic equilibrium as a useful tool in addressing questions that are relevant to the economic profession. He qualifies the tool represented by economic equilibrium as a model connected to a specific theoretical apparatus, which, although abstract and often remote with respect to the actual state of affairs, has reverberations on the real world of economics. How these reverberations come about, case by case, is not always obvious because the links between economic theories and actual economic states of affairs are tortuous, and their robustness varies in degree. This fact explains why the concept of equilibrium has been endowed with different connotations, sometimes incompatible with one another, which reflect the different levels of complexity of the economic problems that are being addressed in each case. On Backhouse's account, the question of the ontological status of economic equilibrium is a legitimate one, but the concept can be meaningfully discussed even without addressing that question. The focus of discussion, in fact, should be on the usefulness of the concept of equilibrium as a problem-solving tool, *vis-à-vis* alternative schemes, most notably game theory, which have been put forward in the last decades.

In Chapter 9, 'Equilibrium analysis: a middlebrow view', Warren Samuels sets forth to disentangle the various aspects of the bundle of disagreement surrounding the concept of economic equilibrium. These, he shows, relate to dichotomies such as that between equilibrium as a tool or as an element of reality, between economics as the analysis of conceptual models or of actual states of affairs, and between induction and deduction in the scientific discourse. Samuels's analysis is underpinned by a philosophical position whose starting point is the consideration that economics, as a social science, is 'made, not found'. This consideration has a bearing on the question of the empirical adequacy of economic theories that is at the heart of the controversy between realists (such as Lawson) and instrumentalists (such as Backhouse) on the interpretation, and goal, of economics. Samuels stresses that, contrary to what often claimed, it is impossible to keep ontological and epistemological considerations apart, as these constantly interplay with one another, as well as with the complexity of the phenomena. Within this philosophical and methodological framework, Samuel's preference is to talk in terms of disequilibration, disequilibrium and equilibration rather than in terms of the existence, uniqueness and stability of the equilibrium solutions (but he stops short of claiming superior ontological status for his approach over the other).

Jim Thomas discusses the role of the concept of equilibrium in econometrics in Chapter 10, 'Equilibrium in economics, stability and stationarity in econometrics'. After recalling the three components that, according to Ragnar Frisch, contribute to a real understanding of the quantitative relations between economic variables, that is, statistics, economic theory and mathematics, Thomas points out the imbalance in the way in which those components are rated in the profession, which causes theorists to occupy an intellectually higher position than data gatherers. This state of affairs is partly due to the difficulty (sometimes the impossibility) of measuring a number of key economic variables, such as, for instance, utility, 'normal' or 'excess' profits and 'real' rates of interest, which make the job of the data gatherers all the harder. After discussing the deployment of mathematical analysis in the framework of mainstream economics, and its extension to heterodox economics, Thomas notes that the existence of stable relations between non-stationary variables points to the need for econometricians to devise new theories, or to further develop already existing ones, which would not depend on static equilibrium. The fact that, so far, econometricians have relied on models from existing economic theories – rather than developing their own ones – often led to problems when the models were found not to contain essential features of the phenomena they were meant to portray. This realisation often resulted in adjustments of the models, or in the re-evaluation of problematic features, such as, for instance, autocorrelation, which had previously appeared to be weaknesses in need of elimination.

Victoria Chick addresses the question of the several meanings attributed to economic equilibrium in Chapter 11, 'Equilibrium in economics: some concepts and controversies'. Although Chick's review of the meanings of economic equilibrium is not organised along chronological lines, it none the less includes contributions from the main protagonists of twentieth century economics. She claims that it is equally inappropriate to defend, or to criticise, the concept as if it were one and the same thing, and suggests that, in discussing the ways in which the concept has been deployed, care should be given to the specific meaning attributed to it in each of those ways. Another relevant point of this chapter is the author's emphasis on distinguishing the 'equilibrium method', as theorising aimed to give only equilibrium solutions, from the equilibrium point that a theory may display alongside disequilibrium and adjustment. Chick also hints to how the belief in economic equilibrium offers a way to ignore power relations, ruled out in competitive analysis, and income distribution, ruled out by the representative agent, thereby hinting to the need to address the question of the ideological components that underpin widely shared assumptions in economics, such as that of equilibrium.

The role of ideology in economics is the focus of Chapter 12, 'Heavens above: what equilibrium means for economics' by Alan Freeman. Freeman's basic point is that the notion of equilibrium has a different status in economics from that of any concept (including equilibrium) in the natural sciences. In his view, equilibrium is used in economics in a dogmatic way, that Freeman associates with religion, citing the example of the Catholic church being against Galileo's defence of heliocentrism. In Freeman's analysis, the 'temporal' approach to economics is set in opposition with the equilibrium, or 'steady state', approach (a view that would not apply in the natural sciences), in this way strengthening his case for equilibrium in economics having very little (if anything) to do with equilibrium in the natural sciences.

Andy Denis in Chapter 13, 'The hypostatisation of the concept of equilibrium in neoclassical economics', offers another characterisation of the meanings of economic equilibrium, which include definitions of equilibrium in physics taken from Simpson and Weiner's (2000) *OED Online*. However, Denis's main point is that neoclassical economics – here exemplified by the work of Robert Lucas – has treated the concept of equilibrium in a way that amounts to its 'hypostatisation'. He further maintains that the 'hypostatisation' of the concept exemplifies the contrast between 'formal' and 'dialectical' modes of thought in economics, urging heterodox economists to embark on a research programme aimed to build and deploy a 'dialectical notion of equilibrium'.

References

Ackerman, F. and Nadal, A. (2004), *The Flawed Foundations of General Equilibrium*, Routledge, London & New York.

Addleson, M. (1995), *Equilibrium versus Understanding*, Routledge, London.

Arrow, K. and F. Hahn (1971), *General Competitive Analysis*, Elsevier North-Holland, Amsterdam.

Bacon, F. (1620), *Novum organum*, trans. and ed. P. Urbach and J. Gibson (1994), Open Court, Chicago and La Salle, IL.

Blaug, M. (1978), *Economic Theory in Retrospect*, 3rd edn, Cambridge University Press, Cambridge.

Bowley, M. (1973), *Studies in the History of Economic Thought before 1870*, Macmillan, London.

Bridgman, P.W. (1927), *The Logic of Modern Physics*, Macmillan, New York.

Clower, R, and A. Leijonhulfvud (1975), 'The coordination of economic activities: a Keynesian perspective', *American Economic Review*, 65, 182–8.

Descartes, R. (1637), *Discours de la méthode*, in E.S. Haldane and G.T.R. Ross (1911), *The Philosophical Works of Descartes'*, 1, 81–130, Cambridge University Press, Cambridge.

De Vroey, M. (2002), 'Equilibrium and disequilibrium in Walrasian and neo-Walrasian economics', *Journal of the History of Economic Thought*, 24 (4), 405–26.

Donzelli, F. (1986), *Il concetto di equilibrio nella teoria economica neoclassica*, La Nuova Italia Scientifica, Rome.

Donzelli, F. (1997), 'Pareto's mechanical dream', *History of Economic Ideas*, 5 (3), 127–78.

Dorfman, R., Samuelson, P.A. and Solow, R.M. (1958), *Linear Programming and Economic Analysis*, McGraw-Hill, New York.

Duhem, P. (1886), *Le Potentiel thérmodynamique et ses applications*, Paris.

Edgeworth, F.Y. (1881), *Mathematical Psychics*, Kegan Paul, London.

Fisher, I. (1892), *Mathematical Investigations in the Theory of Value and Prices*, Transactions of Connecticut Academy.

Fox, R. (1974), 'The rise and fall of Laplacian physics', *Historical Studies in Physical Sciences*, 4, 89–136.

Gallavotti, G. (1999), *Statistical Mechanics*, Springer, Berlin.

Gibbs, J.W. (1875–78) [1928], 'On the equilibrium of heterogeneous substances', *Transactions of the Connecticut Academy of Arts and Sciences*, 3, 108–343, in *The Collected Works of J.W. Gibbs*, Yale University Press, New Haven, CT.

Gibbs, J.W. (1902), *Elementary Principles in Statistical Mechanics*, Yale University Press, New Haven, CT.

Hodgson, G.M. (1993), *Economics and Evolution. Bringing Life back into Economics*, Polity Press, Cambridge.

Horwick, P. (1993), *World Changes. Thomas Kuhn and the Nature of Science*, MIT Press, Cambridge, MA.

Hoyningen-Huene, P. (1993), *Reconstructing Scientific Revolutions. Thomas S. Kuhn's Philosophy of Science*, trans. A.T. Levine, University of Chicago Press, Chicago.

Ingrao, B. and G. Israel (1990), *The Invisible Hand. Economic Equilibrium in the History of Science*, MIT Press, Cambridge, MA.

Jevons, W.S. (1879) [1970], *The Theory of Political Economy*, Penguin, Harmondsworth.

Kuhn, T. (1957), 'Energy conservation as an example of simultaneous discovery', in M. Clagett (ed.), *Critical Problems in the History of Science*, University of Wisconsin Press, Madison, WI, 321–56.

Kuhn, T. (1962), *The Structure of Scientific Revolutions*, University of Chicago Press, Chicago.

Machlup, F. (1963), *Essays on Economic Semantics*, Prentice-Hall, Englewood Cliffs, NJ.

Mandler, M. (1999), *Dilemmas in Economic Theory. Persisting Foundational Problems of Microeconomics*, Oxford University Press, Oxford.

Marshall, A. (1890) [1949], *The Principles of Economics*, 8th edn, Macmillan, London.

McKenzie, L. (1954), 'On equilibrium in Graham's model of world trade and other competitive systems', *Econometrica*, 22, 147–61.

Mirowski, P. (1989), *More Heat than Light. Economics as Social Physics, Physics as Nature's Economics*, Cambridge University Press, Cambridge.

Mosini, V. (2002), 'Was the methodology behind electrodynamics inductive or deductive?', *Physis*, 39, 441–67.

Mosini, V. (2005), 'On the interplay between evidence and theory: Dr Hahnemann's homeopathic medicine', *Physis*, 42 (2), 513–37.

Nadal, A. (2004a), 'Contradictions of the open economy model as applied in Mexico', in F. Ackerman and A. Nadal (eds), *The Flawed Foundations of General Equilibrium*, Routledge, London & New York, 133–48.

Nadal, A. (2004b), 'Freedom and submission', F. Ackerman and A. Nadal (eds), *The Flawed Foundations of General Equilibrium*, Routledge, London & New York, 181–202.

Newton, I. (1687), *Philosophiae Naturalis Principia Mathematica*, trans. A. Motte (1846), Adee, New York.

Popper, K. (1963), *Conjectures and Refutations*: *The Growth of Scientific Knowledge*, Routledge and Kegan Paul, London.

Schumpeter, J.A. (1910), 'Marie Esprit Léon Walras', reprinted in J.A. Schumpeter (1951), *Ten Great Economists from Marx to Keynes*, Oxford University Press, Oxford.

Schumpeter, J.A. (1954), *History of Economic Analysis*, Oxford University Press, Oxford.

Walras, A. (1873), 'Letter to Albert Aupetit, December 1, 1907' (n. 1666), in W. Jaffé (ed.) (1965), *Correspondence of Léon Walras and Related Papers*, 3 vols, North-Holland, Amsterdam.

Walras, L. (1909), 'Economique et mécanique', *Bulletin de la Société vaudoise des sciences naturelles*, 15, 313–25.

Weber, M. (2004), *Philosophy of Experimental Biology*, Cambridge University Press, Cambridge.

Weintraub, E.R. (1983), 'The existence of a competitive equilibrium, 1930–1954', *Journal of Economic Literature*, 21 (1), 1–39.

Weintraub, E.R. (1991), *Stabilizing Dynamics*, Cambridge University Press, Cambridge.

Part I

The interplay of equilibrium notions between the natural sciences and economics

1 Equilibrium in mechanics and then in economics, 1860–1920

A good source for analogies?

Ivor Grattan-Guinness

It is well known that mathematical economics took much positive influence from classical mechanics, especially from the 1860s until the 1920s, and that equilibrium was a prime target for imitation. After a review of the main traditions of mechanics, this chapter considers the history of its effect upon economics, first by noting some branches of economics so influenced where the effect was far from clear or rapid, and second by considering the place of mechanical principles, especially equilibrium, in the work of some major neoclassical economists. Finally, the merits of the analogies will be considered, and a rather ironic conclusion drawn.

The varieties of equilibrium in mechanics

Mechanics has a very long history; we are concerned here with the developments of it during the later eighteenth and especially the nineteenth centuries, when emerged the versions of which the effects on economics are most apparent. The first feature to emphasise is that Newtonian mechanics was a major version but far from the only one, especially on the Continent, where almost all the main advances were made from the 1740s onwards. For further details of this huge story, see Dühring (1873), Mach (1883) (with caution), Rühlmann (1881–85), Wolf (1889–91), Voss (1901), Duhem (1903), Stäckel (1905), Jouguet (1909), Dugas (1955), Grattan-Guinness (1990a, b, 2005a, 1994a, esp. pts 8 and 9), Roche (1998), Heilbron (2002) and Pulte (2005), and the many further original and historical references given in these sources; and the extensive bibliography to this chapter.

The range of mechanics

First we need briefly to consider the range of phenomena that had come to fall under mechanics. They may be conveniently divided into five branches: the adjectives below are mine.

Corporeal mechanics concerned 'ordinary-sized' objects as found and handled on the Earth: bodies, fluids and elastic surfaces. Sound was then often regarded as part of mechanics (Cannon and Dostrovsky 1981). In *celestial* mechanics the planets and satellites were taken to be point masses; prime concerns included the fine details of their orbits and rotations, the former considered also for comets. *Planetary* mechanics was concerned with the shape of the heavenly bodies: the Earth was the most important one, followed by the Moon. Important topics included precession and nutation, tides, and topography and cartography. Several aspects of *engineering* mechanics involved friction; for example, the stability of embankments and the construction and stability of buildings or structures of various kinds, such as towers, cupolas, arches and bridges. Of the many machines in this branch, several related to water, both in their design and (in)efficiency of their operation: waterwheels, turbines, pumps, valves and pistons. Connected topics included the building and steerage of boats and ships, and the use of sails. Finally, as the least developed branch, *molecular* mechanics treated the interaction of the supposed 'molecules' somehow comprising the intimate structure of matter (in, for example, elasticity and friction studies) and/or the even smaller molecules that (for some researchers) comprised the structure of the assumed aether (Körner 1904).

By 1800 three distinct traditions had emerged, in competition not only over the question of heuristics versus formalisation but also concerning the territory of legitimate application. Let us note them in turn.

Newtonian mechanics

Newton's approach was prominent, especially in celestial and planetary mechanics (Gautier 1817; Todhunter 1873; Greenberg 1995). His laws were at once both mathematical and mechanical. The second one was often used in the form

$$\text{force} = \text{mass} \times \text{acceleration} \tag{1}$$

including by Newton himself; but he actually formulated it in terms of a relationship between increments of impulse and increments of momentum (with mass assumed constant) (Cohen 1971; Brackenridge 1995; Maltese 1992). The first law was well understood to apply both to static and to dynamic equilibrium. However, within dynamics the derivation of some results was problematic, until it was realised (by Leonhard Euler among others) that the principle of angular momentum had to be adopted as a fourth law (Truesdell 1968, ch. 5). The notion of central forces and actions between bodies (balanced by reaction according to Newton's third law) was widely adopted; however, the inverse square law was taken up with more enthusiasm in Britain than on the Continent, where other laws were also mooted (Guicciardini 1999).

Energy–work mechanics

An alternative tradition, with quite a long history, drew upon the relationship between kinetic and potential energies. (I use the modern terms: *vis viva* and *forces vives* then were popular names for the former notion, while the latter, involving (force × distance) in some form or other, received various names.) G.W. Leibniz advocated it in the late seventeenth century as a means of mathematicising René Descartes's vortex theory of celestial motion, which Newton had come to loathe (Bertoloni Meli 1993). This tradition gained its best credentials in engineering and technology; by the 1780s it was elevated into a general approach to dynamics, with special utility in cases of impact and percussion where *dis*equilibrium occurred. A pioneer of this tradition was Charles Coulomb (Heyman 1972), and the main advocate of its generality was Lazare Carnot (Gillispie 1971; Gillmor 1971), both men with strong engineering backgrounds.

One of the strengths of this tradition is that it allowed for the role of friction in the losses of energy and/or work. However, studies of the properties of friction were limited, for it was and remains a major stumbling block in all traditions of mechanics, in all its manifestations; perhaps the greatest advances have come in fluid friction, with the use and adaptations of the Navier–Stokes equations.

Variational mechanics

Energy mechanics challenged not only the Newtonian tradition but especially the third tradition, which grew up from the mid-eighteenth century onwards in reaction against Newton's. Puzzled by the notion of force, Jean d'Alembert proposed that (1) should be taken as its definition; but then some new law is needed to replace it, and he offered a rather incoherent statement, now known as 'd'Alembert's principle', about the relationship between the motions of masses when left in their current state of equilibrium and when affected by imposed actions such as forces or impacts (Fraser 1985).

This tradition also adopted 'the principle of least action', an optimising law formulated during the 1740s with the help of the calculus of variations; 'action' was a technical term, denoting (force × velocity × distance) in a variety of contexts: for example, for infinitesimal displacements ds it required an integral in distance s. As in other contexts in mechanics, some tricky metaphysical issues arose, concerning the relationship between force and substance; here Euler also invoked religious grounds in order to guarantee its generality. However, he used it only fitfully; it was to be utilised comprehensively first by J.L. Lagrange, but in a secular spirit (Pulte 1989).

This new tradition was enhanced by 'the principle of virtual velocities' (not then 'work', a word that hinted at the disliked notion of force): a refinement of d'Alembert's principle, it stated how masses move after disturbance from equilibrium. But it assumed that mechanical situations could always be reduced to equilibrate ones, and that dynamics could be reduced to statics. Various efforts were made to prove it from other statical and dynamical principles, such as that of the lever (Lindt 1904).

This tradition was formulated and developed in algebraic terms. Indeed, it is often called 'analytical', and Lagrange's treatise *Méchanique analitique* (1788) was the definitive account of it for a long time. There are no diagrams in the book, the author tells us early on, and he meant it, seriously. His use of the calculus of variations inspired the alternative adjective 'variational' to characterise this tradition.

A highlight of this book is an analysis, already rehearsed in papers, of the stability of the planetary system, a major use of perturbation theory (Wilson 1980). Rejecting the religious explanation of stability put forward by predecessors such as Newton and Euler, Lagrange thought that it could be *proved* from Newton's laws, together with the assumption that the planets move in the same direction round the Sun. At that time the problem was conceived as showing that the inclination to the ecliptic and the radius vector of every planet will always remain bounded (while not constant). Although not fully sound, his proof brilliantly launched the study of a problem of extraordinary difficulty.

Parallel progresses

All through the nineteenth century these traditions progressed, especially in dynamics. Every aspect was advanced, from theoretical principles through properties of solids and fluids to the precise definition and measurement of quantities (*passim* in Klein and Müller 1896–1935; Schwarzschild *et al.* 1904–34; Royal Society 1909).

Statics benefited greatly in 1803 from Louis Poinsot's theory of the 'couple' (his word), denoting two forces equal in value, parallel but opposite in direction and not collinear (Poinsot 1803). It is strange that this major modification of statics should have taken so long to be recognised. It also bears upon the (partial) understanding of static equilibrium held by economists and many others.

Another oddity was the small response to the 'paradox of statics', as Euler and others called it. This is the fact that it was not possible to analyse the equilibrium of a loaded table with four or more legs; for there were only three basic equations of static equilibrium, so that a further condition of some kind would have to be assumed. A two-dimensional analogue of this paradox obtains for a bench supported on more than two legs. Given the link that will be made by economists between equilibrium and the numbers of unknowns and of equations required to state the theory, it is ironic that insufficient equations are available in this elementary mechanical situation itself.

Among the three traditions, the variational was substantially advanced by the contributions of W.R. Hamilton from the 1830s onwards, which greatly extended the range and techniques of Lagrange's legacy (Prange 1933). All traditions were elaborated in new contexts: continuum mechanics proved some enthralling challenges, especially in fluid mechanics and elasticity theory (Truesdell 1954, 1955, 1960). However, progress was slow on the task of analysing, especially mathematically, the interactions of the molecules which many scientists held to compose the basic components of physical bodies and substances (Weiss 1988; Rowlinson 2002), and the mysteries of the behaviour of materials, especially the many ways in which they rupture and break (Gordon 1976).

Perhaps the most significant mathematical elaboration, which affected all traditions, was the gradual growth of potential theory, especially from the 1830s (Bacharach 1883). Many of its initial contexts came from mathematical physics, which had grown rapidly in the new century, especially in French hands – heat theory, physical optics, and electricity and magnetism, and from 1820 their interaction in electromagnetism and electrodynamics (Grattan-Guinness 1990a, chs 9, 12–14). The last two subjects were new; the others just named grew massively, and not only on the mathematical side but also in their theoretical and experimental aspects (Bogolyubov 1976, 1978; Harman 1982; Garber 1999). The place in them of mechanical principles was very strong, so much so that in the early nineteenth century P.S. Laplace (1749–1827) advocated that all physical as well as mechanical theories should be developed in terms of short-range central forces acting between the elementary 'molecules' of which they were presumed to be composed and the cumulative actions of a body or physical regimes be taken to be the appropriate integral of its basic inter-molecular components. Thus, for example, his theory of light was ballistic rather than waval (Grattan-Guinness 1990a, ch. 7). However, his approach turned out to be less powerful than the competing theories that did not make such assumptions (Grattan-Guinness 1987). But in those theories mechanical notions were sometimes prominent sources of imitation; for example, principles of conservation or least action, and the decomposition of forces.

Another advance, especially in mechanics itself, concerned the types of boundary conditions applied to situations. In particular, in the 1890s Heinrich Hertz stressed 'non-holonomic' conditions on a mechanical system, in which the displacements of its components are constrained by time-dependent conditions (for example, the effect of friction upon rolling on a surface); 'holonomic' conditions leave the system free to move (again for example, smoothly).

Thanks to these advances, physics grew enormously in importance, from a position of inferiority in the eighteenth century that is hard for us to imagine. In particular, energy mechanics and potential theory were brought together in the mid-century by Hermann von Helmholtz and others to create 'energetics', as it came to be known, covering both mechanics and physics (Haas 1909; Caneva 1993). This point bears upon the later influences on other subjects, of which economics is only one; whether they came under the sway of mechanics directly (our main theme), or from physics directly, or from physics *via* mechanics. Mirowski (1989) has much information on these influences, though he might have stressed rather more the differences between them.

Some controversies between the traditions

When large-scale theories are in competition, differences of various kinds arise: legitimacy, relationships between topics, and generality. The relationship between dynamics and statics was a major one: in energy mechanics dynamics dominated, with statics construed as the special case of zero velocity; by contrast, in variational mechanics the claim of reducing dynamic to statics was central. One should note, however, that static equilibrium admits stable and unstable forms, exemplified respectively by a ball sitting in the base of a bowl and on the top of the same bowl upturned on a flat surface.

An important case of this difference concerned the work term $\Sigma_r F_r dx_r$ for forces F_r displaced by infinitesimal distances dx_r. Following Lagrange, variationists assumed that it was always an exact differential; so they equated it to the differential of a potential P,

$$\Sigma_r F_r dx_r = dP \qquad (2)$$

and then integrated (2) to obtain P, when the system of forces F_r was said to be 'conservative'. But supporters of energy/work mechanics could not so proceed; for them P did not exist, and thus (2) could not hold, on the occasions of mechanical impact between bodies, cases that they claimed variationists could not handle (Scott 1970). Energetics physics would reconcile this clash later, since (2) was construed to hold over all forces involved, whether mechanical or physical.

There were also concerns over the status and types of equilibrium. The basic notion of equilibrium was that of coming to rest or being at it (the static version), or moving uniformly (the dynamic version). But along with, or perhaps rather alongside, them came the notion of the *stability* of a dynamical system, especially following the wonderful contributions made by Lagrange. Stability has a literally more dynamic range than equilibrium, a feature brought out further by Henri Poincaré and especially Alexander Lyapunov around 1890, when they individuated several new kinds of equilibrium (Grattan-Guinness 2005c, chs 48, 51 and 68).

One source of controversies was the (non-)effectiveness of each tradition within certain mechanical contexts, especially in dynamics. The Newtonian version was especially strong on planetary and celestial mechanics; but engineering mechanics most often drew upon the energy/work version. On basic 'ordinary-sized' mechanical situations all three might be used, but there was a great difference in practice. In particular, the variational tradition was unsurpassed in contexts formulated in terms of optimisation, and for the systematic organisation of theories ('axiomatisation' is an anachronism); but it was often wanting in *new* problem areas when intuition needed help, and could not properly cope with cases involving impact.

The final issue is a philosophical one: determinism, with special reference in mechanics to teleology. The variational tradition stands out here, mainly for its use of the principle of least action, which states a *macro* criterion for fixing the path taken by the particle under the stated conditions. Teleology does not obtain in the other traditions, because initial conditions have to be specified in addition to the formulae that derive the ensuing motion. However, this point was often overlooked (Popper 1950–51); in particular, the Newtonian tradition has sometimes been given a deterministic interpretation, in a large-scale manner by Laplace. The question of determinism or indeterminism lurks in many kinds of social science, economics included.

Three cases of intermittent interaction between mechanics and economics

After this rather rapid review of a large ensemble of theories, I briefly note here three parts of mathematical economics in which mechanics played a notable role. As a prelude to the somewhat sceptical comments to come, all three stories are intermittent over time. All cases have important French components, associated with the famous engineering Ecole Polytechnique in Paris, which was founded in 1794.

The (economic) efficiency of machines

Engineering mechanics means business, which means profit, which means return on investment. From the late eighteenth century the French linked efficiency with a general mechanical theory, paying attention to factors such as loss of energy on impact and loss of work to overcome friction both in general terms and in particular cases such as equipment with sliding parts or turbines and waterwheels, and also the measure of water flow in canals and pipes (Grattan-Guinness 1990a, esp. ch. 16; Vatin 1993). A pioneer, Joseph de Montgolfier, offered the quip 'the *force vive* is that which can be had for money', which was picked up by Claude Navier, a former student at the Ecole Polytechnique (and an author of the equations for fluids mentioned above). Other former students active in this area included Gaspard Coriolis and Jean Victor Poncelet (1852). It was to be picked up later in other branches of engineering, such as telecommunications.

The same issues concerned scientists and engineers in other countries, though connections between economic and mechanical principles were not so evident, perhaps due to the lower status there of engineering education and institutions. Britain shows a respectable record thanks to the awareness of luminaries such as William Whewell, William Thomson and James Joule, where links with economics were usually made via the labour theory of value (Berg 1980; Wise and Smith 1989–90). But it did not enter the main stream of the later development of mathematical economics (or the purview of many of its historians): among the leading economists only Léon Walras seems to have drawn upon it, and then only to a limited extent, as we shall see in the discussion of economists below.

Linear programming

Together with its non-linear sister theory, linear programming has became a staple component of teaching and practice in mathematical economics, following their rapid development after the Second World War.[1] But the prehistory of linear programming goes back around 150 years, and some of it has connections with mechanics (Grattan-Guinness 1994b). The most striking anticipator is Joseph Fourier in the 1820s, who knew that he had posed 'a new type of question' and had applications in mind. One of his followers was Navier, who used it to offer a solution to the paradox of statics. Another, of especial significance here, was the young Augustin Cournot (1801–77), who worked over several problems in mechanics in Fourier's way (Grattan-Guinness 2005b). Yet Fourier had few other followers. One reason will have been the lack of effective techniques, especially matrix theory, to produce the conceived solutions; yet the virtual lack of later impact is strange – especially with Cournot, whose own contributions to mathematical economics (Vatin 1998), launched only a few years later, included curves of turnover, which also involve convexity in an important way. It seems that Cournot had *forgotten* recent work by Cournot; surely he cannot have noticed but then discarded the bearing of convexity upon optimisation in his new economic contexts. But so it was: there were only a few further pulses of interest in linear programming thereafter; for example, the Farkas lemmas, which date from the 1900s. A similar point can be made about non-linear programming, though with a rather shorter pre-history (Kjeldsen 2000).

Locational equilibrium

This intersection of economics with transport theory is rightly credited principally to Alfred Weber with his writings of the 1920s, and in this case only few partial anticipations are evident. The most remarkable one was effected by two former students of the Ecole Polytechnique. Gabriel Lamé and Emile Clapeyron graduated in the mid-1810s, just at the time of the Catholic Restoration – not propitious for young men with strong socialist tendencies. Luckily the Czar of Russia unwittingly provided a solution by requesting (not for the first time) the French government to send talented engineers to assist in the training of his own corps.

During their residence in St Petersburg from 1820 and 1831 Lamé and Clapeyron produced an impressive range of research papers, in a co-operation that was unusual in itself in the mathematics of the time. One paper contained a complete recognition of the basic principles of locational equilibrium in 1829, a century before Weber. The role of mechanics is central, for the problem is solved by a mechanical simulation on a panel or table, with weights proportional to the importance of the sites suspended from there on strings that are joined together, so that the point of equilibrium is found when the strings are allowed to seek equilib-

1 More precisely, this remark refers to progress in the West. Soviet mathematicians had developed a version of linear programming during the war, for similar motives; but after the war, they faced considerable difficulties implementing it, for it allows the mathematician to make kinds of decision that the Central Committee wished to retain for themselves in their command economy (see, for instance, Novozhilov 1967). The situation is a rare example of mathematics confronting politics.

rium. They described this procedure in their paper, and certain passages suggest that they had actually set up the mechanism. When studying the distribution of piles of stones on roads to facilitate repairs they even posed the grid problem, where the actor himself decides on the frequency of points of location.

However, they published their paper only in the journal of the St Petersburg corps, which gained very few readers. (It is translated with extensive commentary in Franksen and Grattan-Guinness 1989.) Although they clearly saw both the originality and the utility of their theory, for some reason they failed to reprint it in a Paris journal, unlike several of their other collaborative papers. Thus their work seems to have played no role in the later developments. Once again we see economics and mechanics together, with fascinating intellectual possibilities but virtually no diffusion. While the modern theory of economic geography does not rely upon mechanical artefacts (see Smith 1980, for example), the background of mechanics is still noticeable.

Some uses of mechanics in neoclassical economics

> By demonstrating rigorously first the elementary theorems of geometry and algebra, and then the resulting theorems of the calculus and mechanics, in order to apply them to experimental data, we have achieved the marvel of modern industry. Let us follow the same procedure in economics, and, without doubt, we shall eventually succeed in having the same control over the nature of things in the economic and social order as we already have in the physical and industrial order.
>
> (Walras 1890, 1926, p. 471)

The review of mechanics above shows that a massive and also varied ensemble of theories was developed, in a wide range of contexts with plenty of scope for disagreements. The concept of greatest relevance from now on is equilibrium. In an initial foray into a study of its influence upon economics, I consider a few major figures from the neoclassical tradition. (I follow practice in using 'neoclassical', which is due to Thorstein Veblen 1900, but Alfred Marshall's 'marginal' seems better.) On the pertinent general history of economics see, for example, the appropriate parts of Backhouse (1985), Blaug (1968), Howey (1960), Hutchinson (1953), Ingrao and Israel (1990), Spiegel (1991), maybe Schumpeter (1954, pt 5), and the source book Baumol and Goldfield (1968).

I am not in a position to assess the *overall* merits or otherwise of the economists' theories; I focus upon the place in them of mechanics, which deserves rather closer attention than it often receives in the history of economics. A good *or* bad analogy from mechanics does not make an economic theory good *or* bad in itself (or vice versa), but its place is worth considering.

Some of the appeals to mechanics (and/or physics) were general admiration of mechanical theories; their (supposed) certainty and generality, the rigour of deduction from premises, and in some cases (especially energy/work mechanics) the self-evidence of the premises and the consequent results. But appeals were also made to specific principles and/or methods, and the discussion below deals exclusively with examples of these more specific concerns.

Utility in Jevons

Neoclassical economists, taking as prime concept the utility of economic actors, had to find a basic criteria for equilibrium different from that of the equality of supply and demand. Among the pioneers Stanley Jevons (1835–82) gave mathematics the greatest role. He brought the differential and integral calculus into play, but also drew upon mechanics (Maas 2001); before he started to publish on general economics in 1862 (Grattan-Guinness 2002), he had already written on the mechanical balance. His theory was based upon 'utility', a Benthamite notion drawing upon both pleasure and pain, which he saw as normally obeying the law of diminishing returns: that its derivative (marginal utility) increased to some maximal magnitude but that its second derivative decreased. There is an obvious analogy here with the deceleration of a moving particle, but he seems not to have drawn it. The curve corresponding to such a function is concave or convex to the axes, as he showed in diagrams sometimes; convexity was then a recognised feature of theorising in economics, and also in linear programming for the very few who practised it.

Jevons saw economic actors as trying to maximise their respective utilities, but he had considerable difficulty in reconciling it with the theory of supply and demand. He associated the process of maximisation with statics: it is somewhat akin to the techniques in variational mechanics, though not necessarily so influenced. He decided to identify the situation of equilibriate trading of two commodities by the equality of the ratio of the quantities traded and the inverse ratio of their respective 'final degrees of utility' (that is, the derivatives of the traders' utility functions with respect to those commodities at the time of exchange) (White 2004). This condition does not have any corresponding general result in mechanics.

Other points of possible analogy include associating (or not) curves of indifference with equipotential curves and surfaces. Their chief initiator, Jevons's partial follower in utility Francis Edgeworth (1845–1926), did not press this link, though he based much of his theory upon variational methods (Hamilton had been a family friend), especially the principle of least action; he also allied a 'perfect field of competition' with the motion of a 'continuous' (incompressible?) fluid (Edgeworth 1881, esp. pp. 16–30). On his position see Mirowski (1994).

Equilibrium and utility in Walras

A notable deployer of mechanics was Léon Walras (1834–1910). His work is still the subject of much discussion, as is testified by the large reprint of recent commentaries (Walker 2001) and a sympathetic survey of many of his main procedures (van Daal and Jolink 1993).

Between 1854 and 1858, when in his early twenties, Walras was an external student at the Ecole des Mines in Paris, one of the specialist engineering schools to which graduates of the Ecole Polytechnique passed as internal students. A reform of the courses took place in 1856, though their overall content does not seem to have altered much; a summary history of the courses is given in Aguillon (1889, pp. 660–9). No record appears to survive of Walras's apparently lacklustre activities there, but some educated guesses can be made. As an external student, he should have taken the 'preparatory' courses in mathematics, physics and chemistry, of which the mechanics part was quite wide-ranging, especially in dynamics. He could also have heard some of the main 'special' courses: the one on 'exploitation of mines and machines', taught until 1856 by the distinguished engineer and graduate of the Ecole Polytechnique Charles Combes, included some specialised topics in mechanics; and that on 'legislation and industrial economy', taught by one de Villeneuve, included a basic treatment of economics.

So it is likely that the young Walras knew some economics and quite a bit of (the French tradition in) engineering mechanics. Later he corresponded with (at least) Jules Dupuit, a graduate of the Ecole Polytechnique who passed his career as a roads and bridges engineer and later became an important figure in the economics of machines described above.

Another important early influence on Walras was Poinsot's superb textbook on statics, apparently the eighth edition of 1842 (the edition that I also own, I was pleased to discover!). The main attraction was not the opening chapter on the couple but the second one on questions of static equilibrium, where Poinsot often wrote equations involving linear combinations of terms (as used also in $(2)_1$) because he was balancing static moments (Bailhache 1975). There is an analogy here with economics, in that (distance $\times$ force = moment), the mechanical situation of the lever, from which the word 'equi-librium' comes, takes the same mathematical form as (unit price $\times$ number of units = outlay or income).

In this review I draw largely upon the 'fourth definitive edition' (1926) of Walras's major book on economic theory. The quotation at the head of this section shows how fervent was his advocacy of the major role of mathematics in the prosecution of economic theory (1926, arts 138, 370). He claimed it to be essential for the clear formulation of the law of supply and demand (art. 131), for example, and for the determination of not only equilibrate prices but also the laws of their variation (art. 370). He even criticised Carl Menger for not using mathematics (art. 164).

Among the various branches of mathematics mechanics took prime place for Walras. He distinguished dynamic from static equilibrium, on the grounds of being dependent on time or not (art. 74); perhaps he had studied something about (non-holonomic) constraints. The distinction was very important to him; the real world of 'economic *dynamics*' (art. 74) was time-dependent, and the resort to considerations based upon statics a decided simplification (arts 266, 322).

For Walras equilibrium was important because it had to furnish the environment within which economic activity could take place, especially purchase and consumption. A market trading in various commodities was in equilibrium when the effective demand for each commodity (that is, the demand for a fixed number or quantity of it at a determined price) was equal to its effective supply (arts 130, 42): he seems to have paid more attention to demand than to supply.

Walras interpreted both demand and supply in a community of economic actors as aggregates of the respective demands and supplies of its individual members. This use of aggregation legitimated his use of summations and linear equations. It also recalls molecular mechanics and physics, where cumulative action on or by a body is understood as a sum or integral over its supposedly basic 'particles'; Laplace's approach, mentioned above, was an example of this way of theorising. Maybe Walras was aware of such practices.

Walras also gave an important place to utility, and its maximisation by economic actors. A major notion in the setting of prices was the 'scarcity' of a commodity for an actor, essentially the derivative of his utility function. Walras's theory of equilibrium was based upon actors offering and changing trading prices by trial and error (*tâtonnement*), and equilibrium required each economic actor to maximise his own utility. Walras was aware that any state of equilibrium should itself be independent of the sequence of trial-and-error values that happened to have been used in its determination (this theorem was a basic component of the theory of limits since A.L. Cauchy in the 1820s); that it might take unstable as well as stable forms, depending upon the properties of the pertaining demand and supply curves; and indeed that equilibrium might not obtain at all. A necessary condition for two commodities to be in 'general' or 'perfect equilibrium' was similar to Jevons's, namely that the ratio of their unit prices equalled the ratio of those prices relative to a third commodity (art. 111).

A puzzling feature of Walras's theory is his explicit elimination of production time of a commodity (arts 207, 251). For contact with reality here seems slight; is, for example, a shipbuilding yard supposed to imagine that it can manufacture a ship that quickly? The assumption is especially surprising in an economist who stressed the place of time in theory in general. Maybe he was trying to avoid involving money, or developing a theory of capital; but such unwillingness should have been manfully overcome. Perhaps he was trying to maintain analogies with mechanics, where indeed no analogy with production time seems evident; but if so, then it was an unfortunate loyalty. Among successors to his approach the Swede Knut Wicksell did try to marry Walras's general approach to a theory of time-dependent capital, in his *Lectures on Political Economy* (1901).

In his last writing on economics Walras (1909) restated his belief in mechanics as a source for economics. In addition, presumably drawing upon the fairly recent spread of vector methods in mathematics (and specifically in economics by Irving Fisher), he claimed that scarcity was like a vector in having a direction (for example, I desire your product, not vice versa); in earlier writings he had likened scarcity to velocity or to heat. But the importance in mathematics of vectors lies in the properties of their algebra, such as composition and the scalar and vector products of two vectors. What corresponds to these properties in economics? If nothing, then the analogy is rather weak.

Equilibrium and 'index functions' in Pareto

Walras's successor at Lausanne University, Vilfredo Pareto (1848–1923), continued the reliance upon mechanics, as one would expect from someone with a considerable engineering background. On occasions Pareto also expressed his allegiance to d'Alembert's principle, which not only belongs to the variational tradition but also affirms the reducibility of dynamics to statics. In his textbook on economics he made explicit the analogy by imagining 'a man sliding down a slope on a sledge, while another man descends the same slope on foot, stopping at every step'. The latter situation 'represents a series of (discrete) successive positions of equilibrium' in 'broken movement'; and it 'is precisely this – a series of positions of equilibrium – which we study in political economy'. Presumably he had in mind, say, market trading, which is disturbed when one stall holder suddenly halves some of his prices; after some time trading settles down again, though maybe not in the same state of balance as before. By contrast, for Pareto 'the man on the sledge is a continuous movement which, if we study it, involves us in a problem of dynamics', for he is the mechanician (Pareto 1896, art. 587).

However, some reservations are in place. First, what corresponds in trading of any kind to the continuous and uniform action of gravity? Second, and more important, *the man sliding on a sledge is not in equilibrium*. No bones are smashed (we presume), and one could analyse the conservation of energy during his smooth descent; but none of the forms of equilibrium mentioned above is involved. It seems that Pareto confused the distinction between dynamic and static equilibrium with that between dynamic situations with or without impact.

Pareto had a fine opportunity to publicise his theory to mathematicians when he was invited to produce an article for the great German *Encyklopädie der mathematischen Wissenschaften*. Whether on his own or the editors' initiative, he did not offer a general article on mathematical economics but confined himself to 'Applications of mathematics to national economy'. His piece was quite short (Pareto 1902) and largely confined to his own approach, though he also provided a good bibliography of others' work. His version of utility was the 'ophelimity' of an economic actor, the desire for benefit and pleasure, which is to be maximised; Pareto related it to the freedom of choice and to lines of indifference. His account was confined to 'static' equilibrium, with 'dynamic' equilibrium handled only in a brief final part. There he stressed empirical work on economic crises: for a theoretical basis he appealed to the principle of virtual velocities, which shows his preference for the variational tradition.

Pareto's essay does not seem to be well known; but for the French edition of the encyclopaedia he produced a much more ambitious account (Pareto 1911), which has become fairly familiar. Unfortunately the project was abandoned shortly after the end of the Great War, and his article may have been a casualty. For it ends somewhat inconclusively on a new topic in its last article with, as it happens, a full sentence on the bottom line of page 640 of the volume; but this is the end of a thirty-two-page signature, which was the manner of production of both encyclopaedias. Thus the end of the text was probably not the end of the essay. But enough was printed for the principal points to be grasped.

The essay was a mercifully concise review of theories largely developed in earlier work, usually by Pareto himself. In its opening article he stated that he was exclusively concerned with static economic equilibrium, and he noted similarities with mechanics.

The main change relative to the German piece was that in the intervening years Pareto had abandoned ophelimity in favour of the 'index function'. An economic actor handles commodities denoted by variables x, $y, \ldots$, with certain given values at the start of his trading. Setting the commodity x as money, Pareto drew upon a neoclassical tradition practice set in train by Jevons by defining prices of y, $z, \ldots$ as the negative of the respective partial derivatives of x with respect to each one. (The minus sign was introduced in order to give positive prices; for the money value of a commodity usually decreases, and so its function has negative gradient.) He then formed a suite of equations relating the prices and the initial and subsequent (variable) quantities of each commodity. Eliminating the initial values of y, $z, \ldots$ from the suite yielded an equation relating these subsequent quantities to their prices and the initial value of money; and since the latter were partial derivatives, he had obtained a linear first-order partial differential equation. Integrating it and then taking its total differential gave him an equation of the form (2):

$$0 = q_x dx + q_y dy + \ldots, \tag{3}$$

where the coefficients were functions of all variables (including x) and also of the initial value of x. He then eliminated the initial value of x also, upon the possibly dubious claim that the price of any commodity lying between its buying and selling values did not 'generally' depend upon any initial value, money included. Allowing for the possible need of an integrating factor in (3), he wrote its integral as

$$\text{`}F(\phi) = c\text{' (a constant), where } 0 = \phi_x dx + \phi_y dy + \ldots \tag{4}$$

$F(\phi)$ was the 'index function' relative to x of the economic actor. F had to satisfy only a few conditions on its total differential dF, and so was not unique; the burden of this rather bemusing theory fell upon ϕ, a function of the other variables but *not* of the initial value of x. The principal condition governing the actor's decision regarding a commodity, say y, was that he was in equilibrium if the differential increase dy in y left F stationary, that is, $dF = 0$. 'The function F is thus an index of the individual's movements' (Pareto 1911, arts 2–5). Now (4) takes the form of a work function in mechanics, with its integral interpretable as a potential;[2] indeed, the whole analysis looks mathematically much like a piece of variational mechanics using principles such as d'Alembert's or virtual work. However, Pareto did not rely upon mechanics but instead drew upon the calculus of functions of several variables. He went on to consider various relationships between the variables and their partial derivatives around assumed points of (seemingly static) equilibrium and properties of the associated indifference curves, with ophelimity now taken to be just one kind of index function (arts 18–19).

Pareto also considered various aspects of supply and demand, and of production. The most durable part is the theory of optimality named after him, whereby a community achieves 'maximal ophelimity' when 'it is impossible to change by a slight amount in such a way that the ophelimities enjoyed by each individual, neglecting those that remain constant, all increase or all decrease' (art. 28). If any mathematical analogy comes to mind, it would be saddle-point optimal points of a function of several variables, maybe with constraints; no obvious analogue comes to mind from mechanics, whose place in this essay was confined to the observation that the theory was applicable to mechanical businesses involving technology, such as a mill (art. 29) – a sign of the reduction of its place in mathematical economics that belonged to the new century.

Mechanics as a source of emulation or of corroboration?

It is quite understandable historically that economics, a struggling discipline, should have turned to a glamorous and transparently successful companion such as mechanics, and later also to physics when it too gained high status, as major sources of notions and theories to imitate. In this section I consider types of (in)effective imitation.

There are two stages of influence of mathematics upon economics. One concerns the use and handling of numbers in data, in contexts such as the testing of an economic theory. Here one uses not only arithmetic but maybe also other branches such as statistics and numerical methods. The main concern here is the role of mathematics in the earlier stage of theory formation in economics.

Let us consider in quite general terms the types of influence – positive and/or negative – that one theory may have upon another one. An attractive part of the philosophy of science, and mathematics in particular, nevertheless it has not gained the attention that it deserves; the remarks that follow draw upon the sketch given in (Grattan-Guinness 1993). The basic notion is that of 'structure similarity' between theories, namely the extent to which they may make (or not make) similar assertions in their different contexts; that is, how a theory means (or does not mean) in various different contexts. For example, Pareto's equation (3) is a sum in which each term has its own interpretation in economics; but there are contexts

2 A later case is the hydraulic machine developed around 1950 by A.W.H. Phillips at the London School of Economics (Morgan and Boumans 2004). It allowed three-dimensional modelling, an important improvement on the norm; but the caveats rehearsed in this section about forming analogies still apply.

where the individual terms of a sum have clear mathematical meanings but do not carry the physical readings that apply to the sum itself.

Let us take two (components of) theories, A and B, either in settled form or in process of development, possibly though not necessarily mathematical or economic, but with different ranges of application. The (lack of) quality of the theories, or the level of competence with which analogies are made, are not at issue here. Several types of influence, which are not mutually exclusive, can be distinguished: I state them in terms of A influencing B, but the converse influence, or interactions between the two (again positive or negative), may also obtain.

1 *Reduction.* A not only actively plays a role in the formation and development of B, but the theorist also hopes to *reduce* B to the remit of A. Analogies become special cases of A in B.
2 *Emulation.* A actively plays a role in the formation and development of B, with resulting structural similarities, but reduction is not asserted or maybe even sought. Analogies are exactly that.
3 *Corroboration.* A plays little or no role in the formation and development of B; but the theorist draws upon similarities to A, maybe including structural ones, to develop B further and thereby enhance the measure of analogy between B and A.
4 *Instantiation.* A and B have certain notions N in common, thereby creating analogies. But each occurrence of N is seen as an example of its great generality, which surpasses the remits of A and B.

The central concern of this chapter is forms of equilibrium, and the extent and ways in which mechanics provoked their study in economics. The theories come mainly from mechanics or from economics, with the differential and integral calculus sometimes also present. Let us consider some instances.

The early stages of locational equilibrium show reduction of economics to mechanics, since the theory depends upon the weights falling into a state of static equilibrium; but it is the *only* case of which I am aware. In mainstream neoclassical economics, I doubt if it was ever intended; if so, then the fate of Laplace's molecularism of physics should have been a warning! Interaction between the two fields is evident in the case of machine efficiency.

Usually the influence was from mechanics to economics. Emulation surely occurred in, for example, in Walras's early reading of Poinsot, which implanted mechanics centrally in his thought, leading to active influence in his later work; his call to arms of 1890, quoted at the head of the previous section, is clearly emulative. Mirowski (1989) seems to argue for the emulation of physics (and mechanics) in the development of theory by Walras (and other economists); by contrast, Jolink and van Daal (1989) advocate that much corroboration is present. I suspect that both types of influence may have been in place, and that Walras may not have known, or remembered, which one was in play at each stage; he may not even have had in mind the distinction between the types when preparing his theories. With Jevons and Pareto, corroboration may have been more marked; but again, emulation played a role (Pareto's index functions, for example), and the available evidence may not always allow us to detect the instances.

The status of universality or generality is also worth noting. Each of the three traditions of mechanics rehearsed at the start of this article claimed a wide compass for its operation, although the other two disputed such pretensions! Universality was asserted, especially in the mid nineteenth century, for the constancy of energy in 'any' system. This claim had affected other fields; in particular, some economic theories tried to give a similar status to value (Mirowski 1989, ch. 4). Neoclassical economists seem not to have stressed constancy to this extent, but they instantiated other very general notions such as optimisation, in emulation of various techniques in mechanics and other parts of mathematics. In linear programming both economics and mechanics instantiate convexity and optimisation, notions general enough to be of importance elsewhere also. A wide-ranging entropy law was in place in energetics, to buttress the claims of generality, but no corresponding notion has emerged in economics, either in the period studied here nor to my knowledge ever since. Hence the generality which Walras sought cannot be achieved, at any rate not yet.

Finally, one may wonder about the extent to which economists had mastered the mechanics that they wished to emulate or corroborate. Usually the control was adequate for the (modest) purposes at hand; but Pareto on means of descending a mountain is one exception. However, as a general point, imperfect understanding of theory A does *not* necessarily cause B to be defective.

Sources of effective imitation

Largely analogies

The mention of physics in the last paragraph suggests a useful meta-analogy between the influences of mechanics upon physics and upon economics. As was noted above, the great rise of physics, especially mathematical physics, from the 1800s drew heavily upon various mechanical principles (Sommerfeld 1903–26 *passim*; Warwick 2003): indeed, I characterise mathematical physics as 'mechanics in fancy dress' in order to emphasise that mechanical notions play important roles alongside the laws that are proper to these branches of physics themselves. The magnitude of the influence may have encouraged neoclassical economists heavily to invoke both mechanics and physics but, as was suggested especially in the last section, effective influence was much more restricted. Let us now consider some particular features.

On equilibrium itself, mechanical stability, as characterised earlier, is more dynamic a concept; it is a pity that it did not capture more attention from the economists, especially in the exploration of conditions to achieve and maintain economic 'equilibrium'. Even then, though, the gap between mechanical and economic stability is still impressive: Walras's theory of trial and error did not draw upon mechanical modes of equilibrium or stability in any great detail.

One criticism of economics, whether mathematical or not, is that it makes (and made) unrealistic assumptions: ideal market, perfect competition, and so on. Mechanics may take some of the blame, with its notorious light strings mounted over inextensible pulleys lifting smooth masses in a vacuum, and so on. But with some care good analyses can be still be made in mechanics, concerning quite light strings mounted over sturdy pulleys and lifting rather smooth masses in still air; and experimental testing was of a high standard (see Bell 1973) in continuum and solid body mechanics. So the ideal and the real mechanical worlds are not too far apart. Can the same be said of the ideal and real economic worlds? Walras on (no) production time is a ludicrous assumption.

The main issue here is *testability* of a theory against information obtained from experiment and observation. Economics is criticised, often though not always fairly, for a disinclination to test its predictions against information. Now the contrast with mechanics is not as stark as might be imagined. In the celestial and planetary branches testing could be severe, even on occasion involving strings of decimal places; but there and elsewhere testing was only partial. For example, much experimental work in continuum mechanics yielded information on, say, the deformation and rupture of elastic solids, or the location of the peaks of waves in the motion of large fluid bodies, that could be laid against theoretical predictions; but the alleged arrangement and derangement of the supposedly basic molecules of the continuous substances involved were not really testable. A similar remark applies to any theory in mechanics or mathematical physics that drew upon the structure, molecular or not, of the assumed aether. Further, both subjects were cursed often enough with what I call 'notional' applications, where lengthy analyses of, say, the rings of Saturn or the distortion of the shape of the sextant by exposure to the Sun produced impressive formulae but no useful means of contact with information. Finally, quite often formulae such as series or integrals could not be precisely evaluated for the given values of its constants and variables, so that approximative and numerical methods had to be developed in partial compensation; this need, together with the unavoidable imprecision of data drawn from information, lessened the severity of the testing.

To an extent occurring largely after the period studied here, some other terms from mechanics have endured in economics; most frequently in talk of 'economic forces', and also 'elasticity' of supply and demand, the 'accelerator' in monetary theory, and 'frictions' such as premiums to pay on buying money, or mismatches between the skills needed for unfilled posts and those possessed by the potential employees. But the influence from mechanics was and is slight, barely reaching the level of corroboration – just as well, especially with the difficulties attending friction pointed out above! Similarly, the many analyses of business cycles appear not to have drawn upon cycles in thermodynamics – and indeed there do not seem to be any useful analogies to draw from the adiabatic and isothermal parts of the latter cycle.

The final analogy here is *linearity*. It became almost a dogma in mechanics and (mathematical) physics during the nineteenth century, even though scientists knew that the world was actually not a linear place (Grattan-Guinness 2006).

Linear forms also played an important role in mathematical economics, in particular in Walras's and Pareto's general equations. Now this is quite reasonable when calculating the total cost or price of a commodity that is set at the same price for each item, as with Walras, for example; but its place in the more theoretical aspects, such as the principle of virtual velocities, is much more questionable. Further, in mechanics and physics itself non-linearity has gained a much higher status (West 1985), partly because computers now allow many algorithms and other techniques to be effected in practice. For several decades economics has also favoured other procedures, such as game theory and a wide range of statistical techniques (themselves partly inspired by statistical mechanics); with some honourable exceptions such as Jevons, they were absent from the period when mechanical principles held prime place.

On the use of the calculus in economics

Some of the linear equations used by Walras and Pareto were differential ones, which come from the calculus, which was often used fruitfully, and without appeal to mechanics. For example, marginal utility was taken to be a derivative even though a tiny forward difference was really involved, or it was assumed that some economic function of time (or another variable) was continuous whereas actually it was micro-discontinuous. One can readily forgive economists such licence, which can be found in mechanics and mathematical physics itself: the differential (and integral) calculus is a far more powerful theory to work with than are the difference and summation calculi.

Yet conceptual difficulties could arise. In particular, some differential forms such as Pareto's (3) may not be exact as they stand, and so cannot be integrated directly; but this becomes possible if they can be multiplied through by a function, known as an integrating factor. (Some differential equations do not always have such a function.) But what sense do the resulting formulae make as economics? This question was forcefully posed around 1900 by the mathematician Hermann Laurent to both Walras and Pareto, who did not respond adequately (Mirowski 1989, pp. 243–8). One possible response is to say that, while the initial equation and its solution have to make sense as economics, the lines of deduction in between them need *not* meet this requirement. Several topics in mathematics itself show this feature; for example, Boolean algebra, and operator methods of solving differential equations. The same point can be made for other uses of the calculus, and the solution proposed: for example, using Lagrange multipliers to express constraints (Baxley and Moorhouse 1984) where their status in mechanics itself can be somewhat obscure; or using the implicit function theorem, which gives sufficient conditions for converting a relationship between several variables into one of them being a single-valued function of the others over some neighbourhood of their values.

Largely dis-analogies

Apart from specific contexts such as early locational equilibrium, *any* proposed influence from mechanics, and from physics in general, should be approached with great caution (compare Israel 1996). Indeed, my own reading of economics, not only the authors discussed above, often forced disanalogies to the fore.

Take as an example the important notion of interaction. Surely the modes evident in mechanical and physical situations cannot match, or even resemble, either the numerous types of both personal and interpersonal action of which human beings and communities are capable, or the speed of their deployment. Concerning feedback, for example, many mechanical and physical systems and artefacts have servomechanisms; the historically classic case was a governor mounted on a steam engine, and acting as a safety device. Later on, feedback and other kinds of loop were a major feature of electrical networks, and now of computers also. But human interactions and reactions in, say, a trading or marketing floor, or indeed in any socially based activity, are *immeasurably* more complicated, with aetiology difficult or even impossible to determine. Influence from P to Q or from Q to P, or interaction between them, or all of these – in many cases, who knows which obtained? Such questions leave far behind Walras's assumption of the cumulative utility of a community, noted earlier.

Again, an important method of analysing equilibrium in market trading is by constructing demand and supply curves. Cournot led the way in 1838 with his turnover curves, and later Walras in 1874 and then Marshall in 1890 adapted them to the theory of 'scissors' curves with which we are now familiar; equilibrium occurred at the point(s) of intersection as long as demand was increasing and supply decreasing there. Various types of market were considered, such as monopoly, duopoly, *n*-opoly, barter, fiat money and commodity money (not necessarily in that historical order: see, for example (Blaug 1968, chs 9–10 *passim*)). While the notion of balance is central here, the details attending the versions of balance or equilibrium used in mechanics are lacking: the closest versions may be stability as described earlier, and perhaps oscillatory static. Similar points seem to apply to the later use, from J.R. Hicks onwards, of intersecting curves relating investment to savings or liquidity to money supply. A more important mathematical feature seems to be the question of whether these curves are (locally) convex or not.

These reservations, and similar ones about other features, do not depend upon the important findings in recent decades that cast doubt on the existence of economic equilibria, the failure of the process of trial and error to converge to them, and the apparent economic meaninglessness of various mathematical theorems about them (see Ackerman *et al.* 2004 for a critique). However, quite understandably, the mechanically minded economists of that time underrated such reservations: the lure of potential mechanical glamour was too great to avoid corroboration and even emulation in the senses presented in the previous section. They (and also others not cited here) seem to have appealed quite sincerely to mechanics in general, and equilibria in particular, and daringly when principles such as least action and virtual velocities were invoked. However, they made much less use of mechanics than they claimed in their appeals, as was pointed out by some of the specialists in mechanics and/or physics who took notice of economics (Ingrao and Israel 1985); and often they drew upon only the simplest cases of equilibria.

While neoclassical economists sincerely felt themselves to be influenced by mechanics, the active role played by mechanics was far less than their claims suggest, and often it served more to console than to emulate. But this restricted use of mechanics is very welcome, because appropriate. My point is not that all forms of equilibrium analysis should be avoided in economics (the stance taken in Ackerman *et al.* 2004), but that mechanics and physics were, and are, very unreliable sources of emulation and even of corroboration for equilibria in economics. I take this view not only for the history of mechanics outlined in this chapter but also for later developments of the subject, including very interesting recent ones (for example, Noll 1974).

Adam Smith was partially motivated by mechanical analogies to moot the idea of the invisible hand guiding economic activities (Nadal 2004). However, perhaps it is not a hand at all, at least not one placed on any mechanical tiller.

Bibliography

An asterisked reference is not cited in this chapter but is an important source for the history of mechanics and related parts of engineering and physics.

Ackerman, F. *et al.* (2004), *The flawed foundations of general equilibrium*, Routledge, London.

Aguillon, L. (1889), 'L'Ecole des mines de Paris. Notice historique', *Annales des mines* (8) 15, *Mémoires*, 433–686. Syllabi of the courses for 1889 given on pp. 94–362.

Bacharach, M. (1883), *Abriss der Geschichte der Potentialtheorie*, Thein, Würzburg.

Backhouse, R. (1985), *A history of modern economic analysis*, Blackwell, Oxford.

Bailhache, P. (ed. and comm.) (1975), *Louis Poinsot. La théorie générale de l'équilibre et du mouvement des systémes*, Vrin, Paris.

Baumol, W.J. and Goldfield, S.M. (eds) (1968), *Precursors in mathematical economics. An anthology*, London School of Economics and Political Science, London.

Baxley, J.V. and Moorhouse, J.C. (1984), 'Lagrange multiplier problems in economics', *American Mathematical Monthly*, 91, 404–12.

Bell, J.F. (1973), *The experimental foundations of solid mechanics. Encyclopaedia of physics*, 6a, pt 1, Springer, Berlin.

Berg, M. (1980), *The machinery question and the making of political economy, 1815–1848*, Cambridge University Press, Cambridge.

Bertoloni Meli, D. (1993), *Equivalence and priority. Newton versus Leibniz*, Clarendon Press, Oxford.

Blaug, M. (1968), *Economics theory in retrospect*, 2nd edn, Heinemann, London.

Bogolyubov, A.N. (ed.) (1976), *Mekhanika i fizika XVIII b*[*eke*], Nauk, Moscow.

Bogolyubov, A.N. (ed.) (1978), *Mekhanika i fizika vtoroi polovini XVIII b*[*eke*], Nauk, Moscow.

Brackenridge, J.B. (1995), *The key to Newton's dynamics*, University of California Press, Berkeley, CA.

Caneva, K.L. (1993), *Robert Mayer and the conservation of energy*, Princeton University Press, Princeton, NJ.

Cannon, J.T. and Dostrovsky, S. (1981), *The evolution of dynamics. Vibration theory from 1687 to 1742*, Springer, Heidelberg.

Cohen, I.B. (1971), 'Newton's second law and the concept of force in the Principia', in R. Palter (ed.), *The* annus mirabilis *of Sir Isaac Newton, 1666–1966*, MIT Press, Cambridge, MA, 143–85.

Dugas, R. (1955), *Histoire de la mécanique*, Griffon, Paris. (English trans.: Central, New York, 1957.)

Duhem, P. (1903), *L'Évolution de la mécanique*, Joanin, Paris. (English trans.: Sijthoff and Noordhoff, Alphen aan den Rijn, 1980.)

Dühring, E.C. (1873), *Kritische Geschichte der allgemeinen Principien der Mechanik*, Grieben, Berlin.

Edgeworth, F.Y. (1881), *Mathematical psychics. An essay on the applications of mathematics to the moral sciences*, Kegan Paul, London.

Euler, L. (1983), *Leonhard Euler. Beiträge zu Leben und Werk*, Birkhäuser, Basel.*

Franksen, O.I. and Grattan-Guinness, I. (1989), 'The earliest contribution to location theory? Spacio-economic equilibrium with Lamé and Clapeyron, 1829', *Mathematics and Computing in Simulation*, 31, 195–220.

Fraser, C. (1983), 'J.L. Lagrange's early contributions to the principles and methods of mechanics', *Archive for history of exact sciences*, 28, 197–241.*

Fraser, C. (1985), 'd'Alembert's principle, the original formulation and application in Jean d'Alembert's Traité de dynamique (1743)', *Centaurus*, 28, 31–61.

Garber, E. (1999), *The language of physics. The calculus and the development of theoretical physics in Europe, 1750–1914*, Birkhäuser, Basel.

Gautier, A. (1817), *Essai historique sur le problème des trois corps, ou dissertation sur la théorie des mouvemens da la lune et des planètes, abstraction faite de leur figure*, Courcier, Paris.

Gillispie, C.C. (ed.) (1971), *Lazare Carnot, savant*, Princeton University Press, Princeton, NJ.

Gillmor, C.S. (1971), *Charles Augustin Coulomb. Physics and engineering in eighteenth century France*, Princeton University Press, Princeton, NJ.

Gordon, J.E. (1976), *The new science of strong materials, or Why you don't fall through the floor*, 2nd edn, Penguin, Harmondsworth.

Grall, B. (2004), *Economie de forces et production d'utilité*, Presses Universitaires de Rennes, Rennes.*

Grattan-Guinness, I. (1984), 'Work for the workers: advances in engineering mechanics and instruction in France, 1800–1830', *Annals of Science*, 41, 1–33.*

Grattan-Guinness, I. (1987), 'From Laplacian physics to mathematical physics, 1805–1826', in C. Burrichter, R. Inhetveen and R. Kötter (eds), *Zum Wandel des Naturverständnisses*, Schöningh, Paderborn, 11–34.

Grattan-Guinness, I. (1989), 'Modes and manners of applied mathematics: the case of mechanics', in D. Rowe and J. McCleary (eds), *History of modern mathematics*, II, Academic Press, New York, 109–26.*

Grattan-Guinness, I. (1990a), *Convolutions in French mathematics, 1800–1840. From the calculus and mechanics to mathematical analysis and mathematical physics*, 3 vols, Birkhäuser, Basel, and Deutscher Verlag der Wissenschaften Berlin.

Grattan-Guinness, I. (1990b), 'The varieties of mechanics by 1800', *Historia mathematica*, 17, 313–38.

Grattan-Guinness, I. (1993), 'Structure-similarity: between mathematics and philosophy', in J. Czermak (ed.), *Proceedings of the XV International Wittgenstein Symposium*, Hölder-Pichler-Tempsky, Vienna, I, 317–33.

Grattan-Guinness, I. (ed.), (1994a), *Companion encyclopaedia of the history and philosophy of the mathematical sciences*, 2 vols, Routledge, London. (Repr. Johns Hopkins University Press, Baltimore, MD, 2003.)

Grattan-Guinness, I. (1994b), '"A new type of question": on the prehistory of linear and non-linear programming, 1770–1940', in E. Knobloch and D. Rowe (eds), *History of modern mathematics*, III, Academic Press, New York, 43–89.

Grattan-Guinness, I. (1995), 'Why did George Green write his essay of 1828 on electricity and magnetism?', *American Mathematical Monthly*, 52, 387–96.*

Grattan-Guinness, I. (2000), 'Daniel Bernoulli (1700–1782) and the varieties of mechanics in the eighteenth century', *Nieuw Archief voor Wiskunde*, 5, 242–49.*

Grattan-Guinness, I. (2002), '"In some parts rather rough": an unknown manuscript version of Stanley Jevons's *General Mathematical Theory of Political Economy* (1862)', *History of Political Economy*, 34, 685–726.

Grattan-Guinness, I. (2005a), 'Classical mechanics as a formal(ised) science', in B. Loewe (ed.), *Foundations of the formal sciences*, to appear.

Grattan-Guinness, I. (2005b), 'Cournot on mechanics, 1826–1834, especially using inequalities', *Revista Brasiliera de Historia da Matematica*, 5, to appear. (French trans. in T. Martin (ed.), *Actualité de Cournot*, Vrin, Paris, to appear.)

Grattan-Guinness, I. (ed.) (2005c), *Landmark writings in Western mathematics, 1640–1940*, Elsevier, Amsterdam.

Grattan-Guinness, I. (2006), 'Differential equations and linearity in the nineteenth and early twentieth centuries', in a volume dedicated to the memory of A.P. Yuskekvich, Brepols, Turnhout, to appear.

Greenberg, J. (1995), *The problem of the Earth's shape from Newton to Clairaut. The rise of geomechanics in eighteenth-century Paris*, Cambridge University Press, Cambridge.

Guicciardini, N. (1999), *Reading the Principia. The debate on Newton's mathematical methods of natural philosophy from 1687 to 1736*, Cambridge University Press, Cambridge.

Haas, A.E. (1909), *Die Entwicklungsgeschichte des Satzes von der Erhaltung der Kraft*, Hölder, Vienna.

Harman, P.M. (1982), *Metaphysics and natural philosophy. The problem of substance in classical physics*, Harvester, Brighton and Barnes and Noble, Totowa, NJ.

Heilbron, J. (general ed.) (2002), *Storia della scienza*, V, *L'età dei lumi*, Enciclopedia Italiana, Rome. (Large part on mathematics.)

Heyman, J. (1972), *Coulomb's memoir on statics. An essay on the history of civil engineering*, Cambridge University Press, Cambridge.

Howey, R.S. (1960), *The rise of the marginal utility school, 1870–1889*, Kansas State University Press, Lawrence, KS.

Hutchinson, T.W. (1953), *A review of economic doctrines*, Clarendon Press, Oxford.

Ingrao, B. and Israel, G. (1985), 'General economic equilibrium theory. A history of ineffectual paradigmatic shifts', *Fundamenta scientiae*, 6, 1–45, 89–125.

Ingrao, B. and Israel, G. (1990), *The invisible hand. Economic equilibrium in the history of science*, MIT Press, Cambridge, MA.

Israel, G. (1996), *Le Mathématisation du réel*, Seuil, Paris.

Jolink, A. and van Daal, J. (1989), 'Léon Walras's mathematical economics and the mechanical analogies', *History of Economics Society Bulletin*, 11 (1), 25–32. (Repr. in Walker 2001, I, 93–100.)

Jouguet, E. (1909), *Lectures de mécanique. La mécanique enseignée par les auteurs originaux*, II, Gauthier-Villars, Paris. (Vol. I (1908) covers the seventeenth century.)

Kjeldsen, T.H. (2000), 'A contextualised historical analysis of the Kuhn–Tucker theorem in nonlinear programming', *Historia mathematica*, 27, 331–61.

Klein, C.F. then Müller, C.H. (eds) (1896–1935), *Encyklopädie der mathematischen Wissenschaften*, IV, *Mechanik*, 2 pts, Teubner, Leipzig and Berlin. (Massive and irreplaceable survey.)

Körner, T. (1904), 'Der Begriff des materiellen Punktes in der Mechanik des achtzehnten Jahrhunderts', *Bibliotheca mathematica*, (3)5, 15–62. (Also published Gera, as a Kiel University doctorate.)

Kötter, F.W.F. (1892), 'Die Entwicklung der Lehre vom Erddruck', *Jahresbericht der Deutschen Mathematiker-Vereinigung*, 2 (1891–92), 77–154.

Lindt, R. (1904), 'Das Prinzip der virtuellen Geschwindigkeiten. Seine Beweise und die Unmöglichkeit seiner Umkehrung bei Verwendung des Begriffes "Gleichgewicht eines Massensystems" ', *Abhandlungen zur Geschichte der Mathematik*, 18, 145–95.

Maas, H. (2001), 'Mechanical reasoning: Jevons and the making of modern economics', University of Amsterdam doctorate.

Mach, E. (1883), *Die Mechanik in ihrer Entwicklung historisch-kritisch dargestellt*, 1st edn, Brockhaus, Leipzig. (Overrated. Later editions to nineth, 1933. Various translations.)

Maltese, G. (1992), *La storia de «F = ma». La seconda legge del moto nel XVIII secolo*, Olschki, Florence.

Mirowski, P. (1989), *More heat than light. Economics as social physics, physics as nature's economics*, Cambridge University Press, Cambridge.

Mirowski, P. (1994), 'Introduction', in (ed.), *Edgeworth on choice, economic hazard and statistics*, Rowman and Littlefield, Lanham, MD, 1–79.

Morgan, M.S. and Boumans, M. (2004), 'Secrets hidden by two-dimensionality: the economy as a hydraulic machine', in S. de Chadarevian and N. Hopwood (eds), *Models: the third dimension of science*, Stanford University Press, Stanford, CA, 369–401.

Nadal, A. (2004), 'Freedom and submission. Individuals and the invisible hand', in Ackerman *et al.* (2004), 181–201.

Noll, W. (1974), *The foundations of mechanics and thermodynamics. Selected papers*, Springer, New York.

Novozhilov, V.V. (1967), *Problemy izmereniya zatrat i resul'tatov pri optimal'nom planirovani*, Economica, Moscow. (English trans. *Problems of cost–benefit analysis in optimal planning*, International Arts and Sciences Press, White Plains, NY, 1970.)

Pareto, V. (1896), *Cours d'économie politique*, I, Rouge, Lausanne.

Pareto, V. (1902), 'Anwendungen der Mathematik auf die Nationalökonomie', in *Encyklopädie der mathematischen Wissenschaften*, I, 1097–1120 (article 1G2).

Pareto, V. (1911), 'Economie mathématique', in *Encyclopédie des sciences mathématiques*, tome 1 (4), 591–640. (Complete? Partial English trans. in Baumol and Goldfield, 1968, 49–95.)

Poinsot, L. (1803), *Eléments de statique*, 1st edn, Calixte Voll, Paris. (Many later editions.)

Poncelet, J.V. (1852), 'Examen critique et historique des principales théories ou solutions concernant l'équilibre des voûtes', *Comptes rendus de l'Académie des Sciences*, 35, 495–502, 531–40, 577–87.

Popper, K.R. (1950–51), 'Indeterminism in quantum physics and in classical physics', *British Journal of Philosophy of Science*, 1, 117–33, 173–95.

Prange, H.F.W.G. (1933), 'Die allgemeine Integrationsmethoden der analytischen Mechanik', in Klein and Müller (1896–1935), pt 1, sec. 2, 505–804 (article IV 12–13).

Pulte, H. (1989), *Das Prinzip der kleinsten Wirkung und die Kraftkonzeptionen der rationalen Mechanik*, Steiner, Stuttgart.

Pulte, H. (2005), *Axiomatik und Empirie. Eine wissenschaftstheoriegeschichtliche Untersuchung zur mathematischen Naturphilosophie von Newton bis Neumann*, Wissenschaftliche Buchgesellschaft, Darmstadt.

Roche, J.J. (1998), *The mathematics of measurement. A critical history*, Athlone Press, London.

Rowlinson, J.S. (2002), *Cohesion. A scientific history of intermolecular forces*, Cambridge University Press, Cambridge.

Royal Society (1909), *Royal Society of London. Catalogue of scientific papers, 1800–1900. Subject index*, II, *Mechanics*, Royal Society, London. (Repr. Scarecrow, Metuchen NJ, 1968.)

Rühlmann, M. (1881–85), *Vorträge zur Geschichte der theoretischen Maschinenlehre und der damit in Zusammenhang stehenden mathematischen Wissenschaften*, 2 pts, Schwetschke, Brunswick.

Schumpeter, J.A. (1954), *History of economic analysis*, Allen and Unwin, London.

Schwarzschild, K, Oppenheim S. and von Dyck, V.W. (eds) (1904–34), *Encyklopädie der mathematischen Wissenschaften*, VI, pt 1, *Geodäsie und Geophysik*, pt 2, *Astronomie*, Teubner, Leipzig and Berlin.

Scott, W.L. (1970), *The conflict between atomism and conservation theory, 1644–1860*, MacDonald, London, and Elsevier, New York.

Smith, D.M. (1980), *Industrial location*, 2nd edn, Wiley, New York.

Sommerfeld, A. (ed.) (1903–26), *Encyklopädie der mathematischen Wissenschaften*, V, *Physik*, 3 pts, Teubner, Leipzig and Berlin.

Spiegel, H.W. (1991), *The growth of economic thought*, 3rd edn, Duke University Press, Durham, NC.

Stäckel, P.G. (1905), 'Elementare Dynamik der Punktsysteme und starren Körper', in Klein and Müller (1896–1935), pt 1, sec. 1, 435–684 (article IV 6).

Szabo, I. (1977), *Geschichte der mechanischen Prinzipien und ihrer wichtigsten Anwendungen*, Birkhäuser, Basel.

Todhunter, I. (1873), *A history of the mathematical theories of attraction and figure of the earth from the time of Newton to that of Laplace*, 2 vols. Macmillan, London. (Reprinted Dover, New York, 1962.)

Truesdell, C. (1954), 'Rational fluid mechanics, 1687–1765', in Euler *Opera omnia*, sec. 2, XII, Orell Füssli, Zurich, vii–cxxv.

Truesdell, C. (1955), 'Editor's introduction' on sound and fluid mechanics, in Euler *Opera omnia*, sec. 2, XIII, Orell Füssli, Zurich, vii–cxviii.

Truesdell, C. (1960), *The rational mechanics of flexible or elastic bodies, 1638–1788*, Orell Füssli, Zurich (as Euler *Opera omnia*, sec. 2, XI, pt 2).

Truesdell, C. (1968), *Essays in the history of mechanics*, Springer, Berlin.

van Daal, J. and Jolink, A. (1993), *The equilibrium economics of Léon Walras*, Routledge, London and New York.

Vatin, F. (1993), *Le travail. Economie et physique 1780–1850*, Presses Universitaires de France, Paris.

Vatin, F. (1998), *Economie politique et économie naturalle chez Augustin-Antoine Cournot*, Presses Universitaires de France, Paris.

Veblen, T.B. (1900), 'The preconceptions of economic science' III, *Quarterly Journal of Economics*, 14, 240–69.

Voss, A.E. (1901), 'Die Prinzipien der rationellen Mechanik', in Klein and Müller (1896–1935), pt 1, sec. 1, 3–121 (article IV 1).

Waff, C. (1976), 'Universal gravitation and the motion of the moon's apogee: the establishment and reception of Newton's inverse-square law, 1687–1749', Johns Hopkins University doctorate, Baltimore, MD.*

Walker, D. (ed.) (2001), *The legacy of Léon Walras*, Edward Elgar, Cheltenham and Northampton, MA.

Walras, L. (1909), 'Economique et mécanique', *Bulletin de la Société vaudoise des sciences naturelles*, 15, 313–25. (Repr. in *Metroeconomica*, 12 (1960), 3–11.)

Walras, L. (1926), *Eléments d'économie politique pure, ou théorie de la richesse sociale*, posthumous 'definitive' edn, Pichon, Paris, and Rouge, Lausanne. (English trans. *Elements of pure economics or the theory of social wealth*, Allen and Unwin, London, and Kelley, New York, 1954. Includes data on the earlier four editions, 1874–1900.)

Warwick, A. (2003), *Masters of theory. Cambridge and the rise of mathematical physics*, University of Chicago Press, Chicago.

Weiss, B. (1988), *Zwischen Physikotheologie und Positivismus. Pierre Prevost (1751–1839) und die korpuskularkinetische Physik der Genfer Schule*, Lang, Frankfurt.

West, B.J. (1985), *An essay on the importance of being non-linear*, Springer, New York.

White, M. (2004), 'A grin without a cat: W.S. Jevons, elusive equilibrium', in T. Aspromourgos and J. Lodewijks (eds), *History and political economy. Essays in honour of P.D. Groenewegen*, Routledge, London, 97–117.

Wilson, C.A. (1980), 'Perturbation and solar tables from Lacaille to Delambre: the rapprochement of observation and theory', *Archive for history of exact sciences*, 22, 53–188, 189–304.

Wilson, C.A. (1985), 'The great inequality of Jupiter and Saturn: from Kepler to Laplace', *Archive for history of exact sciences*, 33, 15–290.

Wise, N. with Smith, C. (1989–90), 'Work and waste: political economy and natural philosophy in nineteenth-century Britain', *History of science*, 27, 263–301, 391–449; 28, 221–61.

Wolf, C.J.E. (ed.) (1889–91), *Mémoires sur le pendule précédés d'une bibliographie*, 2 pts, Gauthier-Villars, Paris. (Includes extensive introduction.)

2 Between economics and chemistry

Lavoisier's and Le Chatelier's notions of equilibrium

Bernadette Bensaude-Vincent and Valeria Mosini

This chapter discusses Lavoisier's and Le Chatelier's notions of chemical equilibrium, and their respective interplays with economic equilibrium. We argue that Lavoisier's notion of chemical equilibrium derived from an economical approach to chemistry. However, rather than suggesting a direct influence of economics upon chemistry, we emphasise the migration of concepts within a historical context. We also discuss an influence in the opposite direction, from chemistry to economics, implicit in Samuelson's use of the Le Chatelier principle of mobile equilibrium. We express reservations on whether the appropriation of the principle from chemistry to economics was justified.

Two notions of equilibrium in chemistry

The static notion of equilibrium as a balance of forces has been fundamental to chemistry for a long time. Before the law of chemical equilibrium was formulated in the late nineteenth century, the practice of balancing the weights of reactants and products had become some sort of 'mental gesture' that shaped almost all chemical practices. Presenting Lavoisier's balance sheet method, we argue that the balance was more than just a technical tool, in that it provided an abstract notion to mediate among the various realms of nature, as well as among the various aspects of the Enlightenment culture.

The dynamic notion of chemical equilibrium that emerged in the second half of the nineteenth century resulted from the application of thermodynamic and kinetic considerations to questions of chemical reactivity. The law of mass action – formulated by Guldberg and Waage in 1864 – deals quantitatively with the influence of the concentrations of reactants and products on the final equilibrium. The question of the influence of other parameters, such as pressure, temperature, and volume, on equilibrium is described in a qualitative manner by the Le Chatelier principle, formulated in 1884.

Lavoisier's static notion of equilibrium: balancing gains and losses

The etymology of the term 'equi-librium' refers to the image of equal beams (*libra*), i.e. to the image of a lever, or balance. Equilibrium was first and foremost a 'method' based on the use of balances in the chemical laboratories, and the balance, as a technical tool, became part of a cognitive strategy for understanding chemical changes.

The case of Antoine-Laurent Lavoisier (1743–94) is of special interest to understand the interplay between chemistry and economics on the question of equilibrium. This is because Lavoisier pursued a double career: as a chemist, he was a member of the Académie des Sciences, but he was also a tax collector[1] and authored a number of *Mémoirs* in political economy,[2] with the balance creating a link between these two careers (Bensaude-Vincent 1993). As a financier, Lavoisier used accounting methods, that he exported into chemistry by listing the quantities of the inputs (reagents) and outputs (products) of the chemical reactions in two columns, as if on a balance sheet (Dujarric de la Riviere 1949).

Lavoisier was not the first chemist to use balances in the laboratory, not even the first one to use other precision instruments (Bensaude-Vincent 1992; Holmes 1998). A number of chemists before him – or against him during the controversy over the existence of phlogiston – used gravimetric methods for exploring chemical reactions. Although spectacular sometimes, chemical transformations are black box processes. With Lavoisier, the balance became a method of knowing, a strategy for understanding what happened in chemical reactions (see Multhauf 1962). In particular, by weighing inputs and outputs Lavoisier understood the role of gases in processes such as combustion and calcinations, and confirmed Guyton de Morveau's observation – which appeared in the 'Dissertation sur le phlogistique', the first essay in Morveau's *Digressions Académiques* published in 1772 – that metals increased their weight upon calcinations (Brock 1992). Lavisier's next step was to bring a direct challenge to the phlogiston theory (Stahl 1730), according to which metals released phlogiston on calcinations, and should, therefore, lose weight when heated. In a sealed note addressed to the Académie on 1 November 1772, Lavoisier advanced the (revolutionary) hypothesis that processes like combustion and calcinations implied a combination with air.[3]

Lavoisier used the balance, and the gravimetric criterion behind it, for several purposes: for exploring the nature and proportion of the constituents of compounds, for predicting new phenomena, and for corroborating hypotheses based on philosophical postulates that made the verdict of the balance incontrovertible (Daumas *et al.* 1959). As in the case of the matter conservation principle

1 This dual career was by no means an exception in late Enlightenment France (Gillispie 1980, 2004).

2 For critical biographies of Lavoisier see Guerlac (1975) and Donovan (1993).

3 On Lavoisier's first attack on the phlogiston theory see Guerlac (1961). For a comparison between Lavoisier's and Stahl's philosophical approaches see Metzger (1930).

> Nothing is ever lost, either in art or in nature. We can state as a basic postulate that, in all operations, an equal amount of matter exists before and after the operation, that the quality and quantity of principles are the same; only changes, only modifications take place. It is on this conviction that the entire art of chemical experimentation is founded. One must always assume the equality between the principles of the bodies that one examines and those that one obtains through analysis.
>
> (Lavoisier 1789a, 2, p. 101, our translation)

which, in Lavoisier's formulation, acquired an essentially operational value, thus providing the basis of the art of experiment; it also allowed the writing of chemical equations and the characterisation of compounds on the basis of the proportions of their components. All this created the basis for the 'new' language of chemistry, forged in the *Méthode de nomenclature chimique*, published in 1787 by Lavoisier himself, together with Louis-Bernard Guyton de Morveau, Claude-Louis Berthollet and Antoine de Fourcroy.

Notably, Lavoisier's use of the balance, and the consequent writing of chemical equations, were rooted in the philosophy of Etienne Bonnot de Condillac. In line with it, Lavoisier assumed algebra to be a universal method in which analysis acted as a 'lever of the mind' that lifted the 'unknowns' by the weight of the 'knowns' (Roberts 1992). Undoubtedly Lavoisier's balance sheet method was very powerful and brought about simplicity in chemistry. Yet it had a cost. It created a timeless equilibrium that eliminated temporality from chemical systems. Change was not as relevant as permanence, and equilibrium represented what could be grasped while the process whereby it was reached remained undisclosed (Wise 1993). Moreover, addressing equilibrium as the most important aspect of reactivity discarded as irrelevant the chemical puzzle of why the properties of 'mixts'[4] differ from the sum of the properties of the mixts' components.

Lavoisier extended the notion of equilibrium far beyond the realm of chemical reactions: balancing equations became a kind of programme (or obsession) behind most of his work, whatever the field to which the equations applied. For instance, as a landowner, Lavoisier became interested in farming, and developed a rational agricultural system that consisted in giving, for each parcel of land, the quantitative records of the inputs (seeds, fertilisers, water and work) and outputs (harvest yields) (Lavoisier 1788). In this way, he extended the method of balancing gains and losses to exchanges between the mineral and the vegetable realms. In his physiological studies on animal respiration, Lavoisier, like most of his contemporaries, assumed respiration to be a kind of combustion, and designed a method for measuring the physiological work done by the animal through the quantity of oxygen (then 'named vital' air for its fundamental role in

4 The terms 'mixt' was synonymous with compound. Notably, it was Lavoisier who replaced the former term with the latter, in line with his attitude to logical reasoning, which prescribed proceeding gradually from the simple to the complex, in this way redefining compounds as the union of two, or more, components (Duhem 1902; Bensaude-Vincent 1997).

respiration) spent during the effort associated with the work. With his collaborator Armand Seguin, he tried to extend this method to evaluate the work done by a man giving a speech, a musician playing an instrument, or, even, a meditating philosopher, a writer, a composer of music (Lavoisier 1789b).

Lavoisier's attempt to balance body and mind was in line with his previous attempt to balance nature and society by assuming that regulatory mechanisms exist, similar to the balancing acts of Nature – exemplified, for instance, by indigestion stopping animals from engaging in excesses and gluttony – which prevent human societies from collapsing. In his writings on political economy, Lavoisier expressed views that echoed the physiocrats' claim of a natural order at play in economics. In line with François Quesnay's *Tableau économique*, published in 1758, he described economic activity as a circulation of fluids, a kind of hydrodynamics, which led to the establishment of a balanced trade. He held that human intervention could only slightly influence the 'natural balance' in favour of one's own interest by weighing the effect of the different measures and counter-measures that would maintain the equilibrium of the political machinery. For Lavoisier, the model statesman worked hard behind the stage, in the silence of his study, to maintain a natural equilibrium in the circulation of goods and money, his task basically consisting in making the calculations necessary to restore the balance after each economic transaction. Trade and economic exchanges followed mathematical equations, and the political game was reduced to a mechanism for regulating the economic flux by balancing the periods of wealth with those of decline (Lavoisier 1771). To describe the succession of economic periods in history, Lavoisier spoke of 'revolutions', without attributing to the term the idea of radical change, but using it as synonymous with cycles, in the same way as Copernicus had done in *De revolutionibus*.

If Lavoisier is considered the founder of modern chemistry it is mainly because of the rationalisation he introduced into the discipline. Using the balance, he discarded the mysterious properties and oddities previously attributed to the chemical substances. He conceived of equilibrium as a balance between quantities, thus turning the concept of equilibrium into a 'mediator' (in the literal sense, i.e. with reference to the Latin term *medius* or middle). The balance became a *middle* between any two things, and was endowed with the power of making those things commensurable. Actually, for Lavoisier, the balance did more: it mediated between the concrete and the abstract, nature and society, description and prescription (Wise 1993). This a-temporal notion of equilibrium, or balance between action and reaction, was an all-pervading model in the Enlightenment, whether in mechanics, electricity, chemistry or political economy (see also Wise *et al.* 1989–90).

Reversible reactions and the dynamic notion of chemical equilibrium

From the 1860s onwards, the chemists started applying thermodynamics to the study of chemical reactions. Their aim was, to a certain extent, similar to

Lavoisier's: it related to predicting the state of equilibrium reached upon reaction from a given initial mixture. As we spell out here, like Lavoisier's balance, thermodynamics provided indirect information on what occurred in the black box represented by chemical reactions, thereby enabling the chemists to circumvent the puzzle represented by 'affinities', the 'elective attractions' attributed to individual substances in their mutual interactions. These, although studied intensively in the eighteenth century, had remained mysterious and unexplained. Once the idea, formulated by J. Thomsen (1826–1909) – that the heat developed in a reaction (called the 'decrease of energy') was a measure of the forces of affinity at play – was accepted,[5] the chemists no longer needed speculating about affinities to predict the direction of reactions, and could rely on Marcellin Berthelot's principle of maximum work, which stated that 'all chemical changes performed without intervention of external energy tend to the production of the body, or system of bodies, which releases most heat' (Berthelot 1864, p. 399, our translation).

In order to understand some important developments occurring at the same time, we need to take a step back to the incomplete reactions that Claude-Louis Berthollet had studied in his *Essai de statique chimique* (1803). He had noticed that the quantity of reactants had a crucial influence on the outcome of reactions, especially with regard to reactions that occur in nature but not in the laboratory due to their requiring very large quantities of reactants. On Berthollet's account, the outcome of chemical reactions does not depend only on the affinities of the substances, since the presence of a large amount of a given substance may compensate for its weak affinity for another substance, shifting the direction of reaction towards products that would not be expected on the basis of the substances' affinities alone (1803).

The reactions in which Berthollet became most interested were reversible ones; he thought that these represented the rule, and that complete reactions were the exception, in this way stepping out of mainstream thinking at the time that regarded reversible reactions as resulting from anomalous cases of chemical affinities. Berthollet's ambition was to formulate general rules that could account for the variety of chemical reactions; together with Pierre-Simon Laplace, he founded the Societé d'Arcueil, whose programme, inspired by a 'Newtonian dream',[6] was to submit chemical and physical phenomena to a single law, promoting the study of a 'chemical mechanics' that would cover equilibrium processes, as well as irreversible transformations (Goupil-Sadoun 1977). In this respect, Berthollet's philosophical approach may be seen as anticipating Comte's positivism (1830–42), which aimed to discover general laws expressed by mathematical equations rather than searching for ultimate causes.

The reversible reactions that had interested Bertollet in the early 1800s came under intense scrutiny in the mid-1850s, when it became apparent that reversible

5 Thomsen developed this idea in a number of papers published between 1859 and 1873, under the collective title 'Thermochemische Untersuchungen', in *Poggendorffs Annalen der Physik*.

6 On Berthollet's and Laplace's 'Newtonian dream' see Crosland (1967) and Bensaude-Vincent and Stengers (1996).

reactions correspond to a dynamic equilibrium being established between a forward and a backward reaction.

Primacy on defining chemical equilibrium as a dynamic balance between two opposing reactions still occurring after equilibrium has been reached, probably goes to A. Williamson (1851), while M.J. Malaguti (1853) pointed out that equilibrium is reached when the velocities of the two opposing reactions became equal. The formalisation of the notion of chemical equilibrium, however, is due to the collaboration between two Norwegian scientists: C.M. Guldberg (1836–1902), professor of applied mathematics at the University of Christiania, and P. Waage (1833–1900), professor of chemistry at the same university. Researching chemical affinities, they came to enunciate the law of mass action in a paper read before the Norwegian Academy in 1864 and published the following year in the Academy's Proceedings. The gist of the law is that the chemical action is proportional to the active mass, the latter being the number of molecules in unit volume.[7] In Guldberg and Waage's own terms:

> When two substances A and B are transformed by double substitution into two new substances A′ and B′, and under the same conditions, A′ and B′ can transform themselves into A and B ... the force which causes the formation of A′ and B′ increases proportionally to the affinity coefficient for the reaction $A + B = A' + B'$ but depends also on the masses of A and B. *We have learned from our experiments* that the force is proportional to the product of the active masses of the two substances A and B.
>
> (Quoted in Partington 1964, IV, p. 590, emphasis added)

Notably, Guldberg and Waage came to the formulation of the law of mass action after carrying out more than 300 quantitative experiments, and the law was corroborated by data from other scientists (Dubus 1853; Scheerer 1860). In 1878, J.H. Van't Hoff formulated the law of mass action on the basis of considerations of chemical kinetics, and, on all evidence, independently of Guldberg and Waage's formulation. A few years later, in his *Etudes de dynamique chimique* published in 1884, he tackled the question of how the temperature affects the equilibrium between two different states of matter (or systems), enunciating a 'principle of mobile equilibrium'. The principle states that, if the temperature of the systems is dropped, equilibrium is restored by a shift toward the system whose formation releases heat; conversely, if the temperature of the systems is raised, equilibrium is restored by a shift towards the system that requires absorption of heat. In 1879 G. Robin put forward a principle similar to Van't Hoff's but related to pressure; it stated that an increase in pressure favours reactions occurring with diminution of volume. These principles, and other, similar, ones, may be seen as special cases of the principle of chemical equilibrium, put forward by Le Chatelier in 1884. Before discussing the principle, it is appropri-

7 On account of being published in Norwegian, the law started to circulate widely only when F.W. Ostwald discussed and further corroborated it with new data in a publication in German (Ostwald 1877).

ate to briefly recall some aspects of Le Chatelier's personal and intellectual biography.

Chemical equilibrium, and the factors affecting it

H.L. Le Chatelier (1850–1936) was born to a family of distinguished scientists: his father and one of his uncles were engineers, another uncle was an architect, and they all shared the same view: that science and its industrial applications should proceed in close association, frequently and freely influencing one another. Le Chatelier became interested in science from an early age, and, as a student at the Ecole Politéchnique, was influenced by Comte's positivism (Leichester 1970). In 1877 he became professor of general chemistry at the Ecole des Mines, a post he kept until retirement in 1919, while being appointed professor of general chemistry also at the Sorbonne in 1907, when he became a member of the Académie des sciences. Throughout his career, he held important positions as government adviser on scientific and technical questions, and was interested in the organisation of scientific research, as his (1925) *La Science et l'industrie* and (1928) *Le Taylorisme* testify.[8]

Le Chatelier's doctoral thesis was on the setting of hydraulic cements; it dealt with questions such as the cement's chemical composition (plaster, gypsum, calcium silicates and alluminates, and more), and the role of external factors – such as atmospheric pressure and humidity – relevant to the setting process. Among his early interests were high temperatures processes; in 1882, the knowledge acquired in this field earned him, together with F.E. Mallard,[9] an appointment from the government to investigate the cause of repeated, disastrous, explosions in mines. The investigations were successful and shed light on the conditions for the combustion and explosion of mixtures of gases that formed in the mines. Le Chatelier was asked by some industrialists to look into a problematic reaction: that of iron oxides with carbon monoxide occurring in a furnace. The problem with this reaction was that the expected products, iron and carbon monoxide, were accompanied by a considerable quantity of carbon dioxide when they emerged from the furnace. It was believed, at first, that the presence of carbon dioxide at the end of the process meant that this required more time and energy to be completed; however, taller furnaces, which prolonged the

8 In it Le Chatelier investigated the question of creating a proportionate relation between the cost of research laboratories and the expected profits resulting from the innovations introduced. Following F.W. Taylor, he advocated a rigid division of labour, convinced that this would bring uninterrupted advancements in knowledge. The main aspects of the book may be summarised as follows (1) Good science grows out of industrial projects (illustrated with historical cases such as those of Lavoisier, Carnot, Sainte-Claire Deville and Pasteur), (2) Like natural phenomena, industrial phenomena are ruled by general laws, which link the relevant parameters of the production process with the quality and cost of the final products, (3) Science is the study of natural laws, i.e. of necessary relations that hold between phenomena, whatever the nature of the objects covered by the phenomena, (4) Scientific method is a means to increase the efficiency of scientific research as well as of industrial production.

9 His colleague professor of metallurgy at the Ecole des Mines.

process, did not lead to the desired outcome. After carrying out further investigations, Le Chatelier attributed the presence of carbon dioxide at the end of the process to the reaction being reversible and leading to an equilibrium. He approached the question of the effect on equilibrium of parameters other than the quantity of reactants, and came to the enunciation of the principle that bears his name. It states that:

> Every system in *stable chemical equilibrium* submitted to the influence of an exterior force which tends to cause variation either in its temperature or its condensation (pressure, concentration, number of molecules per unit of volume), in its totality or only in some of its parts, can undergo only those internal modifications which, if they occur alone, would bring about a change of temperature or condensation of the opposite sign to the one resulting from the external cause.
>
> (Le Chatelier 1884, p. 787, our translation, emphasis added)[10]

In mechanics, the term 'stable equilibrium' is easily understood as the kind of equilibrium of a body so placed that, if disturbed, it returns to its former position. The Le Chatelier principle gives a qualitative account of how chemical, rather than mechanical, systems at stable equilibrium react to regain a state of stable equilibrium once this had been disturbed.[11] The principle is descriptive and qualitative, and this was seen as a major limitation at a time when it was paramount to describe phenomena in mathematical terms.

However, the application of the principle to a variety of industrial processes contributed to increasing the yield of reactions, thereby optimising those processes. Notably, the methodology behind the principle was very much in line with the prevailing one at the time: a *fin de siècle* positivism such as that of Henri Sainte-Claire Deville (1818–81),[12] whose writings Le Chatelier admired, and discussed with three of Sainte-Claire Deville's disciples, Troost, Debray and Hautefeuille, who sat on his doctoral thesis committee (Letté 2004).

In line with Sainte-Claire Deville's *fin de siècle* positivism, Le Chatelier made it clear that he had come to the enunciation of his principle independently

10 Notably, the Le Chatelier principle is at the basis of feedback processes, such as those that enable living organisms to maintain the value of their parameters quasi-constant, a phenomenon known as 'homeostasis' (see Jarvis and Mosini, this volume).

11 In both cases, mechanical and chemical, a system is in stable equilibrium when its configuration corresponds to a minimum of the potential energy.

12 A professor at the Ecole Normale Supérieure from 1851 to 1880, and at the Sorbonne from 1866 to 1880, Sainte-Claire Deville avoided theoretical issues and impressed a strong empirical character to his work and lectures, suggesting banishing altogether from 'positive' chemistry the notion of atomicity, that he regarded as an occult force. He advocated a supposedly 'theory-free' research programme, largely resting on the measurement of observable parameters such as those of thermodynamics (Sainte-Claire Deville 1857, 1869). In this respect, *fin de siècle* positivism represented a stronger version of Comte's original formulation (Comte 1830–42), which did not systematically object to using unobservable entities in the scientific discourse, and accepted the atomistic hypothesis (Bensaude-Vincent 1999).

of any hypotheses on the nature of chemical interactions (Le Chatelier 1885). He was not deluding himself: the principle rested mainly on observations relative to applied investigations on as diversified topics as the conditions for the setting of cements, high temperature processes and reversible reactions. (On Le Chatelier's view on the interplay between evidence and theory in science, see his 1888 book.)[13]

The Le Chatelier principle and the Le Chatelier–Samuelson principle: what do they have in common?

In his *Foundations of Economic Analysis* (1948), Samuelson addressed the question of how the equilibrium of a system is displaced by comparing the case in which no auxiliary constraints are imposed on the system with the case in which constraints are imposed. He regarded this type of question as being 'important in thermodynamics as well as in economic systems' (Samuelson 1948, p. 36), and held that the question admits of a simple answer, which is provided by a theorem on mathematical functions. Given a function z, if all its unknowns x_i are independently variable, a maximum is determined by the equilibrium conditions that the partial derivative of the function with respect to all variables x_i be equal to zero. If a constraint is imposed that connects one variable with its conjugate parameter, so that the variable assumes fixed value, the equilibrium conditions are modified (see Samuelson 1948, pp. 30–8 for details), and a 'general theorem' is enunciated, which, as Samuelson added in a footnote, 'corresponds to some of the phenomena which fall under the heading of the celebrated principle of Le Chatelier' (Samuelson 1948, p. 38).[14] On the question of the relation between his theorem and the Le Chatelier principle, Samuelson acknowledged inspiration from 'Professor E.B. Wilson's suggestion that this [principle] is essentially a mathematical theorem applicable to economics' (Samuelson 1948, p. 81).[15] Samuelson granted the above theorem the status of a 'principle', and dubbed it 'the Le Chatelier–Braun principle',[16] adding that

> its economic significance may be summarised as follows: if, in a given position of equilibrium, a (compensated) change in price is made, the resulting

13 On the question of the interplay of evidence and theory in bringing about scientific knowledge see Mosini (2002) and Mosini (2005).

14 Elsewhere Samuelson claimed that his theorem captured the 'abstract structure' shared by all equilibrium systems that qualify for being described by the Le Chatelier principle (Samuelson 1960a, p. 1).

15 Professor Wilson had taught Samuelson at Harvard, having, in turn, been taught at Yale by one of the giants of chemical physics of all time: J. Willard Gibbs. Yet Wilson's position – that Samuelson, at this stage, reported without further specifications – is rather surprising given that, as we pointed out, the Le Chatelier principle was qualitative and had not been mathematically formalised.

16 We found no reference in Samuelson (1948) for the name Braun added to Le Chatelier's in relation to the principle.

> change in amount demanded of that good will be greater if the individual is not subjected to the extra constraints of rationing than if he is subjected to such constraints; furthermore, the introduction of each new constraint will make demand still more inelastic.
>
> (Samuelson 1948, pp. 168–9)

Samuelson returned to the question of the application of the theorem to other economic systems, claiming, for instance, that it could be used to cover 'analysis of input–output, multi-sectoral Keynesian multiplier systems, and general demand analysis involving gross substitutes' (Samuelson 1960b, p. 368). In a further attempt to illustrate once more with an economic example his interpretation of the Le Chatelier principle, Samuelson (1972) considered the following. Take a production process involving two inputs, labour and land. The initial prices are the wage (p_1) and the rent (p_2) and the initial quantities are, respectively, q_1 and q_2. Samuelson set the example in the Marshallian short run, in which factor inputs (such as labour and raw materials) may be altered, but in which there are fixed factors (land, capital, etc.) that cannot be changed. Fixing the quantity of land imposes one binding constraint on the production process, while p_1, p_2 and q_1 are all free to vary. Considering the effect of a change in p_1 on q_1, he showed that

$$(\partial q_1/\partial p_1)_{q2} \leq 0 \quad (1)$$

Now consider the same change in p_1, but with the additional constraint that p_2 is now fixed. Then, according to what he re-dubbed the 'Le Chatelier–Samuelson principle',

$$(\partial q_1/\partial p_1)_{p2} \leq (\partial q_1/\partial p_1)_{q2} \leq 0 \quad (2)$$ [17]

The first thing to note about the conclusions that Samuelson drew on the basis of the 'Le Chatelier–Samuelson principle' is that the same conclusions could have been derived on the basis of mathematical considerations alone. This is because imposing a binding constraint on a function will restrict the range of optimum values with respect to the unconstrained function, and probably rule out the unconstrained solution. Imposing yet a further binding constraint will restrict the range of possible optimum values further. So, what, if anything, does the Le Chatelier–Samuelson principle add to mathematical analysis, and, more important, was Samuelson's reading of the Le Chatelier principle correct?

To discuss the latter point, we refer to the elaboration of the question of the applicability of the Le Chatelier principle to economics spelled out in Samuelson's 1972 paper, which hints at the aspect of Professor Wilson's teaching connected with the Le Chatelier principle. Samuelson recalled being

17 We modified Samuelson's notation v_1 and v_2 to represent the quantities, used in the 1972 paper, with the standard notation: q_1 and q_2.

> struck by his [Wilson's] statement that the fact that an increase in pressure is accompanied by a decrease in volume is not so much a theorem about a thermodynamic equilibrium system as it is a mathematical theorem about surfaces that are concave from below or about negative definite quadratic forms. Armed with this clue, I set out to make sense of the Le Chatelier Principle.
>
> (Samuelson 1972, p. 254)

We do not wish to comment on Wilson's statement, which clearly attributed more importance to the structure of scientific laws than to their empirical content;[18] the real problem, which, as we spell out later, is a direct consequence of Wilson's position, comes with Samuelson's next sentence in the same passage: 'Let me now enunciate a valid formulation of that [Le Chatelier] principle' (Samuelson 1972, p. 254). That formulation in the 1972 paper is long; a concise version is in Samuelson (1960b), form which we quote: 'Squeezing a balloon will decrease its volume more if you keep its temperature constant than it will if (by insulating it) you let the squeezing warm it up' (Samuelson 1960b, p. 368).

As we mentioned earlier, the Le Chatelier principle refers to systems in *stable equilibrium*, and an inflated balloon is a system *not* in stable, but in *unstable*, equilibrium; the effect of squeezing it depends on various factors: the intensity of the pressure that goes with the squeezing, the resistance of the rubber the balloon is made of, the quantity of air initially present in it (whether it corresponded to the maximum that the balloon could take without exploding, or not).

The crucial difference between a system in stable equilibrium and one in unstable equilibrium is that, for reasons having to do with stability in relation to energy content, while the former, as long as the exogenous shocks exerted on it are of moderate import, tends to revert to the previous equilibrium state, the latter has no tendency to do so, and will, in fact, either evolve towards a different unstable equilibrium, or reach stable equilibrium in a way that may imply its own destruction (as in the case of the balloon exploding, or going flat if the internal pressure was to be reduced by letting air out of it).

The analogy between thermodynamic and economic systems that Samuelson established is, in actual fact, between systems in unstable equilibrium; his considerations of the effect of any further constraint being introduced on those systems (on top of the one – or more – constraint(s) required to keep the systems in the unstable equilibrium they are in) are correct. But the thermodynamic systems to which the Le Chatelier principle applies have reached a state of stable equilibrium on account of internal relation between their component parts, as opposed to being kept in the specific unstable equilibrium by external constraint(s). As the previous paragraph indicates, systems in stable equilibrium

18 This position is highly debatable inasmuch as the gas laws of thermodynamics – to which Wilson was referring – largely resulted from empirical work, which was mathematically formalised only at a late stage.

have a built-in (natural, one might say) tendency to restore equilibrium, while those to which the Le Chatelier–Samuelson principle refers have not.

Samuelson's interpretation of the range of systems covered by the Le Chatelier principle is a case in point for being ultra-cautious about treating theories as uninterpreted mathematical formalisms.[19] The properties of entities matter a lot to their adequate description: borrowing from other domains requires semantic, on top of syntactic, analogies, as the case of systems in stable or unstable equilibrium shows.

The question of the different methodologies, respectively, behind the Le Chatelier principle, and the Le Chatelier–Samuelson principle, is also worth mentioning. The former resulted from the huge experimental work carried out by Le Chatelier in various branches of applied science; it related to, and complemented, as it were, the law of mass action that Gouldberg and Waage had established on the basis of over 300 experiments that were inspired, or corroborated, by countless other experiments carried out by other scientists working on reactivity and affinities.

By contrast, the so-called Le Chatelier–Samuelson principle was introduced on the basis of a purported analogy between the mathematical description of thermodynamic and economic systems that Samuelson repeatedly claimed, for instance, with his statement that the Le Chatelier's 'principle reflects a mathematical theorem about matrices connected with definite quadratic forms. And since quadratic forms of this type are intimately involved in economic maximising problems, it is not surprising that the Le Chatelier principle should have found many applications in theoretical economics' (Samuelson 1960b, p. 368).[20] In the same paper, Samuelson stated that the mathematical isomorphism between thermodynamics and mathematical economics creates an analogy between the two disciplines that would not be challenged even by the possible failure to find analogies between the parameters – which reflect the properties of the entities – that appear in the theories (Samuelson 1960b). As this, and other, similar, considerations suggest, Samuelson was reasoning about 'abstract' mathematical analogies,[21] thereby showing that the Le Chatelier–Samuelson principle was born out of the deductive methodology.

Conclusion

We wish to conclude by pointing out some common aspects between the epistemologies underlying the two concepts of equilibrium outlined here. Lavoisier and Le Chatelier were concerned, one might say obsessed, with rationalisation. *Ratio* means rapport, quantification, mathematisation. Both men had a deep faith in mathematics, and used the concept of equilibrium to quantify chemical reactions. Lavoisier's all-pervasive balance method relied on the assumption that matter is conserved, an assumption that provided him with a means of universal

19 For a history of mathematical economics, see Weintraub (2002).

20 With reference to the theorem introduced in his 1948 book.

21 For the difference between 'abstract' and 'concrete' formal analogies, see Redhead (2001).

commensurability. On his account, all sorts of phenomena – oxidation, the work of an artist, the growth of a plant – could be compared by means of weighing. Even an imponderable substance such as caloric could be 'weighed', as it were, by the use of a calorimeter. Le Chatelier's concept of equilibrium was haunted by the acknowledgement of the inevitability of losses in physical processes, sanctioned by the second principle of thermodynamics. The realisation of the only partial inter-conversion of heat and work prompted his quest for the optimisation of chemical reactions, as well as of other processes of industrial interest (Chaudron *et al.* 1937). Lavoisier's and Le Chatelier's rationalising ambitions exemplify a specific feature of the technocratic world view developed by the French elite in the nineteenth century, which created continuity between the *ancien régime* and the Third Republic through the philosophy of the Enlightenment.

In methodological terms, Lavoisier and Le Chatelier conceived of the interplay of evidence and theory as being shifted towards evidence, while Samuelson, with his attempt to lump the behaviour of chemico-physical and economic systems together under the same umbrella, took the opposite stance.

References

Bensaude-Vincent, B. (1992), 'Between chemistry and politics: Lavoisier and the Balance', *Eighteenth-century, Essays and Interpretation*, 33, 217–37.

Bensaude-Vincent, B. (1993), *Lavoisier. Mémoires d'une révolution*, Flammarion, Paris.

Bensaude-Vincent, B. (1997), *Eloge du mixte. Matériaux nouveaux et philosophie ancienne*, Hachette Littératures, Paris.

Bensaude-Vincent, B. (1999), 'Atomism and positivism: a legend about French chemistry', *Annals of Science*, 56, 81–94.

Bensaude-Vincent, B. and I. Stengers (1996), *A History of Chemistry*, Harvard University Press, Cambridge, MA.

Berthelot, M. (1864), *Leçons sur les méthodes générales de synthèse en chimie organique*, Alcan, Paris.

Berthollet, C.L. (1803), 'Essai de statique chimique', De Demonville, Paris.

Brock, W.H. (1992), *The Fontana History of Chemistry*, Harper Collins, London.

Chaudron, G. and R. Dubrisay (1937), 'Henry le Chatelier et l'industrie chimique', *Revue de métallurgie*, special issue: a la mémoire de Henry le Chatelier, January, 55–62.

Crosland, M. (1967), *The Society of Arcueil: A View of French Science at the Time of Napoleon*, Harvard University Press, Cambridge, MA.

Daumas, M. and D.I. Duveen (1959), 'Lavoisier's relatively unknown large scale experiment of decomposition and synthesis of water, February 27–28 1785', *Chymia*, 5, 111–29.

Donovan, A. (1993), *Antoine Lavoisier. Science, Administration, and Revolution*, Blackwell, Oxford.

Dubus, H. (1853), 'Ueber chemische Verwandtschaft', *Annalen der Pharmacie*, 85, 103–34.

Duhem, P. (1902), *Le Mixte et la combinaison chimique*, English trans. (2002) P. Needham, *Mixture and Chemical Combination, and Related Essays*, Kluwer, Dordrecht.

Dujarric de la Riviere, R. (1949), *Lavoisier économiste*, Masson, Paris.
Gillispie, C.C. (1980), *Science and Polity in France at the End of the Old Regime*, Princeton University Press, Princeton, NJ.
Gillispie, C.C. (2004), *Science and Polity in France. The Revolutionary and Napoleonic Years*, Princeton University Press, Princeton, NJ.
Goupil-Sadoun, M. (1977), *Le Chimiste Claude Louis-Berthollet, 1748–1822. Sa vie, son oeuvre*, Vrin, Paris.
Guerlac, H. (1961), *Lavoisier. The Crucial Year*, Cornell University Press, Ithaca, NY.
Guerlac, H. (1975), *Antoine-Laurent Lavoisier, Chemist and Revolutionary*, Scribner, New York.
Holmes, F.L. (1998), *Antoine Lavoisier. The Next Crucial Year, or the Sources of his Quantitative Method in Chemistry*, Princeton University Press, Princeton, NJ.
Lavoisier, A.L. (1771), 'Fragments d'un éloge de Colbert', in *Œuvres*, VI, 109–24, (1862–96), II, 812–23, Imprimerie impériale (renamed Imprimerie nationale in 1871), Paris.
Lavoisier, A.L. (1788), 'Résultats de quelques expériences d'agriculture et réflexions sur leurs relations avec l'économie politique', in *Œuvres* (1862–96), II, 812–23, Imprimerie impériale, Paris.
Lavoisier A.L. (1789a), *Traité éléméntaire de chimie*, in *Œuvres* (1862–96), I, Imprimerie impériale, Paris.
Lavoisier, A.L. (1789b), 'Mémoire sur la respiration des animaux', in *Œuvres* (1862–96), II, 688–703, Imprimerie impériale, Paris.
Le Chatelier, H. (1884), 'Sur un énoncé général des lois de l'équilibre chimique', *Comptes-rendus de l'Académie des sciences*, 99, 786–7.
Le Chatelier H. (1885), 'Sur les lois numériques des équilibres chimiques', *Comptes-rendus de l'Académie des sciences*, 101, 1005–7.
Le Chatelier M. (1888), *Recherches expérimentales et théoriques sur les équilibres chimiques*, Dunod, Paris.
Le Chatelier, H. (1925), *Science et industrie*, Flammarion, Paris.
Le Chatelier, H. (1928), *Le Taylorisme*, Dunod, Paris.
Leichester, H.M. (1970), 'Le Chatelier, Henry Louis', in C.C. Gillispie (ed.), *Dictionary of Scientific Biography*, VII, 116–20.
Letté, M. (2004) *Henry Le Chatelier (1850–1936) ou la science appliquée à l'industrie*, Presses Universitaires de Rennes, Rennes.
Malaguti, M.J. (1853), 'Exposition de quelques faits rélatif à l'action réciproque des sels solubles', *Annales de chimie et physique*, 37, 198–206.
Metzger, H. (1930), *Newton, Stahl, Boerhaave et la doctrine chimique*, Blanchard, Paris.
Mosini, V. (2002), 'Was the methodology behind electrodynamics inductive or deductive?', *Physis*, 39, 441–67.
Mosini, V. (2005), 'Evidence against theory or evidence without theory? The case of Dr Hahnemann's homeopathic medicine', *Physis*, 42 (2), 513–37.
Multhauf, R.L. (1962), 'On the use of the balance in chemistry', *American Philosophical Society Proceedings*, 106, 210–18.
Ostwald, F.W. (1877), 'Ueber den Einfluss der Basis auf die relative Affinitat der Sauren', *Annalen der Physik und Chemie*, 2, 429–54.
Partington, J.R. (1964), *A History of Chemistry*, Macmillan, New York.
Petit, A. (1995), 'Les mouvements positivistes', in I. Poutrin (ed.), *Le XIXe siècle*, Berger-Levrault, Paris, 473–92.

Redhead, M.L.G. (2001), 'The intelligibility of the universe', in A. O'Hear (ed.), *Philosophy at the New Millennium*, Cambridge University Press, Cambridge, 73–90.

Roberts, L. (1992), 'Condillac, Lavoisier, and the instrumentalization of science', *Eighteenth Century: Theory and Interpretation*, 33, 252–71.

Sainte-Claire Deville, H. (1857), 'De la dissociation ou décomposition spontanée des corps sous l'influence de la chaleur', *Comptes-rendus de l'Académie des sciences*, 45, 857–61.

Sainte-Claire Deville, H. (1869), *Lecons sur l'affinité professées devant la Société chimique le 28 février et le 6 mars 1867*, Hachette, Paris.

Samuelson, P.A. (1948), *Foundations of Economic Analysis*, Harvard University Press, Cambridge, MA.

Samuelson, P.A. (1960a), 'Structure of a minimum equilibrium system', in R.W. Pfouts (ed.), *Essays in Economics and Econometrics*, University of North Carolina Press, Chapel Hill, NC, 1–22.

Samuelson, P.A. (1960b), 'An extension of the Le Chatelier principle', *Econometrica*, 28, 368–79.

Samuelson, P.A. (1972), 'Maximum principles in analytical economics', *American Economic Review*, 72 (2), 249–62.

Scheerer, T. (1860), 'Versuche ueber die Menge der Kohlensaure, welche bei hoerer Temperatur aus kohlensauren Alkalien durch Kieselsaure und andere Oxyde ausgetrieben wird, nebst Folgerunngen hinsichtlich der atomistichen Zusammensetzung der Kieselsaure', *Annalen der Pharmacie*, 116, 129–60.

Stahl, G. (1730), *Philosophical Principles of Universal Chemistry*, English trans. P. Shaw, J. Osborn & T. Longman, London.

Weintraub, E.R. (2002), *How Economics became a Mathematical Science*, Duke University Press, Durham, NC and London.

Williamson, A. (1851), 'Suggestions for the dynamics of chemistry derived from the theory of etherification', *Proceedings of the Royal Institution*, 2, 90–4.

Wise, N. (1993), 'Mediations: Enlightenment balancing acts, or the technologies of rationalism', in P. Horwich (ed.), *World Changes. Thomas Kuhn and the Nature of Science*, MIT Press, Cambridge, MA, pp. 207–56.

Wise, N. and C. Smith (1989–90), 'Work and waste: political economy and natural philosophy in nineteenth-century Britain', *History of Science*, 27, 263–301, 391–449; 28, 221–61.

3 The ubiquity of the notion of equilibrium in biology, and its relation with equilibrium in economics

Louise Jarvis and Valeria Mosini

Our starting point in this chapter is the ubiquity of the notion of equilibrium in the study of nature, particularly in biology. To focus discussion on specific examples, we have chosen the self-regulating process – known as 'homeostasis' – by which living organisms keep the value of their physiologically relevant parameters *quasi*-stable, and the equilibrium of costs–benefits analyses of neo-Darwinian accounts of genetic evolution and behavioural ecology. We also draw attention to the reciprocal exchange of concepts between economics and biology characteristic of the second half of the nineteenth century, and to the peculiar way in which concepts were backed up in one discipline by being applied in the other, before actually being validated in *either* discipline.

The assumption of equilibrium has been embedded in the description and study of nature from the start, forming part of the teleological explanations of natural events invoked by the Greeks, and of the theological accounts given by the Scholastic philosophers (Egerton 1973; Cuddington 2001). Countless examples of equilibrium have been discussed in biology and related disciplines, most of which have been taken to be synonymous with 'natural balance'.[1] Today these notions of equilibrium as balance have come to constitute a tenet of the popular understanding of natural phenomena. The media constantly try the new technologies for their possible interference with the equilibrium of nature, and the public are urged to prevent and repair environmental damage by helping to restore the balance of nature. In this way, the notions of equilibrium and balance in nature have become invested with cultural value.

However, no single or simple notion of equilibrium underlies biological thinking, because countless equilibrium processes, acting and interacting in a complex orchestration, occur in living organisms. Some equilibria are static, others dynamic; some emerge from the interaction of just two factors, while

1 For examples from ecology, see Pimm (1991).

others depend on many. There are physical and chemical equilibria that underpin the biological ones, and there are physiological and bio-economic equilibria between organisms. Finally, there are the very discrete equilibrium processes that drive the genetic make-up of individuals and their species populations. It might be argued that everything in biology is about equilibrium, that biology is the study of equilibria in nature inasmuch as an environment conducive to life – as we know it – emerged from the combined balances of meteorological, geological, chemical and ecological cycles.[2]

In this chapter, we consider two ways in which the concept of equilibrium is deployed in biology. One has an empirical, the other a theoretical, basis; one is dynamic, the other static. The former relates to the observation that all physiologically relevant parameters of living organisms have quasi-constant values, the latter to the use of costs-benefits analyses in neo-Darwinian theorising.

'Homeostasis': equilibrium observed

As contemporary physiology texts put it (see, for instance, Withers 1992), the homeostatic activity that enables living organisms – which are 'open' systems in their exchanging matter and energy with the environment – to retain their structure and functions is regulated by a complex array of endocrine and nervous system receptors and effectors. When the receptors 'detect' a change in the value of a physico-chemical parameter, the effectors – which may be glands that release hormones that influence cellular processes, or muscles that perform physical functions – trigger the processes that induce a corrective response. Here, we give a few examples of the complex and often interrelated processes through which homeostasis is achieved.

Homeothermic organisms deploy homeostatic processes to maintain a relatively constant internal body temperature, despite the daily and annual variation in the temperature of the environment. In the case of mammalian temperature regulation, thermo-receptors located on the skin and in the hypothalamus, acting together, gauge the temperature difference between the body and the environment. Depending on the action required to keep the body temperature quasi-constant (either cooling or conserving warmth), the hypothalamus triggers nervous messages that dilate or constrict the peripheral blood vessels, induce sweating or shivering, or, for some species, raise or lower the body hairs.

The regulation of blood sugar levels is an example of homeostatic control conducted via the endocrine system. In this case, chemeoreceptors in the pancreas 'detect' the sugar level in the blood; depending on the action required for the maintenance of equilibrium, the pancreas secretes one of two hormones. If there is too much sugar in the blood, insulin is released; if there is too little sugar,

2 The role of equilibrium and balance in biology came under scrutiny in the late twentieth century when it appeared that 90 per cent of all the organisms that had ever lived had gone extinct. This realisation did not appear commensurate with the notion of a grand balance in nature, and some biologists began to seek interpretive models that rely less on those assumptions (see, for instance, Cooper 2001 and Cuddington 2001).

glucagon is released. Both these hormones target the liver, which is the actual effector of blood sugar homeostasis. If the liver 'detects' insulin, it starts storing away the available glucose as glycogen; if it 'detects' glucagon, this indicates that the body requires glucose, and the liver begins to break down the previously stored glycogen, to release glucose into the blood stream.

The complex chemical processes that allow cells to respire, metabolise foodstuff and release energy are also under homeostatic control, which is achieved by negative feedback. If the end product of a metabolic pathway begins to build up, its excess combines with the regulating enzyme(s) that initiated the metabolic chain, thereby stopping it. When, in fact, the end products have been fully used in further pathways, the regulating enzyme(s) are freed, and the pathway begins to function anew.[3]

With this picture of homeostasis in the background, we come to recalling how homeostasis was discovered. It was Claude Bernard (1878–1913), the founder of experimental physiology, who first became aware of the fact that a state of constancy in the physico-chemical constituents of living organisms is essential to survival, and it was Walter Cannon (1871–1945) who coined the term 'homeostasis' to describe the self-regulating process that ensures the quasi-constant state.

Bernard's experimental work investigated a wide range of medical and physiological functions: digestion, the working of the nervous system and the functioning of the liver, pancreas and heart being some. It was on the basis of huge evidential support that, in 1866, Bernard prepared a *Rapport* for the Ministry of Education, published the following year, in which the view was advanced that a *milieu intérieur* exists in living organisms, which ensures constancy of the organisms' components.

It is worth recalling that Bernard was a wonderful experimentalist, endowed with a sceptical attitude towards accepted theories, but also critical of Comte's positivism. For him, the scientific method consists of three stages: observation, hypothesis, experiment. The third stage is necessary to confirm, or reject, the second stage, and both are initiated by *observation*, something at which Bernard excelled. So much so that it has been pointed out that the decisive turning point in his discoveries was 'his extraordinary capacity for noting, in the course of an experiment, a fact that was somewhat marginal and did not accord with the prevailing theory' (Grmek 1970, p. 32).

Like Bernard, Cannon did not develop his researches in a systematic fashion but, in fact, often as a result of 'chance observation that other investigators might have ignored' (Benison and Berger 1970, p. 73). Like Bernard, Cannon was interested in digestion and the working of the nervous system, and, once more like Bernard, he was an extremely skilled experimentalist, to the point of being able to remove the entire sympathetic nervous system[4] from a live animal,

3 Homeostasis also controls cell division; cancer results from a malfunctioning of the feedback mechanism that regulates cell growth.

4 The sympathetic system is part of the 'autonomic system', whose name indicates that it acts automatically, without direction from the cerebral cortex.

and experiment on the effects of its removal.[5] Investigations carried out for over a decade led Cannon to the view that the function of the sympathetic system is that of keeping a state of constancy as the one described by Bernard as *milieu intérieur*.

Cannon's first mention of the term homeostasis is to be found in a short paper published in a volume in honour of physiologist Charles Richet (Cannon 1926). A full description of the various aspects of homeostasis is in his 1932 book, tellingly entitled *The Wisdom of the Body*, which describes the formation of a stable medium (the 'fluid matrix') and the several ways in which the medium is kept quasi-constant, with examples relating to the content of water, salt, sugars, proteins, fat, calcium, and more.

The process that led Cannon to discover the relation between homeostasis and the sympathetic system was long, and its various stages are difficult to trace back. The relation became apparent only slowly, and it was not until research on the activity of the sympathetic system in providing stability for the organism was published that the connection between the activity of the system and the emergence of those regulatory mechanisms was understood. As Cannon himself recalled, he and his team had been working on the role of the sympathetic system in maintaining steady states without knowing it; then facts already discovered took a new meaning, which eventually led to the appreciation of the role of the sympathetic system in bringing about homeostasis as if through a process of 'inductive unfolding' (Cannon 1932, p. 268). Hence Cannon's discovery came about as a instance of the bottom-up approach to science, which included wide-ranging, sometimes even unplanned, observation, upon which causal hypotheses were based, and thoroughly tested.

Reciprocal exchange of equilibrium concepts between biology and economics

The reciprocal exchanges between biology and economics have been extensively discussed by Geoffrey Hodgson:

> The two-way relationship between biology and economics dates from the very emergence of these modern sciences in the eighteenth and nineteenth centuries.... The flow of ideas from 'natural economy' to 'political economy' was in both directions, illustrating some key conceptual resonances between these two disciplines.
>
> (Hodgson 1993, p. 55)

The starting point of the exchange between biology and economics has often been identified with Mandeville's claim (1724) that the division of labour in the societies, together with self-interest (interpreted as greed), would contribute to

5 The whole idea is repellent to our minds, although it did not stir much opposition in those days. In point of fact, we can find partial consolation in the fact that the removal had much less dire effects than might be expected.

prosperity. Mandeville's claim was inspired by considerations on the working of animal societies, in particular that of bees. Inspiration from the work of nature was also behind the physiocrats' claim that economic phenomena are ruled by the same principles as natural phenomena.[6] The view that, if unperturbed by constraints and interventions, the economy would behave as a natural system and, therefore, tend towards equilibrium,[7] quickly spread. As a reaction to the government's of the time interventions on mercantilism, *laissez-faire* economics emerged, which held that self-interest and the power of competition are the driving forces towards economic equilibrium, and that this, in turn, would bring about improved living conditions for all.

In *The Wealth of Nations* (1776), Adam Smith promoted and popularised *laissez-faire* economics. Like the majority of his contemporaries, he was influenced by Newtonian science and the philosophy underlying it, and assumed that, just like laws of nature exist that bring about equilibrium in the physical world, so it would be for the economic world. Smith was also influenced by earlier theorists who had claimed the tendency towards a kind of natural balance in economies (see Hodgson 1993). For him, this natural balance would result from the interplay between enlightened self-interest and competition, which, acting like an invisible hand, would harmonise the needs of all.[8]

As *laissez-faire* economics became popular, its effects started being discussed with contrasting opinions. For many, it was a good thing because it promoted competition, which appeared to be the driving force for the achievement of economic equilibrium, while for others it was harsh and cruel, since it reduced state support for the poor as part of the limitation of government intervention. However, two aspects of *laissez-faire* economics, the notion of competition and that of limited resources, were going to exert profound influence outside economics, most notably on biology, thus starting the next stage of exchange between the two disciplines. The crucial figures in this process were Herbert Spencer (1820–1903) and Charles Darwin (1809–82).[9]

Spencer conceived of a unified science of natural and social phenomena; by combining the notion of balance in nature with findings from the new discipline of thermodynamics, he concluded that progress was an unavoidable aspect of reality 'Progress, therefore, is not an accident, it is part of nature: all of a piece with the development of the embryo or the unfolding of a flower' (Spencer 1855, p. 65).[10] For Spencer, natural balance and evolution[11] had not just shaped the physical world; they had also established the pattern by which society and

6 Francois Quesnay's *Tableau economique* of 1758, for instance, was inspired by studies on blood circulation.

7 In 1710 Lord Shaftesbury described the attainment and maintenance of equilibrium and balance in economies of self-interest as a feature of the 'will of Nature'.

8 For further characterisation of Smith's views on economic equilibrium, and the way to achieve it, see Dixon and Wilson's chapter.

9 Although, for Marshall (1904), Spencer's contribution was more important than Darwin's.

10 For discussion of the role of the notion of progress in Spencer's thinking, see Mayr (1992).

11 A term that he used as early as 1852 (Hodgson 1993, p. 81).

culture change, so that economies don't just mirror nature in their behaviour, but emerged by a similar process. Spencer reasoned that the balance of nature was due to an equilibrium between destructive and constructive forces. Extending to biology the emphasis on competition of *laissez-faire* economics, he conceptualised the notion of the 'survival of the fittest' in the natural world, albeit without exaggerating it; for instance, he acknowledged that competition created fluctuations in organisms' numbers, but claimed that, when viewed over long periods, amidst those fluctuations was a point of equilibrium (Spencer 1882).[12]

Notably, although Spencer often compared human society to living organisms, and used concepts from energetics (Capek 1961), his thinking remained deeply embedded in nineteenth century mechanicism (Whitehead 1926; Bannister 1979). Accordingly, his ontology was atomistic, in that, while he acknowledged the existence of relations between entities,[13] and granted those more emphasis than Darwin did (Hodgson 1993), he gave primacy to the entities' 'intrinsic' properties, currently defined as properties that are always displayed independently of anything else (Kim 1982).

As to Darwin's theory of natural selection (1859), some historians of science see it as the outcome of his coming in contact with the harsh social conditions that *laissez-faire* economics had brought about (Desmond and Moore 1991). In 1838, two decades before his theory of evolution by natural selection was published, Darwin had read Thomas Malthus's (1826) work on population, which argued that, in societies, the resources available would always be inadequate to satisfy everybody's needs. Malthus concluded that competition would be inevitable, with the strongest prevailing. Darwin combined Malthus's ideas about competition and limited resources with the appreciation of variation in natural populations he had acquired during his world travels, as a young man, aboard HMS *Beagle*.[14] He identified competition as the culling force, or natural selection, that drove biological evolution and achieved equilibrium by acting on the variation in populations and preventing the survival of those individuals least able to compete in the context of limited resources.

Darwin's (and Wallace's 1905) constant worry to resist linguistic expressions that may hint at a 'selecting' deity[15] was part and parcel of the material-

12 Spencer's notion of fluctuations around equilibrium had a considerable impact on the emergence of population biology and early ecology in the first decades of the twentieth century. In particular, chemist, mathematician and ecologist Alfred Lotka took Spencer's argument about equilibrium and, using differential equations, created a predictive model of the predator–prey interaction. His model, which took account of the various aspects of the interaction, such as, prey density, predation rate, predator mortality, and reproduction of the predator per unit of prey consumed, revealed the interaction to be characterised by cyclic fluctuation about equilibrium (Lotka 1925). (For further discussion, see Keeton and Gould 1993.)

13 For discussion of the distinction between intrinsic and relational properties on the two separate questions, not to be conflated, of reality and knowledge, see Mosini (2006), and references therein, especially Lenzen (1931) and Margenau (1950).

14 For discussion of Darwin's ability to transfer concepts across disciplines, see Ghiselin (1969) and La Vergata (1985).

15 Famously, the word 'selection' (Waters 1986).

istic stance that so much contributed to the success of evolutionary thinking in the twentieth century. However, the truly 'revolutionary' step, which paved the way for Darwin's presenting mankind as but one of the animal species in *The Descent of Man* (1871), had occurred with the assumption that human societies are in all respects comparable with animal societies (see Mandeville), which had deprived mankind of the special place in the animal kingdom that theology attributed it, at a time when science and theology were still intertwined.

This short account of reciprocal exchanges between economics and biology cannot fail to mention the fact that, in the late Victorian period, metaphors from Darwin's own economically influenced theory of biologic evolution began to travel back into economics. The most important figure in this respect is Alfred Marshall (1842–1924),[16] who explored biological theories to find ethical solutions to the problems posed by a pure 'survival of the fittest' social cull. For Marshall, biological theories were a great source of metaphors and analogies for economists (Niman 1991); those, rather than the physical sciences, should guide economic theory: 'The Mecca of economists lies in economic biology' (Marshall 1890, p. xiv). Marshall followed Darwin in seeing the evolutionary process as one of gradual changes,[17] rather than one as characterised by abrupt leaps. His search for inspiration from biology was somewhat frustrated by the confusion arising from the several competing evolutionary paradigms (Bowler 1988), and the ultimate essence of his analysis remained 'mechanical, addressing equilibrium outcomes' (Hodgson 1993, p. 101). But Marshall can be said to have prepared the ground for the introduction of bionomics and ecological economics in the twentieth century, which were also fostered by further developments within biology itself, such as, for instance, the growing importance of population biology, and the tremendous breakthroughs in genetics.

Notably, the assumption underlying *laissez-faire* economics, that the various forces at play would reach equilibrium – in the same way as equilibrium is reached in the natural world – by balancing each other under the guidance of self-interest and competition, implied a twofold speculative leap. First, because, at the time, equilibrium in nature had just begun to be described in scientific terms, and only to a modest degree, and the corresponding theoretical notions were far from being developed in all their aspects; second, because there was no empirical, theoretical or logical reason for assuming that human societies would behave as animal societies, as Mandeville, for instance, did. The first point implied that what was a pre-theoretical principle for proto-scientists, equilibrium as the balance observed in nature, became a theoretical milestone of 'natural' economics. The second point implied that the analogy between natural and economic phenomena was postulated without justification, and endorsed without discussion.

16 For the influence of evolutionism on Cournot, see Vatin's chapter.

17 For the role of gradualism in Darwinian evolutionary theory, see Desmond and Moore 1991.

The account of reciprocal exchanges between economics and biology just given has a further interesting aspect: it suggests that concepts travelled across the two disciplines and were backed up in the one discipline by being applied in the other before actually being validated in any one discipline.[18] In this way, a top-down methodological approach was enforced, which contrasts the bottom-up methodological approach of the Bernards and the Cannons.

We turn now to another example of the top-down methodological approach, represented by equilibrium as the result of costs–benefits analyses.

Equilibrium as the result of costs–benefits analyses

Between the 1930s and the 1950s, important developments in Darwinian thinking took place, which benefited from the population biology studies of R.A. Fisher, Sewall Wright and J.B.S. Haldane, among others. The notion of a bio-economic equilibrium emerged from costs–benefits analyses, and was first applied in genetics, socio-biology, and behavioural ecology. In the 1960s, biologists began to base their explanations for some puzzling adaptations on the trade-offs between the energy associated with developing the aspects and behaviours related to the adaptations in question and the resulting survival and reproductive advantages (see especially Tinbergen 1963a, b).

Taking into account the formidable breakthroughs of the 1950s and 1960s, biologist Richard Dawkins proposed the 'selfish gene' theory (1976), which shifted the emphasis of evolutionary history and adaptation away from the organism and towards the genetic material that codes for it. In Dawkins's interpretation, it is the DNA that is prior, rather than the organism it codes for. This shift of emphasis rendered the organism a kind of 'machine' that the DNA builds to best enable its own survival and perpetuation, which depends upon the achievement of an equilibrium between the cost of the machine the DNA builds and the benefits that the machine confers it. This equilibrium implies countless trade-offs resulting from the gradual rise and selection of beneficial characters, and the deletion of non-beneficial ones. Every modification, adaptation and development that appears in the organism represents an instantiation of DNA's own perpetuation device; in its most extreme form, the organism is just the throw-away survival machine of the genetic code. For Dawkins, 'survival of the fittest' means the DNA sequence that builds the machine that proves most successful at perpetuating and duplicating itself.

Here we give two examples – sexual reproduction and altruistic behaviour – of how the notion of equilibrium that emerged from costs–benefits analyses within the selfish gene paradigm is deployed.

18 The view that competition for limited resources was an essential element of evolution, as Darwin assumed, has, in recent times, been challenged by several historians and philosophers of biology (see, for instance, Lewontin 1978, 1980, and Sober 1981).

The economy of sexual reproduction

Sexual reproduction, so widespread among living organisms – whether animals or plants – constitutes a problem that requires explanation because it is a much less efficient means of producing large quantities of offspring than asexual reproduction. Moreover, the genetic blending that occurs during fertilisation means that successful DNA sequences are broken up and altered before they reach the next generation. Each sex cell contains only half the parental DNA, and is combined at random with half from the other parent. There is a chance that blending will dilute beneficial parental traits, and it is even possible that any new combination traits will be deleterious and render the young less fit than either of their parents. Hence sexual reproduction may be said to imply potential disadvantages when compared with asexual reproduction.

The selfish gene theory explains the prevalence of sexually reproducing organisms by showing that the genetic recombination inherent in fertilisation, which produces offspring that are different in varying degrees and traits from either of their parents, does, in fact, have benefits. It does so by showing that the variations between parent and offspring, and between the offspring themselves, allow the organisms to use the environment and the resources available to them in a highly effective manner (see, for instance, Ridley 1995). It was Darwin (1859) who noted that the environment is so complex and varied that even the very smallest area may contain many micro-habitats, differing from one another in tiny degrees. These tiny differences are mirrored by the variation between organisms and their offspring, which potentially allow the organisms to diffuse into the marginally different niches that the microhabitats offer. Thus parent and offspring are forced slightly less into competition with one another, as the small variations they display enable them to nest in slightly different micro-niches in the highly varied environment. Reducing competition between parent and offspring is an excellent way to boost the success of offspring generations. So, although fewer offspring are produced sexually, their fitness is improved by not having to compete so strongly with their parents and amongst themselves. Although being different from a successful parent may be costly, the costs may be balanced (or overridden) by the advantages related to the ability for the individual to utilise a slightly different micro-niche from its parents.[19]

Altruistic behaviour

Another problem for evolutionary biologists was represented by intra- or interspecies 'altruistic' behaviours. Costs–benefits analyses suggest that these

19 Moreover, the variation between parent and offspring afforded by sexual reproduction is beneficial in the evolutionary arms race that organisms engage in with predators and parasites that are constantly adapting to better use the organisms either as prey or as hosts (Van Valen 1973). So, although there is a cost attached to introducing variation into a genome that proved successful in the parent, there is a benefit in terms of the offspring's ability to better evade parasites and predators (Hamilton and Howard 1994).

behaviours only give the impression of some sort of self-sacrifice, while having a discreet reproductive benefit for the 'giver' (Keeton and Gould 1993).[20]

Consider the intra-species altruism exemplified by care relationships within families. In the same way that reproduction promotes the future of the individual's genome, so altruism promotes the future of the portions of the genome that different individuals in the same family share, and the selfish gene theory suggests that helping family members can be the same as helping oneself. The more genetically related two individuals are, the greater degree of altruism is warranted between them in terms of overall genome prosperity. A sexually reproducing organism shares about 50 per cent of its genes with its young. Siblings that share both parents also share 50 per cent of their genes with each other. On the selfish gene theory, it is good to have a child, but it is also good to have a sibling. Also, an organism will care for its grandchildren, since, put simply, two grandchildren are worth one offspring in selfish gene terms. The costs–benefits trade-offs for the selfish gene mean that it is not always best for an organism to reproduce itself directly by producing offspring, and that, in fact, it may prove better to direct resources towards assisting sibling production; it is better to have many siblings than only one or very few offspring. And the rule extends to more remote members of the family as well, and applies, for instance, between cousins and even more remote relatives (Krebs and Davies 1978).

Recall that, on the selfish gene theory's account, it is not the prosperity of the individual that is paramount, but the prosperity of the genes that the individual organism is built to serve. Those genes are not only within that particular organism, but also within the other organisms related to it, and so the selfish gene is served by altruism. Therefore, the true measure of the success of a gene is not whether an individual organism hosting it survives and reproduces, but whether the gene is passed on to more individuals in the next generation (Cronin 1991).

As an example of inter-species 'altruism', consider 'mutalism', a relationship in which symbiosis is achieved between two unrelated organisms belonging to different species, of which 'cleaning symbioses' provide the simplest illustration. Clown fish live amongst the tentacles of the sea anemone, cleaning their hosts of trapped particles, while themselves feeding on that debris and taking refuge amongst the anemones' stings. Similarly, the gut bacteria of humans and the cellulose-digesting bacteria of ruminants perform digestive functions for

20 The cost/benefit *equilibria* of family groups were first explained and given a mathematical treatment, by the 'kin selection' theory, which expressed the cost/benefit balance with the equation $R \times B > C$, in which R is a measure of relatedness, B is a measure of reproductive gain, and C is the cost to the altruist organism (Hamilton 1964a, b). Hamilton's theory offers an explanation as to why certain individuals in a colony of ground squirrels or meerkats act as lookouts at the expense of spending their time foraging for food or resting, and give alarm calls when danger approaches at the expense of their own concealment from a predator. The animals in those colonies are closely related, and so, for example, making an alarm call that might jeopardise an individual's own life might serve to protect the lives of the siblings, cousins, offspring and grandchildren with which it cohabits. Hamilton's theory has also been used to explain the apparently mystifying arrangement in colonial insect populations, in which the vast majority of individuals do not reproduce (Krebs and Davies 1978).

their host, while themselves being provided with food and a habitat. Organisms that live symbiotically exist in equilibrium with one another. As soon as that equilibrium is broken the symbiosis is lost. For example, if one organism begins to take more from the other than it offers in return it begins to tend towards a state of parasitism, which is a non-equilibrium relationship of costs and benefits between two organisms. If one organism ceases to benefit from the relationship with another organism without being harmed by it, 'commensualism' is established, which is illustrated by the growth of barnacles on the bodies of whales, and by orchids using trees as bases for their growth.

Summing up, altruistic behaviours, and co-operative interactions in general, within and between species require that the costs and benefits involved balance each other.

Conclusion

There are so many equilibria, whether within, or between, biological systems that the notion of equilibrium may be said to be ubiquitous in biology. Those equilibria are nested and overlaid, and the overall balance of nature is attributable to this wide variety of interacting processes occurring in a great orchestration.

The two concepts of equilibrium in biology that we have chosen to discuss, homeostasis and balance in costs–benefits analyses, differ from one another in a relevant way in their having emerged in different methodological frameworks, respectively, the bottom-up (one may say, inductive) and the top-down (one may say, deductive) one. There is no question that the inductive and the deductive methodologies are not totally independent from one another, in that elements of both methodologies interplay in almost all instances of scientific research that is made possible by that very interplay. However, where the emphasis between the two methodologies lies is in many ways an important point, and has been used, for instance, in discussing the current state of economics (Lawson 2003). Equilibrium as in homeostasis was first observed, and later understood and reconstructed, mainly on the basis of pre-theoretical, causal, arguments. By contrast, the balance of neo-Darwinian costs–benefits analyses, which provides a compelling and fascinating account of many states of affairs, is mainly theory-dependent. This is by no means a unique case; on the contrary, the twentieth century has witnessed a constant shift towards theory in the interplay with evidence (see, for instance, Franklin 1986).

That shift, however, may have major consequences in cases in which the corroboration of theories by data is impossible or highly controversial, as, for instance, in economics. Hence, in such cases, caution should be exerted in discussing theoretical notions of equilibrium, such as the balance of costs–benefits analyses of neo-Darwinian accounts. One may even wish to go back to Newton's prudent attitude against theoretical explanations, and his refusal to accept the view that 'it is thus because it cannot be otherwise', to which he added that 'it may not be effectual for determining truth to examine the several ways by which phenomena may be explained unless where there can be a perfect enumeration of all those ways' (Newton 1672, p. 320).

What was Newton saying there? He was saying that there may be *several* explanations for the same set of phenomena, and that, at any one time, one cannot be certain that those *several* explanations exhaust the entire range of possible explanations. In this way, in a very concise, and effective, manner, Newton stated the thesis of the under-determination of theories by data that has come to form one of the cornerstones of twentieth century philosophy of science.[21] Equally important, the above claim also conveys Newton's firm view that scientific knowledge has *always* a provisional character, i.e. that 'if no exception occurs from phenomena, the conclusion may be pronounced generally. But, if at any time afterwards, any exception shall occur from experiments, it may then begin to be pronounced with such exceptions to occur' (Newton 1730, p. 404).

It is on this word of caution towards the role of theoretical explanations in science that we wish to conclude, suggesting that it may provide a good starting point to re-address the question of how the balance between evidence and theory is currently understood in economics.

References

Bannister, R.C. (1979), *Social Darwinism. Science and Myth in Anglo-American Social Thought*, Temple University Press, Philadelphia.

Benison, S. and A. Clifford Berger (1970), 'Cannon, Walter Bradford', *Dictionary of Scientific Biography*, III, in C.C. Gillispie (ed.), Scribner, New York, 71–7.

Bowler, P.J. (1988), *The Non-Darwinian Revolution: Reinterpreting a Historical Myth*, Johns Hopkins University Press, Baltimore MD.

Cannon, W. (1926), *Hommage à Charles Richet*, A. Pettit (ed.), Presse Institut, Paris.

Cannon, W. (1932), *The Wisdom of the Body*, Norton, New York.

Capek, M. (1961), *The Philosophical Impact of Contemporary Physics*, Van Nostrand, Princeton, NJ.

Cooper, G. (2001), 'Must there be a balance of Nature?', *Biology and Philosophy*, 16, 481–506.

Cronin, H. (1991), *The Ant and the Peacock*, Cambridge University Press, Cambridge.

Cuddington, K. (2001), 'The "balance of nature" metaphor and equilibrium in population ecology', *Biology and Philosophy*, 16, 463–79

Darwin, C. (1859), *On the Origin of Species by Means of Natural Selection, or the Preservation of Favoured Races in the Struggle for Life*, Murray, London.

21 The thesis of the under-determination of theories by data is usually attributed to philosophers like Popper and Goodman, or, at most, traced back to Poincaré (see, for instance, Laudan 1998). In fact, as we just indicated, priority for the enunciation of the thesis goes to Newton, and it seems right to give him credit for it. A wider form of that thesis, known as 'the Duhem–Quine thesis', holds that, since theories come to be tested only in conjunction with auxiliary hypotheses, if the theory is refuted, it is unclear whether this depends on the theory or on the auxiliary hypotheses, and, in general, it is possible to readjust those auxiliary hypotheses, and rescue the theory (Duhem 1906; Quine 1953). Notably, while the thesis of the under-determination of theories by data as stated by Newton only suggests to attribute scientific knowledge provisional character, without doubting it before contrary evidence crops up, the Duhem–Quine thesis lends itself, and has been used, to support scepticism.

Darwin, C. (1871), *The Descent of Man, and Selection in Relation to Sex*, Murray, London.
Dawkins, R. (1976), *The Selfish Gene*, Oxford University Press, Oxford.
Desmond, A. and J. Moore, (1991), *Darwin*, Penguin Books, London.
Duhem, P. (1906), *La Théorie physique. Son objet et sa structure*, Chevalier et Rivière, Paris.
Egerton, F. (1973), 'Changing concepts of balance of Nature', *Quarterly Review of Biology*, 48, 322–50.
Franklin, A. (1986), *The Neglect of Experiment*, Cambridge University Press, Cambridge.
Ghiselin, M.T. (1969), *The Triumph of the Darwinian Method*, University of California Press, Berkley, CA.
Grmek, M.D. (1970), 'Bernard, Claude', *Dictionary of Scientific Biography*, I, in C.C. Gillispie (ed.), Scribner, New York, 24–34.
Hamilton, W. (1964a), 'The genetical evolution of social behaviour' I, *Journal of Theoretical Biology*, 7, 1–16.
Hamilton, W. (1964b), 'The genetical evolution of social behaviour' II, *Journal of Theoretical Biology*, 7, 17–52.
Hamilton, W. and J. Howard (eds) (1994), 'Infection, polymorphism and evolution', *Philosophical Transactions of the Royal Society of London, Series B*, 346, 267–385.
Hodgson, G.M. (1993), *Economics and Evolution. Bringing Life back into Economics*, Polity Press, Cambridge.
Keeton, W. and J. Gould (1993), *Biological Science*, Norton, New York.
Kim, J. (1982), 'Psychophysical supervenience', *Philosophical Studies*, 41, 51–70.
Krebs, J. and N. Davies (1978), *Behavioural Ecology*, Blackwell Science, London.
Laudan, L. (1998), 'Underdetermination', in E. Craig (ed.), *Routledge Encyclopedia of Philosophy*, Routledge, London, 527–30.
La Vergata, A. (1985), 'Images of Darwin: a historiographic overview', in D. Kohn (ed.), *The Darwinian Heritage*, Princeton University Press, Princeton, NJ, 901–72.
Lawson, T. (2003), *Reorienting Economics*, Routledge, London & New York.
Lenzen, V.F. (1931), *The Nature of Physical Theory*, Wiley, New York.
Lewontin, R. (1978), 'Adaptation', *Scientific American*, 239, 212–30.
Lewontin, R. (1980), 'Sociobiology: another biological determinism', *International Journal of Health Sciences*, 10, 347–63.
Lotka, A. (1925), *Elements of Physical Biology*, Williams and Wilkins, Baltimore, MD.
Malthus, T. (1798) [1926], *An Essay on the Principle of Population, as it Affects the Future Improvement of Society*, Macmillan, London.
Malthus, T. (1826), *An Essay on the Principle of Population*, Murray, London.
Mandeville, B. (1724) [1970], *The Fable of the Bees*, P. Harth (ed.), Penguin, Harmondsworth.
Margenau, H. (1950), *The Nature of Physical Reality*, McGraw-Hill, New York.
Marshall, A. (1904), 'On a national memorial to Herbert Spencer', *Daily Chronicle*, 23 November.
Marshall, A. (1890) [1920], *Principles of Economics*, 8th edn, Macmillan, New York.
Mosini, V. (2006), 'Relational properties and the question of realism in science', in C. Garola and A. Rossi (eds), *The Foundations of Quantum Mechanics. Historical Analysis and Open Questions*, World Scientific, Singapore, 260–73.
Newton, I. (1672) [1776], 'Letter to Oldenburg', *Isaaci Newtoni opera quae extant omnia commentaries illustrabat*, S. Horsley (ed.), Nichols, London, IV, 320–7.
Newton, I. (1730) [1952], *Optiks. A Treatise of the Reflections, Refractions, Inflections and Colours of Light*, Dover, New York.

Niman, N.B. (1991), 'Biological analogies in Marshall's work', *Journal of the History of Economic Thought*, 13 (1), 19–36.

Paley, W. (1803), *Natural Theology or Evidences of the Existence and Attributes of the Deity, collected from the Appearances of Nature*, Faluder, London.

Pimm, S. (1991), *The Balance of Nature? Ecological Issues in the Conservation of Species and Communities*, University of Chicago Press, Chicago.

Quine, W.V. (1953), *From a Logical Point of View*, Harvard University Press, Cambridge, MA.

Ridley, M. (1995), *The Red Queen, Sex and the Evolution of Human Nature*, Penguin, London.

Smith, A. (1776) [1986], *The Wealth of Nations*, Penguin Books, Harmondsworth.

Sober, E. (1981), 'Holism, individualism, and the units of selection', in P.D. Asquith and R. Giere (eds), *Philosophy of Science Association 1980*, II, Philosophy of Science Association, East Lansing, MI, 93–121.

Spencer, H. (1855), *The Principles of Psychology*, Williams and Norgate, London.

Spencer, H. (1882), *First Principles*, Appleton, New York.

Tinbergen, N. (1963a), 'On aims and methods of ethnology', *Zeitschrift für Tierpsychologies*, 20, 410–33.

Tinbergen, N. (1963b), 'The shell menace', *Natural History*, 72, 28–35.

Van Valen, L. (1973), 'A new evolutionary law', *Evolutionary Theory*, 1, 1–30

Wallace, A.R. (1905), *My Life. A Record of Events and Opinions*, 2 vols, Chapman and Hall, London.

Waters, C.K. (1986), 'Natural selection without survival of the fittest', *Biology and Philosophy*, 1 (2), 207–25.

Withers, P. (1992), *Comparative Animal Physiology*, Saunders College Publishing, New York.

Part II

Equilibrium in pre-neoclassical economics

4 'Sympathy', 'character' and economic equilibrium

William Dixon and David Wilson

In this chapter we address A. Smith's and T. Chalmers's notions of economic equilibrium as a 'natural concord' made possible by the capacity referred to by Smith as 'sympathy' and resulting in what Chalmers referred to as 'character'. The Smith–Chalmers view suggests a much richer picture of human agency in economic affairs than the egoistic theory put forward by T. Hobbes, and largely endorsed by neoclassical economics. We compare criticisms of the latter characterisation of human agency, made from a sociological standpoint, with that of social psychologist G.H. Mead, in which we find echoes of Smith's and Chalmers's views.

Neoclassical economics has an understanding of equilibrium that transcends human agency. We do not mean by this to rehearse the usual charge against it for not saying how its agents reach equilibrium, or how, having reached it, they stick with, or return to, it in the face of exogenous shocks. Rather, our point is that neoclassical agents seem to lack some of those basic human capacities that are required to enable their effective co-ordination. Further, we argue that, having said too little (in actual fact, nothing) about the foundational role of 'sympathy' (as Smith called it) in human co-ordination, neoclassical economics fixes the origins of General Competitive Analysis in the work of A. Smith (Arrow and Hahn 1971). It also claims too much in regard to the powers with which it endows human agency in its economic dealings, for instance, when positing economic actions and interactions as being 'actuated *only* by self-interest' (Edgeworth 1881, p. 16, our emphasis). Indeed, as Smith himself recognised, to say that an agent is self-interested is to say something about why she would want to act, not how she is able to do it. *Contra* Edgeworth, human agents *cannot* be *actuated* only by self-interest: presumably Edgeworth here meant to say 'motivated by self-interest and capacitated by the power of reason', for it is something like this formula that underpins the modern economic paradigm, and enables proponents like I. Fisher to conceive of human-interactive events as 'correspond[ing] to the mechanical equilibrium of a particle' (Fisher 1925, p. 11).

The formula that equates human agency with particle-like behaviour has long given offence to many, both within and without the bounds of economic discourse. Indeed, from without, the offence seems to have given rise to a whole new discipline of sociology, which, in the hands of its classical practitioners, endeavours to fill out the excessively 'lean' version of economic agency of the neoclassical paradigm with more capacities on the motivational, and fewer on the rational, side. In the next section we rehearse some of their arguments. A closer look at some of this theorising, however, shows that it is not the neoclassical description of economic agency as such that is taken to be objectionable but, rather, the assumption that economic behaviour can, of itself, constitute and maintain society. For this reason, the sociological imagination does not so much challenge the understanding of action and interaction of neoclassical economics as supplement it. Some critics of the neoclassical conception of economic agency and equilibrium (for example, Durkheim, more of which below, Sen 1988 and the self-styled socio-economists Etzioni and Lawrence 1991), whilst contesting its abstraction from moral/social issues, fail in our view to realise the significance of this abstraction. The key to understanding this failure, we claim, is that the agent of neoclassical theory is not so much under-motivated as under-capacitated. As we argue below, this point was apparent to earlier generations of economic theorists, in particular, to Marshall and, through Beveridge, to Keynes, who took an interest in the issue of 'character' as the idea that economic equilibrium depends on the behaviour of agents whose competence cannot be simply characterised as, and reduced to, an instrumental, or strategic, rationality. It is not difficult, if one goes back beyond the neoclassical revolution, to find writers on economic matters who believed that there is more to human beings than a simple calculating *ego* (see, for instance, R. van den Berg's and F. Vatin's chapters). But, to find a coherent theoretical alternative to the neoclassical orthodoxy, we argue, one should return to the political economy of A. Smith and T. Chalmers, whom we read through the action theory of social psychologist G.H. Mead. Our reading suggests an understanding of human action and interaction that cuts through the sterile debates on the moral basis (or otherwise) of economic behaviour that have accompanied neoclassical economic equilibrium theorising up to the present time.

Hobbes's 'homo economicus' and its malcontents

In order to understand Smith and his fellow political economists, we need to recall that their discourse originated in reaction to the rampant egoism that, according to Hobbes and his followers, underpins most (if not all) human interactions. Hobbes's version of political economy may have been criticised for many reasons, but for Smith the decisive factor was one of common sense: the 'natural concords' that human beings are evidently capable of achieving are simply beyond the capacity of the Hobbesian actors (Smith 1759, p. 22). Having criticised Hobbes's theory of human actors capacitated only by a rational egoism, Smith set out in *The Theory of the Moral Sentiments* (henceforth *TMS*) to provide a more adequate account of human agency. But, almost at once, he was badly misunderstood. This became clear in responses to the subsequent publication of *The Wealth of Nations* (henceforth *WN*). In his review of this work, Feder detected a willingness 'to trust too much to the harmony of individual interests in producing naturally by their free action general good' (Feder 1777, quoted in Montes 2003, p. 68). Hildebrand's mid-nineteenth century assessment left even less to the imagination: in a remarkable turn of phrase, he claimed that Smith and his disciples attempted to 'transform political economy into a mere natural history of egoism' (Hildebrand 1848, quoted in Montes 2003, p. 70). Thus, in barely more than two generations, Smith's reaction to egoistic social theory has been all but forgotten and *WN* itself was being read as an exercise in enlightened Hobbesianism.

Durkheim's sociology fed off this misunderstanding. For Durkheim, sociology was required as a reaction to what he took to be the starting point of political economy: Hobbes's essentially unsocial self. Like Smith, Durkheim rejected such a starting point as a possible basis for the explanation of a spontaneous social order. Hobbesian egoism 'detaches the individual from the rest of the world . . . closes off every horizon [and] leads directly to pessimism' (Durkheim 1887, p. 94). But Durkheim took Smith, *qua* political economist, to be part of the problem rather than the basis of a solution. The manner in which Durkheim himself dealt with this issue set the tone for sociology as well as for some significant critical interventions within economics itself. For Durkheim, what he took to be the prevalent characterisation of the human actor as calculating ego was not so much wrong as incomplete; consequently, the answer to the question of how human society arises and reproduces itself is to somehow supplement self-interest with other, more socially oriented, concerns. It is clear that 'these *two* springs of behaviour have been present from the very beginning' (Durkheim 1895, p. 145, our emphasis). Where there is only ego, where, in Durkheim's words, there is only 'interest', we are back in the discredited territory of Hobbes, 'for where interest alone reigns, as nothing arises to check the egoisms confronting one another, each self finds itself in relation to the other on a war footing' (Durkheim 1895, p. 152). On Durkheim's account, it is not just that the needs and wants brought into conformity through the social process are richer and more complex than Hobbes's selfish *ego*; rather, the social process depends, for its very existence, on characteristics additional to those that define the Hobbesian actor. For Durkheim, the acquisition of character, for want of a better term, is about the *how*, rather than just the *what*, of co-ordination; character is the element which was missing in Hobbes's theory, that enables human agents to co-ordinate. Durkheim thought that his richer, more complex, conception of human agency would solve the problem of viable social behaviour but his conception of the 'social fact' as *sui generis* did not achieve that goal. Asserting the importance of studying the social fact in its own right, as 'irreducible' to 'the psychic nature of the individual' (Durkheim 1887, p. 62), and examining social facts in this way, he circumvented the issue as to how we get from the individual to the society by effectively refusing to engage with it. It turns out, then, that

Durkheim's apparently methodological decision was a substantive one, a decision that derived from a particular kind of understanding of the relationship between individual and society. 'A social fact', he said, 'is to be recognised by the power of the external coercion which it exercises' (Durkheim 1895, p. 56); it originates and operates independently of the power of individuals. Social properties emerge just as the properties of an alloy like bronze differ from the properties of the alloy constituent metals (see Durkheim 1895). Thus what is distinctive for Durkheim about human, as opposed to other animal societies, is that human co-ordination, rather than being instinctive, internally driven, is 'imposed . . . from the outside', 'added on to his own nature' (Durkheim 1895, p. 248). But, in positing a sociology, literally, a logic of the social, that works independently of the (self-)interest-driven psychology of the individual, Durkheim, far from transcending Hobbes's egoism, left its theoretical foundations intact. Effectively, Durkheim's explanation of society substituted for one 'social fact' (the Hobbesian social contract) another one of his own making. For Durkheim, like Hobbes, factors that are supposed to lie outside human nature become the basis of his explanation of society.

It might be said that an attractive feature of Hobbes's egoistic theory – one which, arguably, helped the latter to resurface as the bedrock of neoclassical economics – is that it did postulate an agent at ease with herself. On the other hand, Durkheim was right to point out that such an agent is congenitally incapable of *inter*acting effectively, unless supplemented with additional character traits. But, as we suggest above, it is in this process of supplementation that the agent is in danger of losing her integrity. On Durkheim's account, her character traits – those 'morals', 'norms', 'values' of which sociologists and socioeconomists speak – are supposed to be acquired, imposed, from the outside, added on to her 'own nature', and, for this reason, can hardly be said to be her own.

As we argue in the next section, Smith's political economy has the decisive advantage over both Hobbesian theory and the sociological/socioeconomic reaction to it, of postulating an agent who, like the Hobbesian agent, and *contra* the reaction to it, is comfortable with herself and her actions, but, unlike the Hobbesian agent, is also naturally capable of successful interactive behaviour.

A. Smith: equilibrium through 'sympathy'

The aspect of Smith's *TMS* that most interests us here is the view that the human self and its acts involve the taking in, and, thus, the pre-reflective anticipation, of the attitudes of others. Smith called this process of pre-reflective anticipation 'sympathy', taking it to be not just one of a number of attitudes that the self might strike in relation to others, but to represent the core around which the human self and its interest are constituted, the condition that underlies all human action.

Smith opened *TMS* on typical moral-philosophical terrain. First, what do we consider right and wrong in regard to 'tenor of conduct'? In other words, '[w]herein does virtue consist'? And, second, how do we come to see things in that virtuous way? 'By what power or faculty of mind . . . is this character, whatever it be . . . recommended to us?' Or 'how and by what means does it come to pass that the mind prefers one tenor of conduct to another?' (Smith 1759, p. 265). How, in other words, is moral judgement possible? Smith claimed that the distinction between the forms of behaviour that are recognised as moral, and the faculties that make this recognition possible, is immanent in moral discourse itself, and that, for this reason, it always and everywhere finds practical application. What Smith claimed, however, is that 'moral-philosophical systems' do not always (or usually) recognise this natural difference, and that this is a major (perhaps the major) source of error. So, for example, benevolence (in the appropriate context) is often identified both as a form of moral conduct and as the cause of moral conduct. Or, again, self-love (and again in the appropriate context) is viewed both as a form of moral conduct and as its cause.[1] Smith's explicit recognition of a distinction between the 'what' and the 'how' of moral judgement implied that, while human beings recognise (in the appropriate contexts) benevolence and self-love as virtues, these virtues do not by themselves make moral judgement (or conduct) possible. In other words, the explanation – as against a mere explication – of moral judgement is to be found elsewhere.

Smith's palpable concern with moral judgement raised a second issue, since judging is not the same thing as feeling. This is because judging requires more (or possibly other) than feeling: it implies reflecting, considering and deciding on feelings. Assuming that the title of *TMS* was deliberately chosen suggests that, for Smith, feelings or 'sentiments' are involved in our capacity for moral judgement, which, therefore, rests on our capacity for moral feelings. My feeling or sentiment, however, is not of a deliberate kind, and turns from moral disposition into judgement only when my ongoing pre-reflective state is disturbed by a certain incongruity. In my normal pre-reflective mode, I 'expect', or I have 'hopes' (Smith 1759, p. 221) in regard to your conduct, and, so long as my hopes are confirmed, no moral judgement ensues. Indeed, it is only when I am 'surprised' by your behaviour, only when I am 'astonished and confounded' (ibid., p. 27), 'enraged', filled with 'wonder and surprise' (ibid., p. 31) by your conduct, when I fail to 'anticipate' your response or reaction, that a moral judgement is formed. Normally I just feel, and feeling is not considering, let alone judging. How, then, does the individual come by the moral sentiments that constitute her ongoing, pre-reflective state, and that, when disturbed, provoke a moral judgement? According to Smith, this is through 'sympathy', a term that he did not use to mean 'pity and compassion', or a 'fellow-feeling with the sorrow of others', as in everyday language, but to mean a sense of organic connection between human beings, the capacity to feel with,[2] to establish a 'fellow-feeling'. Sympathy is thus taken to mean 'our fellow-feeling with any passion whatever'; we sympathise, when we 'bring home' to ourselves the case of another: sympathy is the capacity for 'entering into' another's situation (Smith 1759,

1 One need hardly add that, ironically, Smith's project itself has subsequently been read in these conflated terms. Indeed, such a reading seems to be the source of the much discussed *Das Adam-Smith Problem* (see Montes 2003 for a recent summary of the relevant literature).

2 From the Greek σύν παθέω.

pp. 10–11). This does not mean that I sympathise with any benefit you may receive: in some cases, I recognise your benefit, but I cannot sympathise with it. However, I can, and do, sympathise with your gratitude, with how you *feel* about the benefit. Otherwise expressed: for Smith there is an organic connection between myself and how you feel (about a certain form of conduct that affects you). But your feeling (or rather how I suppose you feel) and myself can be organically connected only if your feeling is somehow inside myself. And 'your feeling, inside myself' constitutes what Smith calls the 'impartial spectator', the 'man within the breast' (see, for example, Smith 1759, pp. 129–32). Now 'your feeling, inside myself' is not the same as your actual feeling, which, as such, cannot be inside myself. Smith's impartial spectator is neither a part of the 'I' nor a part of the 'you', but, rather, an 'us' that is part of the self. Smith's impartial spectator is a metaphor of the norms we live by, and we come to live by these norms because they are rooted in us as the 'man within the breast'. It is a moot point whether Smith thought of these rules as absolute or relative. Either way, he did not think of them as external rules that we are forced to adhere to, or as rules to which we agree to conform, upon reflection. These rules inhere in me: they are my rules, they do not just enable me to judge, they enable me to act. The 'man within the breast' is me, and accompanies me everywhere. In that sense Smith's otherwise admirable terminology is misleading, for the 'man within the breast' is no man (but rather a constituent part of a man), no more than the man whose breast he inhabits would be a man without him. The human being can no more act according to the passions alone (egoistic theory) than according to the impartial spectator, or rather according to his representative, the 'man within' (traditional moral theory). Smith put it thus:

> [the actor] lower[s] his passion to that pitch, in which the spectators are capable of going along with him. He must flatten, if I may be allowed to say so, the sharpness of his natural tone, in order to reduce it to harmony and concord with the emotions of those who are about him ... [And] ... [i]n order to produce this concord, as nature teaches the spectators to assume the circumstances of the person principally concerned, so she teaches this last in some measure to assume those of the spectators.
>
> (Smith 1759, p. 22)

Note that Smith's actor is not undergoing a strategic 'lowering of tone'; she does not have an act in mind which she modifies, having first reflected on the other person(s)' initial response, though of course this can happen too. Rather she has anticipated the other person(s)' response in her mind: her lowering of tone comes naturally. Nature teaches to act with the other person(s)' responses in mind, and vice versa, and all this is instinctive: '[w]e are *immediately put in mind* of the light in which he will view our situation, and we begin to view it ourselves in the same light; for *the effect of sympathy is instantaneous*' (Smith 1759, pp. 22–3; our emphasis).

T. Chalmers: equilibrium through 'character'

Like Smith, Chalmers drew attention to a form of self that has the feelings and attitudes of others in mind, alongside his own ones; one who cannot help but act in anticipation, or expectation, of a certain response, one who cannot conceive of the act without a sense of reaction of the other. It is only such a self as this that can sustain a world without external direction or regulation. Only such a self is able to develop the character appropriate to the various situations met with, because it is only by taking in the feelings of others that the human actor has the intrinsic capacity to learn and adjust. This acting is moral to the core but not in the sense of it adhering to some universal standard. Rather, for Chalmers, as for Smith, the human act is intrinsically moral in virtue of the fact that it always embodies a sense of what is expected of her and others. In other words, for Chalmers, character develops from human interactions. As expectations with regard to a conduct are more or less confirmed, that conduct begins to become a habit. In this way a person gradually builds up a collection of habits. As we will show below, for Chalmers 'character' is the learnt disposition to act in a particular, and predictable, way.

Like Smith, Chalmers also took such a self as the basis of political economy and its science. For him, the key to the formation and reproduction of a liberal political economy is the reproduction of an acting self capable of nurturing and sustaining the equilibrium characteristic of economic and political order, which, in his mind, was a liberal economic order. Our interest is in how Chalmers, like Smith before him, imagined the virtues that would bring about equilibrium and order to be inculcated. How does one come by these virtues that Chalmers referred to as 'character'? In *On the Adaptation of External Nature to the Moral and Intellectual Constitution of Man* Chalmers addressed just this issue by investigating the 'affinities between man and his fellows, that harmonise the individual with the general interests' (Chalmers 1833, I, p. 10); to this end, it is necessary to understand the 'moral constitution of man' rather than 'the moral system of virtue' (ibid., p. 11). Concern with the latter would ask 'What is virtue?' but Chalmers's interest was in 'the mental process by which man takes cognisance of virtue' (ibid., p. 1; see also pp. 55–8). The cultural basis of the free market would have to be formed on this mental process, which presupposes a self with the capacity and need for self-development, culminating in the formation of character. It is essential, however, that this process should not be looked at in isolation: 'the main tendencies and aptitudes of his moral constitution should be looked for in connection with his social relationships, with the action and reaction which takes place between man and the brethren of his species' (ibid., p. 8). These interactions Chalmers considered to be the 'proper theme of our volume' (ibid., p. 162); they constitute what he called 'conscience' (ibid., p. 60), elsewhere the 'voice within every heart', the 'guide or governor' (ibid., p. 62, and p. 71). Conscience for Chalmers, then, is summoned from within, but it is not determined from within. It is rather constituted by the 'actings and reactings that take place between man and man in society'

(Chalmers 1833, I, p. 162), receiving its 'impulse and . . . direction from sympathy with the consciences around it'; conscience, for Chalmers, is the social taken into oneself, the 'reciprocal play of moral judgement . . . maintain[ing] . . . its freshness and integrity' (Chalmers 1833, I, p. 169). Through conscience, each one acts 'under the observation and guardianship of his fellows . . . each man lives under a consciousness of the vigilant and discerning witnesses' (ibid., pp. 169–70). It is this vital 'law of interchange of mind and mind' that ensures that no one is 'left to the decay and the self-deception of his own withering solitude' (ibid., p. 170), thus multiplying the 'pleasure of virtue as also the sufferings of vice' (ibid., p. 172). As conceived by Chalmers, the 'delicate mechanism' corresponding to the reciprocity of minds is the intrinsic form of the self, which, left to its own devices, ensures social coherence by making self-action something very different from a mass of chaotic experiments taking place on, and in, a hostile world. Left to its own devices, then, this 'mutual acting and reacting of . . . emotions', this 'law of interchange of mind and mind', does 'form the materials of a society that can stand' (Chalmers 1833, I, pp. 210–11).

According to Chalmers, conduct conducive to a liberal order cannot be legislated for, or demanded from without, the self, because any attempt to institute good behaviour would destroy the good. It is not possible to 'translate beneficence into the statute-book of law, without expunging it from the statute-book of the heart' (Chalmers 1833, II, p. 24). Law that makes virtue an object of compulsion destroys it. This 'law of the heart' for Chalmers, however, by no means makes one a Humean slave of the passions. Whatever is within, for Chalmers, cannot only be passion (with or without the capacity for instrumental reasoning) because, as Hume went on to show, people's acts are not ultimately acts of volition. In distinguishing emotion (which is not in itself determinate of action) from will (which is), Chalmers did not mean to rehearse standard moral-philosophical themes, which set the moral act against what one is inclined to do: Chalmers did not mean to substitute for an *ego* buffeted by external rules an *ego* buffeted by internally generated rules. To sum up, for Chalmers, actors capable of sustaining a liberal political economy develop a 'character', which enables them to act in a free, yet responsible, way, and this is what brings about economic equilibrium and harmonious social coexistence.

Remnants of Smith's and Chalmers's views on equilibrium

Notwithstanding Smith's and Chalmers's convincing critiques of egoistic theory, neoclassical economics, which claimed Smith as one of its seminal figures, resurrected the Hobbesian theory of behaviour that Smith's and Chalmers's arguments on the role of sentiment in the formation and reproduction of society aimed to lay to rest. However, the neoclassical, and more particularly the Walrasian, notion of equilibrium as a strategically rational accomplishment did not spell the end of that earlier conception of economic equilibrium as a 'natural concord' brought about by the formation of a particular kind of character. Ironically perhaps, remnants of that earlier, ethically capacitated, view of equilibrium surfaced in the work of A. Marshall. From the start, Marshall's concern was with practical ethics, and his interest in economic thought was driven to the question of the formation of character (Groenewegen 1995, p. 141). In the *Principles* Marshall wrote that 'man's character has been moulded by his every-day work', and noted that 'the conditions which surround extreme poverty, especially in densely crowded places, tend to deaden the higher faculties' (Marshall 1890, pp. 1–2). He noted that, even outside the *residuum*, outside what today might be called the underclass, many could not make 'the best of their mental faculties' due to overwork, lack of education or leisure, and concluded that 'the study of the causes of poverty is the study of the causes of the degradation of a large part of mankind' (Marshall 1890, p. 2). He thus urged to discuss economic matters in the light of the consideration that a man's character is 'a product of the circumstances under which he has lived' (ibid., p. 631).[3] Marshall went on to develop an analysis of different time periods that he saw as supplementing Ricardo's lopsided 'long-run' view that, on his account, had taken too much for granted in the matter of character. This is because investigating circumstances required investigating actual processes over time, rather than assuming an adjustment process towards any long-run equilibrium values that could be presupposed. Marshall's realisation that the individual is formed by his circumstances, that is to say, by 'short run' situations, in particular by poverty, is the reason why time was to became a central element in his analysis. However, for Marshall, the distinction between 'short-run' and 'long-run' was not in itself sufficient in that it did not capture the real developments that occur over time, even though it provided an adequate approximation for certain analytical purposes: 'Fragmentary statical hypotheses are used as temporary auxiliaries to dynamical – or rather biological – conceptions' (Marshall 1890, p. xiii). Economics should be concerned with human beings who 'change and progress', so that the central issue must be 'living force and movement' (ibid., p. xiii). Despite conceding that treating problems of economics in terms of 'statical equilibrium . . . alone can give us definiteness and precision of thought', he warned that static equilibrium only represented a starting point towards 'a more philosophical treatment of society as an organism' (ibid., p. 382). He could not conceive of a 'more calamitous notion than that abstract, or general, or "theoretical" economics was economics proper' (Marshall 1925, p. 437). On his account, the equilibrium method applied to economic matters in the standard neoclassical approach offered little, as 'pushed to its more remote and intricate logical consequences, it slips away from the conditions of real life' (Marshall 1890, p. 382).

Arguably, remnants of the earlier, ethically capacitated, view of equilibrium advocated by Smith and Chalmers are also to be found in the post-neoclassical works of W. Beveridge and J.M. Keynes. Both authors held that a viable form of economic equilibrium depends in an essential way on the formation of an agent whose competence cannot be simply characterised as, and reduced to, an

3 This reference to circumstance as character-forming was itself to become the basis for an understanding of economic process that would be fully developed by Beveridge and Keynes.

instrumental or strategic rationality. Furthermore, they held that, whatever else it is that makes a competent economic actor and interactor, it is not a supplement to self-interest, nor something that holds self-interest in check. Whenever this 'character' is present in the economic agent, it really does dwell within the agent, who is comfortable with it. It is Keynes who is remembered as the economist of unemployment *par excellence* (see Keynes 1936), though it was, in fact, Beveridge (1930) who, for the first time, made unemployment a key concept in economic thought. At first sight, his categorisations appear similar, although couched in old-fashioned language, to the classifications that form the basis of the mandatory chapter on unemployment of current (mainstream-oriented) economics textbooks. Yet closer inspection reveals something peculiar to Beveridge's discussion of unemployment: the question of its moral causes. Prefiguring the theoretical import that Keynes would give to the distinction between short-run and long-run, Beveridge wrote that 'the forces which constantly tend to adjust demand and supply work only in the long run. There are forces as constantly tending to disturb or prevent adjustment' and crucially these counterforces often had 'a run long enough to determine the fate of individuals' (Beveridge 1930, p. 14). For Beveridge, short-run imperfections have long-run consequences because, in compromising the ability of the individual labourers to meet their needs, and to fulfil their responsibilities within the system, they can, and do, undermine the labourers' independence. Keynes expanded on, and clarified, this point in the *General Theory*: short-run analytics should not be thought of as representing the accidental fluctuations of economic magnitudes around their already determined long-run values. Rather, the short-run situation, informing how people are disposed to act, effectively determines the long run. Indeed, as Keynes pointed out, when commenting in the early 1930s on the adjustment taking place under the gold standard, the balancing of capital and current accounts was 'to the detriment of the working classes' and on the backs of a part of the working population 'who suffer the misery and deterioration of character that follows' (Keynes 1973–79, XX, p. 97). Both Beveridge and Keynes, then, aimed to secure the basis for an adequately functioning capitalist economy, which they understood, as did Chalmers, as requiring the establishment of conditions that would enable individual choices to be made in a free, yet responsible, way.

G.H. Mead: equilibrium as the outcome of a complex social process

As we mentioned in the introduction to this chapter, sociological or socio-economic criticisms of economic thought in regard to its treatment of co-ordination tend to be theoretically under-resourced. This is because, in attempting to modify the calculating ego of the agent of neoclassical economics, these criticism concentrated on *motivation*, as supplement, complication or socialisation, effected by an unexplained 'outside'. In fact, the operational significance of the ethical depletion of the neoclassical equilibrium economic agent is at the level of capacity rather than motivation, a fact recognised by Marshall, Beveridge and

Keynes, albeit without these authors offering a *general* theory of human interaction within which their special case of a competent economic agency would find a place. As we discuss hereafter, a general theorising of the human act that offers a way out of the sterile egoism versus moralism debate between neoclassical economics and its malcontents is to be found in the work of the twentieth century social psychologist George Herbert Mead (1863–1931).

Mead belonged to the broad current of post-Kantian thought which addressed the presuppositions of intellectual activity, especially with respect to action. Of particular concern to him was the relation between knowing and doing. For Kant, thought must stay within the realm of the experiential for it to have any purchase. But, this apart, the being, doing or acting of the knowing subject (should) play no further role in the determination of her thought, whether theoretically or practically oriented. On the contrary, in the case of theoretical reason, experience is itself the synthesis of transcendental concept and intuition. Likewise, Kant's take on practical reasoning made a positive virtue out of the individual, abstracting from those very features of her situation those that are not common to all. Indeed, this is the central message of the second *Critique* (Kant 1788). Notably, Kant's separation of the capacity of knowing from practical engagement was the issue within which Mead framed his pragmatically inspired social psychology. For him, the meeting of minds that successful interaction presupposes comes earlier than the calculative and/or conventional taking account of the responses of others. There is no preconceived act that the agent modifies in the light of others' reactions, or passions that are tamed by social interaction in order for successful co-ordination to take place. For Mead, how others might respond to one's behaviour is not by way of some afterthought – though it can be that as well – but by way of something already built into the structure of the human act (Mead 1925).

Mead distinguished three forms of being: inorganic, organic and, as a special case of the latter, human being, characterised by the capacity for reflective thought. Even in the case of inorganic matter – say, for example, in the action of light on a photographic plate or, again, in the action and reaction of substances in chemical processes – the key to an adequate understanding of events, he argued, is the idea of process, of interaction, of 'sociality'. This is because the emergent state of affairs, as the outcome of environmental stimulation and individual response or (re)action, is one that modifies both the individual and the environment. What Mead took to be true of the inorganic holds *a fortiori* for the organic life form and its environment. It is not merely that organism and environment are (or should be thought of as) constitutive of one another, as is the case with what Mead called 'inanimate being', but, rather, that the organism selects its environment, as it were, by constituting it in such a way that it stimulates or releases impulses immanent in the living form itself. Thus, as Mead put it, '[i]n the twisting of a plant towards the light, the later effect of the light reached by the twisting controls the process' (Mead 1945, p. liii). Or, again:

> a digestive tract creates food as truly as the advance of a glacial cap wipes out some animals or selects others which can grow warm coats of hair. An

> animal's sensitiveness to a particular character in an object gives the object in its relation to the animal a particular nature.
>
> (Mead 1922, p. 158)

So Mead claimed that 'sociality' is a property of all action, inorganic as well as organic, one that indicates no more than a relation between the individual and the environment. In *The Genesis of the Self and Social Control*, however, he distinguished different types of sociality. In the case of organic beings, he wrote:

> [a] social act may be defined as one in which the occasion or stimulus which sets free an impulse is found in the character or conduct of a living form that belongs to the proper environment of the living form whose impulse it is.
>
> (Mead 1925, p. 263)

This of course takes us no further than the instance (given above) of the flower 'twisting towards the light' and thus selecting its environment so as to provide itself with energy. Notably, no consciousness or thought is involved in this process; rather, organic beings and environment are attuned to one another through the physiology of the former. The same may also be said of that class of acts which, though social in the more usual sense of entailing co-operation between individuals belonging to the same group, relies on physiological differentiation alone. To be sure, in this case the completion of the (complex) act comprises a succession of (more elementary) operations carried out by various members of the group, and, thus, '[t]he objective of the act is then found in the life-process of the group ... not in those of the separate individuals alone' (Mead 1925, p. 264). In such cases, the actions of the ant or bee in achieving the social object, the construction and running of the nest or hive, are produced by the differentiated physiological characteristics of the various agents collaborating towards the same goal.

The distinctiveness of the human social act becomes apparent once it is recognised that the physiological differentiation that enables the social acts of many other creatures is not available in this case. On the contrary, successful interaction for human beings must mean that each actor *somehow* has in mind the social object that his/her action will help to construct. In this case the social act would be one which the 'different parts of the act which belong to different individuals should appear in the act of each individual' (Mead 1925, p. 264). By phrases such as 'different parts of the [social] act ... should appear in the act ... of each individual' or should appear 'in [her] experience', Mead meant something like the following: in doing what I do, I (pre-reflectively) anticipate, or expect, that the situation which would arise from the completion of my act will call out in you the response necessary for social completion. In other forms of life, in which the success of the social act is underwritten by an evolutionary process which ensures a certain distribution of physiological characteristics acting as *stimuli* across the group to elicit the responses necessary for the completion of the act, there is no idea in any of the individual collaborators what success or completion might mean. In human society, however, in which physiological differentiation plays little or no role, it is of the essence for successful co-ordination that each individual has *somehow* in mind the social object which his/her action will help to construct. We should clarify the significance of the qualification *somehow* just given. Mead did not mean that successful co-ordination always and everywhere depends on each of the individual actors having a conception of the greater good to which their own activity contributes. There is not necessarily a grand social act in which the individual's act is inscribed, but each act, whether initiated solely by the individual or not, is, and cannot be other than, social. Mead's point was that, whether she reflects or not, the human actor *does* take account of the likely response by others to her act. Whatever the ostensible aims or purposes of her act, then, Mead suggested that the human actor cannot help but put herself in the place of the other to see how her action will be received, and that this *instinctive* re-positioning shapes her act. For Mead, human activity is characteristically minded, rather than physiologically differentiated, in a way that is not simply purposeful. Of course, we do have an interest, and we do set out to consider the means of achieving it. Indeed, Mead's version of how the self comes to think and act suggests that some of that thinking and acting will be about and directed towards others. But before all this, there must first be a self, and Mead's self *is* 'an individual who organises his own response [thought out or otherwise] by the tendencies on the part of others to respond to his act' (Mead 1925, p. 267), by a 'sympathetic placing . . . in each other's roles, and finding thus in [its] own experience the response of others' (Mead 1922, p. 162). Put otherwise, Mead's self is both an 'I' and a 'me': an active, passionate, one might say, partial, side of being that organises his responses in accordance with a passive, impartial counterpart. Indeed, such a complexity seems inescapable if the idea of self-consciousness is to be taken seriously. For to say that the 'I' sees itself in the act, or to say that the act is mine, is to somehow sense an entity, the 'me', to which the act responds or answers, an entity that is reproduced and/or refurbished in the process, but is somehow distinct from it. But how is this seeing or sensing of myself possible, if not through the 'mirror' of your attitudes and responses to it?

In claiming that the self is irreducibly social, Mead meant to imply neither that human beings are essentially benevolent, nor that even the most 'private' of actions has consequences for others. Rather, he suggested that the self is irreducibly social in virtue of the fact that the characteristically human form of acting presupposes a *pre-reflective* anticipation of the responses of others. 'If we are to co-operate successfully with others, we must in some manner get their ongoing acts into ourselves to make the common act come off' (Mead 1925, p. 263). But could not a similar sentence be found in Smith's *TMS*, or in Chalmers bizarrely entitled *The Political Economy of the Bible*?

Conclusion

It is one of those nice ironies in social thought that those, like Durkheim, who criticise the lean, abstract, agency that came to form the basis of modern economic equilibrium theory on the grounds that it dehumanises human agency put in its place a creature so much *less* able, *less* capable, than the neoclassical *homo economicus*. In any case, the very leanness of the neoclassical system of atomic or particulate behaviour is, for the economic equilibrium theorists, its strength, not its weakness, or lack. The critics mistake form for content, motive for capacity. Modern *homo economicus* is a *way* of acting that can accommodate any socially conditioned *why* of acting. Morgenstern, like Walras before him (for one), did not doubt that 'individual motivation might be influenced by imitation, advertising, custom, etc.' (Morgenstern 1974, p. 10). But what he did doubt is that these influences 'change the formal properties of the process of maximizing' (Morgenstern 1974, p. 10). For the neoclassical Morgenstern, the point is that the *formal* properties of the process of maximising, a process in itself devoid of ethical substance, is the condition of all our doings, whether ethical or not. It is as if ethical orientation intruded into this 'formal process' so as to give it determinate content. Critics miss the point by half when they claim that the agent of neoclassical theory is too self-interested: the decisive assumptions of neoclassical economic equilibrium theory are about *how* we humans are *able* to act and interact, not about why we would want to.

It is another of those nice ironies that the action theory that underpins neoclassical economic equilibrium analysis is not, as repeatedly claimed (see, for instance, Arrow and Hahn 1971, p. 1), a development of Smith's social theory, but, rather, one that resuscitates the Hobbes–Mandeville view of human agency that Smith (standing on the shoulders of earlier Hobbes critics) thought he had discredited once and for all. But the proto-sociologists weren't listening. For Durkheim, economic agency meant Hobbes. And from that questionable premise he drew the conclusion that a purely *economic* equilibrium is untenable. As a matter of fact, Hobbes himself had shown that the very concept of a spontaneous order – a concept that was to become the *Leitmotif* of the new science of economy – was untenable on the basis of his characterisation of human nature. But the more enlightened of the political economists were well aware of all this, which is why theorists like Smith looked for a different understanding of how human beings act and interact on which to found their new science. In fact, it is probably fair to say that, until Hobbesianism reasserted itself in the guise of neoclassical economics (Marshall excepted), few writers in political economy were thinking of human agency in Hobbes's terms. But still, to deviate from Hobbesian assumptions is one thing; to provide a viable theoretical alternative is quite another. Smith, Chalmers and Mead attempted to do so by showing that the natural concord that ensures equilibrium in economic transactions is achieved by agents that, against Fisher's account (1925), do *not* correspond to the mechanical equilibrium of a particle.

References

Arrow, K. and Hahn, F.H. (1971), *General Competitive Analysis*, Holden-Day, San Francisco.

Chalmers, T. (1833), *On the Adaptation of External Nature to the Moral and Intellectual Constitution of Man* (vols I–II), Bridgewater Treatise I, Bridgewater Fund, Edinburgh.

Chalmers, T. (1844), 'The political economy of the Bible', *North British Review* 2 (3), pp. 1–29.

Beveridge, W. (1930), *Unemployment. A Problem of Industry*, Longman, London.

Durkheim, E. (1887) [1972], *Selected Writings*, ed. A. Giddens, Cambridge University Press, Cambridge.

Durkheim, E. (1895 [1982], *The Rules of Sociological Method and Selected Texts on Sociology and its Method*, ed. Steven Lukes, Macmillan, London.

Edgeworth, F.Y. (1881), *Mathematical Psychics. An Essay on the Application of Mathematics to the Moral Sciences*, Kegan Paul, London.

Etzioni, A. and P.R. Lawrence, eds. (1991), *Socio-economics. Towards a New Synthesis*, Sharpe, London.

Fisher, I. (1925), *Mathematical Investigations in the Theory of Value and Prices*, Yale University Press, New Haven, CT.

Groenewegen, P. (1995), *A Soaring Eagle. Alfred Marshall, 1842–1924*, Edward Elgar, Cheltenham.

Hobbes, T. (1651) [1991], *Leviathan*, ed. (with introduction) Richard Tuck, Cambridge University Press, Cambridge.

Hume, D. (1739) [1973], *A Treatise of Human Nature*, ed. (with an analytical index) L.A. Selby-Bigge, Clarendon Press, Oxford.

Kant, Immanuel (1788) [1956], *Critique of Practical Reason*, Bobbs-Merrill, New York.

Keynes, J.M. (1936), *The General Theory of Employment, Interest and Money*, Macmillan, London.

Keynes, J.M. (1973–79), *Collected Writings of John Maynard Keynes*, ed. D. Moggeridge, Macmillan, London.

Marshall, A. (1890) [1956], *Principles of Economics*, Macmillan, London.

Marshall, A. (1925), *Memorials of Alfred Marshall*, ed. C. Pigou, Macmillan, London.

Mead, G.H. (1922), 'A behaviouristic account of the significant symbol', *Journal of Philosophy*, 19, 157–63.

Mead, G.H. (1925), 'The genesis of the self and social control', *International Journal of Ethics*, 35, 251–77.

Mead, G.H. (1945), *The Philosophy of the Act*, ed. Charles W. Morris, University of Chicago Press, Chicago.

Montes, L. (2003), '*Das Adam Smith Problem*. Its origins, the stages of the current debate, and one implication for our understanding of sympathy', *Journal of the History of Economic Thought*, 25 (1), 63–90.

Morgenstern, O. (1974), *Selected Economic Writings*, in A. Schotter (ed.), Princeton University Press, Princeton, NJ.

Morris, W. (1945), 'Introduction' to Mead (1945).

Ricardo, D. (1951), *The Works and Correspondence of David Ricardo*, P. Sraffa (ed.), Cambridge University Press, Cambridge.

Sen, A. (1988), *On Ethics and Economics*, Blackwell, Oxford.

Smith, A. (1759) [1976], *The Theory of Moral Sentiments*, D.D. Raphael and A.L. Macfie (eds), Oxford University Press, Oxford.

Smith, A. (1776) [1986], *The Wealth of Nations*, Penguin Books, Harmondsworth.

5 Economic equilibrium in the French Enlightenment: the case of A.N. Isnard

Richard van den Berg

In this chapter I discuss the social and economic ideas of an early contributor to equilibrium theory, the French engineer Achilles Nicolas Isnard (1748–1803), in the context of his overall scientific production. In this way, I show that Isnard developed sophisticated views about human decision-making processes. While he claimed that producers and consumers make decisions on the basis of personal interests, he qualified these as being supported by unreflective, impulsive or habitual, action and concluded that only conduct motivated by an 'interested' choice that is 'fortified by virtuous habits' leads to socially desirable outcomes. This concern with the motivations of humans engaging in social transactions stands in strong contrast with modern economic equilibrium theory.

In 1781, a work in two volumes entitled *Traité des richesses* was published in Lausanne, Switzerland. Its author, the thirty-three-year-old Achilles Nicolas Isnard, was a provincial engineer trained at the École des Ponts et Chaussées, where he had excelled at mathematical subjects.[1] In several places in the *Traité* Isnard applied mathematics to support economic reasoning. In particular, he applied algebra to demonstrate the notion of market equilibrium, and presented examples of mathematical relations between production, relative prices and distribution. It is for the algebraic demonstration of market equilibrium that Isnard is chiefly remembered. In the twentieth century, some influential historians of economic thought convincingly argued that Isnard's use of simultaneous equations to demonstrate economic equilibrium anticipated, and actually influenced, the general equilibrium theory of Léon Walras (1834–1910) (see esp. Schumpeter 1954; Jaffé 1969; Ingrao and Israel 1990).

In this chapter I look beyond Isnard's early contribution to equilibrium theory, placing it in the larger context of his overall social thought. The *Traité des richesses* was a wide-ranging work, somewhat similar in scope to Adam Smith's *Wealth of Nations*, published only five years earlier. What is more, a

1 For Isnard's biography, see Van den Berg (2006).

few years after *Traité des richesses* came out, Isnard published the *Cathéchisme social* (1784), in which he spelled out his moral theory. These two works together form a single account of what Isnard called, in the preface of the *Traité*, the 'science of man' (Isnard 1781, I, p. vii). Isnard was a strong supporter of the new doctrine of economic liberalism, the theory of *laissez-faire*, a social philosophy that had steadily gained influence during the Enlightenment period, through the works of Vincent de Gournay (1712–59), François Quesnay (1694–1774), Jacques Turgot (1727–81) and, above all, Adam Smith (1723–90). The belief in the possibility of establishing a 'natural' economic order was a key element of this social philosophy. While this belief was widespread in early modern European thought, a largely novel contribution to it was the idea that order, or socially beneficial arrangements and outcomes, may result from the pursuit of individual economic motives. Isnard's mathematical analyses (for instance, of how marketed quantities of various goods establish relative prices 'between themselves', or of the tendency towards a uniform rate of profit throughout the economy) represented ways to formalise this belief in the possibility of an 'unplanned order'.

What has gone almost unnoticed among commentators on Isnard's writings is that he did not only use mathematics to support his liberal views, but also developed an original theory of human motivation. A central element in this theory is the distinction between reflective or calculating action, on the one hand, and unreflective or habitual action, on the other. As may be expected of a *laissez-faire* theorist, he claimed that many decisions of individual economic agents are based on reflections of personal 'interest', in this way making the exercise of economic power a restrained and calculated business. However, interestingly enough, he also maintained that there are clear limitations to the scope for calculating action. In the *Cathéchisme social* he stated that:

> [t]hose [writers] who have regarded self-love as the only motivating force of actions have extended their doctrine too far by denying the existence of moral sentiments, or at least by reducing them to the cold effects of interested reflection [*froids effets d'une réflection intéressée*].
>
> (Isnard 1784, p. 80)[2]

One of the main reasons for Isnard to emphasise the importance of unreflective, impulsive, or habitual, motives for human action was that, in his view, social morality cannot be based on the motives of self-interest alone. Rather aptly for an engineer, who for most of his career was employed in hydrological projects, he held that the selfish passions need 'canalising':

> we have not yet achieved the science of man and of that what is right for him. Let us study nature, let us study its workings and its ways, let us stop its harmful effects and employ its means to useful effects. Let us divert the

2 All translations form Isnard's works are my own.

> torrents which ravage our houses and our fields, let us push back the seas that flood our shores, but let us take care that the canals that fertilise our fields are fully filled.
>
> (Isnard 1781, I, p. vii)

More specifically, Isnard highlighted the need for the moral education of citizens, by instilling appropriate 'virtuous habits' that 'hem in' the self-interested, calculating behaviour of man.

At first sight, Isnard is indeed a precursor of modern equilibrium theory, a writer who, as Jaffé put it, 'blazed [a trail] in advance of Léon Walras's construction of an elaborate mathematical highway' (Jaffé 1969, p. 40). However, further reading of Isnard's writings, particularly his theory of human motivation, leads to some surprising conclusions. The agents of his economic theory are sophisticated beings: in addition to being mere calculators of individual advantages, their behaviour is moulded by habitual social codes.

In the next section, I focus on the importance of motivations of personal 'interest' in the economic theory of the *Traité des richesses.* I will then discuss the moral theory of the *Cathéchisme social*, and draw some conclusions.

Human motivation and deliberation in the *Traité des richesses*

In the small body of literature about Isnard's economic writings very little attention has been paid to the kind of decision making he assumed individuals and groups to engage in. The focus has almost exclusively been on the, admittedly remarkable, formal analyses of market exchange and production. The praise for the engineer's achievement as a mathematical economist is high indeed. The fact that he successfully used simultaneous algebraic equations to justify the notion of market equilibrium constituted, according to one commentator, 'one of the most important contributions in the history of the development of mathematical economics' (Theocharis 1983, p. 62). Other authors pointed out that 'Isnard was . . . the first to suggest the condition of equality between the number of equations and the number of unknowns that, until the early twentieth century, was to remain the theory's only answer to the problems of the existence and uniqueness of the vector of equilibrium prices' (Ingrao and Israel 1990, p. 64).

However, the recognition of Isnard's contribution to economics is almost completely limited to this *formal* analysis. It is quite commonly believed that his theory was somehow devoid of more substantial *economic* reasoning. For instance, Baumol and Goldfeld criticised Isnard's procedure of calculating equilibrium prices by assuming as given 'fixed and unexplained quantities offered in exchange' (Baumol and Goldfeld 1968, p. 253). This raises the question what the considerations of traders are, prior to offering specific quantities to the market. And this kind of economic theoretical discussion, it is alleged, Isnard did not provide. Jaffé (1969, p. 25) attributed this deficiency to the absence in Isnard's work of an articulated utility theory, and Hébert stated that it 'remained for Walras to add the engine of utility maximization' (Hébert 1987, p. 1004) to Isnard's equilibrium analysis. The view that Isnard's contribution, while significant from a formal point of view, lacks an *economic* underpinning is, in the opinion of the present writer, the result of a highly selective and anachronistic reading of the *Traité*. Reading the work as a whole, one encounters many passages in which Isnard attributed specific economic objectives and motives to individual agents and groups, infusing his theory with a discernible economic logic (although not one based on utility maximising).

A good example of how there is more to Isnard's ideas than a first reading suggests is his treatment of the fixed and, supposedly, 'unexplained' quantities offered in exchange. While it is true that in his algebraic analysis of exchange he assumed *given* traded quantities, just as he assumed *given* relative prices in his analysis of production, he did not really leave either unexplained. Indeed, there are in Isnard's work clear, if not fully determinate, relations between the 'spheres' of exchange and production. Schematically these relations may be represented as in Figure 5.1. The diagram is based on one of Isnard's numerical examples in which a total of forty physical units of one commodity (M) and sixty physical units of another commodity (M′) are produced by two 'sectors' (Isnard 1781, I, p. 36). Each sector retains ten units of its own produce to be used as inputs in the next round of production; the remainder is sold in the market. In order to continue production each sector also has to purchase inputs produced by the other sector (10 M′ and 5 M respectively). In addition, exchange does not only take place in order to satisfy the reciprocal input requirements of the sectors, since each has produced in excess of the requirements for 'simple' reproduction (25 M and 40 M′ respectively).

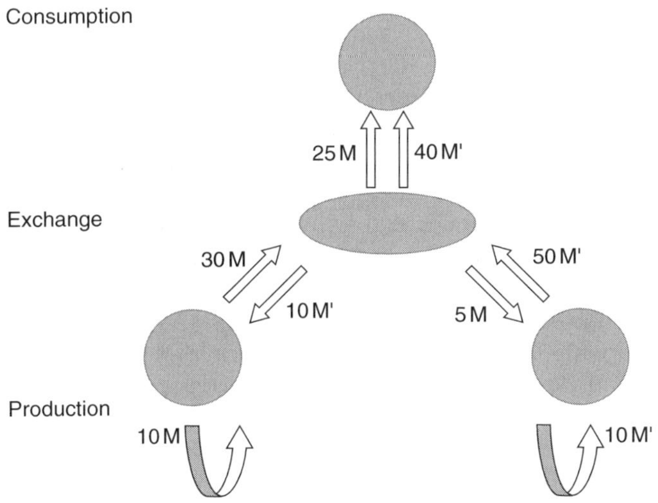

Figure 5.1 Relations between the spheres of exchange and production.

That Isnard intended to explain the determination of quantities brought to the market is clearly indicated. Just before beginning his algebraic analysis of exchange by assuming three fixed quantities, *a*, *b* and *c*, of different kinds of commodities, he stated: '[w]e will *later* determine the quantity of commodities produced and brought to the market' (Isnard 1781, I, p. 19, emphasis added). Some pages later, in his discussion of production, he comes back to this remark when he notes:

> As we *have seen* [i.e. in the analysis of market exchange], the values of products are established without the costs or expenditures of producers being considered in the deal: but those [producers] *will not produce useful things, if they do not expect to recover their costs*, that is to say, the value of the advances necessary to the existence of that commodity. One has to assume therefore that the value of a commodity is at least equal to the costs of production. [But] this value can also surpass the value of those costs. When this is the case, the difference is for the producer the revenue that he draws from his enterprise.
>
> Those costs consist of the purchase of raw produce, which he has to employ or consume in production in payment for the labour of men or of workers, and of fixed capital.
>
> (Isnard 1781, I, pp. 34–5; emphases added)

This passage suggests a clear relation between production decisions and the 'market realisation' of the value of the quantities supplied to the market. Even though *for theoretical convenience* Isnard worked with fixed marketed quantities (*offres*) in his analysis of market exchange, he envisaged a process whereby those quantities adapt. This adaptation is the result of the comparisons made by each producer between the costs incurred in production and the sales value of the products. It may be argued that Isnard considered the process of reproduction as a sequential one, wherein costs are incurred in the production of goods prior to their sale in the market, and wherein production is adapted in response to prices realised in the market. Consequently, Isnard did not conceive of a *general* equilibrium system in which there is a *simultaneous* determination of quantities and prices.[3] However, this does not mean, of course, that decisions about quantities offered to the market are *unrelated* to information about prices.

Isnard's description of how produced quantities adapt to prices realised in the market is an example of the kind of calculating behaviour that is ascribed repeatedly to economic agents (most commonly 'producers') in the *Traité*. The engineer's attention for the comparison between the 'necessary price' of products (i.e. the price required to cover all advances) and the market price is of course not unique. Indeed, it can be found in the contemporaneous physiocratic literature generally.[4] However, compared with the physiocrats, Isnard is much more pronounced in his view that it is the desire for profit, i.e. a positive difference

3 This point is made more fully in Van den Berg (2006).

4 For a longer discussion of the physiocratic 'theory of value' see Van den Berg (2004).

between sales value and costs, which motivates producers. He stated in general terms that '[i]t is the hope of the producer to obtain through sale the reimbursement of his costs *and* a share of disposable wealth, to be used for enjoyment or saving, which motivates him to undertake productive activities' (Isnard 1781, I, p. 144, emphasis added). The profit seeking of individual entrepreneurs should be relied upon to co-ordinate the production of the various commodities for which there is an effective demand in society:

> The reproducer [*reproducteur*] only acts in response to the sale of his products. It is necessary for the production of any thing that its value is at least equal to that of the costs necessary to its existence; if consumption and sale do not assure it its value, the production stops, because the producers seek to employ their funds more usefully.
>
> (Isnard 1781, I, pp. 96–7)

Note that the last remark implies not only that producers are assumed to adjust produced quantities in response to the profitability of their existing activities, but that they may reallocate their capitals to alternative activities. Indeed, Isnard also discussed a general tendency towards a uniform rate of profit in a manner that reminds one of Turgot:

> Fixed capitals distribute themselves to serve the different uses in agriculture, industry and commerce in such a way that their values will be in the same ratio to the offers made in exchange for their products less the costs of upkeep, repair and replacement, so that the ratios of funds to the interest will be uniformly the same in the different enterprises. This uniformity is achieved, and equilibrium establishes itself, because funds make themselves available, and flow to the places where the interest is highest, and because like things have the same value. When things have a higher price in one place than in another, they flow there and equilibrium is re-established.
>
> (Isnard 1781, I, 48–9)[5]

The profit motive, or the desire for 'disposable wealth', is assumed to influence the decisions of producers in a number of other ways. Not only did Isnard describe how it directs producers in their decisions on how much to produce and where to invest their capital, it also leads them to adopt cost saving techniques. There is a strong normative notion in the *Traité* that the primary purpose of the reproductive system is to increase the production of 'disposable wealth' (i.e. 'final' consumption goods). This view was stated, for example, in the following, rather physiocratic-sounding, passage:

> Among the total mass of wealth we will make a distinction between that [part] which is employed in production and that employed for the

5 For a comparison between the theories of capital of Isnard and Turgot see Van den Berg (2005).

> enjoyment and consumption of men. The former is necessary to production the latter is disposable. *One should employ as much wealth as possible in production in order to increase general wealth. But economy dictates that the employment of productive expenditures is directed in such a way that the costs are as small as possible relative to production.*
>
> (Isnard 1781, I, p. xv, emphases added)

While Quesnay and his followers translated a similar objective into the need to increase agricultural production, and adopt the most economic agricultural techniques, Isnard had a much more general understanding of what constitutes 'wealth'.[6] He expressed the conviction that producers generally can be relied upon to adopt cost-saving techniques, since '[e]very individual, trying to obtain the largest benefits at the smallest possible costs, enters into the smallest details of productive economy in order to succeed in this' (Isnard 1781, I, p. 189). He applied this argument, for example, in his discussion of labour-saving machinery, arguing that whatever techniques save on production costs, and result in a larger disposable product, will be adopted by producers and be beneficial to consumers.[7] Thus, Isnard assumed producers to be reliable calculators in decisions ranging from the determination of output levels, allocation of capital and choice of technique. In fact, the engineer argued quite explicitly that individual entrepreneurs, guided by their 'hope of profit and economy', do a better job directing economic activities than a central 'administrator' could ever do:

> [T]he profits of production blossom, thanks to trade. *The sum of the private calculations of merchants and producers is more reliable than the calculation of a drafter of prohibitive laws can be.*

6 Immediately after the sentences cited above he distances himself from the physiocratic theory of productivity and distribution. He continues: 'It is a mistake to maintain that there is any kind of wealth that does not yield a net product, or a product above costs. Of all particular kinds of products, one part belongs to production, the other to enjoyment. The sum of the parts belonging to production forms the general mass of the costs of production, the sum of the other parts forms the general mass of disposable wealth. The values of individual products determine the share of the total mass of disposable wealth that devolves to each producer. This share varies with the difference between the values of products and of the objects necessary to production, which the producer has to purchase.' Isnard's mathematical analysis of production and distribution explains these views admirably. For a comparison between Quesnay and Isnard on these points see Steenge and Van den Berg (2001).

7 See Isnard (1781, I, pp. 80–2, 170–4). 'The principles of economy dictate in all workshops, in all activities and to all men to execute all works at the least possible costs, [and] to increase disposable wealth relative to the costs of production . . . (pp. 170–1) 'The goal of the activities of agriculture, industry and trade is a continued supply of consumption goods [*jouissances*]; the general aim of producers is to supply consumption goods at the least possible cost. If in an enterprise two horses produce more than ten men, the producer will choose the horses as agents of his production. If in a workshop a wheel, a lever, a windlass or any machine substitutes the work of twenty men and costs less to maintain, [then] the producer will employ this machine and will dismiss the twenty workers. The general laws have to be the result of these particular principles' (p. 81; cf. p. 171).

> A renowned Author complains that by allowing freedom one confides the interest of the State to the ignorance of private interest. It seems to me that *the sum of knowledge that traders acquire through exercise and experience, and the speculations that are dictated by their interests, far exceed the views of an administrator*. And that *there is a lot of presumption in believing that one can be powerful enough to direct the private operations of trade by general orders, in such a manner that the nation as a whole derives a greater advantage than through the course of private industry*. Trade honours the Sovereign that protects it, but it will not recognise a general director of its operations.
>
> (Isnard 1781, I, p. 189, emphases added)

Isnard applied to specific questions the liberal argument that individual producers and traders 'dictated by their interests' are more reliable in delivering socially desirable outcomes than 'prohibitive' laws. In discussing the guilds and the policing of markets, he even extended this reasoning to 'non-price factors' such as the quality of commodities. He maintained that exclusive privileges and inspections cannot be justified by the argument that they are a means of barring incompetent or unscrupulous producers from selling shoddy goods. 'Errant' sellers will be more effectively excluded through the natural effects of competition:

> in the case of liberty [the exclusion of unreliable sellers is] a result of the efforts of producers and sellers to attract buyers by means of the better quality of products and merchandises and by means of the reputation acquired through these efforts in those arts, which, it has been believed, should be subjected to inspections of police in favour of buyers with little experience.
>
> (Isnard 1781, I, p. 230)[8]

8 The mention of 'buyers with little experience' (*acheteurs peu expérimentés*) is interesting. Isnard makes a clear distinction between what a modern theorist would call 'search goods' and 'experience goods', or in his own words between markets where 'everyone can be the judge or connoisseur of the merchandise one buys' and markets 'where not all men are equally connoisseurs'. It is in the latter situations that reputation becomes an important factor: 'Industry, reputation, trust, an advantageous location, and often word of mouth [*le babil*] determine the popularity of craftsmen and merchants. Industry without trust will have little custom in professions where not all men are equally connoisseurs, or where they do not simply have to satisfy their personal tastes. Unlimited competition is advantageous to production and consumption in all arts and crafts where everyone can be the judge or connoisseur of the merchandise one buys. In the other [professions] where the fear of being deceived accompanies the desire to buy, the reasons that lead the craftsman or the merchant to merit the trust of the public and that give a natural exclusion to unknown [sellers] are also favouring consumption. If it is by the improvement and good quality of merchandises that craftsmen and merchants try to get known and exclude errant merchants, and not by laws emanated from the authorities, then it is clear that consumption will gain benefits that are less assured under a regime of prohibitions' (Isnard 1781, I, pp. 229–30). Note that the last sentence implies only a qualified endorsement of free competition: one could take it to mean that if sellers do *not* compete on quality intervention may be justified.

If this reasoning seems too uncritical, it should be pointed out that, in his moral theory, Isnard devoted further attention to the exclusion of opportunistic behaviour (see below, p. 108). More generally, the moral theory of the *Cathéchisme social* does much to qualify the impression one may get when reading some of the above passages from the *Traité des richesses* that the engineer advocated an almost unrestrained economic freedom for citizens to pursue their 'private interests'. I am not suggesting here that the views in the *Cathéchisme* are at odds with those of the *Traité*: there is no reason to suppose an 'Achilles Isnard problem', similar to the old 'Adam Smith problem' according to which the worldly outlook of the *Wealth of Nations* was in conflict with the more idealistic views of human nature in the *Theory of Moral Sentiments*. Instead, not unlike Smith, Isnard's book on the moral sentiments should be seen as providing a more general and richer social theory that supplements his economic doctrines.[9]

Reflective versus unreflective actions in the *Cathéchisme social*

One of Isnard's main objectives in the *Cathéchisme social* was to delineate the proper domain for deliberate, calculated, human action. He insisted that much human action, and moral action in particular, is not motivated by self-interested reflection.[10] Isnard developed his ideas on impulsive and deliberate behaviour from a sensationist perspective that was quite commonly accepted at the time. A strong influence of Condillac's philosophy of the development of mental capacities, and sometimes even hints of the more radical materialist views of writers like Helvétius, Holbach and La Mettrie, can be found in *Cathéchisme social*, especially in the first few chapters. Isnard affirmed that the human mind 'only receives its ideas from the senses' (Isnard 1784, p. 16), developing its faculties in response to sensations. Humans, in common with animals and plants, possess a natural aptitude to recognise sensations as being either agreeable or disagreeable, i.e. they are

> endowed with instinct, that is, the faculty to act in order to enjoy or avoid impressions that are received. Sentient beings have received from nature the faculty to avoid what is contrary to them and to be attracted to what agrees with them.
>
> (Isnard 1784, p. 17)

Rejecting the view of instinct as a 'premonition or a predetermination that is independent from sensations and knowledge', Isnard maintained that it is a faculty that evolves as sensations become more complex and refined: 'the

9 For a discussion of Adam Smith's moral philosophy see Dixon and Wilson's chapter.

10 He presented his theory as an attempt 'to defeat two erroneous opinions' in vogue amongst Enlightened authors of his day. One was that free will is an illusion, and that man is 'subjected to superior forces' in all his decisions. The other was that 'man deliberates in all his actions and that he is always determined by his apparent [personal] interest' (Isnard 1784, p. 43).

instinct grows relative to the passions of which sentient beings are susceptible. Man perfects his instinct through the perfection of his sensory faculties' (Isnard 1784, p. 21). Like other sensationist authors, Isnard held that higher mental faculties, such as representation and reflection, also derive from more primitive instinctive powers of response to sensations, and claimed that humans developed a superior capacity for representing and recalling sensory impressions.[11] This capacity allows them to compare ideas, or 'represented sensations', an exercise that Isnard called 'reflection' and 'judgement', attributing to it men's faculty to engage in deliberate or reasoned action.[12]

To some extent, sensationist philosophy challenged the Cartesian dualism of body and mind by holding that higher mental faculties, such as 'reflection', also derive from more primitive powers of response to sensations (cf. Israel 2001, p. 517). In making this point (1784, pp. 21 ff.), Isnard agreed with Helvétius that 'pleasure and pain are the motivating forces, not only of instinct, sentiments and passions, but also of the will' (1784, p. 80). At the same time, however, he emphasised the differences in the workings of instinct, which acts on immediate and bodily sensations, and the will, which 'acts by virtue of reflection'.[13] It should be noted that this distinction is strongly reminiscent of Quesnay's distinction between *la liberté animal*, which is a mechanical power of decision that takes into account only 'physically good and bad' (Quesnay 1756, p. 796) and *la liberté morale ou d'intelligence*. To Isnard, as to Quesnay, the term 'freedom' was almost synonymous with 'deliberation': '[t]he freedom of man consists in his power to deliberate and choose. If he has within himself a power that chooses and decides then he is free' (Isnard 1784, p. 39; cf. Quesnay 1747, p. 748; 1765, pp. 48–9). Possession of this faculty of 'deliberation' does *not* mean that man can ever free himself from 'motives', i.e. that he has a capacity for 'disinterested' or 'selfless' choice, as Isnard specifically stated:

> From the fact that man never decides without a motive and without interest, [some writers] have concluded that he would not be free. But freedom does *not* consist in the capacity to decide without a motive.
>
> (Isnard 1784, pp. 38–9; emphasis added)[14]

11 Isnard acknowledged that some animals also possess limited representative faculties, thus endowing them with 'a kind of foresight, a sense of future need' (Isnard 1784, p. 19).

12 'The exercise of reflection and judgement is reason. One part of the functions of reason is to compare the motives of actions, to choose or decide upon the ends and means, or to deliberate and to discover what is true and what is false. Reason often compares two ideas to a third one in order to determine the relation between the first two. This operation of reason is called reasoning. The faculty of deliberation, which is enjoyed by reason, is called freedom. The will is a faculty of the mind by which it decides and by which it chooses or opts ends and means' (Isnard 1784, p. 23).

13 'There is one motivating force which is moved immediately by sensations, ideas and passions, and which has the title of instinct, and one which is moved by reason or by the comparison of sensations and ideas, and which has the title of will' (Isnard 1784, p. 42).

14 On this point Isnard was in almost perfect agreement with Quesnay (1747, pp. 747–8, and 1765, p. 49 n.).

On his account, freedom consists, in fact, in the ability to compare, choose between and direct various motives and passions. Deliberation provides man with a *combat des passions*, or what Hirschman (1977, p. 38) described as 'a disciplined understanding of what it takes to advance one's power, influence and wealth'.

> It is through the exercise of this faculty [i.e. deliberation] that [man] becomes the master of his actions and opposes the effects of the instinct and the passions, or the impulses of his organs. Through reflection he establishes in himself a means of resisting [*un combat*] the passions. When he is excited by violent desires, the imagination brings about new ideas that stimulate the right passions to counterbalance those desires. Through judgement he decides which actions are harmful and which actions are useful.
>
> (Isnard 1784, pp. 37–8)

Summing up, for Isnard 'freedom of choice' is a degree of autonomy which derives from the ability to hold blind passions at bay, and to turn them into considered interests.[15] As we saw, it is this capacity for interested decision making which Isnard assumed in many places in the *Traité des richesses*. However, perhaps surprisingly, Isnard equally emphasised in the *Cathéchisme* that a large part of human behaviour is unreflective. It is one of his main aims in that work to delineate when actions are and when they are not (or: should . . . should not be) the result of self-interested deliberation

> We will prove bit by bit that man masters his physical impulses by deliberating about the interested motives that are present and tangible and about interested motives that are remote. [However] [w]e will also prove that man is often led by the impulses of his sentiments and his passions, before making use of reflection and of his faculty of deliberation.
>
> (Isnard 1784, pp. 43–4)

In arguing that '[m]an is often led more by his passions than he is directed by a recognised utility [*utilité reconnue*]' (1784, p. 79) Isnard's principal point was not so much that man would possess 'selfless' passions. As noted earlier, Isnard assumed that man is motivated in *all* his actions by impulses of pleasure and pain. Instead his primary concern was with the contrast between the actions that are, and those that are not, preceded by a mental process of deliberation or calculation of interests.[16] In this context Isnard highlighted the great influence of habit on human decision making.[17] Habit is seen as a factor that can reinforce

15 This conviction can be found in the physiocrats and indeed in a long line of French social thought that descended principally from Jansenist theologians (see Heilbron 1998).

16 I argue below that, in this respect, his preoccupations differed from those of Adam Smith.

17 He is likely to have taken over the emphasis on the importance of habit from writers, Holbach and Condillac among them, who called on the force of habit, i.e. routines established through repeated impressions and actions, to explain seemingly innate dispositions of humans and animals (see Jimack 1996, pp. 259–60).

both instinctive and reflected action. In general, habit 'is produced through the repetition of sensations, ideas and actions'. The very repetition of ideas or actions accustoms the body and the mind to them and disposes them to repeat them in the future.[18] Hence habit reinforces the power of the instinct 'to influence the actions of men and animals without the participation of the will' (1784, p. 32). At the same time, however, habit is an instrument that man can consciously employ to shape his conduct: 'It is by means of habits contracted by the will that it counteracts the dangerous effects of the instinct, and *as a result of the effects of reflection man acquires an instinct that is different from the one received from nature*' (1784, p. 33, emphasis added). While man requires a conscious effort to acquire 'good habits', once established these no longer necessitate 'reflection' at every step. In particular, habituation can serve to curb the opportunistic aspects of man's calculating behaviour.

Self-love versus egoism

I discussed in the second section of this chapter that, in the *Traité des richesses*, Isnard repeatedly professes his belief that individual producers and consumers should be left free to pursue their private interests in the ways they see fit. However, this was not an unqualified belief, for he acknowledged that individuals may well be tempted to press their own advantages in an asocial or 'opportunistic' manner. In fact, he suggested that such behaviour is deep-seated:

> The eradication of vices such as bad faith, disregard of agreements and duties, untruthfulness, ambition or intrigue, which harm the interests of fellow citizens, and the hatred that is the result of these vices, is much more difficult than [the eradication] of intemperance, against which nature itself has provided a curb in each individual's urge for preservation.
>
> (Isnard 1781, I, p. 100)

In the *Cathéchisme social*, Isnard suggested that the reason why such 'vices' are difficult to eradicate is that they are the result of an exaggerated form of self-love, or 'exclusive self-love', namely egoism. The egoist is '[s]omeone who relates *all* his actions to his personal interests . . . when he practises social virtues, it is because he instantly perceives their utility' (Isnard 1784, pp. 239–40).

18 Adding a clear materialist touch, Isnard envisaged the formation of habit through repetition as a physical process: 'it is not difficult to conceive that the repetition of those movements makes the molecules of the fluid that is exercised more supple, by diminishing friction, by augmenting fluidity, or by removing the molecules that may hinder action. Through the effects of habit, the instinct thus increases its power to influence the actions of men and animals without the participation of the will. The repetition of exercises, the repetition of movements of the limbs, and the repetition of an infinite number of operations of the body and the mind establishes in the animal faculties an aptitude to produce the same movements with more facility and prior to any deliberation' (Isnard 1784, p. 32).

> [The egoist] is so accustomed to calculating the result of all his actions that his mind is committed to calculation when nature is about to produce a sentiment. The sentiments lose out through detrimental habits. Egoism is a self-love that is so exaggerated that it extinguishes most of the virtuous sentiments, and so blind that it neglects the interest of society, which is necessary to his personal interest.
>
> (Isnard 1784, p. 239)

Isnard's critique of 'egoism' was not based on a belief that there is a need in society for disinterested public-spiritedness among citizens. Classical republican ideals, such as can be found for example in the works of Mably (see Wright 1997), are largely absent from his writings.[19] The virtuous man that Isnard contrasted with the egoist is a man who is also motivated by self-love:

> Not all men who are motivated by self-love are at the same time egoists. Someone who is led by self-love to prefer the happiness that the social virtues cause to the enjoyments the procurement of which are in his physical and momentary interest is not egoistic but virtuous and sociable.
>
> (Isnard 1784, p. 239)

If a truly 'virtuous and sociable' person is no less 'led by self-love' to practise social virtues, what then distinguishes him from the egoist? To some extent it is the fact that sociable man is more 'enlightened' in the pursuit of his interests: instead of a narrow calculation of personal interests, he takes into account the damage that his self-seeking actions may do to the society on which he depends. Instead, the 'free-riding' egoist who 'tries to enjoy the advantages of society without contributing to its costs' risks 'destroying the bonds of society' (Isnard 1784, pp. 239, 240). Another difference between the two kinds of men is at least as important. The sociable man has preserved or practised his virtuous *sentiments*. It is only through 'detrimental habits' that the egoist is completely given over to calculation. As discussed in the previous section, Isnard insisted that not all human action is calculating; much of it is impulsive or habitual. While on numerous occasions humans indeed act deliberately, i.e., according to their interests, it is only a long-standing 'habit of completely neglecting the interests of others [that] normally extinguishes and destroys the natural faculties for producing virtuous sentiments' (Isnard 1784, p. 239). Thus egoism is not a 'natural' disposition but an exaggerated tendency acquired through practice and the formation of 'bad' habits. It is nurtured through bad examples and bad teachings. One of the vices that 'normally accompanies exclusive self-love or egoism [is] greed or an excessive desire for goods and wealth . . . Greed normally produces avarice, cupidity, covetousness, a passion for gambling, and immoderate ambition' (Isnard 1784, p. 241). 'Cupidity' is a desire for wealth that does not stop short at dishonourable methods; it is, to borrow an expression, 'self-interest

19 At the beginning of the revolution Isnard (1789) published a stinging criticism of J.J. Rouseau's concept of the 'general will'.

seeking with guile': '[Cupidity] urges the sacrifice of an honourable state to a lucrative state . . . leads by an indiscernible slide to injustice . . . it makes the soul venal and extinguishes a great part of the distinguished sentiments' (Isnard 1784, p. 242). This vice is reinforced through examples of influential citizens and the state:

> Public cupidity influences individuals. When one sees in the great and good an immoderate passion for the acquisition of wealth, a taste for financial enterprises and lucrative projects, when government renders cupidity less odious by encouraging it in certain classes of society and by permitting the growth of that vice in the capital, when it spreads to the highest classes whose distinction is based more on great sentiments than on the enjoyment of wealth, then that vice will soon become general in society and will produce other vices and the corruption of morals.
>
> (Isnard 1784, p. 242)

It is not only the bad practical examples of the great and good that encourage the spread of egoism: the philosophical doctrine that all actions, moral ones included, are self-interested is also dangerous to the sentiments in that it encouraged 'enlightened' man to calculate, instead of acting well on impulse:

> The maxims that have been published about interest are extremely dangerous because of the sophisms that are deduced from them. Those sophisms have not a little contributed to annulling the sentiments. It has been declared that man is only motivated by his interest and that that motive should be the basis of morality. Unfortunately, it has been concluded from this opinion that by deciding according to his interest, man acts according to his nature, and that whenever one is truly persuaded that one acts according to one's true interest, one does never contravene the fundamental rule of morality. From those false conclusions and false judgements with regards to interest has resulted the beginning of a revolution that is fatal for the sentiments that used to inspire great acts in men.
>
> (Isnard 1784, pp. 77–8)

According to Isnard, in weighing up his personal advantages man is too easily swayed by material gains and sensual pleasures to believe that morality can be based simply on the calculation of personal interests:

> It is easy to make false calculations in the search for true interests. A bad action may procure a depraved man a great sum of physical pleasures and enjoyments. He only has to be a little inclined to vice for there to be falsity in his judgement. The morality that is founded solely on interest would have some effect on his conduct only if he believed that the regret [for his actions] could not be effaced by the multitude of sensual pleasures which he could enjoy as the result of his bad action. He only has to stray a single step

> from the route indicated by the morality that is based solely on interest to wander on to the dangerous path of egoism.
>
> (Isnard 1784, p. 78)

Individual human reason provides an unreliable basis for morality, precisely because, by being too calculating, it can fall prey to seemingly advantageous choices, which, in fact, turn out to be a delusion.

Moral behaviour as habit

Instead of attempting to found morality on rational calculation, one should rely, in Isnard's opinion, on the guidance of 'virtuous habits'. As we saw, he acknowledged that habits, inculcated through the repetition of actions, dispose humans to a kind of decision making that does not require the intervention of human reason. It is possible to reinforce such habitual behaviour with regard to moral action: 'Man is born with the aptitude to become virtuous or depraved. His sentiments are turned towards vice or virtue depending on the *habits of vice or of virtue* which he acquires' (Isnard 1784, p. 77, emphasis added).

Through exercise and instruction one can establish something akin to a 'moral sense': '[t]he habit of distinguishing between good and bad can give to the mind a *finesse* of tact that makes it suited to this operation prior to the exercise of reflection' (Isnard 1784, p. 49; see also Conclusion). The moral education Isnard proposed consists partly in the encouragement of 'natural sentiments', such as friendship, gratitude, fatherly and motherly love, which are 'more often an effect of nature than of reflection' (Isnard 1784, p. 76).[20] However, more important in a developed society is that citizens get themselves accustomed to the 'reflected virtues' (*vertus réfléchies*). These are the virtues that are necessary for the persistence of society. As was noted, Isnard argues that man's freedom consists in his ability to weigh his various interests, a competence which is based on his superior 'faculty of foresight and of the representation of sensations with the aim of comparing them to present sensations' (Isnard 1784, p. 40). Through these powers of foresight and deliberation humans realise that they do not only possess immediate physical needs, which they could satisfy 'alone and isolated in a forest', but develop more refined needs and desires, which they can only hope to satisfy within society. As a result, they come to understand that the persistence of society is in their own best self-interest.

The principal virtue that guarantees the persistence of society is '[j]ustice [which] is founded on the utility of society, and on the necessity of the determination of reciprocal rights and the safeguarding of those rights' (Isnard 1784, p. 190). Isnard clarified the distinction between justice, a necessary and enforceable virtue, and benevolence and charity, merely laudable virtues, which can also be found in the physiocrats, as well as in Smith, and which was generally

20 Such virtues are natural because they 'can be observed in their purest form among animals and children' (Isnard 1784, p. 76).

'a most important premise in post-Grotian jurisprudence' (see Hont 1987, p. 255; cf. Haakonssen 1985, p. 66).[21] However, in an apparent criticism of Scottish moral philosophy,[22] Isnard emphasised that humans do not have a strong 'natural' inclination towards the observance of justice: '[t]he virtues that are necessary to the order of society are the ones that are most difficult to inculcate, because man does not always feel this necessity as forcibly: nature is more open to the sentiments' (Isnard 1784, p. 190).[23] It is for this reason that every citizen requires a moral education to instil 'virtues fortified by habit' (Isnard 1784, p. 127). While, with hindsight, individuals may well recognise that 'the determinations of their present interest harmed the general interest', it is impossible for them to always foresee these effects (see Isnard 1748, pp. 84–5). Therefore citizens are advised to adopt a general 'plan of conduct' in their youth and follow, regardless of their benefits on individual occasions, a 'code of laws according to which one regulates one's judgements, one's deliberations and one's actions' (Isnard 1784, p. 85). By adhering to this code, its observance becomes habitual. In this manner man can lead his self-seeking urges into virtuous channels:

> In order to be virtuous, and remain virtuous, man ... has to keep, through habit, the course of the virtuous sentiments that nature has given him, and curb the vicious dispositions that may assail him, of which there are seeds just as there are of virtues...
>
> (Isnard 1784, p. 126)

What are, more specifically, the virtues necessary for the order of society? Justice in the first place consists of absolute respect for private property rights. Furthermore, there are virtues 'analogous with justice': 'sincerity, candour, fairness, and truthfulness', or more generally 'probity' or integrity. Man should

21 'Charity and beneficence inspire the relinquishing of rights, while justice prescribes the conservation of rights. ... There are virtues that do not depend on strict and necessary duty. However, all men have a right to the exercise of justice and analogous virtues' (Isnard 1784, p. 189). According to Isnard, the duties of charity, for example in cases of food shortages, can never overrule the duties of justice: 'Morality and humanity preach in favour of charity. However, legislators have never stated that hunger justifies theft or the violation of property' (Isnard 1781, I, p. 194). Similarly, the sovereign should guarantee justice not subsistence: 'It is the consequence of [a] false principle that Sovereigns are convinced that they are the distributors of the goods produced on the land and that they owe their subjects their subsistence. It is the duty of Kings to guarantee their subjects the enjoyment of the largest possible product of their labours ... through protection and the administration of public expenditure: but it is not the duty of Kings to provide subsistence to their peoples' (Isnard 1781, I, pp. 8–9).

22 'Justice is principally a virtue of reflection: it is only linked to the sentiment by the analogy that it can have with the love for the general good. Those philosophers who have founded [justice], like other virtues, on a universal benevolence, and have attributed to that sentiment its origin, have rid justice of one of its principal properties, that of being one of the first products of human reason' (Isnard 1784, pp. 189–90).

23 Here Isnard is in agreement with the physiocrats, who stressed the importance of education for the observance of property rights (see Albertone 1986).

make sure he becomes 'thoroughly penetrated by, and convinced of, the need to respect [those virtues]' for three reasons:

> The three principal causes that make probity necessary are (1) the interest man has in inspiring trust with the aim of the advancement and prosperity of his civil business, (2) the interest of man in earning the esteem and the recognition of society, aiming to preserve social order, and (3) the satisfaction the virtuous man experiences through the exact observance of the rules of conduct which will lead him to true happiness in life, or the approval of his conscience.
>
> (Ibid., p. 198)

The three reasons mentioned in this passage, relative to why citizens are inclined to exercise commercial virtues, neatly sum up the different dimensions of Isnard's theory of human motives and action. In the first place, individuals often choose to act in a trustworthy manner in economic life because they calculate that it is in their personal interest to do so. Isnard explained the economic benefits of acting with probity in a manner that almost reads as 'saving on contract costs':

> Someone who conducts his business candidly and fairly encounters a great ease in doing business [*terminer les affairs*] because of the trust he engenders. Someone who has acquired *a reputation of candour and fairness through the repetition of virtuous acts* will encounter an even greater ease, because he finds that his reputation is well established. Someone who is natural and open and who is recognised as such in society has *fewer obstacles to overcome* in business, because he is *exempted from having to dispel distrust.*
>
> (Isnard 1784, p. 195, emphases added)

As I mentioned earlier, Isnard had acknowledged in the *Traité des richesses* that the establishment of reputation is in the considered self-interest of traders.[24] This, however, is not the only reason why successful citizens refrain from pursuing their private interests in opportunistic ways. A second motivation for doing so is that 'reflected virtues' (*vertus réfléchies*) instruct man that he should not engage in practices that undermine society. An understanding of the possible consequences of egoistic behaviour for the social system as a whole does not come naturally but arises only from reflection upon the fundamental rules of society. The second motivation differs from the first in that it involves deliberation about more remote consequences of one's actions, requiring instruction in the principles of society, and for this reason is a more enlightened form of self-interest. The third motivation differs from the first two, in the sense that is it unreflective. Part of the reason why virtuous people

24 A difference is that the advantage of reputation highlighted in the *Traité* is that it helps to reduce competition (from unscrupulous traders), while in the *Cathéchisme* the greater ease in concluding contracts is given as the principal benefit.

refrain from opportunistic behaviour is independent of calculations about extrinsic costs or benefits. Probity is a virtue inculcated by habit, which through 'a certain study during one's youth' can be perfected to 'scrupulousness' (Isnard 1784, pp. 199–200).[25] It is 'the satisfaction the virtuous man experiences through the exact observance of the rules of conduct' that leads him to 'internalise' this behaviour and make it into a virtuous *habit*. This character of genuine integrity, experienced as contributing to fulfilment in life, led Isnard to compare probity with honour:

> Honour is for people of the highest rank a sentiment that is analogous to what probity is in the class of people who are engaged in the production of wealth. . . . Honour is for the nobility what probity is for ordinary people [*le peuple*].
>
> (Isnard 1784, pp. 198–9)

Honour is the opposite of a reflected virtue, it is impulsive, pursued for its own sake and regardless of consequences. In Isnard's view the commercial virtues of 'sincerity, candour, fairness, and truthfulness' should have this character too.

Conclusion

According to Hirschman's (1977) influential thesis, the emergence of the intellectual discipline of political economy during the Enlightenment was accompanied by a new image of man. Man could be trusted, it came to be believed, to pursue his acquisitive urges in a disciplined manner. He was judged generally to be able to curb destructive passions himself by acting according to his 'interests'. As capitalism started to become a dominant social force, man was recast, according to Hirschman, as a calculating actor who had a firm grip on his impulsive urges, especially there where they may otherwise have socially harmful effects. The new image of man was important for the 'new science' of political economy in two ways. First, if individuals calculate their most favourable courses of action, the collective outcomes of these actions may be understood, perhaps not as planned but at least as regular and logical. For example, the crucial economic idea that profit rates in different sectors of the economy tend to equilibrate depends on the assumption that owners of capital are reliably calculating where to invest their funds most profitably.

Second, the new image of man acting according to his interests also casts him as a reliable partner in a moral sense. For example, by reflecting on the potential harm to their reputation, merchants would refrain from dishonest practices. However, it is in particular in this second respect that one may doubt whether

25 'A merchant, for example, who discloses all the circumstances that may affect the price of the thing put up for sale shows a probity that takes the title of scrupulousness. A scrupulous man does justice to all people who co-operate to the success of an enterprise or the actions from which he receives the fruits. A scrupulous man does not attempt to pin the blame of an unjust acquisition on others' (Isnard 1784, p. 199).

social philosophers of the Enlightenment, even ones known as *laissez-faire* theorists, did not have a wider conception of human motivation. For example, when Adam Smith pleaded for the establishment of the 'obvious and simple system of natural liberty', he counted on a sociable and morally responsible exercise of this liberty by individual citizens. Most modern literature on Smith acknowledges that his moral theory played a role in providing his liberal economic convictions with a foundation in sociability and citizenship. In this chapter, I put forward a similar thesis with regard to Isnard's political economy. In contrast to Smith's work, Isnard's has never been studied in a comprehensive manner.[26]

It is interesting to note that the engineer was well disposed to the Scottish moral sense theories of which Smith's 'system of sympathy' was a sophisticated version. Generally speaking, French philosophers and economists of the time had difficulties accepting the Scottish notion of a moral sense. As Faccarello and Steiner (2002, p. 72) explained.[27]

> [French] commentators just did not understand a key point of Scottish philosophy: the construction of a moral theory that did not derive from reason . . . according to the commentators Smithian sympathy could not in itself provide an adequate foundation to his argument, but had to be derived from something else – from reason.

Isnard's assessment of the idea of a moral sense is considerably more positive:

> Hutchetson [*sic*] and the Shafteburists [*sic*] argued that there is in the mind a faculty to discern good and bad which is independent from any reflection; that the functions of this faculty are analogous to those of the senses and that good and bad [actions] cause involuntary sensations of pleasure and aversion. This subtle idea has not been much adopted. The habit of distinguishing between good and bad can give the mind a *finesse* of tact that makes it suited to this operation prior to the exercise of reflection. But this faculty is not at all innate, and man can distinguish between good and bad only after having received instruction about the relationship of good and bad.
>
> (Isnard 1784, p. 49)

What Isnard liked especially about the moral sense theories was the notion that the moral faculty may be 'involuntary', i.e. 'independent from', or 'prior to', reflection. Man is (or should be) motivated by moral sentiments that complement his conscious calculations of personal benefit. Besides this very important similarity there are some significant differences in Isnard's moral theory as compared with that of Smith. Let me briefly mention two. First, in arguing for human motives other than 'interests', Isnard concentrated on the distinction

26 As an indication of the extent of the neglect of Isnard's work: I have been unable to find a single discussion of the content of the *Cathechisme social* in the secondary literature.

27 Ando (1993) put forward a similar thesis.

between 'reflective' (interests) and 'unreflective' (sentiments, habits) motives, rather than, as Smith did, on the distinction between 'partial' and 'impartial' judgement and action.[28] Second, Isnard does not posit an 'innate' moral sense. Commenting on the Scottish notion, Isnard objected that an 'unreflective' moral sense can only be the product of a '*habit* of distinguishing between good and bad'. This seems to imply that, compared with Smith, Isnard had a weaker belief in 'automatic' checks built in that would prevent individuals from the socially harmful pursuit of their own self-interest. He thought, in fact, that men could, indeed, become accustomed to egoistic, or opportunistic, calculating behaviour, and that 'virtuous habits' should be inculcated through education and example to prevent this from happening, and to make self-interest socially beneficial.

In conclusion, where does all this leave Isnard's reputation as an early forerunner of general equilibrium theory? Undoubtedly, his attempt to use a system of simultaneous equations in order to illustrate the notion of market equilibrium, though very brief, remains a crucial step along this particular path in the history of economic thought. However, exclusive attention on the engineer's contribution to mathematical economics has left Isnard seriously underrated as a social theorist. In sharp contrast with most modern equilibrium theory, the specific motivations of humans engaging in social transactions were an important theme in Isnard's writings. As an early proponent of economic liberalism one of his main concerns was to formulate a social code of conduct for citizens that would be acceptable in a commercial economy. This is a concern that seems alien to the equilibrium models of modern economic theorists. That does not mean, however, that Isnard's views are irrelevant to modern commercial society. Indeed, the opinion that the private calculations of self-interest by producers and consumers need to be complemented with a solid moral education, inculcating unreflective social virtues, sounds surprisingly up-to-date.

28 This is clear, for example, in the following passage critical of Helvétius: 'It is said that self-love is the motive for all men's actions, and that men always decide on the basis of the pleasure that they hope for and the pain that they fear. *Admitting the truth of the second part of this proposition, the first is not a necessary consequence of it.* As we have seen, while man is motivated by a sensation that is suitable and analogue to his sentient being, he is not therefore [always] motivated by self-love. *Only in the case of acts and movements that require reflection could one suppose such a cause*, and even then the power of the sentiments will often get the upper hand over the effects of reflection. There are manifold cases where the motives of interest give way to the impulses of sentiment. There are also many cases where sentiment act prior to reflection taking place' (Isnard 1784, pp. 74–5, emphases added).

References

Albertone, M. (1986), 'Instruction et ordre nature: le point de vue physiocratique', *Revue d'Histoire Moderne et Contemporaine*, 33, 589–607.

Ando, T. (1993), 'The Introduction of Adam Smith's Moral Philosophy to French Thought', in *Adam Smith. International Perspectives*, ed. H. Mizuta and C. Sugiyama, Macmillan, Basingstoke and London, 199–211.

Baumol, W.J. and Goldfeld, S.M. (1968), *Precursors in Mathematical Economics. An Anthology*, London School of Economics and Political Science.

Faccarello, G. and Steiner, P. (2002), 'The Diffusion of the Work of Adam Smith in the French Language: An Outline History', in *A Critical Bibliography of Adam Smith*, ed. K. Tribe and H. Mizuta, Pickering & Chatto, London, 61–119.

Haakonssen, K. (1985), 'Natural Law and the Scottish Enlightenment', in *Man and Nature*, ed. D.H. Jory and C. Stewart-Robinson, Academic Printing and Publishing, Edmonton, Alta.

Hébert, R.F. (1987), 'Isnard, Achylle Nicolas', in *The New Palgrave. A Dictionary of Economics*, ed. R. Eatwell *et al.*, Macmillan, London, I, 1004–5.

Heilbron, J. (1998), 'French Moralists and the Anthropology of the Modern Era: On the Genesis of the Notions of "Interest" and "Commercial Society"', in *The Rise of the Social Sciences and the Formation of Modernity*, eds J. Heilbron, L. Magnusson and B. Wittrock, Kluwer, Dordrecht, 77–106.

Helvétius (1773), *De l'homme, de ses facultés intellectuelles et de son éducation*, La Société Typographique, London.

Hirschman, A.O. (1977), *The Passions and the Interests. Political Arguments for Capitalism before its Triumph*, Princeton University Press, Princeton, NJ.

Hont, I. (1987), 'The Language of sociability and commerce: Samuel Pufendorf and the theoretical foundations of the "Four Stages Theory", in *The Languages of Political Economy in Early-Modern Europe*, ed. A. Pagden, Cambridge University Press, Cambridge, 253–76.

Ingrao, B. and Israel, G. (1990), *The Invisible Hand. Economic Equilibrium in the History of Science.* MIT Press, Cambridge, MA.

Isnard, A.N. (1781), *Traité des Richesses contenant l'analyse de l'usage des richesses engénéral et de leurs valeurs; les principes et les loix naturelles de la circulation des richesses, de leur distribution, du commerce, de la circulation des monnoies et de l'impôt, et des recherches historiques sur les révolutions que les droits de propiété public et particulier ont éprouvées en France depuis l'origine de la monarchie.* London and Lausanne.

Isnard, A.N. (1784), *Cathéchisme social, ou Instructions élémentaires sur la Morale sociale, à l'usage de la jeunesse*, Guillot, Paris.

Isnard, A.N. (1789), *Observations sur le principe qui a produit les révolutions de France, de Genève et d'Amérique dans le dix-huitième siècle*, Malassis, Évreux.

Isnard, A.N. (1791), *Les Devoirs de la seconde législature ou des législateurs de France*, Mecquignon, Paris.

Israel, J.I. (2001), *Radical Enlightenment. Philosophy and the Making of Modernity, 1650–1750*, Oxford University Press, Oxford.

Jaffé, W. (1969), 'A.N. Isnard, Progenitor of the Walrasian General Equilibrium Model', *History of Political Economy*, 1, 19–43.

Jimack, P. (1996), 'The French Enlightenment: Deism, Morality and Politics', in *British Philosophy and the Age of Enlightenment*, ed. S. Brown, Routledge History of Philosophy V, Routledge, London, 251–73.

Quesnay, F. (1747) [1888], 'La Liberté', Oncken *Œuvres économiques et philosophiques de F. Quesnay*, Baer/Peelman, Frankfurt/Paris, 747–58.
Quesnay, F. (1756 [1888], 'Evidence', Oncken *Œuvres économiques et philosophiques de F. Quesnay*, Baer/Peelman, Frankfurt/Paris, 764–97.
Quesnay, F. (1765) [1962], 'Le droit naturel', in *The Economics of Physiocracy*, ed. R.L. Meek, Edward Elgar, New York, 43–56.
Schumpeter, J.A. (1954), *History of Economic Analysis*, repr. 1994, Routledge, London.
Smith, A. (1759) [1976], *The Theory of Moral Sentiments*, eds D.D. Raphael and A.L. Macfie, Oxford University Press, Oxford.
Smith, A. (1776) [1976], *An Inquiry into the Nature and Causes of the Wealth of Nations*, eds R.H. Campbell, A.S. Skinner and W.B. Todd, Oxford University Press, Oxford.
Steenge, A.E. and Van den Berg, R. (2001), 'Generalising the *Tableau économique*: Isnard's *Système des richesses*', *International Journal of Applied Economics and Econometrics*, 9 (2), 121–46.
Theocharis, R.D. (1983), *Early Developments in Mathematical Economics*, Macmillan, London and Basingstoke.
Van den Berg, R. (2004), '"*Un état de pleine concurrence*": old and new controversies about the Physiocratic theory of value', *Économies et sociétés*, 35 (8–9), 1431–57.
Van den Berg, R. (2005), 'The Theory of Money, Interest and Capital in the French Enlightenment', paper presented at the 2005 ESHET conference in Stirling.
Van den Berg, R. (2006), *At the Origins of Mathematical Economics. The Economics of A. N. Isnard*, Routledge, London.
Whatmore, R. (2000), *Republicanism and the French Revolution*, Oxford University Press, Oxford.
Wright, J.K. (1997), *A Classical Republican in Eighteenth-Century France*, Stanford University Press, Stanford, CA.

6 Influences on the economic theory of A.A. Cournot

Mechanics, physics and biology

François Vatin

This article is concerned with the epistemological bedrocks of Cournot's work. This author has often been interpreted in terms of a mechanistic notion of economic theory founded on models of equilibrium; however, his line of thought was richer and more complex. To appreciate this, it is necessary to discuss not just his first book on economics, published in 1838, but also the two later ones, published in 1863 and 1877, together with his other scientific and philosophical works. In this way, the emphasis on equilibrium disappears, and is replaced by an energeticist philosophy inspired by Leibniz, which connects physical with organic phenomena, and economic with social ones.

Interpreting Cournot

Antoine-Augustin Cournot (1801–77) is an essential thinker in nineteenth-century France. Educated at the Ecole Normale in Paris, he began a career as a mathematician, publishing in mechanics and probability theory; he then became Professor of Mechanics and Analysis at Lyons (1834), Rector of the Académie de Grenoble (1835) and General Inspector of Mathematics (1836). For a long time he was president of the jury for the teaching diploma in mathematics, a competition for recruiting teachers for secondary and higher education. Little sympathetic to the regime of the Second Empire, he left Paris in 1854, ending his career as Rector of the Académie de Dijon.

Today Cournot is mainly known for his probability theory (Cournot 1843), and for his fundamental work in mathematical economics, *Recherches sur les principes mathématiques de la théorie des richesses* (Cournot 1838), on account of which he has been considered a precursor of neoclassical economics.[1] However, this evaluation of Cournot is made at the cost of a truncated reading of his writings, which, from the mid-1840s onwards, were devoted to a comprehen-

1 It was Walras (1878) and Jevons (1879) who started this evaluation of Cournot, nowadays widespread, by according him a high place in their theoretical pantheon.

sive attempt at a philosophical synthesis of the kind of Auguste Comte's (Vatin 2003). This synthesis was fully developed in the *Traité de l'enchaînement des idées fondamentales dans les sciences et dans l'histoire* (Cournot 1861), in which Cournot sketched a *fresco* of knowledge, which, going from mathematics to history, included physics and biology. A mechanicist by formation, he developed in this book an organic representation of the history of societies[2] that led him to re-discuss economic theory in a new book, *Les Principes de la théorie des richesses* (Cournot 1863), published some twenty-five years after the *Recherches*. This book has received much less attention from modern economists than the 1838 one, perhaps because Cournot did not use mathematical methods in it.[3] However, the book is very rewarding, and, if read in the light of Cournot's overall philosophical thinking, shows continuity in Cournot's epistemology through an energeticist philosophy inspired by Leibniz.

I argue that it is in the light of this energeticism that Cournot successively drew upon mechanics, biology, political economy and history. In proposing this reading, I dissociate myself from scholars such as Claude Ménard, who claimed that an 'epistemological rupture' occurred in Cournot's work, from the mechanicism of his early years to the biologism of his mature period: 'The systems of forces that served to think of the mathematical *equilibria* of 1838 was replaced by the metaphor of the social body, susceptible to explain the unpredictability and discontinuity of economic phenomena' (Ménard 1978b, p. 29, my translation; see also Ménard 1978a). My interpretation of Cournot's epistemology leads to a reassessment of the role of the notion of equilibrium in his economics. For I show that, although with the methods introduced in 1838, Cournot contributed much to the elaboration of modern models of economic equilibrium, and indeed continues to inspire game theorists in the modern epoch (Schmidt 1992), his overall epistemology was not mechanistic, either in physics or in economics, and he regarded the use of static models of equilibrium as only a first step towards laying down a dynamical theory of the phenomena under investigation. Indeed, in his 1838 book, Cournot criticised as trivial the idea of an equilibrium between supply and demand, to which he attributed only a rhetorical meaning.[4] As for his *Principes* of 1863, it was largely directed against Frédéric Bastiat, the liberal apologist of the time,[5] and supported the conceptions of Friedrich List, the founder of the German historical school. Thus regarding Cournot as a precursor of the Walrasian conception of economic equilibrium is mistaken; indeed, Cournot resisted the pressure exerted by the young Walras in 1873–74 to persuade him to lend his scientific authority to Walras's mathematical theory of general equilibrium (Vatin 1998, 2005a).

2 This theme was going to gain success in England with Herbert Spencer, but also in France (Becquemont and Muchielli 1998; Vatin 2005b).

3 Economists usually ignore Cournot (1861, 1863) as mere rewritings of Cournot (1838); Cournot himself was partly responsible for this misinterpretation (Vatin 1998, 2000a).

4 One must not forget that Cournot, whose economic convictions were protectionist, always opposed the liberal idea of free trade.

5 Frédéric Bastiat (1801–50), journalist and politician, incarnated militant economic liberalism in mid-nineteenth century France.

In the next section I discuss in detail, and challenge, the thesis that an epistemological rupture occurred in Cournot's thinking.

Cournot: from mechanicism to organicism?

At the beginning of the twentieth century, many philosophers wrote exegeses of Cournot's thought, albeit without discussing its evolution. Cournot, for his part, had not made matters simple, for he never acknowledged changes in the epistemological approach that underpinned his work, which was published over thirty years (from 1851 to 1875). Changes did, in fact, take place, if only because of the care with which he kept abreast of scientific developments: his silence on any such changes ought to be taken either as suggesting that he did not acknowledge them, or that he saw them as being consistent with each other. Hence the task for the historian was one of either rediscovering a concealed consistency in Cournot's work, or explaining its evolution. The philosopher Gaston Milhaud is probably the first scholar who addressed the question posed by those changes. Without questioning the evolution of Cournot's thinking, Milhaud (1911) underlined the presence of an energeticist element in it, as early as 1951, in the *Essai sur les fondements de nos connaissances et sur le caractère de la critique philosophique*, which anticipated Cournot's later vitalism.[6] Why did Cournot's vitalism develop only at a late stage? Milhaud's answer to this question is essential to this chapter. He claimed that the fundamental difference between the 1851 and the 1861 books was due to the introduction of the paradigm of energetics in physics more than to the growing importance of biology (Milhaud 1927). Milhaud also underlined that Cournot's study of man underwent an important evolution. In 1851, he saw the study of societies as an extension of that of psychic life; in 1861, he derived social organisation directly from biology according to a wholistic scheme, which excluded psychology from the general field of knowledge.[7] Seeing in Cournot's late vitalism a continuation of his energeticism, as Milhaud did, implies the view that, at root, Cournot's views did not really change.

I, in fact, approaching the matter from the point of view of industrial mechanics, claim that the introduction of thermodynamics meant so much to Cournot's conceptual universe because he was somehow prepared for it.[8] For, in his early scientific works, he had advocated a philosophy of mechanics that broke free

6 François Mentré came to the same conclusion (Mentré 1927), after having claimed the opposite some twenty years earlier (Mentré 1908). Later exegeses of Cournot are rather divided on the continuity/discontinuity question. Some authors, the economists especially, are interested only in the first Cournot, and overrate his mathematical rationalism; others, a minority, see only the second Cournot, and cast him as a forerunner of Bergson's vitalism (see Lévêque 1938).

7 On the same question, Mentré had to say: 'As a matter of fact, the *Traité* is original in so far as it sets the study of social man before that of man as an individual,' concluding that 'it is not because of the discovery of vitalism that the *Traité* innovates relative to the *Essai*, but because vitalism is applied to social phenomena' (Mentré 1927, p. 40, my translation). However, Mentré's analysis did not go as far as Milhaud's, since it ignored the evolution of Cournot's views on physics.

8 My reading is based on Vatin (1993), in which I deal with the genesis of industrial mechanics.

from the eighteenth century rationalism embodied in analytical and energy mechanics.[9] Far from adhering to the Cartesian scheme that reduced physics to mechanics and mechanics to rational mechanics, as early as 1834 Cournot became interested in industrial mechanics, a discipline that revolved around Leibniz's concepts of 'active force' and 'work', bridging the phenomena of inanimate matter with those of life (Cournot 1834). About the biological concept of 'vital force', Cournot stated that:

> It was necessary, that after the fashion of the physicians' active force, the most active of forces, that which creates organic types, ran out in exertion, and that, once spent in a certain way, it could not be spent in another.
>
> (Cournot 1872, p. 381)[10]

And on the connection with the notion of physical force: 'The idea of force takes its source primarily in the intimate feeling we have of our power as a mechanical agent, and in the effort or the muscular tension which is the organic condition to exercise this power' (Cournot 1851, p. 153). Thus, for Cournot, Leibniz's energeticism set up a link between the mechanical and the biological domains, and, as I spell out in the next section, created a 'social cosmology'.

Cournot's references to Leibniz are important to me, as I believe them to be the key to interpreting Cournot's thinking over time (see also Robinet 1981). In his 1861 *Traité*, Cournot distinguished three metaphysical categories: 'ontology', 'transcendental dynamics' and 'teleology', respectively built around the concepts of 'substance', 'force' and 'finality'. He specified that 'The first type adapts better to material or purely physical facts, the third to biological facts; the second, for which we made our Leibnizian preference clear, has the merit of adapting equally well to both' (Cournot 1861, p. 295). On Cournot's account, a synthesis between mechanical and biological patterns could be achieved through Leibniz's dynamicism, in particular through the notion of 'superior dynamics', which, he thought, rules 'the moral world as much as the physical world, and explains the most delicate phenomena of the body as well as the motions of the inert masses' (Cournot 1851, p. 194).

My thesis that Cournot's thinking was based on a version of Leibniz's energeticism contradicts the view, advanced by other authors, that there were two quite separate strands to Cournot's thinking, one mechanistic, the other biological.

9 Cournot was initially a specialist in mechanics, in which he defended his thesis. He wrote a whole series of articles and reviews in this field between 1826 and 1829 in the *Bulletin des sciences mathématiques, astronomiques, physiques et chimiques*, edited by Baron de Ferussac between 1824 and 1832 (Grattan-Guinness 2005). On the various traditions in eighteenth century mechanics, see Grattan-Guinness's chapter in this volume.

10 All translations from Cournot are my own.

Mechanics and social biology

It might be argued that, together with Comte, Quételet and Spencer, Cournot was one of the founders of sociology. Inspired by Vicomte Louis de Bonald's 'reactionary' thought,[11] Cournot rejected the concept of a universal man advanced by the French revolutionaries: 'Individual man from the point of view of science is a mere abstraction. Where can you find him? At what time did he appear in the world? What race does he belong to? In which environment did he develop?' (Cournot 1861, p. 309). In the *Essai* (1851), he had not yet given a place to psychology, that he considered to be a link between biology and the zoological sciences,[12] and, in the 1861 *Traité*, disregarded psychology as a possible link between the sciences of nature and the science of man, holding that man cannot be studied apart from society:

> It is not only true to say, as has been said all along, that man is made for social life, a character common to other species, but it is also true that individual man, with his well known refined abilities, is a product of social life, and that social organisation is the true organic condition for the emergence of these higher abilities while there is nothing similar with other living species.
>
> (Cournot 1861, p. 297)

This statement would have been applauded by Marx as well as by Durkheim. It set up an epistemological sociology that was against the tradition established by the philosophers of the eighteenth century, who, following the *Idéologues*, put the sentient man at the heart of their theoretical system. But the main parallel is with Auguste Comte. This is because, in the 1861 *Traité*, Cournot evoked the idea of a 'social physics', without specifying if he used the term with reference to Comte or to Quételet, both of whom had used it, the former in 1822, and the latter in 1835. In the *Essai* Cournot used the idea of a social physics to try to justify a parallelism between the physico-mathematical sciences and the 'mathematisable' part of the sciences of man, a use that suggests a reference to Quételet. Later on, however, Cournot associated the notion of social physics with the birth of the 'industrial society' as Comte understood it:

> In short, the result of civilisation, population and industrial development should be to substitute for a hierarchical constitution of the society, founded on the concept of law as determined by us, a classification taking into consideration necessary facts and laws very much similar to those govern-

11 For the influence of counter-revolutionary thought, especially that of Bonald (1754–1840), see Nisbet (1966, 1978).

12 In his 1851 *Essai*, Cournot presented a classification of sciences that was reminiscent of Francis Bacon's, Jeremy Bentham's and André-Marie Ampère's. He followed Ampère's definition of 'noological sciences' as the sciences of 'thought', including in this 'all the faculties of sense and all those of will' (Ampère 1834, p. 28).

> ing physical facts; hence the name of 'social physics', put forward by a few writers, which is far from being inaccurate.
>
> (Cournot 1861, p. 427)

If, however, Cournot did not adopt 'social physics' as one of the founding concepts of his epistemology, it is because, for him, societies, initially suitable to be described by biological models, would progressively come closer to resembling mechanical ones:

> Human societies are both organisms and mechanisms. One cannot assimilate them, especially in their final stages, to a living organism, but one would be more mistaken still in misunderstanding, in their first stages, their great similarity to a living organism.
>
> (Cournot 1851, p. 304)

Initially, Cournot thought that this continuous transition from biological to mechanical models was advanced enough in economics to justify its mathematisation, attempted in his 1838 book. However, on the basis of the analysis in the (1861) *Traité*, Cournot became convinced that the process of rationalisation was not, in fact, as advanced as he had thought, and disowned his previous attempt at mathematical formalisation (Vatin 2000b).

This double aspect of human societies, biological and mechanical, led Cournot to conceive of the history of civilisation according to a threefold scheme that he developed in the fifth part of his 1851 *Essai*. According to it, we are living a historical phase that follows a pre-historical one, that of organic humanity, and precedes a post-historical one, that of mechanical humanity, characterised by totally rational behaviour. It is the tension between the mechanical and the biological aspects of human societies that provokes the ups and downs of history. When reason will triumph, human society will be totally mechanised, and history will amount to a 'news sheet' listing facts, which would not be events, in the standard sense of the term, because they would not possess a historical sense. Cournot did not see this 'end of history' as a 'happy future'; hence the 'conflict' between rationalism and vitalism in his philosophy should not be exaggerated: the opposition of the two notions does not imply two distinct periods in his thought, nor does it create a clear-cut dividing line between inert sciences and the sciences of life and society. For Cournot, historicity does not *specifically* belong to the biological and social frame: the physical world also has a history that cosmology describes. In the end, the opposition between physics and biology is determined by another, more general, opposition that he mentioned as early as 1851: that between the 'theoretical' (that is, in their logical construction) sciences and the 'cosmological' (in their empirical foundation) sciences. For Cournot, the *a priori* rationality of the laws of the physical world does not have the absolute value that Descartes and Kant attributed to it.

I turn now to examining Cournot's reception of Darwin's theses.

Cournot, 'scientific Darwinism' and 'social Darwinism'

In spite of his Catholic faith, Cournot displayed evolutionist convictions in his (1851) *Essai*, in which he formulated a theory that may be seen as similar to Darwin's, although it contained an account of adaptation that might be similar to Lamarck's (see also Mentré 1908, 1927; Milhaud 1927).[13] If Cournot was somewhat reserved about Darwin's ideas, that he discovered after writing his *Essai*, his criticism did not proceed from a downright theological rejection. Despite the Church's reluctance, he accepted the progress achieved by natural sciences in the course of the eighteenth and nineteenth centuries on the appearance of life on Earth and on the sequences of animal species including man. If, as a Christian, Cournot doubted the simian origin of man (as Darwin understood it), he did not formulate this as a major philosophical objection (Cournot 1872).[14] It was on epistemological grounds that he rejected Darwin's theory. His criticism, developed between 1872 and 1875, was based on two objections. The first one was this:

> What becomes of the beauties of organic creation in a system that is only concerned with the functional unity of the organs? Is it not judging improvements of living Nature as one blames some economists to judge the improvements of human society only according to an account of products and consumption?
>
> (Cournot 1872, p. 365)

At first sight, this argument looks rather theological; it becomes more poignant if understood as a criticism of Bastiat's 'economic optimism' (Bastiat 1850) developed in the (1861) *Traité*. For Cournot, in human economy (and also in natural economy), Leibnizian harmony cannot depend only upon economic factors. He questioned Darwin's naturalist economy ('fitness'), while accepting its application to human societies, that is to say, he accepted 'social Darwinism' but rejected the idea that this could be deduced from 'scientific Darwinism'. Yet he adopted, and applied to human societies, some of Darwin's ideas; for instance, that of a 'struggle for existence' and that of the 'survival of the fittest'. One may be surprised to see 'social Darwinism' develop in Cournot's thought, given that he rejected scientific Darwinism. In fact, such surprise would be unjustified. This is because Cournot did not believe that Darwin's natural selection principle explained major effects ('macro-evolution'), while acknowledging that it provided an appropriate frame to conceive of 'minor' ones ('micro-evolution') such as those concerning man in historical times. Cournot's second

13 Following Jean-Claude Pariente (note in Cournot 1851, p. 501), Cournot was inspired here by Etienne Geoffroy Saint-Hilaire's *Principes de philosophie zoologique* (1830). Notably, Isidore Saint-Hilaire, son of Etienne Geoffroy, was a friend of Cournot's, and himself a naturalist with a Christian faith. Conry (1974) pointed out the affinity between Cournot's evolutionist conceptions and those of the botanist Charles Naudin. It does not seem that the botanist and the philosopher ever came into contact. They may have both been inspired by Geoffroy Saint-Hilaire.

14 This paragraph is summed up and reshaped in Cournot (1875).

objection to Darwin's theory related to the scant palaeontological evidence in its favour; he also challenged Lamarckian evolutionism: taking the elephant's trunk as an example, only the initial and final states seem 'adapted'; what about the intermediate states (Cournot 1851)? Finally, as an underlying theme, what Cournot rejected in evolutionism, whether Darwinian or Lamarckian, was mechanicism, which he contrasted with the vitalist principles of his epistemology:

> Virtue of germ, tendency to improvement, marvellous co-ordination cannot come from outside causes, or result from a purely mechanical sorting. By changing a sudden transformation into a slow graduation the mechanist explanation becomes less shocking, its coarseness is somewhat dissimulated, although, in depths, one always asks a mechanical cause for what it just cannot give.
>
> (Cournot 1872, pp. 287–338)

Cournot held that the process of natural selection gives only an ancillary explanation, but not the general frame, of the great mystery of evolution; the vitalist epistemology he endorsed was half-way between creationism and transformationism (Conry 1974).

Now we take the question of how Cournot's investigations into the philosophy of sciences and history translated themselves into his late economic thinking.

Thermodynamics, mechanicism and vitalism

Cournot's 'social Darwinism' was linked with an energeticist concern over the possible exhaustion of natural resources:

> Since natural wealth, the most efficient tool of a refined civilisation, exhausts itself gradually and all the more quickly that civilisation and industry progress are greater, it seems that this gradual exhaustion is in the future the greatest danger for civilisation itself as we conceive it, and the most obvious obstacle to the realisation of our assumption of unbounded and endless progress, so naturally suggested by the rapidity of current progress. Hence arise reasons to fear that human industry may be doomed not only to reach a stage where it would cease to make perceptible progress but would even decrease some day, and even disappear just as fire dies out for lack of fuel. But let us drop this subject and let us refrain from indulging in rash and vain conjectures about a too distant future. One should converse neither with princes nor with populace about the likelihood of their death; princes punish such temerity by disgrace, the people take their revenge through mockery.
>
> (Cournot 1861, p. 576)

Cournot's modernity on this issue is striking, albeit not surprising. Since the colonisation process was coming to an end, and the physical and economical finitude of the Earth was coming to the fore, the image of a 'concessionary planet' (Cournot 1872, 1877) became part of European thinking. In this new perspective, the natural limit of economic development was no longer about flows (as with Malthus), but about stocks. Cournot's position was all the more radical because it questioned not only the possibilities of population growth but the very survival of civilisation. In this context, one understands the meeting in Cournot's thinking between thermodynamics and Darwin's ideas, respectively exemplified by the steam engine and the economy of life. Replacing human (or animal) labour with coal might have been expected to free the economic process from the cyclical temporality that characterised animal economy (tiredness, and also the seasonal rhythm of food production). In fact, Cournot extended to physics this conception of wearing out and exhaustion. Thermodynamics and evolutionism, born, more or less, at the same time, proceed from a common philosophy, that of the irreversibility of time, and, in this way, challenge the cosmic position that man claimed for himself. Darwin showed the historical origin of human civilisation while thermodynamics put an end to its development.

Thermodynamics was a central theme in the *Principes* (1863), where Cournot readjusted his views on political economy in the light of the dynamicist philosophy developed in the *Traité* (1861). But his understanding of thermodynamics, and, even more, its application to the phenomena of life that he believed responsible for economic activities, was quite imperfect at the time (Vatin 1998). Cournot found it very difficult to reconcile the principles of thermodynamics with those underlying economic action. Is the latter only transforming natural existing powers, or is it capable of creating new ones? As often when encountering a theoretical difficulty, Cournot sought refuge in epistemology, and contrasted the mechanistic with the vitalistic approaches to political economy and physiology:

> Everything comes short in front of nature's absolute refusal to place at man's disposal the resources, that is to say, forces and necessary materials; this is perfectly obvious and does not ask for commentaries. One cannot say as much about the forces developed by man through his own activity, nor from the stocks and working tools produced by previous work, and kept through foresight, that is to say, capital. While undertaking an analysis of changes affecting the economic system, we should reason as if these changes influenced only the direction of productive forces emanating from man and did not have the property of increasing the very intensity of these productive forces, by raising up inventions, arms, capital, where inventions, arms, capital become really necessary. We approach here the really important question, a question that, actually, has two different solutions, depending on the circumstances, each of which can be asserted absolutely, as a theorem without any consideration of circumstances, so that economists can be sorted out into two schools, two sects, two opposed camps: some consider social economy as a form of physical mechanics in which are taken

> into account only inorganic forces the intensity of which man cannot master, but only change in direction with the help of his engines, the others are dynamicists, or rather vitalists, they take into account external circumstances, chiefly as means of incitement, to bring up to the summit of their energy forces the source of which is internal and is nothing but the very principle of life.
>
> (Cournot 1863, pp. 181–2)

Within economics, Cournot's contrasting the mechanistic with the vitalistic approach may owe a lot to Friedrich List (1841),[15] whom Cournot mentioned in the introduction to the *Principes* as one of the authors who had most influenced his views. On List's account, real 'political' economy, in the sense of national economy, depends on productive forces, while 'cosmopolitan economy', preferred by the English liberal school, depends on 'exchangeable values'. However, the long passage from Cournot above should not be understood only in relation to List. Another quote from the *Traité* helps:

> Hence the germ of two extreme theories, one claiming that value comes (directly or indirectly) from work, the other pretending (or rather having pretended, as this theory is now out of fashion) that human work produces value only if it spends as much on keeping up the worker [. . .]. We face here again this conflict between the idea of force and the idea of material that lies at the bottom of all our physical theories.
>
> (Cournot 1861, p. 449)

We find in the two quotes above the central opposition between a mechanist philosophy of substance ('Cartesianism') and a dynamicist philosophy of force ('Leibnizianism') present in Cournot's philosophy. Indeed, the second half of the quotation from the 1863 book shows that Cournot emphasised this opposition, by presenting a twofold criticism: of the Physiocrats, for exaggerating, 'substance-style', the economic role of the Earth, and of the Ricardians, for exaggerating, 'force-style', that of capital. Thus, comparing the 1861 and the 1863 texts, we see that the Physiocrats are 'mechanist' economists, who deny the capacity of human agency to produce wealth, and restrict it to the transformation of the wealth produced by the Earth; while the Ricardians are 'vitalist' economists, who adjust their argumentation on the productive force of work (and capital that proceeds from it). Such an interpretation is paradoxical and in complete opposition to List's doctrine, where the Ricardians are the symbol of the pure 'theory of exchangeable value'. Therefore, this is probably not what Cournot thought, as he tended, on the contrary, to criticise the Physiocrats and the Ricardians, the former for overstating the limitation in the resources of the Earth, the latter for the limitation in the capital resources. Cournot did not regard these two mistakes as symmetrical. Indeed, in stating that the resources of the

15 See Cournot (1863), p. 3, and Jorland's note on p. 366 of the same volume. List's *Das Nazionale System der politischen Ökonomie* (1841) was translated into French by Henri Richelot in 1851.

Earth are strictly limited, the Physiocrats would be right. However, he thought that their mistake was that of applying to a national scale what makes sense only at the level of the whole planet.

His criticism of the Ricardians was of an altogether different nature, since he felt that, to use Marx's vocabulary, they had 'reified' capital by bestowing upon it a productivity of its own with no relation to how capital is managed by economic agents according to his dynamicism (Cournot 1863). (This criticism actually agrees with List's.) It was a winding path that brought Cournot back to List. In 1861, he had contrasted the Physiocrats' economy of substance with the Ricardians' economy of forces. This would bring the former to substantialist mechanism and the latter to dynamicism. In 1863, reconsidering the matter with List's theory in mind, he reached the following conclusions: the Physiocrats are wrong in remaining attached to a substance philosophy which they applied wrongly by restraining it to the case of one country; and the Ricardians are wrong in transforming force into substance ('reification' of the capital), in this way evading the economy of force, which is the very presupposition of work value. (One cannot help seeing in this rather distorted demonstration a conceptual wavering that recalls Cournot's difficulties in conceptualising thermodynamics.)

The issue here is that of economic dynamics, the main concern in the (1863) *Principes* from which Cournot tended to turn away in 1877.[16] However, his better understanding of thermodynamics enabled him to introduce energeticism more satisfactorily into economic reasoning. He developed an eco-energetic reasoning that considered 'physical' productivity as preliminary to 'economic' productivity (Cournot 1877).[17] He inherited here a typical scheme of nineteenth century engineering thinking. By measuring inputs and outputs in the same unit, it is possible to calculate the 'yield'; in this way, for instance, Thünen calculated the cost of grain transport, taking into account that not only horses but the driver ate some!

The introduction of the concept of energy in the mid-nineteenth century resulted from combined efforts to measure 'yields' in various branches of productive activities.[18] One should not be surprised to see studies on human work, on the steam engine and its consumption of coal ('duty') and on agronomy all come together with the chemist Justus Liebig. Out of all these researches emerged the concept of energy as a universal notion. Thereby 'energeticism' in economic thought at the end of the nineteenth century appears as the direct consequence of the 'economicism' of physical-chemical thought since the time of Lavoisier (see Bensaude-Vincent and Mosini's chapter). It is against that background that the interplay between physics and biology on which Cournot

16 On many items, the 1877 *Revue* tends to get closer to the 1838 *Recherches*, which had been praised in the meantime by the neoclassical authors (Vatin 1998, ch. 3).

17 This thinking scheme proceeds from what Paul Samuelson (1983) defines, commenting upon Thünen, as the 'waning' model.

18 Compare Thomas Kuhn's study (1959), which stressed the contribution of industrial mechanics to the genesis of thermodynamics.

founded economics and social science should be understood. His economic 'vitalism' was, to start with, a 'dynamicism' directly descending from the application of Leibniz's 'superior dynamics' to the phenomena of life and of inert matter. Should we conclude that Cournot, contrary to appearances, remained deeply 'physicalist'? Yes, if by that we mean that physics remained his preferred discipline. No, if we assimilate 'physicalism' to a 'mechanicism' that he never ceased to fight in every field of knowledge. On the other hand, one cannot deny the presence of a biological inspiration in Cournot's social and economic thinking that was sustained by his adherence to Leibniz's energeticism.

This general survey of the epistemology of Cournot enables us to address the question of his treatment of the notion of equilibrium, first in physics, and then in economics.

Cournot's concept of equilibrium in mechanics, philosophy and economics

Contrary to what one might imagine from the standpoint of the interpretation of Cournot as a precursor of neoclassical economics, the term 'equilibrium' is not prominent in his philosophical and economic writings. Surely, he did not ignore this fundamental concept of mechanics but, from his first works, accorded a privileged place to dynamics and concerned himself, in physics, with unstable, more than with stable, equilibrium; rather than reducing dynamics to statics, he construed the latter as a limiting case of the former.[19] This position led him to defend the notion of 'force' (Cournot 1828b) against those, such as Lazare Carnot, who called it 'metaphysical'. In his mature work, in fact, Cournot affirmed the primacy of dynamics over statics by means of explicit reference to Leibniz's philosophy, and to thermodynamics. He opposed static models of equilibrium with a dynamical perspective, which highlighted 'expenditure', and introduced the notion of temporality, that of the arrow of time, in physics and economics:

> When one studies the manner of activating forces and the diverse mechanical effects that they are capable of producing, one is quickly led to envisage force under two different aspects: now as a thing that subsists and that one uses indefinitely without consuming it, as one employs weights in equilibrium with each other; now as a thing that consumes itself *or spends itself*, on account of the very use that one makes of it [. . .]. In establishing this distinction, the mechanicists are entirely in line with the jurists and the economists [. . .].
>
> (Cournot 1861, pp. 81–2)

19 That position led Cournot (1828b) to develop the original concept of 'latent dynamics' to describe states of equilibrium susceptible of being disrupted. As we saw, he took a similar approach in economics.

Against Ménard's contention (1978) that Cournot's (1838) *Recherches* was dominated by a reference to the mechanical concept of equilibrium, I wish to point out that the term 'equilibrium' appeared in this work only on two occasions and was not properly thematised. It was with reference to the conceptions of the oscillation of values about a fixed point, put forward in the eighteenth century, and taken up by Walras under the expression *tâtonnement*: 'Now our analysis does not have in view that this state of equilibrium around which commercial variations occur without ceasing to cause the values of exchange to oscillate' (Cournot 1838, p. 25). The widespread interpretation of Cournot as a theoretician of equilibrium results from a modern re-reading of his work initiated by the neoclassicals at the end of the nineteenth century. Evidence of this can be found in the index of the French edition of the *Recherches*, which contains twenty-two entries for the term 'equilibrium', only two of which concern Cournot's text itself. The others relate to the preface of the editor Gérard Jorland, and to an article by Francis Y. Edgeworth (1897). Curiously, the term 'equilibrium' appears more frequently (fifteen times) in the 1863 *Principes*, which was characterised by the replacement of a mechanical model of equilibrium with biological metaphors of the 'social body'. This apparent paradox can easily be explained: the *Principes* was inspired by Cournot's major epistemological work, the 1861 *Traité*, in which Cournot maintained that, like mechanics, economics consists of kinematics, statics and dynamics (Cournot 1861). Elsewhere he took up the point again, asserting the similarity between economic and mechanical analysis:

> One will thus reason like the geometers who, in order to determine the oscillations of a system of bodies, suppose them to be displaced however little from the position of equilibrium towards which they gravitate without occupying other positions of equilibrium that they may take, in consequence of a complete overturning of the system.
>
> (Cournot 1863, p. 69)

However, Cournot did not consider the concept of equilibrium as a focal point of economic analysis, as Walras (1874) would do. In the *Recherches*, he developed an economic theory that, starting from the model of the monopole, and moving on to the duopole, arrived at 'indefinite competition'. Envisaging as 'natural' not only the uniqueness but also the plurality of *equilibria* in a market, he insisted again on the similarity between the epistemologies of economics and physics:

> The laws of consumption of two articles on two markets may thus be adjusted so that there be not a sole equilibrium, but several or even (under the most singular of all hypotheses) an infinity of possible *equilibria*, without one seeing by reason, drawn from this theory, that the system would fix upon one of these *equilibria* rather than on another one, contrary to the principle that wishes that a determinate system of causes would

> always have a determined effect. There is nothing at the basis of this objection that might weaken the theory. The same difficulty has its analogue in statics, where it concerns equilibrium in the proper sense of the word, and it presents itself every time that assigning conditions for an economic equilibrium is concerned.
>
> (Cournot 1861, p. 219)

Thus, for Cournot, in economics, as in mechanics, equilibrium is only a moment of thought. It is a powerful analytical instrument, of which he did not hesitate to make use while refraining from hypostatising it by making it the focal point of the theory. For Cournot, doing that would be tantamount to handing dynamics over to statics, something he had resisted from his first mechanical works by targeting Lazare Carnot as a follower of Lagrange's. Walras constructed his pure political economics on the model of Lagrange's analytical mechanics (see, in particular, Walras 1898): the static representation of the economy that flows from an epistemology of equilibrium could not satisfy Cournot. For him, the social world is steeped in its historical background, and the resulting dynamics is what needs explaining first. The interpretation of Cournot to the benefit of neoclassical economics underestimates the complexity of the epistemological debates of the mechanicists in the early nineteenth century, on which Cournot initially based his epistemology. No doubt, he approached economics from the viewpoint of the mechanicist, albeit not one that regarded equilibrium as a central concept. On this point Cournot never changed his mind, even in the face of Walras's attempts to lure him into his camp. One might say that Cournot was well advised: Arrow and Debreu (1954) made a powerful attempt at showing the existence of a general equilibrium over all markets in a situation of pure and perfect competition. Although they did not study either the conditions of stability or the problem of the uniqueness of equilibrium, they did not doubt that they would come to prove that general Walrasian equilibrium was indeed unique and stable (Guerrien and Pignol 2000). However, in 1973, Hugo Sonnenschein showed the impossibility of demonstrating the existence of a general equilibrium under perfect, unique and stable competition (see Guerrien and Pignol 2000 for discussion).

References

Ampère, A.-M. (1834), *Essai sur la philosophie des sciences*, Bachelier, Paris.

Arrow, K. and Debreu, G. (1954), 'Existence of equilibrium for a competitive economy', *Econometrica*, 22, 265–90.

Bastiat, F. (1850) [1982], *Harmonies économiques*, Slatkine, Geneva.

Becquemont, D. and Mucchielli, L. (1998), *Le Cas Spencer. Science, religion et politique*, Presses Universitaires de France, Paris.

Comte, A. (1822) [1996], 'Plan des travaux scientifiques nécessaires pour réorganiser la société', in *Philosophie des sciences*, Gallimard, Paris, 235–347.

Comte, A. (1830–42) [1975], *Cours de philosophie positive*, 2 vols, Hermann, Paris.

Conry, Y. (1974), *L'Introduction du darwinisme en France*, Vrin, Paris.

Cournot, A. (1828a), 'Sur la théorie des pressions', *Bulletin de Férussac*, 9, 10–22.

Cournot, A. (1828b), 'Réflexion sur les principes de la mécanique', *Bulletin de Férussac*, 9, 68–74.

Cournot, A. (1834). 'De la mesure des forces et du travail des machines', in Kater and Lardner (eds), *A treatise of mechanics* (French translation by Cournot), Paulin, Paris, 408–41.

Cournot, A.A. (1838) [1980], *Recherches sur les principes mathématiques de la théorie des richesses*, G. Jorland (ed.), Vrin, Paris.

Cournot, A.A. (1843) [1984], *Exposition de la théorie des chances et des probabilites*, B. Bru (ed.), Vrin, Paris.

Cournot, A. (1851) [1975], *Essai sur les fondements de nos connaissances et sur le caractère de la critique philosophique*, J.C. Pariente (ed.), Vrin, Paris.

Cournot, A.A. (1861) [1982], *Traité de l'enchaînement des idées fondamentales dans les sciences et dans l'histoire*, N. Bruyère (ed.), Vrin, Paris.

Cournot, A.A. (1863) [1981], *Principes de la théorie des richesses*, G. Jorland (ed.), Vrin, Paris.

Cournot, A.A. (1872) [1973], *Considérations sur la marche des idées et des événements dans les temps modernes*, A. Robinet (ed.), Vrin, Paris.

Cournot, A.A. (1875) [1978], *Matérialisme, vitalisme, rationalisme. Etude sur l'emploi des données de la science en philosophie*, C. Salomon-Bayet (ed.), Vrin, Paris.

Cournot, A.A. (1877) [1982], *Revue sommaire des doctrines economiques*, G. Jorland (ed.), Vrin, Paris.

Edgeworth, F.Y. (1897), 'La teoria pura del monopolio', *Giornale degli economisti*, 15, 13–21, 307–20, 405–14. (English trans. 'The pure theory of monopoly', *Papers relating to political economy*, 1925, Macmillan, London, I, 111–42.

Grattan-Guinness, I. (2005), 'Cournot et la mécanique (1826–34), et particulièrement son utilisation des inégalités', in T. Martin (ed.), *L'Actualité de Cournot*, Vrin, Paris.

Guerrien B. and C. Pignol (2000), 'La théorie de l'équilibre général depuis 1939', in A. Béraud and G. Faccarello (eds), *Nouvelle histoire de la pensée économique*, III, chapter XXXII, La Découverte, Paris, 379–416.

Jevons, W.S. (1879) [1970], *The theory of political economy*, Penguin, Harmondsworth.

Kater, H. and Lardner, D. (1830) [1834], *A treatise of mechanics* (French trans. by Cournot), Paulin, Paris.

Kuhn, T. (1959), 'Energy conservation as an example of simultaneous discovery', in M. Clagett (ed.), *Critical problems in the history of science*, University of Wisconsin Press, Madison, WI, 321–56.

Lévêque, R. (1938), *L'Élément historique dans la connaissance humaine d'après Cournot*, Belles Lettres, Paris.

List, Fr. (1841), *Das nazionale System der politischen Ökonomie* (*Système national d'économie politique*, French trans. by H. Richelot, Paris, 1851 [1998], Gallimard, Paris).

Ménard, Cl. (1978a), *La Formation d'une rationalité économie. A.A. Cournot*, Flammarion, Paris.

Ménard, Cl. (1978b), 'La solution aux crises, la fin de l'histoire', *Cournot. Etudes pour le centenaire de sa mort*, Vrin–Economica, Paris, 23–30.

Mentré, F. (1908), *Cournot et la renaissance du probabilisme au XIXe siècle*, Rivière, Paris.

Mentré, F. (1927), *Pour qu'on lise Cournot*, Beauchesne, Paris.

Merleau-Ponty, J. (1983), *La Science de l'univers à l'âge du positivisme. Etude sur les origines de la cosmologie contemporaine*, Vrin, Paris.

Milhaud, G. (1911), 'Le développement de la pensée de Cournot', *Revue du mois*, October, 404–27.

Milhaud, G. (1927), *Etudes sur Cournot*, Vrin, Paris.

Nisbet, R. (1966), *The sociological tradition*, Basic Books, New York.

Nisbet, R. (1978), 'Conservatism', in T. Bottomore and R. Nisbet (eds), *A history of sociological analysis*, Heinemann, London, 80–117.

Quételet, A. (1835) [1991], *Sur l'homme et le développement de ses facultés*, Fayard, Paris.

Robinet, A. (1981), 'Leibniz dans l'oeuvre de Cournot', *Studia leibnitiana*, 13, 159–91.

Samuelson, P.A. (1983), 'Thünen at two hundred', *Journal of Economic Literature*, 21, 1468–88.

Schmidt, C. (1992), 'Concurrence, concours de producteurs et mode d'organisation de la production chez Antoine-Augustin Cournot', *Economie et société*, 16 (3), 71–99.

Vatin, F. (1993), *Le Travail, économique et physique 1780–1830*, Presses Universitaires de France, Paris.

Vatin, F. (1998), *Economie politique et économie naturelle chez A.A. Cournot*, Presses Universitaires de France, Paris.

Vatin, F. (2000a), 'Cournot, Tarde et la fin des temps', *L'Homme et la société*, 136–7, 127–56.

Vatin, F. (2000b), 'Cournot. Les *Principes* de 1863: des *Recherches* sans mathématiques?', in P. Dockès *et al.* (eds), *Les Traditions économiques françaises 1848–1939*, CNRS Editions, Paris, 305–21.

Vatin, F. (2003), 'Comte et Cournot, une mise en perspective biographique et epistemologique', *Revue d'histoire des sciences humaines*, 8, 9–40.

Vatin, F. (2005), *Trois essais sur la genèse de la pensée sociologique. Politique, épistémologie et cosmologie*, La Découverte, Paris.

Walras, L. (1874) [1988], *Eléments d'économie politique pure*, in *Œuvres*, VIII, Economica, Paris.

Walras, L. (1878), 'Bibliographie des ouvrages relatifs à l'application des mathématiques à l'économie politique', *Journal des économistes*, (4) 4, 470–7.

Walras, L. (1898) [1992], 'Esquisse d'une doctrine économique et sociale', in *Etudes d'économie politique appliquée*, *Œuvres*, Economica, Paris, X, 405–41.

Part III

Equilibrium in present-day economic theory and practice

7 Tensions in modern economics

The case of equilibrium analysis

Tony Lawson

Modern economics is recognised by many as being in a rather unhealthy state. An often unnoticed manifestation of this is a degree of confusion in the employment of central categories, due in large part to a recurring failure to distinguish properties of models from properties of the social reality the models are thought to capture. I illustrate by focusing on interpretations of economic equilibrium in the modern discipline.

Modern mainstream economists distinguish themselves from both their predecessors and the current heterodox traditions by their insistence on everywhere employing methods of mathematical deductivist modelling. So immersed in these modelling activities are mainstream economists that they regularly, or so I will argue, elide the distinction between properties of their models and properties of the domain of reality that economists are professing to study. Perhaps this might seem defensible if there were no means of accessing social reality other than via such models. However, this is not the case; there are indeed numerous ways of getting to know social reality, as testified by our numerous everyday knowledgeable and skilful activities. Acknowledging this, we might still want to reason that the elision in question need not matter if we have reason to suppose that the methods in question were well tailored to conditions typical of social reality. Once more, though, we know this not to be so. Rather, whilst we shall see that the methods in question are appropriate to closed worlds of isolated atoms (terms I will elaborate upon below), social reality is found to be rather different in nature.

One result of this regular mismatch of method and subject matter is that the mainstream project of modern economics is marked by repeated explanatory failure. This is an issue I have explored at length elsewhere (see Lawson 2003). Here I focus instead on an alternative manifestation of the ill health of the discipline, the tensions, or confusions, that arise just because real-world properties and those of models often become conflated. Such tensions, furthermore, even frequently, carry over to the contributions of heterodox opponents, who often accept mainstream claims at face value and thereby engage in debates that miss the point.

My aim here is elaborate upon these contentions by way of considering how economists have employed one particular, albeit often central, category, that of (economic) equilibrium.

My argumentative strategy is to first identify tensions in the theorising of equilibrium. I then demonstrate that the factors already discussed serve, when further elaborated, to explain the identified tensions.

Equilibrium theorising in modern economics

A review of the contributions to equilibrium theorising in modern economics in fact immediately reveals various *prima facie* problematic features, confusions, or at least curiosities, some of the most significant of which I wish to focus upon here. These are all features that in due course I shall seek to explain.

A first notable feature of the modern discipline is that at any point in time many authors seem incapable of avoiding setting out inconsistent accounts of the nature of their project. In particular many oscillate between (1) supposing that an equilibrium exists and is something to be explained and (2) asserting that the existence of an equilibrium is something to be established.

Thus, for example, Arrow and Hahn, in their *General Competitive Analysis* (one of the seminal contributions to general equilibrium theory), early on claim the heritage of Adam Smith (asserting that 'Smith was a creator of general equilibrium theory' – Arrow and Hahn 1971, p. 2), and note that Smith's project was to explain an *a posteriori* state of affairs that was no part of anyone's design. Indeed, they hold the view that Smith's

> notion that a social system moved by independent actions in pursuit of different values is consistent with a final coherent state of balance, and one in which the outcomes may be quite different from those intended by the agents, is surely the most important intellectual contribution that economic thought has made to the general understanding of social processes.
>
> (Arrow and Hahn 1971, p. 1)

Yet, no sooner do they assign to economics the task of explaining this state of affairs, one they interpret as an equilibrium, than Hahn, writing at the time Arrow and Hahn (1971) would have been in press, warns us to caution against supposing an equilibrium exists:

> it cannot be denied that there is something scandalous in the spectacle of so many people refining the analyses of economic [equilibrium] states which they give no reason to suppose will ever, or have ever, come about. It probably is also dangerous. Equilibrium economics . . . is easily convertible into an apologia for existing economic arrangements and it is frequently so converted.
>
> (Hahn 1970, pp. 88–9)

A second feature of equilibrium theorising in economics is that there are various competing conceptions of equilibrium, with the range of notions apparently resistant to successful systematisation, despite the best efforts of some. The result inevitably is a lack of clarity over what is being discussed. Machlup sums up the situation in complaining that equilibrium is 'a term which has so many meanings that we never know what its users are talking about' (Machlup 1991, p. 43).

A third remarkable phenomenon is that, amongst economists who bother to concern themselves with notions of equilibrium, there is a polarisation of responses. Most contributors are either (1) strongly in favour of retaining some equilibrium notion in economics or (2) strongly against doing so. This polarisation is *prima facie* somewhat surprising in a situation that both lacks a consensus about what the concept means and even supports a widespread awareness that interpretations are indeed multiple. Yet examples abound. Thus it has been claimed, for instance, that 'it is impossible to exclude the terms "equilibrium" and "disequilibrium" from the economist's discourse' (Matchlup 1991, p. 43), that 'wherever economics is used or thought about, equilibrium is a central organising idea' (Hahn 1984, p. 43) and that 'the strongest defence of equilibrium analysis ... is that it is indispensable' (Backhouse 2003, p. 8). In the opposite camp, Kaldor wrote of the irrelevance of equilibrium economics (Kaldor 1972), Robinson stated that the 'metaphor of equilibrium is treacherous' (Robinson 1968, p. 15), whilst Hayek eventually chose to avoid it as 'A somewhat unfortunate term' (Hayek 1968, p. 184).

An interesting aspect of this situation also warranting explanatory comment is that those most insistent on maintaining the notion are contributors to the mainstream project of modern economics, whilst those rejecting the equilibrium notion are mostly associated with modern heterodox traditions. That said, however, I should note that the figures with whom the modern heterodox traditions are most associated were often accommodating of the equilibrium idea initially, before becoming less enchanted over time. This I think is true of the likes of Joan Robinson, Keynes and Hayek, now ineradicably associated with modern heterodox reasoning. Thus, for example, Robinson came to contrast equilibrium theorising negatively with a preferred historical approach, while Hayek, for reasons we will discuss in due course, came to prefer the 'concept of order ... to that of equilibrium' (Hayek 1968, p. 15). This latter set of developments too calls for some kind of explanation or further insight.

My aim in this chapter is precisely to outline one way of rendering the phenomena expressed in these observations intelligible. That is, I want to advance and defend an interpretation of what is going on that can account for the: (1) recurrent incoherences that arise in equilibrium theorising; (2) various competing conceptions of equilibrium; (3) polarisation of attitudes towards equilibrium theorising, including a tendency for heterodox figures to become increasingly sceptical over time. The elaboration of an account that can explain these observed features constitutes the objective of the main body of this chapter. In a final section I draw out some brief implications of the analysis sustained.

Explaining the phenomena noted

My explanation of the phenomena under examination, briefly sketched above, follows from a broad thesis about the nature of modern economics that I defend elsewhere. In this chapter I mostly outline its relevant components. I shall not rehearse previous extended defences of this overall thesis (for this see Lawson 2003, especially ch. 1), although I shall provide some motivation for it. Meanwhile, I do interpret its ability (demonstrated below) to render intelligible the phenomena before us as further evidence of its explanatory power and so adequacy. The relevant components of this broader thesis are as follows:

1. The modern economics academy is dominated by a mainstream tradition the essence of which is an insistence on mathematical-deductive modelling.
2. As an intellectual project, modern mainstream economics is not in a healthy state. (It achieves few explanatory or predictive successes, is plagued by theory/practice inconsistencies, relies on constructs recognised as quite fictitious and generally lacks direction.)
3. The explanation of the situation noted under 2 is that mathematical-deductive methods are regularly applied in conditions for which they are not appropriate.
4. If the heterodox alternatives are defined by a reaction to the mainstream insistence on the ubiquitous employment of methods of mathematical modelling, the explanation of this opposition is a shared vision largely at odds with the (atomistic and closed-system) ontological presuppositions of methods of formalistic modelling.
5. The ontological nature of the heterodox opposition to the mainstream is under-theorised and very often unrecognised within the heterodox traditions themselves, being manifest mostly in the defence of alternative economic categories.

Let me briefly give some feeling for why I accept these particular assessments.

The first claim – that the modern economics academy is dominated by a mainstream tradition that insists that mathematical-deductive modelling be everywhere utilised – surely no longer needs justification. Consider just the observations of Richard Lipsey, author of a best-selling mainstream economics textbook:

> to get an article published in most of today's top rank economic journals, you must provide a mathematical model, even if it adds nothing to your verbal analysis. I have been at seminars where the presenter was asked after a few minutes, 'Where is your model?' When he answered 'I have not got one as I do not need one, or cannot yet develop one, to consider my problem' the response was to turn off and figuratively, if not literally, to walk out.
>
> (Lipsey 2001, p. 184)

Simply put, an *insistence* on formalistic modelling methods whatever the problem being addressed, is an edict accepted by, but only by, the mainstream, and is the only recurring feature of the mainstream (see Lawson 2003, ch. 1).

My second claim – that as an intellectual project modern mainstream economics is not in a healthy state – is again one that needs little substantiation, being a matter that the more reflective of mainstream economists seem increasingly prepared to acknowledge themselves. Thus we find Nobel Memorial Prize winners noting that 'Page after page of professional economic journals are filled with mathematical formulas leading the reader from sets of more or less plausible but entirely arbitrary assumptions to precisely stated but irrelevant theoretical conclusions' (Leontief 1982, p. 104); that 'economics has become increasingly an arcane branch of mathematics rather than dealing with real economic problems' (Friedman 1999, p. 137); that 'Existing economics is a theoretical system which floats in the air and which bears little relation to what happens in the real world' (Coase 1999, p. 2).

Further, the mainstream 'theorist' Ariel Rubinstein admits that 'economic theory has not delivered the goods', adding that 'the link between economic theory and practical problems ... is tenuous at best' (Rubinstein 1995, p. 12). Indeed, he concludes, 'Economic theory lacks a consensus as to its purpose and interpretation. Again and again, we find ourselves asking the question "Where does it lead?"' (Rubinstein 1995, p. 12).

Nor is the problem just the project's lack of direction and limited explanatory and predictive power. In addition, the project's theory and practice are highly inconsistent. For example, econometricians put huge resources into elaborating the methods they take to be appropriate and justified, yet their practices diverge wildly from their own methodological strictures (see e.g. Leamer 1978, p. vi; Hendry *et al.* 1990).

All in all, the discipline is replete with theory/practice inconsistencies, fares poorly by its own criteria and lacks any clear idea as to where it is going. It is also full of anomalies that range over its various sub-programmes. Consider the observations of Richard Lipsey once more:

> anomalies, particularly those that cut across the sub-disciplines and that can be studied with various technical levels of sophistication, are tolerated on a scale that would be impossible in most natural sciences – and would be regarded as a scandal if they were.
>
> (Lipsey 2001, p. 173)

If a summary statement is required it is perhaps provided by Mark Blaug, a methodologically oriented economist, who has spent considerable resources throughout his career attempting to shore up the mainstream tradition. His current assessment runs as follows:

> Modern economics is sick. Economics has increasingly become an intellectual game played for its own sake and not for its practical consequences for

> understanding the economic world. Economists have converted the subject into a sort of social mathematics in which analytical rigour is everything and practical relevance is nothing.
>
> (Blaug 1997, p. 3)

My third claim – that the disarray of modern economics follows because methods of mathematical-deductive modelling are regularly applied in conditions for which they are not appropriate – is something I shall elaborate rather than defend (for a defence also see Lawson 2003, ch. 1).

All methods are appropriate in some conditions and not others. As Keynes long ago in effect recognised, the sorts of mathematical methods economists use presuppose a closed world of isolated atoms. (Keynes focused on the econometrics of Tinbergen, of course.) To describe a causal factor as atomistic in this fashion is not to make a claim about size but to indicate a presupposition that it exercises its own separate independent and invariable effect, whatever the context, thus guaranteeing that under some repeated conditions *x* the same predictable outcome *y* will always follow, so long as countervailing forces are held off. The point, of course, is that social reality does not comprise merely isolated atomistic systems. Indeed, it is easy enough to show that social reality is not only open (it consists of more than systems supporting event regularities), but also structured (irreducible to the course of events), intrinsically dynamic (its mode of being is as a process) and highly internally related (consisting of parts and wholes each constituted though their (ever-changing) relations to other parts and wholes – think of the positions of teachers and students, or employers and employees), amongst much else. From this perspective, it is not at all surprising that attempts to analyse social life using only methods that presuppose a world that is closed and atomistic fare so badly.

The fourth and fifth claims can be run together. Here I am suggesting that heterodox contributions tend to presuppose a shared vision largely at odds with the (atomistic and closed-system) ontological presuppositions of methods of formalistic modelling. Rather, the heterodox contributions tend to advance substantive, methodological and/or policy claims whose ontological presuppositions are essentially those of openness, structure, process, internal relationality, and so on. However (with a few important exceptions, most notably Paul Davidson's (1989, 1996) emphasis on non-ergodic systems), the ontological nature of the heterodox opposition to the mainstream is under-theorised and very often unrecognised within the heterodox traditions themselves.

Thus, in post-Keynesianism we find an emphasis on uncertainty (presupposing openness) in place of risk, in feminism the emphasis is on caring and identity relations (presupposing internal relationality) instead of selfish individuals, and in old institutionalism the emphasis is on the evolutionary method (process) rather than theorising an equilibrating or teleological system. However, as I say, the ontological presuppositions *per se* are rarely emphasised. I believe it is just because the ontological basis of heterodoxy goes unrecognised that its criticisms of the mainstream have usually been less effectual than they deserve.

A brief sketch of my explanation of the state of equilibrium theorising

Here I want to use this five-part thesis (which, as I say, is defended at length elsewhere – see e.g. Lawson 1997, 2003) to explain the phenomena noted earlier. The nature of my argument is perhaps unfamiliar. So it may be useful at this point if I provide a schematic overview of its basic thrust and direction. It runs as follows.

The limited power of formalistic methods to illuminate social reality, the lack of fit of the former to the latter, necessarily results in mainstream economists inventing 'a reality' of a form that their modelling methods can address (i.e. a world of isolated atomistic individuals possessed, for example, of perfect foresight, or rational expectations, omniscience, pure greed, and so forth). But this is not all. It also imparts meaning to macro or system categories of a sort that is driven by the needs or constraints of formalistic modelling (rather than meeting with the more usual, historical or intuitive understandings of such categories). And this happens in ways that are often unappreciated (if ultimately explicable). We shall see that *equilibrium* is one such system category that suffers such a fate (a further one of interest but not considered here is the econometric idea of a data generation process or DGP (see Pratten 2005); another is that of complexity (see Perona forthcoming).

If I can use the term *theoretic* to denote the quality of being a feature of a model and the term *ontic* to denote the quality of being a feature of the world the economist presumes to illuminate, a more succinct way of describing the problem that arises through the prioritisation of the modelling orientation is a conflation of the theoretic and ontic, with the latter reduced to the former.[1] Now, in mostly neglecting to engage in systematic ontological elaboration, the heterodox opposition has tended to take the mainstream constructs at face value, and thereby to counterpoise alternative conceptions at the same (substantive or system) level, mostly failing to appreciate that the two sides to the discussion are talking about entirely different worlds.

Only with a turn to systematic ontology, however, can we make sense of the total situation. For only then are we in a position both (1) to clearly distinguish the ontological presuppositions of the mainstream methods and those guiding heterodox traditions, and (2) to see that they are not only differently derived, but also (given the lack of fit of social reality and the formalistic methods used) necessarily very different in character. And we shall see that it is only through sustaining the theoretic/ontic distinction that we can ultimately comprehensively explain (1) the confusions and inconsistencies as arise, (2) the variety of equilibrium notions on offer and (3) the debates and polarisations (including trends to increased scepticism in the contributions of some) such as are observed. Let me now defend this claim in detail.

1 Elsewhere (Lawson 1997) I have described this error as the *epistemic fallacy*. The fallacy in question is the supposition that questions about being can be always be rephrased as questions about knowledge (of being).

The explanation in detail

In the context of equilibrium analysis my central claim translates into the idea that some conceptions of equilibrium found in the literature are theoretic and others are ontic, where this difference in the nature of the competing conceptions goes largely unnoticed.

To illustrate, we can consider the most frequently occurring examples of contrasted notions of equilibrium in the economics literature, those of *system determinateness* on the one hand and *balance or order* on the other. For an examination of actual texts quickly reveals that those who have emphasised determinateness have mostly meant by this the *determinateness of particular representations or formalisations* of the economy, whilst those who have emphasised balance or order have interpreted this as *an aspect of the economy they are attempting to represent*. While the former is theoretic, a sought-after property of theories or more typically models, the latter is ontic, a property of society that the investigator is seeking to understand and explain.

However, it is a general failure to recognise that this is the nature of the distinction being drawn that has led to such confusion as abounds. Typically, the rhetoric of equilibrium analysis supports images of order or balance whilst its real content has concerned the properties of formalistic models. The failure to distinguish the two in a systematic way has resulted in a literature that is often incoherent, with contributors tending to talk past each other. Ultimately, we shall see, this state of affairs also throws insight on the plethora of equilibrium concepts in contention as well as the polarisations in attitudes to equilibrium theorising.

The equilibrium dichotomy

It is useful, at this point, to consider the classic statement of equilibrium theory in the modern period provided by Arrow and Hahn (1971). This is useful just because these authors start their book with a 'historical introduction' that emphasises precisely the distinction just noted. Indeed, their opening sentence runs as follows:

> There are two basic, incompletely separable, aspects of the notion of general equilibrium as it has been used in economics: the simple notion of determinateness, that the relations describing the economic system must be sufficiently complete to determine the values of its variables, and the more specific notion that each relation represents a balance of forces.
>
> (Arrow and Hahn 1971, p. 1)

If we examine this passage closely we can indeed see the different nature of the two conceptions. The first criterion, *determinateness*, is precisely a property of relations used to describe the economic system, whilst a balance of forces is an aspect of the economy, one that each equation is said to represent. The former is a property of the theoretical conception, the latter thought to be a property of what the theoretical conception is about. The former is theoretic, the latter ontic. Arrow and Hahn, though, like most modern economists, are so much oriented to the theorising aspect that they misunderstand the nature of the difference in the two conceptions they describe. As the noted passage also indicates, they suppose that the difference to which they are drawing attention is one of levels generality. Specifically, they emphasise that the idea of representing a *balance of forces* is a 'more specific notion' than that of 'determinateness'.

Let me be clear on this. *Contra* the sort of interpretation advanced by Weintraub (2005), these authors do not claim that the historically prior notion (or aspects of a notion) concerning a 'balance of forces' has now been replaced by the (more) modern notion (or aspect) of determinateness. Rather, as I say, they merely see the former as being the more specific concept; indeed, they view the two conceptions as incompletely separable aspects of one notion. Now, *contra* Arrow and Hahn, I suggest that the categories in question are after all completely separable notions of equilibrium, that (what I am calling) the ontic notion is not simply (or at all) a more specific notion, but something quite different from the theoretic one. It is clear, though, that Arrow and Hahn do often run the two concepts together (as two inseparable aspects of a one notion) just because the theoretic/ontic distinction is untheorised. Their primary concern is with model properties, with the determinateness of systems of equations. They think that any attempt to theorise the whole of an economic system implies the acceptance of this conception of equilibrium. However, in illustrating the supposedly more specific notion of a balance, they unwittingly provide an ontic formulation:

> In a sense, almost any attempt to give a theory of the whole economic system implies the acceptance of the first part of the equilibrium notion; and Adam Smith's 'invisible hand' is a poetic expression of the most fundamental of economic relations, the equalisation of rates of return, as enforced by the tendency of factors to move from low to high returns.
>
> The notion of equilibrium ('equal weight', referring to the condition for balancing a lever pivoted at its centre) was familiar to mechanics long before the publication of *The Wealth of Nations* in 1776, and with it the notion that the effects of a force may annihilate it (e.g., water finding its own level), but there is no obvious evidence that Smith drew his ideas from any analogy with mechanics. Whatever the source of the concept, the notion that a social system moved by independent actions in pursuit of different values is consistent with a final coherent balance, and one in which the outcomes may be different from those intended by the agents, is surely the most important intellectual contribution that economic thought has made to the general understanding of social processes.
>
> (Arrow and Hahn 1971, p. 1)

This passage (apart from the first clause referring to equilibrium as determinateness) deals solely with the way the economy works. The concern is with the balance of a social system. The focus has nothing to do with properties of models, and everything to do with the forces of society. Yet Arrow and Hahn move from this discussion to immediately suggest that 'Smith was a creator of general equilibrium theory', a purely theoretic notion, indeed confusing the discussion of economic equilibrium. Thus we can see the source of the confusion noted at the outset. Smith and those adopting an ontic orientation are indeed concerned to explain an existing situation. Smith's objective is to explain such economic order as occurs in the social world. By referring to such a state of affairs as an equilibrium, Arrow and Hahn, and others, are thereby suggesting, at this point, that an equilibrium always occurs, and that it is something to explain. However, when they conceive of an equilibrium in terms of a consistency property of their models, as determinateness, their concern is to show that such a property – an equilibrium – exists.[2] Thus the failure explicitly to distinguish the theoretic and the ontic produces conflicting statements about what is going on.

Consider again the passage from Hahn noted at the outset 'it cannot be denied that there is something scandalous in the spectacle of so many people refining the analyses of economic [equilibrium] states which they give no reason to suppose will ever, or have ever, come about' (Hahn 1970, pp. 88–9). Let us once more be clear. When Hahn here refers to an equilibrium that may never come about it perhaps appears, at first sight, that he is using an ontic notion. However, this is not so. He is really saying that, in an imagined world consistent with his model, there is nothing to ensure that an equilibrium position would result. Or more accurately, he is saying that if, for a set of equations used to construct a description of the economy, there is a manner – a specification – whereby the various equations are found to be mutually consistent, then the solution to the consistency question, stylised as an equilibrium, is not a part of the model description, and so not a necessary outcome even in such a counterfactual (closed and atomistic) world as described by the model specification. In short, the equilibrium is merely a solution to a system of equations. It is a vector that renders the equations consistent. Hahn's point is that there is nothing in the apparatus of the model to ensure that even if, *per impossibile*, the model accurately represented the world, the equilibrium situation, expressed by the model's consistency condition, would emerge.

I do not want to suggest that Hahn intentionally misleads, or always fails to acknowledge the limits of his endeavour. Certainly, Hahn seems to have become increasingly clear with the passage of time on what his constructions entitle him

2 For example, they turn next to Walras, to whom, they suggest, the 'full recognition of the general equilibrium concept can be attributed unmistakably' (Arrow and Hahn 1971, p. 3). Here we are in the realm of models. Things are confused because variables in models are referred to as prices, demand and supply, and so forth. However, it is clear from the discussion that when Equilibrium is now conceived of as a set of prices, being those that equate supply and demand on each market under a given set of conditions, the category is a property of models, not to states of affairs they are purported to represent: 'That there was an equilibrium set of prices was argued from the equality of the number of prices to be determined with the number of equations expressing the equality of supply and demand on all markets. Both are...' (Arrow and Hahn, p. 5).

to conclude. Indeed, in an 'Intellectual Retrospect' he is very clear about what is taking place in his theory contributions:

> The great virtue of mathematical reasoning in economics is that by its precise account of assumptions it becomes crystal clear that applications to the 'real' world could at best be provisional. When a mathematical economist assumes that there is a three-good economy lasting two periods, or that agents are infinitely lived (perhaps because they value the utility of their descendants which they know!), everyone can see that we are not dealing with any actual economy. The assumptions are there to enable certain results to emerge and not because they are to be taken descriptively.
>
> (Hahn 1994, p. 246)

It seems reasonable to suppose that, if Hahn had been clearer on this score from the outset, some of the earlier (non-connecting) discussion might have been avoided. Joan Robinson (for example 1978) in particular might have been spared the effort of responding to Hahn in terms of outlining, and defending as more realistic, a particular (ontic) conception of an equilibrium.

To repeat, then, my explanatory thesis (conditioned on the description of modern economics described above) is that in modern economics there is an erroneous (if explicable) tendency to conflate theoretic and ontic features of an analysis. And this thesis can be seen to account for much of the incoherence of equilibrium analysis as abounds.

The remaining problematic features

How does this thesis account for the two remaining sets of observations noted above, namely of:

1 A plethora of competing equilibrium conceptions, especially of those conceptions that can be viewed as versions of system determinateness.
2 A polarisation of orientations, divided amongst mainstream/heterodox lines?

The plethora of conceptions is easily explained. For where equilibrium is merely a solution concept for a model, a property of a system of equations, there can clearly be as many definitions of equilibrium as there are possibilities for system model construction. And scope for the latter seems limitless. This situation is grasped by some but seemingly not by most. Thus a heroic attempt to bring clarity by Machlup ends up doing no more than rendering both the equilibrium as *balance* and equilibrium as *determinateness* notions as theoretic:

> Equilibrium, in economic analysis [is] a constellation of selected interrelated variables so adjusted to one another that no inherent tendency to change prevails in the model which they constitute ... As an alternative

> definition of equilibrium we may propose mutual compatibility of a selected set of interrelated variables of particular magnitudes.
>
> (Machlup 1991, pp. 54–5)

But Dixon, amongst others, hits the nail on the head precisely: 'At its most general, we can say that "equilibrium" is a method of solving economic models. At a superficial level, an equilibrium is simply a solution to a set of equations' (Dixon 1990, p. 356).

It is equally possible to explain our remaining puzzle, the polarisation of attitudes over the relevance of an equilibrium notion. I have already noted that attitudes have tended to divide along mainstream/heterodox lines, with the mainstream, unlike heterodoxy, insisting the equilibrium notion is essential, and with the heterodox opposition to employing this category becoming increasingly marked over time. We now have before us the resources to understand why. Consider, first, the mainstream insistence that the notion of equilibrium be retained. The reason for this must now be clear. For this mainstream project is defined by its insistence that mathematical methods be everywhere and always employed, despite the dearth of explanatory successes to date. But, in a situation where model equations are found almost always to be inappropriate to the analysis of the economic system, what other goal can be accepted for modellers than the questioning of their equations' mutual consistency? Where the emphasis is on a formalistic system, attention is always going to turn to the question of whether the system has some sort of mathematical solution. And the natural, or anyway traditional, way to try and present this as an economic activity is to present the mathematical exercise as the search for an economic equilibrium. Associating the process with Smith is merely an attempt to grant the exercise a historical legitimacy, an endeavour that significantly misleads.

How about the heterodox rejection of the use of the term? If the mainstream was always going to require a notion to express the model-property of consistency or determinateness, was it equally predictable that heterodoxy was always going to abandon the term? The answer I think is yes if not necessarily immediately. I suggested earlier that a feature of the heterodox traditions is that, although they emphasise categories with ontological presuppositions different from those of the mainstream mathematical methods, they rarely acknowledge that this is so. Specifically, the mainstream methods presuppose a closed atomistic reality, whereas heterodox conceptions can be shown to be based on a vision of social reality as open, structured, processual, highly internally related, amongst much else (see Lawson 2003). As I say, though, the ontological basis of the opposition has rarely been explicitly identified.

Even so, heterodox economists have been oriented to ontic elaboration, focusing mostly on equilibrium as a balance, or form of order. In consequence the tension between the conceptions of social order they have been seeking to explain and the more dominant definitions of equilibrium have usually been apparent, even if the ontological basis of the distinction remained untheorised. This has resulted in equilibrium notions being employed, if at all, often in a hesitant and cautious manner. Joan Robinson provides an obvious example:

> The word equilibrium, in ordinary speech, describes a relation between bodies in space. The scales of a balance are in equilibrium when the balance is at rest . . . If we are continually throwing coppers at random into either scale, the balance is continually wobbling and never reaches equilibrium; but, at any moment, there is a definite equilibrium position which it would quickly reach if, from that moment, we left it alone.
>
> (Robinson 1956, p. 57)

She concluded:

> Nor can we apply the metaphor of a balance which is seeking or tending towards a position of equilibrium though prevented from actually reaching it through constant disturbances. In economic affairs the fact that disturbances are known to be liable to occur makes expectations about the future uncertain and has an important effect on any conduct (which, in fact, is all economic conduct) directed towards future results . . . A belief that a particular share is going to rise in price causes people to offer to buy it and so raises its price . . . This element of 'thinking makes it so' creates a situation where a cunning guesser who can guess what the other guessers are going to guess is able to make a fortune. There are then no solid weights to give us analogy with a pair of scales in balance. The metaphor of equilibrium is treacherous . . .
>
> (Robinson 1956, p. 59)

The more the ontic orientation has been manifest in a sustained concern with the nature of the actually existing social order, the more heterodox economists have grasped the irrelevance of the equilibrium framework. Thus, with time, of course, Joan Robinson turned from equilibrium thinking to history.

A second of numerous possible illustrations is provided by the contributions of Hayek. Hayek is especially interesting here in that all along he recognised the theoretic, or *a priori*, nature of the dominant framework, interpreting it as a logic of choice, whilst himself being driven always to provide an ontic account. This is especially true of his work of the late 1930s. Specifically his (1937) 'Economics and Knowledge' paper is a particularly ingenious attempt to reconcile two ultimately incompatible endeavours: an *a priori* logical framework (presupposing a closed system), and a desire for a realistic (open-system) vision of the actual social world.

Early on, Hayek wrote:

> I am certain that there are many who regard with impatience and distrust the whole tendency, which is inherent in all modern equilibrium analysis, to turn economics into a branch of pure logic, a set of self-evident propositions which, like mathematics or geometry, are subject to no other test but internal consistency.
>
> (Hayek 1937, p. 35)

How is the noted tendency to turn economics into a branch of logic to be avoided? How is equilibrium analysis to be rescued as an ontic endeavour, as a project concerned with understanding social reality? Hayek hopes this can be achieved by way of economists seeking out real-world tendencies to equilibrium:

> We shall not get much further here unless we ask for the reasons for our concern with the admittedly fictitious state of equilibrium. Whatever may occasionally have been said by over-pure economists, there seems to be no possible doubt that the only justification for this is the supposed existence of a tendency toward equilibrium. It is only by this assertion that economics ceases to be an exercise in pure logic and becomes an empirical science; and it is to economics as an empirical science that we must now turn.
>
> (Hayek 1937, pp. 43–4)

The story is a long one. But it is sufficient to note here that eventually Hayek accepted that a tendency to equilibrium requires that individuals' expectations of each other become more and more accurate; whilst he admitted to not knowing why or how such an eventuality should come about. As a result, he came close to abandoning the equilibrium project even in this early essay:

> But I am afraid that I am now getting to a stage where it becomes exceedingly difficult to say what exactly are the assumptions on the basis of which we assert that there will be a tendency toward equilibrium, and to claim that our analysis has an application to the real world. I cannot pretend that I have as yet got much further on this point.
>
> (Hayek 1937, p. 47)

Not surprisingly perhaps, this failure spurred Hayek into a form of ontological reasoning. After initially trying to maintain an equilibrium idea, Hayek's ontic orientation led him increasingly to appreciate its limitations. Some time after the 'Economics and Knowledge' paper, in fact, he was emphasising the idea of social order rather than equilibrium: 'The concept of "order", which . . . I prefer to that of equilibrium, has the advantage that we can speak about order being approached to varying degrees, and that order can be preserved throughout the process of change' (Hayek 1968, p. 184).

Eventually, of course, Hayek elaborated a social ontology of rules and other aspects of social structure, and developed his conception of spontaneous order:

> What reconciles the individuals and knits them into a common and enduring pattern of society is that . . . they respond in accordance with the same abstract rules . . . What . . . enables . . . men to live and work together in peace is that the pursuit of their individual ends and the particular monetary impulses which impel their efforts . . . are guided and restrained by the same

> abstract rules. If emotion or impulse tells them what they want, the conventional rules tell them how they will be able and allowed to achieve it.
>
> (Hayek 1976, p. 12)

> A catallaxy is thus a special kind of spontaneous order produced by the market through people acting within the rules of the law of property, tort and contract.
>
> (Hayek 1982, p. 109)

> This is no longer a conception of a state of order in which expectations are always met; rather, it is one in which disappointments are unavoidable: 'In a spontaneous order, undeserved disappointments cannot be avoided. . . . It is only because countless others constantly submit to disappointments of their reasonable expectations that everyone has as high an income as he has.'
>
> (Hayek 1982, p. 128)

With this being so, Hayek's conception is far more in line with the world we daily experience. It is quite different from Hayek's original notion, but reveals the sort of direction that is ultimately to be expected where there is a consistent emphasis on the ontic.

Implications and conclusion

Modern economics is not in a healthy state. And the reason for it is that it, or, rather, the dominant mainstream tradition, defines itself in terms of its method, that of formalistic-deductive modelling, and does so in a context where that method has little application. I have indicated before how this emphasis has resulted in limited explanatory successes, theory/practice inconsistencies and other pathologies. Here I have focused on a further problematic feature created by the mainstream prioritising of modelling over illumination: the confusing of claims about models and their properties with properties of the reality that the models putatively aim to represent.

In truth, modern economics supports two broad sets of traditions, the mainstream project and the heterodox alternatives. The mainstream prioritises modelling whilst the heterodoxy prioritises social illumination. And because the implicit (though rarely examined) ontological commitments of the heterodoxy (of openness, structure, internal relationality and process) are quite different from those (of atomism and closure) presupposed by the mainstream modelling emphasis, the two projects rarely find common ground. However, the true ontological nature of the differences is rarely explored. One of the many debilitating results of this is that when common categories are employed, the real nature of the differences in arguments mostly goes unrecognised, resulting in participants in debates talking past each other. I have illustrated this theme in the context of equilibrium analysis.

If all parties agree that Adam Smith set (and contributed to answering) one of the fundamental questions of economics, namely how the fact of social order emerges in the absence of central or any intentional design, and indeed with individuals pursuing largely independent goals, it is clear that the inheritors of Smith's project are not economic equilibrium theorists concerned with formalistic modelling. Rather, it is those working in the traditions of Marx, Keynes, Hayek, and others, who make the explaining of the actually existing social order the priority. The project of formalistic modelling can be misinterpreted as one concerned with explaining the actual social order only if the atomistic presuppositions of the former go unrecognised, or their irrelevance remains unappreciated. Once we turn to social ontology, to theorising the nature of social reality, the impotence of the equilibrium notion becomes apparent. The real question, Smith's question in modern terms, is how social reproduction of complex, internally related, dynamic social structures occurs in an open world of individuals each seeking to realise his or her own ends. As I say, this eventually was the concern of Hayek and Keynes as well as Marx. How successful they were in the details of their analyses, of course, is a different question.

Bibliography

Arrow, K.J. and Hahn, F.H. (1971), *General Competitive Analysis*, Holden-Day, San Francisco.

Backhouse, R. (2004), 'History and equilibrium: a partial defence of equilibrium economics', *Journal of Economic Methodology*, 11 (3), 291–305.

Blaug, M. (1997), 'Ugly currents in modern economics', *Options Politiques*, September, 3–4.

Coase, R. (1999), Interview with Ronald Coase, *Newsletter of the International Society for New Institutional Economics*, 2 (1), 3–10.

Davidson P. (1989), 'The economics of ignorance or the ignorance of economics?', *Critical Review*, 3, 467–87.

Davidson, P. (1996), 'Reality and economic theory', *Journal of Post-Keynesian Economics*, 18 (4), 479–508.

Dixon, H. (1990), 'Equilibrium and explanation', in John Creedy (ed.), *Foundations of Economic Thought*, Blackwell, Oxford.

Fleetwood, S. (1995), *Hayek's Political Economy: The Socio-economics of Order*, Routledge, London.

Friedman, M. (1999), 'Conversation with Milton Friedman', in B. Snowdon and H. Vane (eds), *Conversations with Leading Economists. Interpreting Modern Macroeconomics*, 124–44, Edward Elgar, Cheltenham.

Hahn, F.H. (1970), 'Some adjustment problems', *Econometrica*, 38, 1–17, repr. in Hahn (1984) (page references to the latter).

Hahn, F.H. (1984), *Equilibrium and Macroeconomics*, Blackwell, Oxford.

Hayek, F.A. (1937), 'Economics and knowledge', *Economica*, 4, 33–54.

Hayek, F.A. (1968), 'Competition as a discovery process', in Hayek (1978).

Hayek, F.A. (1976), 'The mirage of social justice', in Hayek (1982).

Hayek, F.A. (1978), *New Studies in Philosophy, Politics and Economics*, Routledge and Kegan Paul, London.

Hayek, F.A. (1982), *Laws, Legislation and Liberty*, Routledge and Kegan Paul, London.

Hendry, D.F., Leamer, E.E. and Poirier, D.J. (1990), 'The ET dialogue: a conversation on econometric methodology', *Econometric Theory*, 6, 171–261.

Kaldor, N. (1972), 'The irrelevance of equilibrium economics', *Economic Journal*, 82, December. Reprinted in Nicholas Kaldor, *Further Essays on Economic Theory*, Duckworth, London (1978).

Lawson, T. (1997), *Economics and Reality*, Routledge, London and New York.

Lawson, T. (2003), *Reorienting Economics*, Routledge, London and New York.

Leamer, E.E. (1978), *Specification Searches. Ad hoc inferences with non-experimental data*, Wiley, New York.

Leontief, W. (1982), 'Letter', *Science*, 217, 104–7.

Lipsey, R.G. (2001), 'Successes and failures in the transformation of economics', *Journal of Economic Methodology*, 8 (2), 169–202.

Machlup, F. (1991), 'Equilibrium and disequilibrium: misplaced concreteness and disguised politics', in *Economic Semantics*, Transaction Press, New Brunswick, NJ, repr. in Donald Walker (ed.), *Equilibrium*, 3 vols, Edward Elgar, Cheltenham (2000).

Perona, E. (2004), 'The confused state of complexity in economics: an ontological explanation', Faculdad de Ciencas Economicas, Universidad Nacional de Cordoba.

Pratten, S. (2005), 'Economics as progress: the LSE approach to economic modelling and critical realism as programmes for research', *Cambridge Journal of Economics* (forthcoming).

Robinson, J. (1956), *The Accumulation of Capital*, Macmillan, London.

Robinson, J. (1978), 'History versus equilibrium', in *Contribution to Modern Economics*, Blackwell, Oxford.

Rubinstein, A. (1995), 'John Nash: the master of economic modelling', *Scandinavian Journal of Economics*, 97 (1), 9–13.

Smith, A. (1975), *The Wealth of Nations*, Dent, London and Toronto.

Weintraub, R. (2005), 'On Lawson on equilibrium', *Journal of post-Keynesian Economics*, 27 (3), 445–54.

8 Equilibrium and problem solving in economics

Roger E. Backhouse

This chapter argues that the way in which economists use the term 'equilibrium' has to be understood in the context of problem solving. Concepts of equilibrium are used in a pragmatic way to solve problems, which often means that rigour is sacrificed to usability. Whether or not a particular situation is or is not an equilibrium may depend on the choices made by the modeller and is not necessarily of any ontological significance. Economic models should therefore be evaluated solely in terms of their problem-solving ability.

This chapter explores some implications of the claim that economists' use of equilibrium methods should be evaluated according to whether these provide satisfactory solutions to problems that are deemed important by the profession (Laudan 1977).[1] By problems, I mean substantive economic problems, including ones that make sense to non-economists. This will include solving problems of economic policy, but is not confined to that. What it excludes is solving puzzles that have no meaning or significance outside the very narrow disciplinary context in which they arise. Such puzzle solving may be important but only if it contributes, indirectly, if not directly, to solving important problems.[2] I wish to stress that I am suggesting only that economists should provide 'satisfactory solutions' to the problems, not that these be completely solved. Laudan elaborates on this:

> In appraising the merits of theories, it is more important to ask whether they constitute adequate solutions to significant problems than it is to ask whether they are 'true', 'corroborated', 'well-confirmed', or otherwise justifiable within the framework of contemporary epistemology.
>
> (Laudan 1977, p. 14)

1 For a slightly longer discussion of the relevance of Laudan's perspective, see Backhouse (1997).
2 The term 'puzzle solving' is used here in a much narrower sense than in Kuhn (1970).

What gives this claim particular significance in economics is that in it, as in all other fields, problems are not of one kind. Some problems are highly specific whereas others concern answers to more general, more abstract questions. This is explored in the next section, where it is argued that, mainly because of the complexity of the economic world, relationships between different types of problem and the different types of theories that relate to them are much more complicated than might be expected. The variety of the problems that economists face helps explain why they use the term 'equilibrium' in many different ways that are not all consistent with each other. Different concepts of equilibrium are used to solve different problems. This chapter next investigates some of the main ways in which the term 'equilibrium' is used in modern economics. The focus is on concepts of equilibrium in relation to the models with which economists are trying to solve problems,[3] the use of equilibrium methods being appraised in terms of the methods' contribution towards economists' ability to solve problems. Some of the critiques that have been levelled against equilibrium methods are discussed, and some conclusions drawn. The main one is that, because the complexity of the economic world could provide a reason why the logical relations between theories at different levels (in a sense that will be made clear in the next section) are weaker than one might expect, it is argued that this means it is inappropriate to judge economists' use of equilibrium methods against some belief about what the world is like – against some general property of the economic or social world – but against whether they help economists solve the problems that they have set out to solve. This perspective helps remove some of the confusion that has abounded in debates over the role of equilibrium in economics.

A qualification is in order before proceeding. I do not wish to imply that all economics contributes to the solution of interesting and important problems. It is widely held that a significant fraction of what goes on in economics involves solving puzzles that serve no purpose other than to advance the careers of those who solve them.[4] This includes theoretical work that bears no relation to real-world problems, and empirical work where no one (sometimes including the economist who undertakes it) believes the results are robust. Both aspects exemplify what Leontief (1971), in a widely cited presidential address to the American Economic Association, referred to as work based on non-observed facts. I do not wish to deny the existence of such work, much of which is centred on models of equilibrium, or even to suggest that it does not matter. I am simply not concerned with it here.[5] It is commonly accepted that, even in the natural sciences, a

3 To do this is not to make any claim that equilibrium has to be understood in relation to a model, merely that this is a fruitful way of exploring the issue. It may be that there is a sense in which it is possible to speak of equilibrium as a property of the world, and it may be the case that economists do this, but it is not necessary to take a position on it.

4 Of course, there will be great disagreement about which work falls into this category, even though there is general agreement that such work exists.

5 I do not wish to argue that it does not matter. All activity has an opportunity cost. Perhaps more important, such work can still make an impact, either because it takes time before it is discredited, or because false conclusions are drawn from it. But that is a different issue from the one I wish to explore here.

significant number of papers are never cited and are read by very few people. What matters is not these papers, but the small percentage that is significant and which causes knowledge in the subject to advance. In the same way I am concerned with economics that does solve real problems (either directly or indirectly) – with the best examples, not the worst or even (perhaps) the average.

Economists as problem solvers

When confronted with the literature on the existence of competitive general equilibrium, or any one of a hundred other topics in abstract theory, the claim that economists are concerned to solve problems must seem doubtful, unless that is interpreted sufficiently broadly to include theoretical problems generated within the theory itself. Much economic theory is like this: it deals with abstract worlds that in some cases describe no conceivable world, and with problems that do not even make sense outside that theory. However, the claim made here is that the justification for such work is that it helps solve problems that arise concerning the real world.

Consider three types of question. At the most abstract level are questions (call them Type I questions) such as:

1 How is it possible for a system of markets to co-ordinate the activities of billions of individuals without any conscious planning?
2 How can capitalist economies get stuck in situations where productive capacity is lying idle and workers are out of work, even when the world needs the goods that could be produced?

At a less abstract level are questions (Type II) such as:

1 Can policy be used to reduce the level of fluctuations over the business cycle, or is this impossible?
2 Under what conditions is it more efficient to have public services provided by the state and when should they be in the hands of private enterprise?
3 How will a manager's performance be affected by his or her remuneration package? When will payment through share options improve performance and when will it harm it?
4 What rules should be used to determine whether or not take-overs should be allowed?
5 Through what mechanisms can monetary policy affect the level of real activity in the economy?

However, beneath these are the concrete questions (Type III) that concern non-economists.

1 Will George W. Bush's tax cuts stimulate employment in the United States?
2 Would joining the euro raise or lower the standard of living in Britain?

3 What, if anything, should be done about 'fat cat' pay rises?
4 Would privatising the NHS result in better or cheaper health care or would it merely benefit those private firms undertaking it?
5 Will children be better off if they go to university or if they go straight into work at age sixteen or eighteen?

The conventional view amongst economists is that a good way, and perhaps the only way, to solve the concrete (Type III) problems is to tackle some of the more abstract ones. Type II questions concern not specific currency unions, tax cuts or health systems but currency unions, tax cuts and health care provision in general. Above these lie the more abstract, Type I, questions about markets, capitalism and socialism in general. This relationship is shown in the left-hand column of Figure 8.1. An example is provided in Figure 8.2. The relevance of the diagram is that it raises the question of how the boxes are linked. Here, unfortunately, the answer becomes very complicated and all that is possible is to sketch some of the points that arise.

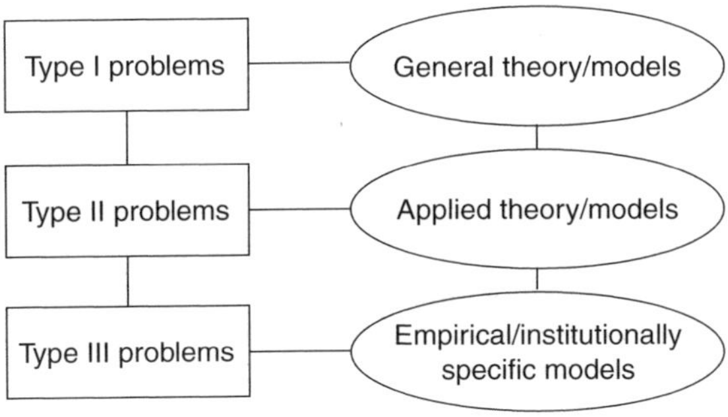

Figure 8.1 Hierarchies of problems and theories.

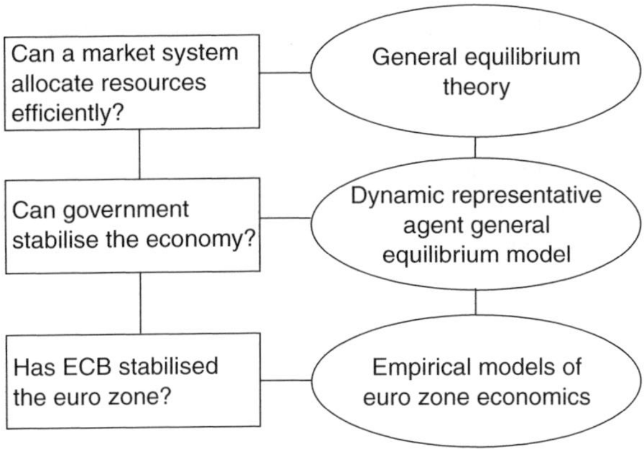

Figure 8.2 Examples of problems and theories.

The 'ideal' is that economists have a general theory (of which the theory of general competitive equilibrium is the prime example) that encompasses all economic questions, and that applied theories are special cases of this general theory. There would thus be arrows running downwards from top to bottom on the right-hand side. In the example of Figure 8.2, the dynamic representative–agent model is a simplified general equilibrium model. In turn, the empirical model is the same model but with numerical parameters substituted for more general ones. This, however, is *at best* an ideal: things never work out like this, for several reasons. One is that the simplifications needed to answer questions at level II dictate that level II models are not just special cases of level I models: though there may be family resemblances, the models are different. Another is that, in order to construct an empirical model, let alone find a satisfactory one, the relationship between level II and level III models is sometimes tenuous.[6] One cannot be derived as a simplification of the other. For the present argument, the more important issue is the relationship between questions and theories and between questions. Here, links run in all directions. Theories suggest questions to be asked (think of arrows running from right to left) and questions suggest theories (arrows running left to right). Some questions in the hierarchy are implied by questions higher up. Some higher questions are generalisations from lower-level questions. Causation, if one may refer to it that way, runs in both directions.

Despite being an extreme simplification, this scheme is useful because it makes the point that relations between theory and problem solving are more complex, and less tidy, than they are sometimes assumed to be. All the links in Figures 8.1 and 8.2 exist but, equally, none of them is either rigid or unidirectional. In particular, theories at levels II and III are driven as much by questions as by theory. General, abstract, theories inform but, typically, do not determine either theoretical or empirical models at the lower levels. Applied theories frequently have to model features of the world that cannot be accommodated within more general models. Theoretical models frequently cannot be applied to data, with the result that empirical models are not special cases of the theoretical models they claim to test. Indeed, this latter gap is so large that one critic (Cartwright 2002) has questioned whether there is any meaningful sense in which one is derived from the other.

Whilst it is possible to see the looseness of the connections in Figures 8.1 and 8.2 as cause for concern, especially when it comes to testing higher-level theories, the other side of the coin is that it increases the scope for real-world problems, determined outside academic economics, to influence theories and models. The result has been that applied theories have proliferated, based on a variety of assumptions that were unknown in the 1960s. Uncertainty, limited information, bargaining, boundedly rational behaviour and other phenomena that cannot be incorporated into general equilibrium theory have become the staple of applied

6 This point has been made by Cartwright (2002). Hoover (2002) makes the point that although these links may not be the rigid ones Cartwright would like to see, there are none the less links.

theory. Different types of model are constructed for different purposes, resulting in enormous variety.

This proliferation of theories and models that cannot be encompassed by any completely general theory extends beyond what is usually considered to be non-mainstream economics. Mainstream economics has, over the last decade or more, continually reinvented, or even subverted, itself, in response to problems arising outside, and within, the discipline, to the extent that it has become hard to say what counts as orthodoxy now. This is one of the main reasons for arguing that economics *is* a problem-solving discipline, driven by substantive problems, and that it is not committed rigidly to one particular framework. In the early 1960s, for example, it would have been arguable that economics was dominated by the theory of general competitive equilibrium – that this was becoming the organising framework for the whole discipline. Many economists do find more abstract questions that arise entirely within the discipline intellectually challenging and their work is dominated by trying to answer such questions using theories that are necessarily highly abstract and make little sense to outside observers. But this tendency has been overridden by the need to solve problems that arise and make sense outside the discipline. I wish to suggest that this has implications for the way equilibrium should be seen.

Equilibrium as a way of solving problems

Most economists, and certainly those who are criticised for their use of concepts of equilibrium, see themselves as concerned with building models, either theoretical ones or empirical ones estimated or calibrated against data. (Perhaps this is the best way to characterise mainstream economics.[7]) These models are mathematical structures that are perceived to reveal something about the world, but are clearly distinct from the world. They are distinct from the world in that they are unrealistic (Friedman 1953) or caricatures (Gibbard and Varian 1978). The obvious sense in which models are unrealistic is that they do not take account of everything: they are simplified representations. However, the unrealism of models goes further in that they may not even model the processes by which real-world agents are believed to achieve the outcomes specified by the models. For example, firms are claimed to behave *as if* they maximise profits: profit-maximisation is assumed to describe behaviour even though managers do not consciously maximise profits – they may not even be able to say precisely what profit maximisation means in a particular context. Alternatively, perfect competition, a market structure in which no agent has any ability to influence price, may describe how market price and output will respond to changes in taxes or technical progress, even though real-world firms have some choice over the prices at which their products are sold.

For economists who model the world in this way, equilibrium is defined in

7 This characterisation is far from perfect, for heterodox economists build models. The term 'mainstream economics' is extremely fuzzy, implying that there may be no ideal definition.

relation to these models. It may be that equilibrium in the model is believed to correspond to equilibrium in the real world in some sense, but there is no necessity for that. The search for equilibrium is primarily a modelling strategy. Being out of equilibrium means that there is unfinished business for the theorist: that the explanation is not yet complete. Thus if supply is not equal to demand, why does price not move towards the equilibrium? If profits could be increased by raising output, why have firms not done so? If the share of profit in income is falling, where will it end? Because economists work with many models, tackling different types of problem and at very different levels of abstraction, they work with many concepts of equilibrium. A short list of some different types of equilibrium gives an idea of this variety.[8]

Partial versus general equilibrium. Partial equilibrium analysis involves a single market, taking changes in the rest of the economy as outside the model, whereas general equilibrium analysis models all markets simultaneously. Clearly, partial equilibrium analysis is more limited in that it rules out important interactions between markets, but it permits more detailed analysis of processes going on within the market that is being analysed.

Perfect versus imperfect competition. Models of imperfect (or monopolistic) competition allow firms to choose the price of their own product, subject to the demand for their product. Imperfect competition is more general, but poses significant additional technical problems, especially in general equilibrium models. To get round these, models have to be greatly simplified, meaning that in some respects, models of perfect competition can be more general.

Short run versus long run. In the real world, activities take place at different speeds, and the distinction between the short and the long run is a way to tackle this problem. The standard application of this distinction is to say that firms can change their price and output very quickly, whereas building new factories or acquiring and installing new equipment takes much longer. Thus a model of the short run takes the capital stock (buildings, machinery and so on) as given, whereas a model of the long run allows firms to choose how much capital to employ. Clearly, the problem of time is a much more general one, and ideally one might have a *continuum* of runs, ranging from the minute-by-minute changing of financial asset prices to the time scale (perhaps decades) over which large-scale investment projects are undertaken.

Inter-temporal equilibrium. Equilibrium over time introduces complications beyond those discussed so far. The first is that time may enter the constraints facing agents: production takes time, so that activities today may affect output or productivity in several years' time; borrowing has to be repaid, which means, for example, that consumers face a lifetime constraint on their spending. The second is that many decisions depend on expectations concerning the future: decisions to invest, or purchase durable goods, depend on expectations of future prices and economic conditions; the value of an asset (whether financial or physical) depends on the income that asset will generate over its lifetime. This means that

8 For another account of this variety, see Chick (this volume).

modelling inter-temporal equilibrium depends on how expectations are modelled, leading to many types of equilibrium.

The simplest way to analyse equilibrium over time is the method of temporary equilibrium: this involves taking those expectations as given – as a parameter – and finding an equilibrium conditional on them. If expectations change, so too will the equilibrium. Another method is adaptive expectations equilibrium: one way to model expectations is to assume that they depend on past values of the variable concerned. There is an infinite variety of possible rules, but a commonly used one is to assume that expectations respond to current variables with a lag. It can be shown that this is equivalent to postulating that expectations depend on all past values of the variable, with recent values being given higher weight than older ones. Because such rules are backward-looking, they may generate expectations that are clearly wrong if there is a clear change in the system. Their attractions lie in their mathematical tractability and in that they base expectations on information that is in principle available to agents.

A third method is perfect-foresight equilibrium, where it is assumed that agents' expectations are correct. Note that no mechanism for achieving this is postulated, though there may be an implicit theory of learning in the background. Related to this is the fourth method, rational expectations equilibrium. This concept of equilibrium, which has become dominant in contemporary macroeconomics, assumes that agents predict everything that they could predict given the information available to them. Formally, it states that agents' expectations are given by the mathematical expectation of the relevant variable, conditional on the set of information. This raises the question of what information should be assumed available to agents, and the strong version assumes that agents know both past values of all relevant variables and the model. Finding an equilibrium involves finding a model such that, if agents use that model to form their expectations (to predict the future), their expectations will, on average, be correct. Errors in agents' expectations should be white noise.

Strategic equilibrium

A further set of equilibrium concepts arises in the context of game theory, which deals with situations where agents have to act strategically. In the classes of model discussed so far, agents are basing their decisions on prices and exogenous factors. However, in many economic situations, agents actions will depend on what they believe other agents will be doing. Suppose there are two agents or players. Player A's optimal strategy depends on what player B does. But player B's decision depends on what he or she believes A will do. Faced with this type of uncertainty, concepts of equilibrium (often referred to as 'solution concepts' to avoid the baggage associated with the term equilibrium) have proliferated. I do no more than mention some examples. These can be divided into two broad categories: non-co-operative and co-operative games.

In non-co-operative games, players decide strategies independently of each other. The most common type of non-co-operative equilibrium concept is the

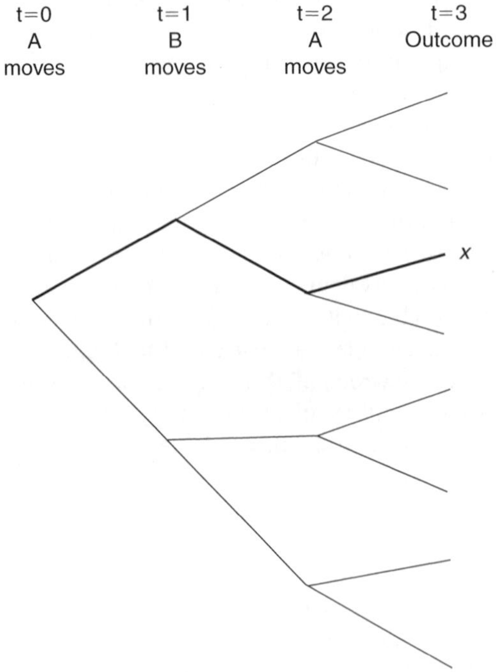

Figure 8.3 Equilibrium in a game with sequential moves.

Nash equilibrium. A Nash equilibrium is an outcome in which each player has chosen the optimal strategy given the strategy that has been played by his opponents. It is an equilibrium because neither player has any incentive to deviate from the strategy he or she has chosen. However, there are many situations where Nash equilibrium does not narrow the range of possible outcomes sufficiently to be of any use, and in response to this many other non-co-operative game concepts have been developed. The aim is to 'refine' the Nash equilibrium by finding additional criteria that the outcome should satisfy.

One example of this refinement of the Nash equilibrium is the sub-game-perfect equilibrium. This uses time consistency and backward induction to narrow the range of solutions that are possible. Suppose two players take decisions sequentially. At time zero player A chooses one of two strategies. At time one, player B plays one of two strategies. Then player A makes a further choice, and so on. The range of possible outcomes can be shown in a tree, as in Figure 8.3. If a particular outcome (say, the one that leads to outcome x) is to be an equilibrium for the whole game, it must also be an equilibrium for the various games of which it is made up – for all the branches of the tree through which it passes.

These types of equilibrium are very different from those found in co-operative games, where players do not act independently and where they may bargain with each other. For example, suppose we have two players bargaining with each other – they each have a stock of goods and are deciding what to exchange and at what price. If exchange is voluntary, we can say that the outcome will be where neither player is worse off than if they exchanged nothing. Typically, this does not determine a unique outcome, merely a range of possible outcomes. This is known as the 'core' of the game. Now suppose that there are three such players. We can apply the same rule that no one can be made worse off by participating. However, here there are additional possibilities. Players A and B might form a coalition and exclude C. Thus no allocation of resources that makes players A and B worse off than they would be if they formed such a coalition can be an equilibrium. Similarly, B and C might form a coalition, or A and C. It can be shown that the possibility of such coalitions causes the core of the game to shrink as the number of players increases. In the limit, as the number of players becomes infinite, the core shrinks to a single point, the competitive equilibrium. In such a model, equilibrium is the set of trades that are blocked by no coalition.[9]

Why the variety of equilibrium concepts matters

Several points need to be made about this discussion. The first is that choice of equilibrium concept matters: moving to a different concept of equilibrium can have a dramatic effect on a model's conclusions. The clearest illustration is perhaps provided by the contrast between adaptive (or, more generally, backward-looking) expectations and rational (forward-looking) expectations. Consider the two systems in Figure 8.4. In Figure 8.4(b), notation PP′ and VV′ refer to 'peak' and 'valley' respectively).[10] In the absence of forward-looking behaviour, configuration (a) is stable and (b) is unstable. The initial point in the diagram depends on past values of x and y, so given the configuration shown in Figure 8.4(a) there will be movement from any initial point towards the equilibrium. In contrast, in Figure 8.4(b), if the initial point is on PP′, equilibrium will be reached, but from any other point the economy will move away from equilibrium.

Now suppose, instead, that we have forward-looking expectations, and that variable y is the variable that responds to expectations (for example, the sterling–dollar exchange rate, or an index of share prices) and that x is a variable that moves more slowly (such as real output, or trade flows). Given an initial value of x, y will jump to the value that agents perceive to be correct.

9 As with non-co-operative games, there are innumerable other equilibrium concepts. It is perhaps worth mentioning the Nash bargain (not to be confused with the Nash equilibrium). This is a solution to a two-player bargaining problem that shows what will happen if the two players have equal bargaining power. Unlike the core, which is typically not unique in the case of two players, the Nash bargain is usually unique.

10 I do not wish to place any economic interpretation on them. Because of economists' fondness for two-dimensional models the solutions to which can be analysed graphically, there are thousands of economic models the solutions of which look like one or other of these diagrams.

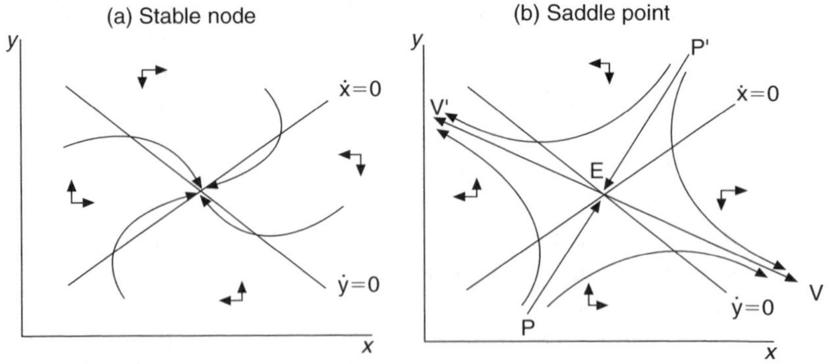

Figure 8.4 Stability with backward and forward-looking expectations.

Figure 8.4(a) poses a problem, for there is an infinite number of values of y that lead to equilibrium, resulting in indeterminacy. In contrast, in Figure 8.4(b), y should jump to the value on PP′, for this is the only value that leads to equilibrium.[11] This means that, with backward-looking expectations, finding a solution to the model involves finding a system such as that described in Figure 8.4(a), whereas under forward-looking expectations it means finding one like that described in Figure 8.4(b).

The second point to be made is that the context is rarely sufficient to determine the equilibrium concept that should be used. Problems can be solved using different models; even within the same type of model, different concepts of equilibrium can be used. There are many reasons for this. Take assumptions about expectations. There are strong theoretical arguments against both rational expectations and backward-looking expectations: both are simplifications that sometimes yield plausible results but in other contexts can yield nonsensical ones. The economist has to decide which is best for the particular problem in hand. Obviously fashion and conventional judgements play a role in economists' theoretical choices, but fashions can and do change, sometimes rapidly: usually it is because certain assumptions are found not to work. How this is done will depend on the level of problem being tackled. For Type III problems, the economist may be able to test alternative models against data, though the Duhem–Quine thesis, stating the under-determination of theories by data, means that inferences about individual assumptions (rational or adaptive expectations) are very much matters of judgement. For Type II problems, on the other hand (and *a fortiori* for Type I problems), such a decision criterion may not be available. Problems concern markets or economies in general, and the appropriate set of assumptions may differ from case to case. All the economist has to go on are theoretical arguments (which may not be decisive) and lessons from individual

11 This overlooks complications, such as why paths that do not lead to E will not be chosen. These complications may matter in evaluating particular models, but this account is sufficient to make the point that the method by which expectations are modelled make a fundamental difference.

case studies (which may not illustrate all possibilities, even when they admit of clear interpretations).

The third point is that the concept of equilibrium, *per se*, carries no ontological baggage. The method of equilibrium analysis, which involves postulating models and then searching for equilibrium, is to do with solving models – with establishing their properties. Equilibrium is defined in relation to the model, and is not necessarily a property of the real world. As an example, take the concept of involuntary unemployment:

> [I]nvoluntary unemployment is not a fact or a phenomenon which it is the task of theorists to explain. It is, on the contrary, a theoretical construct which Keynes introduced in the hope it would be helpful in discovering a correct explanation for a genuine phenomenon: large-scale fluctuations in measured, total unemployment.
>
> (Lucas 1981, p. 243)[12]

Lucas went on to say that it was not meaningful to ask whether a worker was voluntarily or involuntarily unemployed: to talk of involuntary unemployment was simply to abdicate from any attempt to explain unemployment in terms of individual decisions. To talk about equilibrium is to talk about human behaviour. Of course, a specific concept of equilibrium may link closely to an assertion about the real world. Steady-state growth, for example, is an equilibrium concept that has clear implications: measurements tell us whether an economy is in such an equilibrium. What is being claimed here is that there are so many concepts of equilibrium, and so many ways they can be used, that statements about the ontology implied by equilibrium have to be made case by case.

Evaluating economists' use of equilibrium models

Critics of mainstream economics have often focused on the assumption of equilibrium; two of the most well known are Kaldor (1972) and Joan Robinson (1974). There are many reasons why their critiques need to be treated with considerable caution. One is that the term 'equilibrium' has so many meanings that critiques of it can encompass a wide variety of arguments. Kaldor, for example, focused explicitly on general equilibrium theory, by which he meant the theory of Arrow and Debreu. In response, Frank Hahn (1984) pointed out that such models are not intended to depict reality: their point is to provide a counterfactual analysis of what would be required if the economic system were to work perfectly, the failure of these conditions implying that it will be flawed. This meaning of equilibrium in such models bears little relation to that which lies behind Robinson's critique, which focuses on historical time and dynamics. Another important reason for caution is that economists' use of the term 'equilibrium' has changed very significantly since the time of Robinson's work.

12 See De Vroey (2004, ch. 14) for a discussion of Lucas's use of equilibrium.

Robinson's critique focused on the mechanical notion of equilibrium, as it underlies supply-and-demand analysis: equilibrium as a point of rest. In the 1960s (and early 1970s) there was some justification for thinking that this applied to a significant body of economic theory. However, the move towards arguing in terms of inter-temporal equilibrium that took place during the 1970s made it much less relevant. It is natural to think in terms of the equilibrium of supply and demand in mechanical terms as a centre of gravitation. However, in an inter-temporal model, where forward-looking expectations link one period and the next, this may not make sense, for supply and demand do not exist independently of expectations and are as volatile as the prices they are supposed to determine. In an inter-temporal equilibrium, prices and expectations are determined simultaneously and equilibrium ceases to conform to the mechanical analogy: we do not tend towards it. Either we are in it or we are not. Or so it seems. Similar problems arise with strategic equilibria. Mechanical analogies, in any meaningful sense, break down. Furthermore, in models with forward-looking expectations, there is no implication that an equilibrium will be static in any sense: 'The idea that an economic system in equilibrium is in any sense "at rest" is simply an anachronism' (Lucas 1980, p. 708). There are equilibrium models against which Robinson's critique is valid, but it is not a critique of equilibrium in general.

However, what I wish to argue is that equilibrium models should be evaluated not according to whether they conform to beliefs about what the world is like, but in terms of their problem solving ability, where this refers to problems posed by our experience of the real world. If this argument is accepted, it suggests that it is difficult to argue that the use of equilibrium analysis is, *in principle*, flawed. The judgement has to be a pragmatic one – does the use of equilibrium methods work better than other methods? This perspective seems appropriate, given the methodological eclecticism that has characterised economics in the past twenty years: the discipline appears to have been driven by a search for methods that work, not through any commitment to a particular notion of equilibrium. It thus seems reasonable to suggest that it is inappropriate to refer to valid or invalid uses of equilibrium analysis without specifying the problems that are being considered.

Lawson's critique of equilibrium theorising (1997, 2003) is based on the argument that the methods of mainstream economics are mismatched with the reality to which they are being applied. His reasons for this claim have been developed in too much detail for it to be possible to summarise them adequately in a couple of sentences, but in general his argument is that the social realm (the realm to which economics applies) has certain properties and that the methods of mainstream economics rest on assumptions that negate those properties. Deductive theories apply to closed systems, whereas the social realm is open. The social realm is internally related, whereas mainstream theories isolate its various aspects. Human behaviour is transformational, whereas utility-maximising agents with given preferences can do no more than respond rigidly and mechanically to circumstances. Although there are several different aspects to it,

Lawson's argument is essentially ontological. I suggest that, because the social realm is very complex, such a general ontological argument is inappropriate. The salient features of the social realm – and hence the appropriate ontology – cannot be identified in the abstract, but only in relation to specific problems. Interestingly, Lawson does acknowledge that economics has 'modelling successes' but concludes that the conditions under which they occur 'appear *a posteriori* not to be typical of the social realm' (Lawson 2003, pp. 20–1). However, perhaps there is no set of conditions that is 'typical': perhaps the social realm is such that the range of appropriate methods is too large for such a claim to be make sense. Lawson would appear to recognise this, in that he argues for greater pluralism, but the argument presented here raises doubts about the ontology on which his critique of mainstream economics is based. However, my suggestion is that taking seriously the idea that economics is primarily a problem-solving discipline has implications for the principle of ontologically based critiques of economics; it also raises significant questions concerning whether greater pluralism would *in practice* be better than the *status quo*; my suggestion is that there are good reasons why pluralism is probably desirable but pluralism has costs and it is, at least in principle, possible that these costs outweigh the benefits.[13]

Conclusion

This chapter argues the case for taking a pragmatic view, influenced by Laudan (1977), of economic theories and methods, and, hence, of notions of equilibrium. Despite the proliferation of abstract theory, economics is, at heart, a problem-solving discipline in the sense defined above. The attempt to integrate the whole of economics under the umbrella of general equilibrium theory expired more than a quarter of a century ago. Attempts are made to claim that game theory provides an alternative, and more general, organising framework, defining 'the method of economics'. However, as behavioural and experimental economics, not to mention the 'iceberg' of less formal applied work that lies beneath the more visible economic theory, demonstrate, that objective is unlikely to be realised.[14] Not only have consciously heterodox groups proliferated, but so too has variety within the mainstream. The latter has been driven not so much by criticism from outsiders as from the development of new theories and techniques from within – from what has been described as the tendency of mainstream economics to subvert itself deriving theories and methods that call into question ideas that had previously been accepted.[15] Equilibrium has become such an extremely elastic notion, with different concepts of equilibrium being used to solve different problems. Though many economists talk as though they are committed to the notion of equilibrium, the meaning of equilibrium is liable to change when new methods are discovered that enable new problems to be

13 Backhouse (2001) pursues this theme in more detail.

14 Cf. Backhouse (2002, ch. 14).

15 See, for example, Bateman (2004) for an excellent illustration of this.

tackled, and as a result the commitment to equilibrium means little more than a commitment to solving models.

This chapter, therefore, makes two related claims. The first is that a pragmatic or even pragmatist approach centred on solving real-world economic problems fits very well what is going on within economics: that economics is, despite appearances to the contrary, driven by the need to solve problems, and that doing this has so far proved incompatible (except in the short term) with rigid commitment to any one concept of equilibrium. When taken together with the complexity of the socio-economic realm, this explains why concepts of equilibrium and the way in which they are used have proliferated. The second is that such an approach offers an appropriate framework within which to evaluate economists' use of the method of equilibrium analysis. If one accepts this, it becomes very difficult to argue that the method of equilibrium analysis is *in general* flawed or inappropriate for economics; the case for or against equilibrium methods has to be made in relation to specific equilibrium concepts, and it has to be made problem by problem.

References

Backhouse, R.E. (1977), *Truth and Progress in Economic Knowledge*, Edward Elgar, Aldershot.

Backhouse, R.E. (2000), 'Progress in heterodox economics', *Journal of the History of Economic Thought*, 22 (2), 149–55.

Backhouse, R.E. (2001), 'On the credentials of methodological pluralism', in *Economics Broadly Considered. Essays in Honor of Warren J. Samuels*, in J.E. Biddle, J.B. Davis, and S.G. Medema (eds), 161–9, Routledge, London.

Backhouse, R.E. (2002), *The Penguin History of Economics/The Ordinary Business of Life*, London: Penguin Books, Princeton University Press, Princeton, NJ.

Backhouse, R.E. and Laidler, D. (2004), 'What was lost with IS-LM', *History of Political Economy*, annual supplement to Volume 36, *The IS-LM Model. Its Rise, Fall, and Strange Persistence*, M. De Vroey and K.D. Hoover (eds), 25–56, Duke University Press, Durham, NC.

Bateman, B.W. (2004), 'Review of *A History of Post-Keynesian Economics*, by John King', *History of Political Economy*, 36 (3), 581–3.

Cartwright, N. (2002), 'The limits of causal order, from economics to physics', in *Fact and Fiction in Economics. Models, Realism and Social Construction*, U. Maki (ed.), 137–51, Cambridge University Press, Cambridge.

Coats, A.W.B. (2000), 'The progress of heterodox economics', in *Evolution and Path-Dependence in Economic Ideas*, P. Garrouste and S. Ioannides (eds), Edward Elgar, Aldershot.

De Vroey, M. (2004), *Involuntary Unemployment. The Elusive Quest for a Theory*, Routledge, London.

Friedman, M. (1953), 'The methodology of positive economics', *Essays in Positive Economics*, M. Friedman (ed.), Chicago University Press, Chicago.

Gibbard, A. and Varian, H.R. (1978), 'Economic models', *Journal of Philosophy*, 75 (11), 644–77.

Hahn, F. (1984), *Equilibrium and Macroeconomics*, Blackwell, Oxford.

Hoover, K.D. (2002), 'Econometrics and reality', in *Fact and Fiction in Economics. Models, Realism and Social Construction*, U. Maki (ed.), 152–77, Cambridge University Press, Cambridge.

Kaldor, N. (1972), 'The irrelevance of equilibrium economics', *Economic Journal*, 82, 1237–55.

Kuhn, T. (1970), *The Structure of Scientific Revolutions*, University of Chicago Press, Chicago.

Laudan, L. (1977), *Progress and its Problems*, Routledge and Kegan Paul, London.

Lawson, T. (1997), *Economics and Reality*, Routledge, London.

Lawson, T. (2003) *Reorienting Economics*, Routledge, London.

Leontief, W.A. (1971), 'Theoretical assumptions and non-observed facts', *American Economic Review*, 61, 1–7.

Lucas, R.E. (1980), 'Methods and problems of business cycle theory', *Journal of Money, Credit and Banking*, 12 (4), 696–715.

Lucas, R.E. (1981) *Studies in Business Cycle Theory*, MIT Press, Cambridge, MA.

Robinson, J. (1974), 'History versus equilibrium', *Indian Economic Journal*, 21 (3), 202–13.

9 Equilibrium analysis

A middlebrow view

Warren J. Samuels

Controversy over equilibrium analysis is deconstructed, identifying several dichotomies, including equilibrium as an analytical tool and a definition of reality; two different types of realism; study of an actual economy and of a pure a-institutional conceptual model; ontological and epistemological considerations. Further complications include the complexity of the economy, multiple positions on each point; and the pragmatist nature of practice. The economics of disequilibration, disequilibrium and equilibration is advanced as potentially richer than that of determinacy, existence, uniqueness and stability of equilibrium solutions, though neither group has superior ontological status over the other. Also praised is the scope of Vilfredo Pareto's equilibrium analysis.

> There is *no established* economic usage for anything in economics.
>
> (Frank Knight 2005 [1933], p. 35)

The controversy over equilibrium in economics continues, leaving those who care about the issues in disequilibrium or disruption, certainly in disagreement. The controversy has so many elements, so many side issues, and so many differences in definition of so many terms, to which are added unreasonable, even exaggerated, claims, that it is not surprising that any considerable measure of agreement on issues, including just what the issues are, is so difficult to attain.

The bundle of disagreements that must be deconstructed involves the multiple intersections of several dichotomies: one dichotomy distinguishes between equilibrium as an analytical tool and a definition of reality. Another dichotomy contrasts two modes of doing economics, the study of a pure a-institutional conceptual model and the study of actual economies. Equilibrium as an analytical tool can be utilised in both types of studies, though it is frequently associated with the study of a pure conceptual model. Equilibrium analysis can also be applied to the study of actual economies; however, because of its conventional focus on problems of determinacy, existence, uniqueness and stability of equilibrium solutions, its role there has severe limitations because of certain important exclusions. Another dichotomy is that of deduction and induction, complicated by the operation of abduction. The relevant features include the following: that deduction does not yield truth, only validity; that induction is not much use in the case of pure conceptual models; that mathematics is both a tool and a deductive system; that deduction, induction, fact and theory are all theoretical; that each of the combinations of deduction and induction, and fact and theory, involves abstraction but also contributes to the process of abduction; and that, in all the foregoing, the result is fictive and utopian. A further dichotomy which contributes to complexity and disagreement juxtaposes the ontological to the epistemological significance of the foregoing. Still other sources of disagreement include the relevance of pragmatism and the meaning of realism. The basis for these dichotomies and other complications is the enormous complexity of the subject-matter of economics, the wide range of relevant methodological (ontological and epistemological) considerations, and the desire of economists to be recognised as doing science.

One would think that economists, of all people, would most readily appreciate the relevance of the principle of opportunity cost. The adoption of any one definition out of many, any one application out of many, and so on, necessarily incurs the cost of the forgone alternatives. Every forgone alternative necessarily raises problems. If equilibrium analysis centres on the conditions of equilibrium rather than the economics of disequilibrium and of equilibration, inattention to these latter constitutes cost, no less so than ignoring the former. Practitioners of each equilibrist agenda must recognise both opportunity cost and that identifying equilibrium economics in terms of only one use is a matter of selective perception, training and preference. Disagreements also have other sources, including the neoclassical research protocol. The protocol enforces the production of unique solutions in a world in which there are few if any of them. The defence is the same as that of equilibrium economics, namely to serve as a check on reasoning and analysis. Putting the matter that way raises the question of whether equilibrium analysis is a tool (or methodological assumption) or a definition of reality. All these and other issues must be unpacked and deconstructed.

It is because the economy is so complex and so multi-faceted, because each facet can be approached from a number of different standpoints, and because neither any one theory nor any one model can answer all our questions, that theoretical pluralism, pluralism of methods or techniques and methodological pluralism are warranted.[1] '[E]quilibrium *is* a central organising idea' (Hahn 1984, p. 43, quoted by Lawson 2005a, p. 424, emphasis added) and it is indispensable (Backhouse 2004, p. 301). But so too are disequilibrium and

1 Backhouse (2004, p. 297) thus writes, 'Economics is not simple'. In his contribution to this volume, Backhouse writes that 'mainly because of the complexity of the economic world, relationships between different types of problems and the different types of theories that relate to them are much more complicated than might be expected'.

equilibration, for without them equilibrium economics may well be 'irrelevant' and 'treacherous' (Kaldor 1972 and Robinson 1956, p. 59, both quoted by Lawson 2005a, p. 425).

The following attempts to make sense of most of what is involved and to outline a reasonable position. I write as an open-minded eclectic who appreciates the difficulties of being one and who, further, fully accepts the self-referential nature of his own position. For example, I consider my model of the interrelation of legal and economic processes to analyse correctly some of the field's most fundamental elements, but I also appreciate the epistemological and ontological considerations which render the model problematic.

Conceptual and actual economy

Economists pursue two different relevant modes of doing economics. One mode deals with an abstract pure conceptual a-institutional economy bearing no necessary relation to any actual economy. The other mode deals with an actual economy(ies) and the institutional arrangements that both instantiate and distinguish it from other economies. The study of markets can tend to be restricted to a simple, conceptual price mechanism operating in a pure conceptual, a-institutional market, or it can focus on an actual market(s) in all its complexities and include, *inter alia*, the study of the factors – firms, governments, etc. – that help form and operate through actual markets. In the former, resource allocation is a function of the abstract pure conceptual price mechanism without attention to the institutions that in actual economies control the formation of markets and the working of the price mechanism therein.

The foremost expression of these two modes of doing economics has been given by George Shackle:

> There is the world of what we take to be 'real' objects, persons, institutions and events; on the axis of abstract–concrete this world is at the concrete pole. There is the logical or mathematical construct or machine, a piece of pure reasoning, almost of 'pure mathematics', able to exist in its own right of internal coherence, as a system of mere relations amongst undefined thought-entities; this world lies at the abstract pole. And between these two worlds there lies the world of names, linking the real-world elements with the undefined entities of the abstract machine.
>
> (Shackle 1967, p. 294)

Part of the problem of making sense of equilibrium, therefore, is its relation to these two modes of doing economics. This aspect is typically mixed up with other aspects, but deconstruction of equilibrium must proceed one step at a time.

Tony Lawson has, in criticism, made a number of points, in part through underscoring the views of earlier theorists. In his chapter in this book he argues that modern economics fails to distinguish the properties of the models from the properties of the social reality the models aim to represent, and elides altogether the distinction between the two. Elsewhere, Lawson has contrasted the status of determinateness of equilibrium in the two modes of doing economics. Determinateness, he says,

> is precisely a property of relations used to describe the economic system, whereas a *balance of forces* is an aspect of the economy, one that each equation is said to represent. The former is a property of the theoretical conception; the latter is thought to be a property of what the theoretical conception is about. The former is theoretic, the latter ontic.
>
> (Lawson 2005a, p. 431)

Several points. First, those who work in the abstract or conceptual domain have increasingly rebutted criticism by saying that their work is not directly related to the concrete domain of actual economies, though this leaves them open to the charge of being engaged only in puzzle solving. More important, they readily apply reasoning and conclusions from the conceptual domain to the domain of actual economies, typically without attending to Shackle's third domain, 'the world of names, linking the real-world elements with the undefined entities of the abstract machine'. Second, by referring to actual economies as ontic, Lawson is going beyond identifying an aspect of all work (see below) and privileging the status of actual economies because they exist and the conceptual domain is only imaginary. Third, as Lawson argues, the application of equilibrium analysis to the concrete and the conceptual domains involves very different circumstances. Equilibrium readily exists in the conceptual world; it is not an observable feature of actual economies; it is an import from the conceptual to the actual world.

Not surprisingly, therefore, Lawson relishes Hahn's statement that 'it cannot be denied that there is something scandalous in the spectacle of so many people refining the analyses of economic [equilibrium] states which they give no reason to suppose will ever, or have ever, come about' (Lawson 2005a, pp. 433–4, quoting Hahn 1984, pp. 88–9). Actually, there is no reason so to suppose, given the existence of the two domains. But many people have elided or conflated the two. Those working primarily in the conceptual sphere have resisted importation from the concrete sphere of the actual economy, while being willing to export, although now most people recognise the impropriety thereof, given, especially, the a-institutional nature of the concrete sphere.

The accuracy of Hahn's just quoted statement as a positive rather than a normative proposition is underscored by the following more obviously positive propositions: 'Existing economics is a theoretical system which floats in the air and which bears little relation to what happens in the real world' (Coase 1999, p. 2, quoted in Lawson 2005a, p. 427) and, once one abstracts from the first sentence of the following:

> Modern economics is sick. Economics has increasingly become an intellectual game played for its own sake and not for its practical consequences for

> understanding the [actual] economic world. Economists have converted the subject into a sort of social mathematics in which analytical rigor is everything and practical relevance is nothing.
>
> (Blaug 1997, p. 3, quoted in Lawson 2005a, p. 428)

and, straight to the positive point: 'The great virtue of mathematical reasoning in economics is that by its precise account of assumptions it becomes crystal clear that applications to the "real" world could at best be provisional' (Hahn 1994, p. 246, quoted in Lawson 2005a, p. 434). Lawson thus further argues that 'equilibrium is merely a solution concept for a model, a property of a system of equations' (Lawson 2005a, p. 435) and quotes Dixon to that end: 'At its most general, we can say that "equilibrium" is a method of solving economic models. At a superficial level, an equilibrium is simply a solution to a set of equations' (Dixon 1990, p. 356, quoted in Lawson 2005a, p. 435).

Lawson also quotes Hayek:

> I am certain that there are many who regard with impatience and distrust the whole tendency, which is inherent in all modern equilibrium analysis, to turn economics into a branch of pure logic, a set of self-evident propositions which, like mathematics or geometry, are subject to no other test but internal consistency.
>
> (Hayek 1937, p. 35, quoted in Lawson 2005a, p. 438)

and again,

> I am now getting to a stage where it becomes exceedingly difficult to say what exactly are the assumptions on the basis of which we assert that there will be a tendency toward equilibrium, and to claim that our analysis has an application to the real world.
>
> (Hayek 1937, p. 47, quoted in Lawson 2005a, p. 440)

The disjunction between the two domains is raised by Roy Weintraub in his discussion of the applicability of equilibrium, to which end he quotes Dorfman *et al.* (1958, p. 351, quoted in Weintraub 2005, p. 450), who say that 'It is the *model* we are analyzing, not the world'. Weintraub's principal relevant argument is, of course, that Lawson's 'distinction between the theoretic and ontic "nature" of equilibrium in fact reflects the contingencies of how equilibrium was manifest in mathematical discourse in different periods of time' (Weintraub 2005, p. 450). We shall see below that the mathematics can affect the economics, but for now the distinction between the two spheres is itself important.

Roger Backhouse's (2004) paper, which contains a partial defence of equilibrium economics, first notes Joan Robinson's distinction between logical time and historical time; in the present context, this is emblematic of the distinction between conceptual and actual economies (Backhouse 2004, p. 291). He emphasises the problem of 'the relation between economic models and the real world'

(p. 298), though I will show below that the matter is more complicated: the production and use of models, technically defined, takes place in both domains, and are interdependent with each other. Backhouse urges that 'Adam Smith and most of the classical economists', in talking about 'equilibrium, or a center of gravitation . . . were making claims about the real world. . . . In most contemporary economics, on the other hand, statements about equilibrium are typically statements about models . . . [which] refer to properties of abstract systems' (p. 298). Backhouse thus accepts the importance of the distinction between conceptual and actual economies. That his title juxtaposes history and equilibrium, and his text juxtaposes models and the real world, only blends points and interferes with seeing the elements of our problem separately. A particularly interesting illustration of this is his report on Hahn's argument that 'the Arrow–Debreu theorems about Pareto efficiency and general competitive equilibrium show what would have to be necessary if the invisible hand were to operate efficiently. Because the model relies on assumptions that could not possibly be true of any real-world economy, it follows that the invisible hand cannot work perfectly' (p. 298).[2]

Backhouse also acknowledges Christopher Bliss's criticisms of equilibrium economics in which 'things are assumed to be constant which are certainly not constant, though that is indeed a tendency' and 'that factors which ought to be analysed and made the subject of economic theories remain un-analysed or are analysed only crudely' and adds that 'In all these discussions there is a tension between equilibrium being a completely neutral mathematical tool, akin to the concept of a solution, and something with economic content' (Backhouse 2004, p. 300, in part quoting Bliss 1975, p. 125), which helps explain why equilibrium analysis, while used in both domains, is much more used in doing conceptual economics than in studying actual economies (to which some pure theorists likely would reply, so much the worse for the latter). As we shall note below, the significance of mathematics is even greater than this. One aspect centres on the impact of the mathematics on the economic content of the formalist analysis. (Surely the study of actual, as opposed to conceptual, economies is influenced by non-economic considerations; so the impact of mathematics is not unique.) Another aspect concerns the 'many problems for which formal methods cannot yet provide the solution and it seems reasonable to conjecture that *this will always be the case*' (Backhouse 2004, p. 303) – presumably both would also apply to recursive and non-linear mathematics).

In his chapter in this book, Backhouse notes that certain economic models are mathematical structures that are perceived to reveal something about the world while being clearly distinct from the world. In some cases, the models may not even depict the processes by which real-world agents are believed to achieve the outcomes specified by the models, as, for instance, in the case of 'as-if profit maximisation'.

2 Backhouse quotes Hahn thus: 'This negative side of Arrow–Debreu equilibrium I consider almost to be sufficient justification for it, since practical men and ill trained theorists everywhere in the world do not understand what they are claiming to be the case when they claim a beneficent and coherent role for the invisible hand.' (Hahn 1984, p. 52, quoted by Backhouse 2004, p. 298.)

The distinction between the conceptual and the actual economy is important in itself. The distinction does not, however, mean that there is no mutual influence. How each is developed can have influence on economists' work on the other. For example, in a quite different field, we read that 'theoretical models of molecular structure . . . can be carriers of specific information about structures of real molecules', even though, while 'theoretical models can be well corroborated empirically, they cannot be treated as representations of real empirical systems but can play a very important role in experimental practice' (Zeidler 2000, p. 17).

Thus we see that studying the actual (or the concrete) economy and studying the conceptual economies are two different modes of doing economics *and* that the use of equilibrium analysis has different connotations as between them. I have myself earlier written that 'The significance (and limits of significance) of equilibrium results differs between such uses as equilibrium within the confines of a particular model [in the conceptual domain] and equilibrium in the actual economy' (Samuels 1997, p. 78).

Furthermore, *à propos* of the difference between the conceptual world and the actual world, both the actual and conceptual worlds are creations of mankind and do not exist independent of mankind. However, the actual world does exist in the here and now, whereas the conceptual world exists in the here and now only in the minds of its users (as we shall see below) as a tool of analysis. As for the ontological status of equilibrium, it has no existence independent of mankind; in the conceptual world, equilibrium exists only in its contemplation by users of the concept; the world of the actual economy offers almost as much richness. Inasmuch as the conceptual economy is a mental construction of economists, there can be as many conceptual models, theories and concepts as are putatively useful, given the interests of economists. As we shall see below, in this context equilibrium analysis is a tool in both conceptual and actual markets.

Similarly we can distinguish the conceptual notion of a market from actual markets: conceptual markets have no independent existence, existing only in their contemplation by users of the concept; actual markets are driven by institutions/power as well as actions motivated and/or legitimised by the concept; equilibrium analysis can be used as a tool. Our knowledge of conceptual economies is hypothetical; conceptual economies do not exist. Our knowledge of actual economies is severely limited: complicated by deduction yielding only logicality and induction being inconclusive as well as by wishful thinking, normativism and prescriptive versus credentialist epistemology. And economists tend to treat concepts as if they were, or were directly representative of, the actual economy and as if they had ontological existence, which they do not have. (The reader's attention is called to the two different meanings of realism identified below, one as the alternative to pure conceptualism and the other attributing absolute and ultimate ontological status of existence.)

But the conceptual–actual dichotomy is only one dimension of our problem; we have more to unpack.

The ubiquity of abstraction

The conceptual economy is an abstraction from actual economies, in the sense that its component elements are derived from our imagination and intellect applied to our experience with and knowledge of actual economies. The component elements bear no close, perhaps even no remote, relation to any actual economy. It is Alfred Marshall's *ceteris paribus* with a vengeance. The actual economy with which we work, however, the actual economy in our head, so to speak, is also, and necessarily, an abstraction. No mode of doing economics can possibly include every aspect of an economy. Nor would we want it to. It would be too burdensome, much beyond our capabilities and, differently from time to time, our immediate interests. While a pure conceptual economy, properly understood, has no direct connection with any actual economy, the picture of an actual economy abstracts from much, likely very much, of its content. (See Backhouse 2004, pp. 301–2.)

Abstraction can readily become hypostatisation or reification. Generalisations can be made on the basis of examples – or wholes can be constructed from parts – and then the generalisation or the whole can be treated as if it had its own independent existence. As such it can be used, perhaps unwittingly by some, as an idealisation of whatever it covers.

Abstraction, as is taught in Principles courses, is a tool with which the number of active variables is reduced to a manageable few and/or those somehow deemed most important (perhaps on the basis of theory, seemingly involving circularity but actually comprising abduction) and holding the remaining, excluded variables stable or constant under the rule of *ceteris paribus*. Equilibrium analysis, as will be developed below, is also a tool and supplements general abstraction. It is useful in tracing out the logical if not also the substantive consequences of changing one (or more) variables in a model.

Fiction and utopia

Because practitioners of both modes of doing economics deal with abstractions, almost totally so in the case of the pure conceptual economy and largely so in the case of so-called actual economies, the stories they tell qualify as fiction – in the case of an economics deemed scientific, science fiction. I say that not to denigrate but to be accurate and consistent. This is true of neoclassical economics and of every other school of economics – and of every school of every social science. Status emulation, professionalisation and ego, as well as the conventional fiction–non-fiction distinction (which is a matter of usage and not of the ultimate nature of things) – make this hard to accept. Indeed, the description of conceptual economics as dealing with an economy that does not exist, and likely cannot exist, also comports with the definition of a utopia – a good place that is no place (Samuels 2003).

À propos of fiction, we have already seen Lawson's use of statements from Coase ('a theoretical system which floats in the air and which bears little relation to what happens in the real world' (Coase 1999, p. 2, quoted in Lawson 2005a,

p. 427)) and from Hahn ('spectacle of so many people refining the analyses of economic [equilibrium] states which they give no reason to suppose will ever, or have ever, come about' (Hahn 1970, pp. 88–9, quoted in Lawson 2005a, pp. 433–4; Hahn none the less also wrote that 'equilibrium is a central organising idea' in economics (Lawson 2005a, p. 424, quoting Hahn 1984, p. 43)). Lawson also quotes Hayek's indication of his 'concern with the admittedly fictitious state of equilibrium' (Hayek 1937, pp. 43–4, quoted in Lawson 2005a, p. 439). Lawson (2005a, p. 426) himself writes of the neoclassical reliance on 'constructs recognised as quite fictitious'.

Not only has the general term 'fiction' been used but the somewhat more specific terms 'figure of speech' and 'metaphor' also have been used. Several authors have quoted Robinson's dictum that, *à propos* of the balance of forces analogy, the 'metaphor of equilibrium is treacherous' (Lawson 2005a, pp. 425, 437; Backhouse 2004, pp. 293, 294, quoting Robinson 1956, p. 59). Backhouse (2004, p. 293) also cites Machlup to the same effect.

Agreement on the fiction description is obviously found on all sides, shall we say, of the equilibrium issue. Such usage is not confined to economics. *Black's Law Dictionary* treats legal fiction in a manner that, generalising from several case holdings, may be summarised as follows:

> A legal *fiction* is an assumption or supposition or rule of law that something which is or may be false is true, or that a state of facts exists which has never really taken place, or that something is assumed to be true and will not be allowed to be disproved, something which is false, but not improbable.
>
> (Black 1968, p. 751)

The concept of equilibrium is a metaphor, perhaps some other figure of speech. It is also a story design and, as will be seen below, a tool. It is a story design, therefore a tool, in so far as it is used to define economic 'reality' and to structure the stories told by economists. As such, it is one of numerous designs of this kind; it also exemplifies the intellectual prolificacy but also fragility, ambiguity and inconclusiveness of human reason and rhetoric.

Consider the proposition. The invisible hand is the competitive market which generates, *inter alia*, equilibrium. The locution 'invisible hand' is widely seen as a metaphor (or some other figure of speech). The term 'market' is one of some four dozen candidates for the identity of the invisible hand but many people consider that it, too, is a metaphor. The term 'competitive', like the other two, has been defined in numerous ways, and it, too, can be said to be a metaphor. So we may have in the original proposition one metaphor said to be defined by another metaphor which is itself modified by still another metaphor. It is predicaments like this, which are rampant in economics, that render economics ambiguous and unable to answer the problems or questions addressed to it in a dispositive manner. And it is this framework in which equilibrium, perhaps still another metaphor, is embedded. The controversy over equilibrium seems puny in comparison.

The claim may be voiced that the necessity of abstraction does not convey *carte blanche* to invent fictions, especially to make the wrong abstractions. But to claim that a wrong abstraction has been made is to make a substantive claim about a process which in itself (when properly executed, i.e. without technical errors) is not a matter of right or wrong. The abstraction bears no, or no necessary, relation to actual economies. The error arises when a methodological assumption in the conceptual domain is used to describe or otherwise apply to actual economies. In any event, if, as is argued below, equilibrium is principally a tool and not basically a definition of reality, though it can be applied to actual economies, it is largely irrelevant to actual economies in terms of truth versus falsity.

If, as Hahn wrote, equilibrium is a central organising idea in economics, then it is obvious that there is much incoherence in economics; that is certainly the case with another seeming foundational idea, the invisible hand. Yet words are tools too.

Words and language in general both define and structure the world for us. The world may be, ontologically, as a language defines and structures it; but it may not. Language expresses ideas, but these ideas need not and probably never have a given, transcendent, independent existence. Many words used in all schools of economics are primitive terms. They are undefined and their user relies on others to provide definitions satisfactory to them. If primitive undefined term X is given different definitions or identifications by different auditors or readers, it may be said that they all accept X but, because each defines X in their own way, the level of agreement is almost non-existent.

That which is represented by words may or may not be indicative of anything real in what below is called the Realism II sense. To have meaning does not necessarily equate with having reality in that sense.

Fact and theory

It is now widely, if somewhat reluctantly, recognised that fact and theory are not self-subsistent but are interrelated. Facts are theory-laden; they do not impose themselves on a *tabula rasa*. Facts are seen as such on the basis of some theory or other framing device. Theories are derived from facts seen in a particular way. Definitions, in matters that pertain to the present discussion, tend to predicate and give effect to some theory.

Deduction, induction and abduction

Any study proceeds in terms of deduction or induction, or, more likely, their combination, abduction. Deduction is the process of reasoning from premise(s) to conclusions in accordance with a system of logic. Deduction depends upon aprioristic specifications of fact or data, which define the premises, as well as the system of logic. The result of deduction is a valid conclusion. Validity is not, or not necessarily, truth; to call a proposition or line of deduction valid is only to say that its system of logic has been properly used, given the premises from which deduction commenced. Euclidean and non-Euclidean geometries are a case in point. They begin with a fundamental difference in premise and reach diametrically opposite but valid conclusions as to the number of degrees in a triangle. Both happen to be true under certain (and not other) circumstances. Euclidean geometry holds for a plane (two-dimensional); non-Euclidean geometry, for curved space (three-dimensional).

Induction is a process of deriving knowledge from empirical experience based upon a system of handling sense data. Induction depends upon aprioristic deductive theories governing the perception of what is experienced, measured and/or sensed. Each exercise of induction embraces a specific formulation of a particular theory (the hypothesis), the specific domain or social space or data to which it is proposed to apply and by which tested, the specific mode of inductive logic to be used (e.g. statistical techniques), and the decision rule by which the result is to be accepted or rejected. The inductive conclusion may not apply to other formulations of the hypothesis, other domains (data sets), other modes of inductive logic and other decision rules. Strictly speaking, the affirmative conclusion applies to (is true for) only the social space, etc., of the particular test undertaken. Because some other formulation of the test may result in negative conclusions, one cannot conclude on the basis of one or more (but not all possible) affirmative tests that the hypothesis is true, and vice versa.

Also, while one hypothesis could explain a result, a particular result can be generated by several different causes. R or S can lead to T. Whether the instant case of T is caused by R or S becomes the point at issue (for explanatory and/or policy purposes). That R can cause T is not sufficient to conclude that R, rather than S, has caused T in a particular case.

The nature of theory as hypothesis has been examined above. One other term warrants notice: model. A theory as hypothesis has properly all the foregoing elements, from its specific statement to its decision rule. A model, by contrast, is a group of variables structured in a particular way. A model lacks most if not all of the elements of a theory and is therefore inconclusive, especially if it is a tautology or truism. Models require amplification and specification; theories as hypotheses *qua* hypotheses properly come fully equipped. Although models are different from theories and both are means of abstraction, it is possible to think that models are more abstract than theories, because of all the omitted elements; but nothing primary to this chapter turns on that issue. Further, it may be that 'Keynes's obiter dictum about "thinking in terms of models" can only mean thinking in terms of a mathematical model, which is what a rigorous model meant beginning around 1920 outside the UK economics community' (Weintraub 2005, p. 452). I would add that models can be mathematical or discursive, i.e. non-mathematical.

The result is that Truth is extremely difficult to produce.

The conduct of deduction is, therefore, not purely a matter of deduction, and induction is not purely a matter of induction. Deduction depends on induction for its facts and theories; so too does induction depend on deduction, as above. Induction helps supply or inform the premises of deduction; deduction helps supply or inform the hypotheses of induction. The facts of induction are theory-dependent, and the theories of deduction give effect to the readings of fact ensconced within the theories. So deduction and induction are dependent in part on the other. But more is involved than simple propositions, premises and hypotheses, and more is involved than the coexistence of deduction and induction. Abduction is the process of the combination of some form of deduction and some form of induction, and their continuous interaction and revision. Like so many other things, the process is recursive, one of mutual influence or determination, one of over-determination.

Deduction is used in both the conceptual and the concrete domains. Given the nature of the conceptual domain – non-empirical, a-institutional, pure conceptual – induction is inapplicable. Mathematics is a system of deduction, to which validity and not necessarily truth pertains, i.e. not necessarily description or explanation of something in the actual economy. For many centuries it was believed that the correct logicality of Euclidian geometry produced true description. The development of non-Euclidian geometry showed that correct logicality was insufficient to produce true description or correct explanation (Weintraub 2005, pp. 450–1). Truth and not only validity could result only if the geometry was correctly applied to suitable material. Euclidian geometry 'worked' with negligible, even imperceptible, error over a range of distances on Earth only because the curvature of the sphere was slight over those distances.

Lawson properly points to Hayek's position. Hayek is principally concerned with actual economies and the use of equilibrium techniques in their analysis. He differentiates that use from 'the whole tendency . . . inherent in all modern equilibrium analysis, to turn economics into a branch of pure logic, a set of self-evident propositions which, like mathematics or geometry, are subject to no other test but internal consistency' (Hayek 1937, p. 35, quoted by Lawson 2005a, p. 438).

Equilibrium analysis is applicable as a tool (see below) for the study of both pure conceptual and actual economies. In the conceptual domain nothing necessarily pertains to the ultimate nature of things, whereas in the domain of actual economies, careful analysis can distinguish the different status of different things in that respect. Moreover, it is possible for the mathematics to lead the economics along lines quite different from those found in actual economies. That situation parallels Benjamin Whorf's argument with regard to linguistic structure: A language whose sentences have a subject acting through a predicate inculcate a world view in which active agents operate. A language whose sentences do not have a subject acting through a predicate but instead have things simply happening do not have a world view in which active agents operate. The former leads to an activist and the latter to a passive view of individuals in the world and of the world itself (Whorf 1956). In economics, for example, determinism (such as is found in pure mathematical logic) seems to preclude human volition and choice, for example, demand occurs; free will, however, enables human volition and choice – individuals demand. Entrepreneurs are active agents of change; others, so one story goes, are mere passive responders to stimuli.

Returning to Lawson, he has Smith 'concerned with explaining a particular state of affairs' and Arrow and Hahn 'concerned with showing that one exists. That is, Smith is concerned with the ontic, with a real-world state of affairs, whereas Arrow and Hahn are concerned only with whether the model system has a formal property' (Lawson 2005a, p. 433). Except that Arrow and Hahn are dealing with a pure conceptual economy and its formal properties, so that, as above, no connection necessarily exists with an actual economy, surely the determination of existence, (even) in the context of a pure conceptual economy, may be said to have an ontological import, to repeat, in that context. It remains the case, none the less, that substantive ontological questions arise only with an actual economy, i.e. with properties of the economy that the analyst seeks to explain rather than with properties of 'particular representations or formalisations of the economy' (Lawson 2005a, p. 431). One may find it a stretch to contemplate the ontology of the imaginary, an image with no direct connection with an actual economy and therefore a matter of pure imagination and no substance. An ontology of zero (and no prospect of increase) is still an ontology albeit one without substance.

The complication involves how one treats as data the creations of the human mind, including the literature to which this chapter relates: they exist but not in the ontological domain of the ultimate nature of things. Which brings us to ontology (and epistemology), whose relevance has hitherto been begged here. (A different sequence of topics would have had other topics begged at this point.)

Ontology and epistemology: two types of realism

Three types of questions arise. In what sense does the economy exist? And what and how do we know? And how is economics practised, i.e. what are the modes of doing economics? Enormous confusion and incompleteness abound in most answers. I suggest the following.

We have already examined the two modes of doing economics, the study of a pure conceptual economy and the study of the actual economy. This is one pair of alternatives. Those who study the actual economy emphasise realism (to the other's rigour); this orientation of realism – *vis-à-vis* the pure a-institutional conceptual economy – I designate Realism I. A second pair of alternatives involves the juxtaposition of the study of the actual economy to a notion of an absolute ultimate economy, or the natural order of things, which I designate Realism II. The connection between the two pairs is this: the pure conceptual economy may – I stress 'may' because it need not – be taken to be an approximation of the absolute ultimate economy.

Modes of doing economics (I)

1 *First pair.* Pure conceptual economy versus actual economy.
2 *Second pair.* Actual economy (Realism I) versus absolute ultimate economy (natural order of things) (Realism II).

If one equates the study of the pure conceptual economy with the study of the absolute ultimate economy, and one need not do so, then there are three modes of doing economics.

Modes of doing economics (II)
1 Pure conceptual economy.
2 Actual economy (Realism I).
3 Absolute ultimate economy (natural order of things) (Realism II).

Inasmuch as one need not equate the pure conceptual a-institutional economy with the absolute ultimate economy (natural order of things), and because I want to emphasise the two conflicts, I write in terms of the first list.

Ontology

This is the domain of theories of existence, of the nature of reality, here especially the relation of the actual economic system and the conceptual domain to the ultimate nature of reality. If economics deals with prices, the production of bread, money multipliers, production functions, liquidity preference, marginal efficiency of capital, and the like, what is their meaning with regard to existence? Ontology has to do with the sense in which they exist and the sense in which they are real. Metaphysics, a branch of ontology in this respect, has to do with absolutes and ultimates, that is to say, with the ultimate nature of things – things physical (material) and conceptual. The relevant use of ontology is to assert or otherwise establish if something exists, in what sense, and especially, if it has meaning independent of man. Neither the rules of basketball or football, nor the principles of constitutional interpretation and application, nor the several modes of doing economics, nor the economy would exist and have meaning in the absence of man. Natural resources are natural because they exist independent of man, even if man were not or were no longer on the scene, and they are resources because they serve a human function. Without the internal combustion engine and other instruments of technology, the oil found in nature would not be much of an asset. Without man and therefore without the economy of mankind, neither economic equilibrium nor economic disequilibrium nor economic equilibration would exist or have meaning.

Epistemology

Metaphysics makes knowledge claims. So too does the study of the material world. Epistemology has to do with the nature of knowledge, specifically the criteria by which knowledge is accepted as knowledge. Two types of epistemology have arisen. (Does either exist and have an ontological status if man no longer exists?). Prescriptivist epistemology asserts that certain criteria, and only those criteria, elevated over all other criteria, must be met for a proposition to quality as knowledge. Credentialist epistemology holds that propositions may satisfy various different criteria and thereby may qualify as knowledge on the basis of the acceptance of a particular criterion(ia). Prescriptivist epistemology thus affirms an absolute standard; in so far as, however, people differ about which criterion is to constitute the prescription, this approach to epistemology is left in the same position as the credentialist; in both people confront the necessity of choice.

Two types of realism

The economics of the pure conceptual market is explicated using certain analytical tools to ensure logicality, given the specification of the pure conceptualised market. Practitioners of the pure conceptual mode of doing economics may be uninterested in how much and/or how accurately their models reflect the actual economy, preferring the rigour of working with the pure conceptual economy to the putative realism of the actual-economy mode of doing economics. From the point of view, however, of those who prefer to study actual economies, those who work with the pure conceptual economy have given effect to their preference for, and chosen construction of, the pure conceptual economy and thereby diminish (if not exclude) realism and elevate rigour over realism. Realism in this respect or sense, Realism I, connotes the desire and the practice of one mode of doing economics, namely, studying an actual economy. Such realism has to do with the features or properties of the actual economy. Such realism – Realism I – will be put to use, in part, criticising the putatively empty findings of the economics of pure conceptual markets and/or the more grandiose but still putative empty findings of the economics of the natural order of things, the absolute ultimate economy.

The second type of realism, Realism II, affirms the study of the existence of an economy that is given and independent in relation to man. This is the economy of the absolute ultimate reality, the natural order of things. It is neither empirical nor actual, nor need its study pay much attention to institutions, though institutions can be approached in the modes of both Realism I and Realism II. It likely has features in common with the conceptual economy, for both can be seen as having been suggested by a notion of an abstract generic economy.

Tony Lawson is a follower of Realism I. He denigrates the pursuit of the study of the imaginary conceptual economy, preferring realism in the form of studying actual economies. Paraphrasing but rephrasing him slightly, he contrasts the theoretic with the ontic (ontological). The theoretic denotes the features and properties of a model in the mode of economics as the study of the conceptual economy. The ontic denotes the features and properties of the actual economy, the economy he would have economists study. Emphasis on the conceptual economy, he feels, conflates the theoretic and the ontic, 'with the latter reduced to the former' (Lawson 2005a, p. 430; see also 2005b, p. 455).

If ontology is the domain of theories of the various senses of the existence and/or the nature of reality, here especially the relation of the actual economic system to the ultimate nature of reality, then both studies, that of the conceptual economy and that of the actual economy, have an ontological character. One can believe that one's conceptual economy is that of the ultimate nature of reality or that the actual economy is all that exists. From the former viewpoint, there is ontic substance to the conceptual mode of doing economics; the conceptual mode may have no relation to the actual economy but it is, or is close to, the ultimate nature of reality. The problem here is that even if we were all realists in this sense, of Realism II, we likely would disagree as to its content. Numerous versions of the conceptual economy would arise. It is possible to believe that the actual economy is more or less closely akin to the ultimate nature of reality, but most practitioners of the study of the actual economy are, like Lawson, in the camp of Realism I. They would find the ontic quality of the study of the actual economy in the study of the actual economy itself. It would have, in their minds, greater realism than the conceptual mode. They consider the study of the conceptual economy to be without substance, hence to have no ontic quality. From the point of view of ontology as a general philosophical domain, there is an ontological quality to the conceptual economy and its theoretic (in Lawson's sense) practice, but that quality level is that of zero. From the point of view of Realism I, however, only the study of the actual economy has ontic content, and the conceptual mode of enquiry has none, period – hence has no ontological quality. The difference is subtle but obviously important.

Thus Lawson correctly says that 'Smith is concerned with explaining a particular state of affairs' of the actual economy, and that 'Arrow and Hahn are instead concerned with showing that one exists. That is, Smith is concerned with the ontic, with a real world [I prefer actual economy, since "real" has the two senses, Realism I and Realism II] state of affairs, whereas Arrow and Hahn are concerned only with whether the model system has a formal property' (Lawson 2005a, p. 433). He also correctly says of Hayek that 'he recognises the theoretic or *a priori* nature ... [of the conceptual mode], interpreting it as a logic of choice, while being driven himself always to provide an ontic account' (p. 437). And again, 'Hayek is indeed concerned with equilibrium as an ontic notion; he is concerned with prioritising the understanding of real-world situations or causation' (p. 438). Pointing in his own way to zero ontic content, Lawson writes, 'For Hayek seems to accept that the formal logical system of *a priori* considerations must give us an equilibrium notion (one in which different individual plans for action in time are mutually compatible) that is fictitious as a claim about the existing state of affairs' (Lawson 2005a, p. 439). Lawson is therefore able to quote Hayek thusly: 'it becomes exceedingly difficult to say what exactly are the assumptions on the basis of which we assert that there will be a tendency toward equilibrium, and to claim that our analysis has an application to the real world' (Hayek 1937, p. 44, quoted by Lawson 2005a, p. 440; by 'real world' one should read 'actual economy'; the quotation is a splendid example of Realism I's view of the conceptual mode (or Realism II). Such is only to be expected of those 'who make the explaining of the actually existing social order the priority' (Lawson 2005a, p. 443).

À propos of equilibrium, whereas Lawson writes of different definitions or conceptions of equilibrium, I also write of different uses of equilibrium, however defined (see the following section), but the terms can be treated as synonyms and therefore substitutable. Equilibrium analysis can be applied to both the study of the pure conceptual economy and the study of the actual economy. Equilibrium analysis in the study of the pure conceptual economy performs its function of assuring correct rigour but is associated directly with no substance; it is within the domain of Realism II. Equilibrium analysis in the study of the actual economy performs the same function, but is associated with substance; it is within the domain of Realism I.

Lawson also, importantly, writes that his 'central claim translates into the idea that some conceptions of equilibrium found in the literature are theoretic and others are ontic' (Lawson 2005a, p. 430; see also 431). He says that the system determinateness conception typically is theoretic and the balance of forces conception is typically ontic; the former operates principally in the formalisation role, and the latter as an aspect of the actual economy under study. This is a useful dichotomy. It shows the applicability of the equilibrium concept – albeit differently defined – to both modes of doing economics, that of the pure conceptual economy and that of the actual economic system. There is no reason to say, however, that equilibrium – say, as part of the trio of equilibrium, disequilibrium and equilibration – is not a characteristic of the actual economy. Equilibrium may never be attained or be observable but disequilibrium and equilibration are both attained and observable. It is obvious to me that this is an issue of ontology, epistemology and linguistics and as such an example also of potential infinite regress.

Backhouse moves somewhat in this direction. (But his language is unclear with regard to Realism I versus Realism II, though, if pushed, I would say he means Realism I. He says that 'It may be that there is a sense in which it is possible to speak of equilibrium as a property of the world, and it may be the case that economists do this, but it is not necessary to take a position on this (Backhouse, this volume). The question is, what does he mean by 'a property of the world', the actual rather than the conceptual economy or the actual versus the economy in its form as the ultimate nature of things?) In his chapter in this book, Backhouse writes that

> the concept of equilibrium, *per se*, carries no ontological baggage. The method of equilibrium analysis, which involves postulating models and then searching for equilibrium, is to do with solving models – with establishing their properties. Equilibrium is defined in relation to the model, and is not necessarily a property of the real world.

I shall take up the question of whether equilibrium is an analytical tool or a definition of reality (in some sense). It may also be an honorific construct with which to cast lustre on the economic system ('equilibrium is both a technical concept in economic theory and a normative term . . . equilibrium has associations of harmony, balance, consistency' (Backhouse 2004, p. 297)). It surely is taught and used as a definition of reality, as a foundational concept, feature and property *of the system* (which are separable from the properties *of equilibrium*), though perhaps in the form, equilibrium tendency. If people did not use the term in this way, the issue might or might not have arisen but it would largely have withered on the vine. The concept of equilibrium carries whatever ontological and ideological baggage people place on it. In any event, Backhouse goes on to say, 'Of course, a specific concept of equilibrium may link closely to an assertion about the real world' (Backhouse, this volume). He concludes this part of his discussion with the statement 'What is being claimed here is that there are so many concepts of equilibrium, and so many ways they can be used, that statements about the ontology implied by equilibrium have to be made case by case' (Backhouse, this volume). I will take up next the matter of multiple concepts of equilibrium. Suffice it to say that this is a weak, albeit perhaps necessary, argument to make in defence of equilibrium analysis. At any rate, it is not Backhouse's principal argument; to it I turn in the next sub-section.

Weintraub presents a cognate issue. Lawson, he writes, 'has confused ideas about mathematics and the connection of mathematical ideas to economic ideas. As a result, what he identifies as matters of logical necessity [for why, see below] are nothing of the sort, but are, instead, manifestations of quite local and contingent historical circumstances', 'the contingencies of how equilibrium was manifest in mathematical discourse in different periods of time' (Weintraub 2005, pp. 446, 450). I cannot comment on Lawson's and Weintraub's interpretation of the history of mathematics and of its relation to economics. But it is likely clear that the sequence of stages of mathematical enquiry provided the language in which economic ideas were expressed and, if so, it is thereby an example of how the mathematics itself provides content for the interpretation of the actual economy, so that the substance of the mathematical-economic formalism is a function of ideas about the economy and the mathematics of the place and time. As for equilibrium, Weintraub summarises his argument in the terms of an earlier work:

> As equilibrium is dependent for its meaning on the context in which it is found, the meaning of equilibrium changes over time as the texts change. No meaning has a privileged status because of its presumed correspondence to the true equilibrium out there in the world.
>
> (Weintraub 1983, p. 154, quoted in Weintraub 2005, pp. 446–7)

No one would have such worries, I think, if the subject of discussion were the rules of football.

Weintraub also puts to his own use a quote from Dorfman *et al.* (1958, p. 351, quoted in Weintraub 2005, p. 448): 'It is the *model* we are analyzing, not the world.' The three economists may be distinguishing their type of analysis from both the ontic as the study of the actual economy and the ontic as the identification of the ultimate nature of reality. The former is because they are doing the economics of pure conceptual economies; the latter, because they do not identify their model, etc., as the ultimate nature of economic reality.

I must acknowledge that some very important language is handled in an ambiguous manner, leading to considerable uncertainty as to the writer's intentions. Consider the language 'nature of the thing defined', 'intrinsic' and 'nature or real essence' of a thing. In a paper given on 19 September 2005 to the Erasmus seminar on Philosophy and Economics, and a year earlier to the Vancouver workshop on the History and Philosophy of Money, Uskali Maki discussed the 'ontology of money'. Maki says, first,

> Any such definition of *the concept of money* [one using a list of properties] is therefore also a definition of *money*. This means that such a definition is a real definition: a claim about the nature of the thing defined, not just about a concept used to talk about it.
>
> (Maki 2004, p. 3)

And second and third: 'The intrinsic conditions [of money] consist of those properties that constitute the nature or real essence of a thing' (pp. 4–5). Maki is interested in differentiating an 'idealist' account of social reality (e.g. money) that is based on general acceptance or belief. He asks, 'Does money exist? Does it exist in any sense that would satisfy the realist?' (p. 11). Maki also distinguishes between money and money universal, much as one would distinguish between cows and cow-ness. After a carefully and closely reasoned argument, Maki concludes that 'Even if money were completely dependent on people's beliefs for its existence, there is a way in which it [money] could exist objectively' (p. 14). That way is scientific realism, which deals with a 'social world ... dependent on the minds and beliefs of social actors, but ... [which] may be independent of the social sciences...' (p. 14). Whereas

> Purely idealist accounts of social reality make that reality entirely dependent on people's attitudes and acceptances,... it makes more sense to regard it as itself dependent on the system of institutional interconnections.... On this view, money, collective belief, and the system of institutional dependencies mutually shape and condition one another.
>
> (pp. 15–16)

Where does this leave us? In what sense are we to take 'the nature of the thing defined', 'intrinsic' conditions or properties, and 'the nature or real essence of a thing'? If these terms are intended to apply only to the actual economy, the very terms and their nuances seem to point either to a pure conceptual economy or, more likely, to a given, independent, ultimate reality. Maki is trying to distinguish his preferred form of realism from idealism, so the pure conceptual economy is ruled out, leaving a given, independent, ultimate reality. But what does one achieve by, what is added by 'the *nature* of the thing defined', '*intrinsic*' conditions or properties and 'the *nature or real essence* of a thing'? These are philosophically 'strong' terms. Why use them to refer to cowness instead of cows? Why do so, indeed, and then settle for an explanation that includes collective belief and the system of institutional dependences in mutual interdependence? And what is to be said of philosophical efforts to create a *belief* in a particular form of realism that is consistent with Maki's argumentation?

If economists use 'equilibrium', using Maki's reasoning, is it no longer intrinsic? How does one know? What about class and power? Are they intrinsic if we do not use them but not if we do use them? And in what sense, on what level of realism, are 'intrinsic properties' to be understood, that of the actual economy, or that of the ultimate absolute economy? The mystery deepens when the statement is made later in the chapter that 'The variables with which economic models are concerned involve social interactions and human psychology' (p. 21).

The ubiquity of multiplicity and its consequences

Whether we are discussing words, models, theories, facts, etc., the obvious fact is the ubiquity of multiplicity. Not only is there multiplicity of definitions, there is multiplicity of theories, premises, hypotheses, concepts, models and so on. To theoretical multiplicity and methodological multiplicity is added substantive multiplicity along the foregoing lines. Theoretical pluralism, methodological pluralism and substantive pluralism may suggest an embarrassment of riches. They give effect to the complex and multi-faceted character of the actual economy and the many standpoints from which individuals can interpret the actual economy. The same is true of the pure conceptual and the ultimate absolute economies. They lead to several conclusions: the ambiguity and incoherence of the discipline involved; the situation that concepts, models, theories, etc., are not dispositive of the issues to which they are regularly and sometimes fundamentally addressed and therefore are inconclusive; and the need and opportunity for individuals to choose and identify those propositions with which to write *finis* to a problem of inquiry and thereby set their own and others' minds at rest.

This is the situation with equilibrium in economics. Backhouse (2004) has provided, in effect, several lists pertinent to our problem of making sense of the use of the concept. One list concerns the definitions of equilibrium, which include the following (with some overlap):

1. A constellation of selected interrelated variables so adjusted to one another that there is no inherent tendency to change in the model which they constitute.
2. Mutual compatibility of a selected set of interrelated variables of particular magnitudes.
3. System determinateness.
4. Balance of forces or order.
5. Where agents' decisions are compatible with each other and no agent has any reason to change his or her behaviour.

6 Individual optimisation and consistency of plans.
7 All markets clear.

The general problems consequent to multiplicity are implicit in Backhouse's statement that Lucas's 'understanding of the term equilibrium is so different from Robinson's that their use of the same word is confusing' (Backhouse 2004, p. 300).

The second list contains 'four main ideas about equilibrium' (Backhouse 2004, pp. 295–6)

1 The absence of endogenous tendencies for change.
2 Balance of forces.
3 Correct expectations.
4 Meaning that no agent has any reason to change his or her behaviour.

Although I am interested here in multiplicity *per se*, it is noteworthy that equilibrium, whatever else can be said about it, can be and indeed has served as a means of introducing antecedent premises of one kind or another into economic theory. These premises include the honorifics of *laissez-faire*, perfect competition, utility maximisation or rationality, perfect knowledge and selective inclusion of endogenous elements. Several of *these* have multiple meanings and in some cases it is not clear whether an assumption is being made or not (Backhouse 2004, p. 297). But multiplicity itself is a function of the complexity of the economy, its many facets and the many standpoints or perspectives from which they can be viewed and interpreted.

The multiplicity is not produced by superficial or transitory phenomena or considerations. 'If the term equilibrium economics were always used as a shorthand for the same thing', only a 'minor problem' would exist, 'but it is not'. Most economic theories 'may bear [the Arrow–Debreu general equilibrium theory] . . . a family resemblance', but are 'not strictly Arrow–Debreu models . . . not exactly the same' (Backhouse 2004, p. 297).

Another list ensues from consideration of confusion in 'the relation between economic models and the real world'. '[S]tatements about equilibrium', Backhouse goes on to say, 'are typically statements about models . . . [and] refer to properties of abstract systems' (Backhouse 2004, p. 298; NB with regard to the discussion above of properties and like terms). The three items on the list, in summary, are statements about equilibrium that

1 Are believed to apply to no real-world situation (i.e. no actual economy).
2 May or may not apply to the real world.
3 Are believed to apply, if only approximately or under appropriate conditions, to the real world.

Backhouse notes that 'Problems are created because there is sometimes confusion about which category a particular statement falls into' (Backhouse 2004,

p. 298). This is in addition to the problems consequent to the frequent if not usual non-substitutability of definitions of equilibrium; when 'different types of equilibrium . . . emerge when these concepts are applied in different models' (Backhouse 2004, p. 296), and so on. The situation must be seen as even more fluid when one reads Backhouse saying that the meaning and substance of equilibrium vary with differing bundles of included and excluded variables or assumptions. So, for instance, 'Equilibrium in a market where only production costs and preferences are specified is completely different from equilibrium in one where transaction costs and costs of decision making are also included' (Backhouse 2004, p. 302; see also p. 301; Backhouse does not say in what ways they differ).

Let us construct our own list, of the ways in which multiplicity affects the coherence of equilibrium analysis:

1 Varying definitions of equilibrium.
2 Varying beliefs as to the domain to which equilibrium analysis applies.
3 Applying different types of equilibrium in different models.
4 Differing bundles of included and excluded variables and assumptions.

Those four are clearly present in Backhouse's candid survey. A fifth may be only implicit in his discussion and likely should be included in the fourth.

5 Different power (rights) structures yield different cost structures and thereby different equilibria of resource allocations (Samuels and Schmid 1994, 1997).

One of the important insights provided by economics is opportunity cost. One of the limitations of pure conventional equilibrium analysis is that, concentrating on the existence, conditions, uniqueness and stability of equilibrium, it has neglected the study of endogenous disequilibration, disequilibrium, equilibration, multiple equilibria and like topics. Backhouse addresses the general issue. Immediately after noting that in game theory 'it has become well-known that a great variety of solutions is possible and that outcomes are often highly sensitive to small details in the description of the model', he acknowledges that 'when we look for an equilibrium, we are abstracting from the process whereby that equilibrium is reached . . . Assuming equilibrium rather than specifying the process generating it is a simplification that enables us to construct a broader argument' (Backhouse 2004, p. 301).

Four points call out for notice. (1) It is not clear that 'a broader argument' is always correct; broader along one margin but not another, hence opportunity costs. (2) Surely, examining the equilibration process may yield insight into equilibrium *per se*. (3) This language tends to take place with regard to the conceptual domain but is often worded in such a way as to appear to pertain to the actual economy when it does not. (4) This is what used to be called armchair theorising and is now called (after Coase) blackboard theorising, inasmuch as very little if any look-and-see techniques and studies are undertaken of the actual economy.

No wonder that Backhouse writes, 'Equilibrium means too many things...' (Backhouse 2004, p. 303; the sentence continues, 'and is rarely the key point at issue'.) (See the epigraph from Frank Knight.)

The title of Backhouse's 2004 paper is telling; in part, it reads, 'A Partial Defense of Equilibrium Economics.' Among the armament in his intellectual fortress are such lines as:

> It is indispensable.
>
> (p. 301)

> Abstraction is necessary.
>
> (p. 301)

> To focus on [arguments about] equilibrium distracts attention from the substantive issues involved.
>
> (p. 302)

> to use 'equilibrium theory' as the label for the theory under criticism encourages rejection of formal modeling in general.
>
> (p. 302)

And the summation reads, 'There is no argument to be made in principle about the illegitimacy of equilibrium analysis' (p. 301).

Consider the problem of distraction of attention from substantive issues. Assume that two propositions are true: that equilibrium analysis is more at home in the conceptual domain than in the domain of the actual economy, and that the pure theory undertaken in the conceptual domain bears little if any relation to the actual economy. What 'substantive' issues are in danger?

Backhouse desires to limit criticism of equilibrium economics. Such would evidently reduce the multiplicity of positions on equilibrium, yet his defence of equilibrium includes his acceptance of the multiple meanings and usages of equilibrium: 'The variety of the problems that economists face helps explain why they use the term equilibrium in many different ways that are not all consistent with each other. Different concepts of equilibrium are used to solve different problems' (Backhouse, this volume; see also Backhouse 2004, p. 301 and *passim*). If 'Economists should not face a choice between history and equilibrium' (Backhouse 2004, p. 303), why should they be restricted in the criticisms they can make?

To Backhouse, equilibrium is not defined independent of context. 'Equilibrium', he writes, 'is defined in relation to' the models in which it is used. 'The search for equilibrium is primarily a modelling strategy. . . . Because economists work with many models, tackling different types of problem and at very different levels of abstraction, they work with many concepts of equilibrium' (Backhouse, this volume). But 'the context is rarely sufficient to determine the equilibrium concept that should be used. Problems can be solved using different models, even within the same type of model, different concepts of equilibrium can be used.' Surely there is plenty of opportunity for criticism. Should they have to surrender the opportunity to criticise when criticism and dissent are crucial to the growth of knowledge and the health of disciplines (see Samuels 2005, pp. 395–6; Samuels and Fiorito 2006)?

Backhouse uses multiplicity to turn criticism against the critics: One reason 'why their critiques need to be treated with considerable caution . . . is that the term equilibrium has so many meanings that critiques of it can encompass a wide variety of arguments' (Backhouse, this volume). Ironically, Backhouse again gives the opponents of equilibrium economics armament for their attack. If during the last few paragraphs the reader wondered where in all this does the actual economy come through, one answer is that equilibrium analysis is suited to the conceptual mode of doing economics and not, or not much, the mode of the study of the actual economy. But in his contribution to this volume he provides a different answer: 'equilibrium models should be evaluated not according to whether they conform to beliefs about what the world is like' – no mention here of any concern comparable to Maki's – but in terms of their problem-solving ability, where', he adds, 'this refers to problems posed by our experience of the real world'. Throughout his chapter he emphasises how much doing equilibrium economics involves 'matters of judgement' such that if the problem-solving argument is accepted, 'it is difficult to argue that the use of equilibrium analysis is, *in principle*, flawed. The judgement has to be a pragmatic one . . .' His conclusion is that 'Equilibrium has become such an extremely elastic notion, with different concepts of equilibrium being used to solve different problems.' Economics, he writes, is 'driven by the need to solve problems' such that 'a pragmatic or even pragmatist approach centered on solving real-world economic problems fits very well . . .'

I agree with his pragmatist position. (I agree positively and, because (1) I think there is no alternative and (2) find it ubiquitous, I do not need to consider the normative side of the matter.) But how many neoclassical economists would be willing to adopt that position? Heretofore pragmatism has not had such an explicit honorific position. I suppose that Backhouse is making a virtue of necessity: ambiguity, incoherence, inability to dispose of the issues to which equilibrium, etc., are addressed, and the necessity of choice are due, in part, to multiplicity but what 'science' has taken pride in the pragmatic, perhaps even the existentialist, position? Certainly not the mind set which seeks determinate unique optimal equilibrium solutions. Backhouse's affirmations may be more critical than the criticisms of the critics. The idea that 'the choice of equilibrium concept matters', it 'can have a dramatic effect on a model's conclusions' continues the fortress building more or less begun by Milton Friedman's methodology of positive economics. Both move away from realism to pragmatism as a defence of neoclassicism.

At any rate, in his chapter in this book, Backhouse provides yet another list illustrating multiplicity, a list of different types of equilibrium. It includes:

1 Partial versus general equilibrium.
2 Perfect versus imperfect competition.
3 Short run versus long run.
4 Inter-temporal equilibrium.
5 Temporary equilibrium.
6 Adaptive-expectation equilibrium.
7 Perfect-foresight equilibrium.
8 Rational-expectations equilibrium.
9 Strategic equilibrium (Nash equilibrium in non-co-operative games).
10 Sub-game-perfect equilibrium.

to which he could have added

11 Continuous equilibrium (Lucas) (from Backhouse 2004, p. 297).
12 Restorative.

The surprising aspect of multiplicity is not its ubiquity but that in matters of equilibrium, a technical term (unlike the 'invisible hand') and an important foundational concept, we find a primitive term, a term whose meaning is defined differently by different users. That the term remains primitive and without singular definition attests to the continued youthfulness of the discipline, self-congratulatory epistles to the contrary notwithstanding, the fundamental complexity and heterogeneity of the economy, lack of unbiased, open-minded analysis of the concept and/or a core of pragmatic, ultimately agnostic foundations. Machlup's dictum that equilibrium is 'a term which has so many meanings that we never know what its users are talking about' (Machlup 1991, p. 43) suggests that if equilibrium means so many different things, then it can appeal to more people. Meaning all things to all people is not only indicative of a primitive term but a formula for popularity, a concern itself at the heart of the sociology of the discipline.

Equilibrium as tool or definition of reality

Thermometers, of which there are different kinds, give temperature readings but temperature exists independent of our measurements of it. The thermometers have their own independent existence but neither they nor the human temperatures they measure would exist without mankind. Thermometers are tools and the only definition of reality associated with them is Realism I, the actual world.

A carpenter's tools have different functions. The functions and use are due to mankind. The tools would not exist without mankind, although the materials from which they are made would exist without mankind. Other than those materials used by mankind to manufacture the tools, the tools' significance and results are due to mankind. The only definition of reality associated with a carpenter's tools is Realism I, the actual world.

Alfred Marshall created a number of tools for, as it turned out, Joan Robinson's toolkit. Is elasticity of demand or cross-elasticity of demand a tool *or* something which helps define reality in the sense of the actual economy? Without either tool and its measurement, there would still be the human activity that gave rise to it. The development and use of the tools both reflects and selectively channels our definition of reality. The concepts belong to the categories of both tool and definition of reality and the latter is again Realism I, the actual world.

What of the representative firm? Firms exist of varying age and stage of development but the representative firm is a conceptual construction; it is a tool to be used in analysis. Actually it is not quite that simple. The use of the term enables the introduction of certain variables and the exclusion of others into analysis. The term, like elasticity and cross-elasticity, is a tool of model construction, its use a function of designing, and defining, the world in a certain way. The representative firm is to be found in both modes of doing economics, that of the pure conceptual economy and that of the actual economy. That places the term in Realism I.

What about Realism II, ultimate reality? Our notion of ultimate reality, of the ultimate nature of things, can include whatever we want to identify with. Inclusion of the wholly conceptual is perhaps more equivocal than that of key empirical elements. Cows, surely; cowness, doubtful but possible.

Equilibrium, without doubt, is a tool. It enforces logicality, rigour and correctness. It is also a definition of reality. To use equilibrium analysis is to presume that the world has the equilibrium feature (seemingly Realism I) as part of its nature (seemingly Realism II). In fact, though the use of the equilibrium concept alone does nothing to enforce their consideration in analysis, equilibrium is inevitably tied to the much neglected disequilibration, disequilibrium and equilibration. Without the presence of human beings and their buying and selling activities, economic equilibrium does not exist. Given those activities, even if we were unaware of all that equilibrium means, equilibrium would still be a feature of the economy. Clearly it is used as a tool and also helps define reality in both the pure conceptual and the actual economy modes of doing economics. But it is not part of the ultimate nature of things, Realism II.

The realities which equilibrium helps define are certainly the actual economy and the pure conceptual economy. The actual economy exists independent of our perception and definition of it, though it does not exist, I would say, independent of the existence of mankind. The pure conceptual economy is what we make it out to be, but it does not exist independent of our conceptualising activity and our economic activity, and it could be defined in part by equilibrium. Conceptual tools inevitably, I think, help define reality. That is true of Reality II, ultimate reality, which is defined by mankind deliberatively and non-deliberatively. If there is a Realism II it would have to survive the demise of mankind, else it is only a belief, like the rules of poker.

Murray Milgate has written that 'From being the central organizing principle around which the whole of economic theory was organized . . . equilibrium has become a category with no meaning independent of the exact specification of the initial conditions for any model' (Milgate 1987, p. 182, quoted by Backhouse 2004, p. 292). Either way, equilibrium is a tool one of whose functions is to help define reality.

The foregoing speaks, however, in terms of general categories. There are times when equilibrium is a tool and times when it defines reality. The question is about which it is in particular cases, and that is a matter of interpretation. As Backhouse (2004, p. 300) puts it, 'In all these discussions there is a tension between equilibrium being a completely neutral mathematical tool, akin to the concept of a solution, and something with economic content.' Among contemporary contributors to the discussion, Backhouse is perhaps the most insistent on equilibrium as a tool of analysis; for example, the indispensability of equilibrium is as a tool of analysis (Backhouse 2004, pp. 299, 301 and *passim*).

Which raises the question of the neoclassical research protocol. The standard form of doing research within neoclassicism requires that one attain a determinate, unique, optimal, equilibrium result. This requirement can be considered a tool. To attain that result, however, requires – as part of its function as a tool – ruling out of bounds by assumption all those variables that would otherwise prevent reaching unique determinate solutions. This has become a key component of equilibrium economics inasmuch as equilibrium is another part of the protocol. But removing certain variables from economic theory, whether theory in the pure conceptual mode or the actual economy mode, has an effect on the definition of reality. Any variable not included under the protocol will not qualify for the definition of reality. The protocol has a narrowing effect. If the actual economy has not one but several, even numerous, optimal solutions, the protocol serves to hypostatise or reify only one. Knowledge produced under the protocol is that of the pure conceptual mode; it is not consistent with actual economies. Were we to find within neoclassicism the proposition that price structure is a function of the structure of rights, so that the possibility of different rights structures means different optimal equilibrium solutions, the protocol would have evaporated and been discarded. Of course, the change itself would have been due to a change in the discipline's definition of reality; such provides an example of the hermeneutic circle. But it would mean a very different economics; *inter alia*, it would expand Backhouse's lists of multiplicity and be justified by his argument that multiplicity reflects the complexity of the actual economy. If economic theory 'deals with abstract worlds that in some cases describe no conceivable world, and with problems that do not even make sense outside that theory' (Backhouse, this volume), then surely power in the form of rights both describes a conceivable world, i.e. the actual economy, and makes sense even within traditional theory, given a broadening of its scope. The change would change the tool and do so within Realism I. Whether it would come within Realism II is problematic but likely not: the *problem* of the structure of power might well enter Realism II but the structure of power, especially the *status quo* structure of power, would not.

One further point. It is said that equilibrium analysis enforces rigour. Aside from the fact that constructing equilibrium models is not the only way to do economics rigorously, the need for rigour is context-dominated. Imposing the neoclassical research protocol means assuming away everything that would otherwise prevent reaching determinate unique optimal equilibrium results. That both narrows the subject and reduces the respects with regard to which the analysis has to be rigorous.

The ontological claims of orthodox and heterodox economists; pragmatism

The genesis of this chapter was the felt need to make sense of the present stage of the controversy about equilibrium economics. It was also to make sense of the relation of heterodox and orthodox economics on that basis. I now take up the question of the ontological status of the two, with caveats that each group – heterodox and orthodox economists – is heterogeneous and that the limits on enquiry raised above apply to both.

The bulk of this chapter has dealt with equilibrium economics, the economics of orthodoxy. One would expect the members of each group to claim superior ontic (ontological) status. And so they do. This is Lawson's position. I am not sure it is Backhouse's position but he at least seems to lean that way. As we have seen, in one respect at least he and I seem to concur, namely the status of economics as pragmatist.

My view is that the heterodox economist has no greater ontological claim than the traditional equilibrium theorist and the choice between the pure conceptual and actual economy modes is subjective and normative. If one contemplates Realism II, the quest for the ultimate and absolute nature of economic life, then since I find that very little if anything qualifies, neither can claim superior ontological status of that type. If, for example, neither the microeconomics of resource allocation nor the institutional economics of power and rights would exist in the absence of man, even assuming that Realism II makes sense – a question I do not discuss here – then neither orthodox nor heterodox economics can claim Realism II ontological status, hence neither is superior in that respect to the other. One may subjectively prefer equilibrium economics or power-structure economics, but that is insufficient to qualify for Realism II status. And surely to assert such qualification is to render wishful thinking, one's subjective preference, the basis of the ultimate nature of things. Such would be the ultimate hubris.

Orthodox and heterodox economics can qualify only as candidates for Realism I. That is true of both the pure conceptual and the actual economy modes of doing economics. To say that either equilibrium economics or power-structure economics has superior ontological status is likewise to give effect to one's subjective preference. It may be felt that equilibrium economics is more a research objective than a definition of reality. It may be felt that power-structure economics runs deeper than the mechanics of the equilibrating price mechanism, etc. But both equilibrium economics and power-structure economics are tools, both involve abstraction, both evidence multiplicity, both can be practised on one or the other mode of doing economics, and both deal, *vis-à-vis* the natural order of things, with the actual economy and its definition – in short, power-structure economics is both a tool of analysis and a definition of reality. Both practitioners of equilibrium economics and practitioners of power-structure economics are doing what comes naturally (pun intended) to them, i.e. what interests them. If one can teach the economics of full employment at 9:00 a.m. and the economics of less than full employment at 10:00 a.m., then one can teach power-structure economics at 11:00 a.m. One can believe that one is more realistic (in the sense of Realism I) than the others, but none has an existence in the domain of Realism II, and neither has anything but a subjective preference to ground a claim of superiority in Realism I. The 'real' argument is about what should be the subject of analysis. That is a matter of normativism. Giving normativism Realism II status is hubristic.

There is an old quip about someone who sees his own favourite topic and his own favourite conclusion in everything he observes – it is all utility maximisation, it is all sex, it is all power . . . and so on. One favourite topic of mine is what explains what people do. My favourite conclusion is pragmatism. Notwithstanding prescriptive morality, theology, custom and the like, which tend to emphasise received moral rules, etc. (but practise pragmatism, as in the difference between manifest and latent function, for example), it is people's concern with consequences that governs what they do. They may reason within or in the language of received morality but received morality is handled and applied on pragmatic terms. The same is true of equilibrium economics and of power-structure economics, true with regard to the status given them and the conduct of their use by orthodox and heterodox economists respectively. It is also true of law.

One can also say that just as not all aspects of the actual economy are equally amenable to equilibrium analysis, not all are equally amenable to power-structure analysis. Considerations of the division of labour should warrant the practice of both types of analysis and each within both modes of doing economics, pure and actual. It is, ironically, the practice of status emulation which enables the equilibrium economist to claim ontological superiority. The claim of ontological superiority by devotees of power-structure economists is likely fuelled by status emulation. The irony is that the economist seen as orthodox, Adam Smith, and the economist seen as heterodox, Thorstein Veblen, both attributed to status emulation much of what people do.

Conclusion

Economics itself has no transcendent ontological existence. Economics is made, not found. It is continually being made and remade, by efforts to publish that which will be accepted by others sufficiently to make a change in what is considered economics. Models, theories and concepts are instrumental in the contest over the reconstruction of economics and of the economy and polity. They are the terms and frameworks which help us define reality for ourselves, upon which we make choices and act.

Truth in an epistemologically and ontologically conclusive sense is difficult to achieve, yet people have a need to believe. They will adopt whatever proposition or belief satisfies them, quiets the imagination, sets minds at rest, serves as psychic balm, i.e., exemplifying Adam Smith's (1980) argument in his 'History of Astronomy' and George Shackle's in *The Years of High Theory* (1967).

People do have a general need to believe, and disciples of various belief systems compete to satisfy that need. This is all bound up with the structure and the future of the economic system. The difference between theologically based belief systems and economically based ones is that the former is conceptualised in terms of God and the latter in terms of some pure or ideal version of the system.

Equilibrium is a conceptual tool, conclusively dispositive of nothing in a world of multiplicity and in a discipline utilising pure concepts that directly relate to nothing actual at least in the sense that no or little study has been undertaken of the connections and relationships between the pure conceptual world and the actual world. In applying the logical conclusions of deductive analysis to actual economies, there is no proof that the actual economy bears any relevant relation to the conceptual economy. This is especially the case in the absence of much, if any, attention to relating the conceptual economy to the institutional foundations and consequences of the actual economy.

At work are filters and sieves, allowing certain ideas, theories, models, etc., to enter, contend, and survive, and not others. For example, the use of the rationality assumption, maximisation, equilibrium technique(s), the neoclassical research protocol, pure conceptual categories, etc., determines who is insider and outsider, who is orthodox and who is heterodox. In all this, economists are making, not finding the economy to be deployed by economics. This economy may provide only limited, even specious, representation of and not correspondence with reality, applied to the actual economy but, lacking institutional specificity, it has no fundamental connection to it. Economists define the economy for themselves, allowing for some but not all of the complexity of actual economies, i.e., controlled complexity. At bottom is the question, who owns economics?

However much one recognises diversity and multiplicity, and however much they and discussion of alternative interpretations may prevail in a certain segment of the discipline, the prevalent practice of the discipline as a whole is much more monistic. What Joseph Spengler called the problem of order – working out the conflicts between continuity and change, between freedom (autonomy) and control, and between hierarchy and egalitarianism – applies to economics (Samuels 1996). Thus, for example, Backhouse seems willing, however reluctantly, to enlarge the domain of equilibrium economics to the study of disequilibration, disequilibrium and equilibration but more basically seeks to 'preserve the notion of equilibrium as the central category of the analysis' (Giocoli 2003, p. 137).

Although Lawson and Weintraub disagree on what the history shows, it is clear that much history of mathematics and of economics is warranted, even though the influence of mathematics on economics is part of a larger system of relationships. The mathematics used channels the economics. The use of the mathematics of static mechanics, rather than non-linear and recursive mathematics, has led to and/or reinforces the focus on equilibrium and on seeking the conditions of determinacy, existence, uniqueness, stability and optimality of equilibrium. This had led to the exclusion of (1) much of the recursive relationships among variables, (2) non-linear relationships and other aspects of complexity, (3) operation of the adjustment process, (4) factors and forces preventing attainment of equilibrium, (5) determination and path of actual operation of economy, and so on. Further, the economic preconceptions brought to bear channels both the mathematics and the economics, for example Pareto optimality, the neoclassical research protocol and constrained optimisation. How much of economists' mathematical practice is due to the mathematics they use and how much to their own programme become important questions. Formal mathematical modelling *per se* is not the problem, though it contributes to the neglect of topics not readily addressed by the mathematics or the economic preconceptions.

Multiplicity is not to be denigrated. It is one reason why we have an economy and why there are multiple adjustment mechanisms and multiple possible equilibria. In a complex world, different stories need to be told. Consider a simple Keynesian equilibrium/equilibration account. From a period in which $I = S$, a decrease in portfolio investment takes place which leads to more spending on real plant and equipment. This makes $I > S$ which leads to a (further) rise in the marginal efficiency of capital and an increase in income and thereby an increase in consumption. Eventually a new equilibrium takes place in which $I = S$, at a different level than hitherto. If the increase in spending leads to an increase in interest rates, less investment will ensue than just contemplated, with less income and less consumption and saving, with $I = S$ higher than the original and lower than it would have been had the interest rate not increased. This story, and perhaps any one like it ventured by readers, is an example of equilibration and equilibrium. Different substantive assumptions about spending and its consequences yield different equilibrium results. No unique determinate solution here; rather a variety of possibilities depending upon behavioural choices and various micro and macro-level adjustment processes.

Consider that an allocation of resources ensues from a price structure which results from the combination of the structure of rights, costs and individual spending decisions. A change in price structure and/or costs and/or individual spending decisions or in market structures leads to a different allocation of resources. A change in one category of resource allocation may induce another, which initiates a new and different allocative equilibration process and resulting equilibrium allocation of resources. No unique determinate solution here. Rather a variety of possibilities depending upon behavioural choices and various micro and macro-level adjustment processes. This story, and perhaps any one like it ventured by readers, is an example of a change in the economic significance of rights disequilibrating individual opportunity sets, actions constituting disequilibrium and equilibration.

In the second semester of the year-long Principles of Economics course taught by Walter Buckingham Smith at Williams College in the spring of 1930, during a discussion of government promotion of business, Smith is reported to have referred to the 'old mercantilism' still existent in one place on the earth, 'the US Congress' (Samuels and Johnson 2006, p. 99). This is an interpretation of a definition of reality. Another interpretation could be 'business socialism'; still another, 'the political economy of rent seeking' and yet another, 'the operation of representative democracy'. And so on. One can intuit an equilibration process at work in the competition among economic and nationalist interests, the legal framework of the economy being object of capture and use (a competitive, recursive process), a mode of allocating resources and an instrument of manufacturing belief. Equilibrium analysis could thus be applied to any of the multiple definitions of reality. The analysis need not be constrained to seek only unique determinate optimal equilibrium results. The analysis need not be mathematically formalist. The equilibrium analysis should encompass endogenous disequilibrating developments, disequilibrium, equilibration, and adjustment mechanisms, all the while paying attention to the actual factors and forces at work in the economy in which we live. To that end, abstraction would necessarily be used to limit the variables placed and structured within the model, and some if not much of the discussion would be of what here has been called the conceptual mode of doing economics. In this exercise it is neither necessary nor useful to assume given, fully defined rights as one step on the road to a determinate unique result. Rather the analyst assumes, or observes, that questions of rights are never solved once and for all time (Lerner 1972, p. 259; see Sturn 2004, pp. 328–9). Moreover, because of abstraction, it is difficult if not impossible but unnecessary to establish whether the analysis was predicated on a tool or a definition of reality, or whether the use of the equilibrium tool rendered the analysis a pure conceptual definition of reality or was applied to an actual economy. Equilibrium analysis can but need not facilitate rigour in deduction; it can also be a means of achieving realism, but the realism of actual economies without assuming either something absolute or ultimate *or* that the economy of the model reflects the natural order of things.

I surmise that very little if any of the type of criticism and defence against criticism would be felt necessary if Vilfredo Pareto's general equilibrium theory of society had become a, if not the, form taken by economics in the twentieth century (Samuels 1974). Pareto describes and models a society in which power, knowledge (including pseudo-knowledge) and psychology are the three principal social forces or domains, in which, in part, psychology is manipulated in order to influence belief, in turn in order to manipulate power. He examines these variables and these processes using the techniques, non-mathematical to be sure, of equilibrium analysis. His analysis encompasses much of the heterodox topics and heterodox themes heretofore excluded from mainstream, neoclassical economics. Why such exclusion happened is an interesting, indeed important, question, but cannot concern us here. Pareto has provided a set of concepts, a model and a definition of reality, each of which combines equilibrium analysis and the heterodox research agenda. Until now, no participant in the conversation about equilibrium analysis has seen fit to suggest Pareto (the Pareto who goes beyond Pareto optimality). The orthodox economists seem unwilling to apply equilibrium to Pareto's enlarged domain, perhaps because they would have to do equilibrium analysis differently. The heterodox economists seem unwilling to pursue Pareto's enlarged domain in conjunction with equilibrium analysis, perhaps because of the bad taste of traditional equilibrium economics and of Pareto's own efforts to formulate his analysis in a conservative manner. But both set of reservations can be overcome, especially if the neoclassical research protocol is rescinded. One question is, whose economics is it?

Murray Milgate has written that 'From being the central organizing principle around which the whole of economic theory was organized . . . equilibrium has become a category with no meaning independent of the exact specification of the initial conditions for any model' (Milgate 1987, p. 182, quoted by Backhouse 2004, p. 292). Consider the foregoing discussions of multiplicity and its consequences, and equilibrium as tool or definition of reality. Surely it was an exuberant overstatement to make a tool used to enforce logicality and accuracy of consequences into a foundation concept, a central organising principle of all economic theory. Surely, if one considers equilibrium as either or both a tool and a definition of reality, it is ambiguous and incoherent, or, as Machlup wrote, 'a term which has so many meanings that we never know what its users are talking about' (Machlup 1991, p. 43, quoted by Lawson, n.d., p. 4). As a definition of reality it applies to a wide range of phenomena but does not say much about any of them, especially since economists – especially economic theorists – focus on the conditions of determinacy, existence, uniqueness and stability, which are conceptual matters, and largely ignore disequilibration, disequilibrium and equilibration, which are or could be in large part empirical matters. As so many devotees and critics agree, an equilibrium state is non-empirical. Characterising the economy as an equilibrium phenomenon is to impose on a tool a greater interpretive load than the tool can bear, to import from the pure conceptual mode into the actual-economy mode something more metaphysical than real, to ignore the substance of the factors and forces at work in the economy, and to embrace and give effect to the language of belief, ideology and legitimisation. Still, it is an important tool and the fecundity of its uses points to the wide range of its importance, definitional incoherence notwithstanding. What is necessary is a sense of perspective and of limits. If exuberant exaggeration of the claims of equilibrium economics were not made, then it might be more plausible to say with Backhouse (2004, p. 301) that 'There is no argument to be made in principle about the illegitimacy of equilibrium analysis.' If economists were dentists or dental hygienists using certain pointed metal instruments on teeth – picks – or if they were guitar players using certain instruments to pluck strings, would they envelope the science of dentistry or the art of music in stories about their instruments? If I understand the critics the problem is not the illegitimacy of equilibrium analysis – how can one be mad at a tool? Borrowing the well known phrase from Kenneth Boulding (1966), who used it against welfare economics, the problem is the monumental misallocation of resources to recondite issues of the determinacy, existence, uniqueness and stability of equilibrium solutions in comparison with the economics of disequilibration, disequilibrium and equilibration. The neoclassical research protocol is more disturbing than equilibrium analysis *per se*.

References

Backhouse, R.E. (2004), 'History and Equilibrium: a Partial Defense of Equilibrium Economics', *Journal of Economic Methodology*, 11 (3), 291–305.

Black, H.C. (1968), *Black's Law Dictionary*, 4th edn, West Publishing, St Paul, MN.

Blaug, Mark (1997), 'Ugly Currents in Modern Economics', *Options Politiques*, September, pp. 3–8.

Bliss, Christopher (1975), *Capital Theory and the Distribution of Income*, Elsevier, Amsterdam.

Boulding, Kenneth E. (1966), 'The Economics of Knowledge and the Knowledge of Economics', *American Economic Review*, 56 (1–2), 1–13.

Coase, R. (1999), 'Interview with Ronald Coase', *Newsletter of the International Society for New Institutional Economics*, 2 (1), 3–10.

Dixon, H. (1990), 'Equilibrium and Explanation', in J. Creedy (ed.), *Foundations of Economic Thought*, Blackwell, Oxford.

Giocoli, Nicola (2003), *Modeling Rational Agents*, Edward Elgar, Cheltenham.

Hahn, F.H. (1937), 'Economics and Knowledge', *Economica*, 4 (February), 3–54.

Hahn, F.H., ed. (1984), *Equilibrium and Macroeconomics*, Blackwell, Oxford. (Reprint of 'Some Adjustment Problems', *Econometrica*, 38 (1), 1–17.)

Hahn, F.H., ed. (1994), 'An Intellectual Retrospect', *Banca Nazionale del Lavoro Quarterly Review*, September, pp. 245–58.

Kalder, N. (1972), 'The Irrelevance of Equilibrium Economics', *Economic Journal*, 82 (December), 1237–55.

Knight, Frank H. (2005) [1933], 'Notes and other Materials from Frank H. Knight's Course, Economic Theory, Economics 301, University of Chicago, Fall 1933', *Research in the History of Economic Thought and Methodology*, vol. 23-B, pp. 3–86.

Lawson, Tony (2005a), 'The (Confused) State of Equilibrium Analysis in Modern Economics: an Explanation', *Journal of Post-Keynesian Economics*, 27 (3), 423–4.

Lawson, Tony (2005b), 'Reorienting History (of Economics)', *Journal of Post-Keynesian Economics*, 27 (3), 455–70.

Lawson, Tony (2006), 'Tensions in Modern Economics: the Case of Equilibrium Analysis', in V. Mosini (ed.), *Equilibrium in Economics. Scope and Limits*, Routledge, London.

Lerner, Abba (1972), 'The Economics and Politics of Consumer Sovereignty', *American Economic Review*, 62 (2), 258–60.

Robinson, Joan (1956), *The Accumulation of Capital*, Macmillan, London.

Samuels, Warren J. (1974), *Pareto on Policy*, New York: Elsevier.

Samuels, Warren J. (1996), 'Joseph J. Spengler's Concept of the "Problem of Order": A Reconsideration and Extension', in Philip Arestis (ed.), *Employment, Economic Growth and the Tyranny of the Market*, Brookfield VT: Edward Elgar, 185–99.

Samuels, Warren J. (1997), 'On the Nature and Utility of the Concept of Equilibrium', *Journal of Post-Keynesian Economics*, 20 (1), 77–88.

Samuels, Warren J. (2003), 'Utopian Economics', in Warren J. Samuels, Jeff E. Biddle and John B. Davis (eds), *A Companion to the History of Economic Thought*, Malden, MA: Blackwell, 201–14.

Samuels, Warren J. (2005), 'The Role of Government in the History of Political Economy. The 2004 *HOPE* Conference Interpreted and Critiqued by the General Discussant', in Steven G. Medema and Peter Boettke (eds), *The Role of Government in the History of Economic Thought*, annual supplement to Vol. 37, *History of Political Economy*, Duke University Press, Durham, NC, 393–423.

Samuels, Warren J. and Fiorito, Luca (2006), 'Robert Hoxie's Introductory Lecture on the Nature of the History of Political Economy (1916). The History of Economic Thought as the History of Error', *Research in the History of Economic Thought and Methodology* (2006), vol. 24-C, pp. 49–97.

Samuels, Warren J. and Johnson, Kirk D. eds (2006), 'F. Taylor Ostrander's Materials from Economics 1–2, taught by Walter B. Smith, Williams College, Fall 1929 and Spring 1930', *Research in the History of Economic Thought and Methodology* (2006), vol. 24-B, pp. 3–108.

Samuels, Warren J. and Schmid, A. Allan (1997), 'The Concept of Cost in Economics', in Warren J. Samuels, Steven G. Medema and A. Allan Schmid, *The Economy as a Process of Valuation*, Edward Elgar, Lyme, NH, pp. 208–98.

Samuels, Warren J. and Schmid, A. Allan (1974), 'Costs and Power', in Nahid Ashlenbeigui and Young Back Choi (eds), *Borderlands of Economics. Essays in Honor of Daniel R. Fusfeld*, Routledge, New York (1997), 153–70.

Shackle, G.L.S. (1967), *The Years of High Theory*, Cambridge University Press, New York.

Smith, Adam (1980), 'The History of Astronomy', in *Essays on Philosophical Subjects*, Oxford University Press, New York, 33–105.

Sturn, Richard (2004), Book review, *European Journal of the History of Economic Thought*, 11 (2), 328–30.

Weintraub, E. Roy (2005), 'On Lawson on Equilibrium', *Journal of Post-Keynesian Economics*, 27 (3), 445–54.

Whorf, Benjamin Lee (1956), *Language, Thought, and Reality*, MIT Press, Cambridge, MA.

Zeidler, Pawel (2000), 'The Epistemological Status of Theoretical Models of Molecular Structure', *International Journal for Philosophy of Chemistry*, 6 (1), 17–34.

10 Equilibrium in economics, stability and stationarity in econometrics

Jim Thomas

Having defined econometrics, the chapter will discuss a number of economic models that have been used in econometric analysis to show that the concept of 'equilibrium' does not generally appear in the analysis. The recognition that adjustment takes time led to the formulation of models containing lagged values of variables that could be used to model the adjustment process.

What is econometrics?

The origins of 'econometrics' as a formal discipline may be dated with some precision to 1932, when a number of leading economists, including John Maynard Keynes and Irving Fisher, established the Econometric Society.[1] The definition of econometrics that was given by Ragnar Frisch in an editorial in the first issue of *Econometrica*, the Journal of the Econometric Society, in 1933 was:

> Econometrics is by no means the same as economic statistics. Nor is it identical with what we call general economic theory, although a considerable portion of this theory has a definitely quantitative character. Nor should econometrics be taken as synonomous [*sic*] with the application of mathematics to economics. Experience has shown that each of these three viewpoints, that of statistics, economic theory, and mathematics, is a necessary, but not by itself a sufficient, condition for a real understanding of the quantitative relations in modern economic life. It is the *unification* of all three that is powerful. And it is this unification that constitutes econometrics.
>
> (Frisch 1933, p. 2)

1 A considerable amount of quantitative analysis had taken place before the founding of the Econometric Society and some of this material will be discussed in the section on comparative statics below.

There have been many more definitions of econometrics since 1933,[2] some of which are less comprehensive. For example, Malinvaud (1966) takes the view that econometrics may include 'every application of mathematics or of statistical methods to the study of economic phenomena', while Chow (1983) defines econometrics as 'the art and science of using statistical methods for the measurement of economic relations'. I shall concentrate on the definition given by Frisch, because of its emphasis on the three components necessary for econometric analysis.

Frisch's definition refers to the three components necessary for econometric analysis and not to the range of skills required by an individual carrying out an econometric analysis. Historically, there has always been a division of labour, with a considerable degree of specialisation in each of the three areas. Within the academic pecking order, those who specialise in theory have acquired the highest prestige, both in economics and econometrics, while those who collect economic data and/or carry out exercises in applied econometrics struggle in the lower leagues.[3]

To carry out econometric analysis, three things are needed: (1) an economic model written formally in terms of mathematical equations; (2) economic data that relate to the variables that appear in the economic model; (3) relevant statistical techniques to estimate the parameters in the model and test hypotheses. The ordering of the three items is logical, since the relevant data are normally selected after the variables in the model have been specified and they are required for the quantitative analysis to be conducted. However, as I plan to concentrate on (1) and (3), I shall discuss a number of issues relating to economic data briefly here before a more extended discussion of (1) and (3).

Economic data

As was mentioned above, there tends to be a sharp division between economic and econometric theorists and those who gather or generate economic data, with the former tending to regard the latter as a lower class intellectually. As a result the question of how to collect data or evaluate other people's data gets low priority. In relation to the production of economic data, economists are generally hunter-gatherers rather than cultivators of the data fields of economic numbers. Thus:

> Economists are unique among social scientists in that they are trained only to analyze, not to collect data. While psychologists are taught experimental techniques, sociologists learn the vagaries of interviewing, and anthropolo-

2 The survey of 'econometrics' in Pesaran (1998) contains a discussion of alternative definitions. The Introduction to Hendry and Morgan (1995) provides an interesting survey of historical developments in econometrics and the book reprints many classics in the field.

3 There are exceptions to this generalisation, as there are to most such statements. Denis Sargan and David Hendry are examples of outstanding econometric theorists who have also carried out important applied econometric studies.

gists devote much of their time to field work, economists are provided only with the tools for data analysis. One consequence is a lack of scepticism about the quality of the data.

(Reuter 1982, p. 137)[4]

A second point that is very striking is the number of key variables in economics that are hard to define and/or measure empirically. For example:

1 In consumer theory, consumers are assumed to maximise utility (non-observable) subject to the relevant constraints. The non-measurability of utility means that inter-personal comparisons cannot be made, for example, to determine whether net utility is increased if a pound is taken in tax from a millionaire and given to a beggar. This has greatly restricted the contribution that economists can make to discussions of human welfare, despite the Theory of Revealed Preference[5] and many ingenious theoretical compensation schemes.
2 In perfect competition, freedom of entry will ensure that, in equilibrium, an entrepreneur will only earn 'normal' profits, i.e. profits just sufficient to keep him in his particular business, but there is no indication of how to measure 'normal' profits, so that excess profits (i.e. profits in excess of 'normal' profits) may be measured.
3 The '*real*' rate of interest, which plays a crucial role in monetary theory, is defined as the nominal rate of interest (observable) minus the *expected* rate of inflation (non-observable). Some arbitrary procedure has had to be introduced to model or proxy for the unobservable expected rate of inflation before the real rate of interest becomes operational in economic modelling.

Historically, in the 1940s, when researchers at the Cowles Commission[6] began developing econometric theory, they were largely concerned with economic modelling using time-series data (i.e. economic data collected over time) rather than

4 In contrast, some years ago one of my tasks was to teach a non-technical course of statistics to postgraduate economic historians at the LSE. I was using Floud (1974) as my text and planned in one session to use the data from chapter 3 on the geographical distribution of wealth in England based on county assessments of wealth between 1086 and 1843 to explain the use of the correlation coefficient. I assumed we would spend most of the hour on the correlation coefficient, but in the event most of the time was spent in vigorous discussion among the economic historians as to the validity of treating data collected over a period of almost 800 years as being a homogeneous series and very little time was available to discuss the correlation coefficient. This would never happen in an economics seminar.

5 See Richter (1987) for a discussion of this concept.

6 The Cowles Commission was founded in 1932 at Colorado Springs by Alfred Cowles to carry out empirical analysis of economic time series. It moved to the University of Chicago in 1939 and became the centre for theoretical research during the formative years in the development of the new subject of econometrics. In 1955, it became the Cowles Foundation and moved to Yale University, where it continues to carry out research in econometrics.

the random samples beloved of statistical theorists.[7] The use of conventional statistical theory to analyse time-series data raises some difficult philosophical problems that are generally ignored by economists carrying out quantitative analysis. For valid statistical inferences to be drawn from the analysis of sample data, the sample should be drawn from the population by some random process. Economic data collected over time represent a unique set of numbers corresponding to the historical passage of time and it is difficult to argue, for example, that prices, quantities, incomes and rates of interest are random drawings from a normal distribution. As we shall see below, one answer has been to argue, not that economic variables are normally distributed, but that there is a stochastic component in the equation expressing the relationship between the economic variables and that this component represents the net effect of variables and other factors that are not included in the equation. Classical sampling theory is then applied to the stochastic component, the 'random error' in the equation.[8]

Data mining

Another problem with the analysis of one-off historical time series is the temptation to use the data twice: once to formulate a hypothesis and secondly to test the hypothesis. For example, if an economist plots time-series data on pairs of economic variables drawn from a set of 100 variables and at the end of the exercise thinks that there appears to be a linear relationship between two of the variables, s/he may calculate the correlation coefficient from the data or run a regression to estimate a linear relationship. However, applying the conventional standard errors to test the null hypothesis (which assumes that there is no relationship between these two variables) would be invalid, as it would not allow for the probability of finding a significant, but spurious, statistical relationship between two random series drawn from a set of 100 time series. The practice of data mining to find significant relationships raises serious questions over

7 This was true for many years following the development of econometrics in the period during and after the Second World War. Macroeconomic models tend to involve time-series data based on the National Income Accounts, but some studies could involve a cross-section sample of countries' time-series data. Microeconomic models tend to use cross-section data based on surveys/samples of microeconomic units. However, in recent years there has been a growing use of panel data (i.e. a cross-section sample of microeconomic units observed over time).

8 As Qin and Gilbert (2001) suggest, the interpretation of the error term in a regression equation in economics has varied over time. One possible explanation as errors in the measurement of the variables being used in the analysis has not had any general support and 'errors-in-variables' models have not been widely used in econometric analysis. A well known exception is Friedman's critique of the Keynesian consumption function in his theory of the Permanent Income Hypothesis (see Friedman 1957). In the 1930s, some researchers into business cycles, such as Yule and Frisch, interpreted the errors as representing 'impulses' that could cumulate into cyclical movements, but with the pioneering work of Tinbergen (1939) an 'errors-in-equations' interpretation began to dominate econometric analysis. This explains the error term in the regression equation as being the net effect on the dependent variable of the behaviour of all the factors that affect the dependent variable, but which have been excluded from the equation being estimated.

the acceptance of much quantitative economic analysis when conventional statistical tests using conventional probability levels are used to test hypotheses.[9]

Economic models

In general, econometricians have tended to take existing economic theories off the peg to use in the context of particular areas of analysis, carrying over any implicit or explicit assumptions. Economic theory may be divided broadly into two components – microeconomics and macroeconomics. The former tries to explain the behaviour of firms and households or individuals, acting as entrepreneurs, workers or consumers, while the latter tries to explain how economies operate in the aggregate.

Economic variables 'relevant' to a particular economic model are divided into those that are 'endogenous' (i.e. those variables whose behaviour is to be 'explained' by the model) and those that are 'exogenous' (i.e. those variables that are 'given' in relation to the particular model).

For a model to have a solution, there must be as many independent equations as endogenous variables. Equations are divided into three types:

1. Behavioural equations – those that try to explain the economic activities of the economic agents.
2. Identities, e.g. $Y \equiv C + I$ in simple macroeconomic models.
3. Equilibrium conditions, e.g. for a market to clear, price is such that the quantity supplied equals the quantity demanded.

Microeconomic models

Example 1 A simple market model.[10]

(Supply equation) $$Q^S_{(t)} = \alpha_1 + \beta_1 P_{(t)}\ [+ u_{1(t)}] \quad (1)$$

(Demand equation) $$Q^D_{(t)} = \alpha_2 + \beta_2 P_{(t)}\ [+ u_{2(t)}] \quad (2)$$

(Equilibrium condition) $$Q^S_{(t)} = Q^D_{(t)} = Q_{(t)} \quad (3)$$

9 The problem of data mining is discussed in Lovell (1983) and Denton (1985), while Granger and Newbold (1974) present some Monte Carlo results that are relevant to the current discussion. In recent years, the situation has changed and large bodies of economic data exist based on censuses or large random samples of households and firms. Access to such data avoids many of the philosophical problems that arise in trying to justify the use the standard statistical theory of estimation and hypothesis testing to analyse unique, 'one-off' historical data sets and reduces the problem of 'data mining' in some areas of econometric research.

10 Economists tend to formulate models using non-stochastic variables and add an error term to a behavioural equation only if they plan to estimate the parameters in the equation. Econometricians regard economic equations as involving a stochastic component and would therefore include error terms as part of the original specification of the model. As a compromise, I have placed the error terms in square brackets in the behavioural equations.

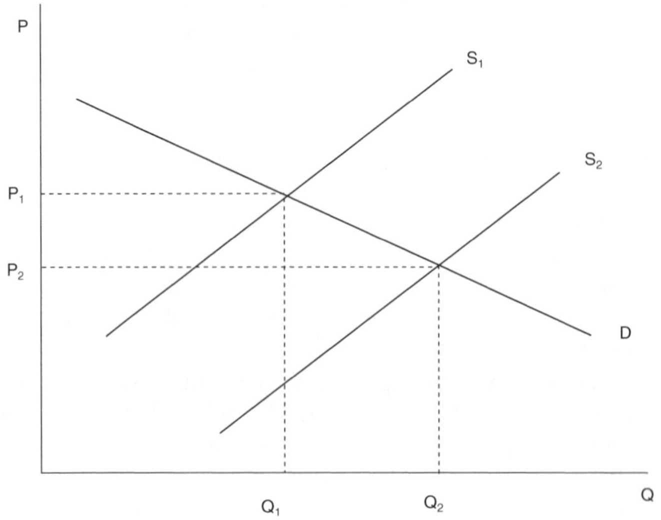

Figure 10.1 Comparative static analysis.

Here there are three endogenous variables, $Q^S_{(t)}$, $Q^D_{(t)}$ and $P_{(t)}$. There are no exogenous variables. The equilibrium condition may be used to replace $Q^S_{(t)}$ and $Q^D_{(t)}$ by $Q_{(t)}$ and then solve equations (1) and (2) to obtain the equilibrium solution that[11]

$$P^e = (\alpha_2 - \alpha_1)/(\beta_1 - \beta_2) \text{ and } Q^e = (\alpha_2\beta_1 - \alpha_1\beta_2)/(\beta_1 - \beta_2) \tag{4}$$

While equation (4) provides the solution to the system of equations defined in equations (1)–(3), observing P^e and Q^e is of little use to the econometrician, as economic relationships cannot be estimated from one observation. Clearly P and Q must vary over time to generate the data necessary for estimation.

Comparative statics is one widely used method of analysing the effects of economic changes, by comparing equilibrium positions. The analysis assumes that we start and finish in equilibrium positions. For example, in the market model, a change in production costs that lowers the price at which each quantity is supplied would shift the supply curve from S_1 to S_2 and lead to a new equilibrium with a larger quantity (Q_2) being sold at a lower price (P_2).

However, the analysis has nothing to say about the process of adjustment between the two equilibrium positions, nor about what happens to prices and quantities if the demand and/or supply functions shift over time. The need to analyse and explain this dynamic process may be illustrated by the problem that faced Henry Moore in an early empirical study of economic cycles in the United States.

11 I have ignored the error terms here to simplify the algebra, as they do not affect the form of the equilibrium solution. The same is true in the discussion of the cobweb model that follows. I shall refer to the error term explicitly when its exclusion from the original formulation of the model affects the stochastic properties of the model.

Henry Moore's perverse demand function for pig iron

Moore (1914), using annual US data from 1871 to 1911, investigated cycles in rainfall in the United States as a potential cause of cycles in the production of agricultural products. By means of periodogram analysis[12] and visual inspection, he found evidence of cycles of length thirty-three and eight years in data on rainfall in Illinois. He then showed that these cycles in rainfall appeared to correspond to similar cycles in the yield per acre of the four main crops in Illinois, namely corn, oats, hay and potatoes. Moore concluded 'that the cyclical movement in the weather conditions represented by rainfall is the fundamental, persistent cause of the cycles of the crops' (Moore 1914, p. 57).

Moore went on to consider how these fluctuations in supply, caused by weather cycles, related to fluctuations in the prices of the products, and this involved an analysis of demand. Moore discusses one immediate problem with carrying out statistical analysis, namely that

> In order that the statistical laws of demand shall have sufficient validity to serve as prediction formulae, the observations must be numerous; and in order to obtain the requisite number of observations, a considerable period must be covered.
>
> (Moore 1914, p. 68)

To meet the difficulty that many factors that affect demand will change over time, he proposed to analyse the relationship between percentage changes in prices and quantities:

> By taking the relative change in the amount of the quantity that is demanded, instead of the absolute quantities, the effects of increasing population are approximately eliminated; and by taking the relative change in the corresponding prices instead of the corresponding absolute prices, the errors due to a fluctuating general price level are partially removed.
>
> (Moore 1914, p. 69)

Moore regressed the annual percentage change in price (y) on the annual percentage change in production (x) for the four agricultural products in his study, using some judicious data mining to choose between linear, quadratic or cubic relationships.[13] The data on the four agricultural products revealed the expected inverse relationship between the two variables. He then proceeded to ask 'Is

12 Periodogram analysis is a mathematical technique that may be applied to time series data to look for cycles and their frequencies.

13 As Moore begins his analysis of the law of demand by stating that the theory of demand relates changes in the quantity demanded to changes in prices, one might expect him to regress quantity on price. It would appear that Moore chose the percentage change in price as the dependent variable in his regressions as he wished to explore the reaction of prices to changes in quantities produced. However, he also estimated relationships between changes in prices and changes in the yield per acre and referred to these relationships as 'demand schedules'.

there any relation between the changing volume of crops and the changing volume of those producers' goods whose fluctuations are generally regarded as indices of the activity of trade?' (Moore 1914, p. 103). To investigate this matter he chose pig iron, as 'It is a common observation of writers on economic crises that the production of pig-iron is an unusually good barometer of trade' (Moore 1914, p. 105). However, the plot of the percentage change in the price of pig iron (y) against the percentage change in production (x) revealed a positive relationship. The regression equation fitted by Moore was

$$y = 0.5211x - 4.58 \ (R^2 = 0.288)$$

Moore's explanation of this apparent contradiction of standard economic demand theory is ingenious, if difficult to follow:[14]

> Upon the assumption that all demand curves are of the negative type, it would be impossible for general prices to fall while the yield per acre of crops is decreasing. In consequence of the decrease in the yield per acre, the price of crops would ascend, the volume of commodities represented by pig-iron would decrease, and upon the hypothesis of the universality of the descending type of demand curves, the prices of commodities like pig-iron would rise. In a period of declining yield of crops, therefore, there would be a rise of prices, and in a period of increasing yield of crops there would be a fall of prices. But the facts are exactly the contrary.
>
> (Moore 1914, p. 112)

Moore's rationale for his upward-sloping demand for pig iron was criticised by Wright (1915), who suggested an explanation in terms of shifts in demand and supply curves over time.[15] A further critique of Moore's work was presented by Working (1927) in an article that made an important theoretical contribution to the development of econometric theory by focusing on the question of 'identification'. How are we to explain the combinations of quantities and prices that are observed over time? One explanation is that the market data collected over time, that is, the observed ($P_{(t)}$, $Q_{(t)}$) combinations, represent a set of moving equilibria, as illustrated in Figure 10.2.

In this example, the demand curves have moved relatively more over time than have the supply curves, so that the observed ($P_{(t)}$, $Q_{(t)}$) slope upwards from the origin, tracing out an approximation to the supply curve, as illustrated in Figure 10.3.

Assuming that these observations represented a supply curve or a demand curve and that data on current prices and quantities alone could be used to estimate these functions was one of the early fallacies in empirical economic analysis.

14 It actually appears in the book before the reporting of the empirical results, so I suspect it represents a piece of *ex post* rationalisation rather than *ex ante* theorising.

15 Wright's review of Moore (1914) is reprinted as chapter 16 in Hendry and Morgan (1995) and discussed in their introduction (pp. 22–4).

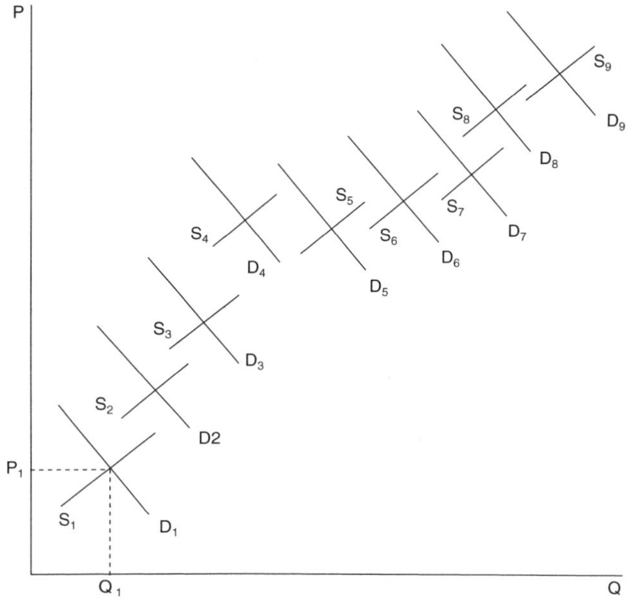

Figure 10.2 Market equilibria over time.

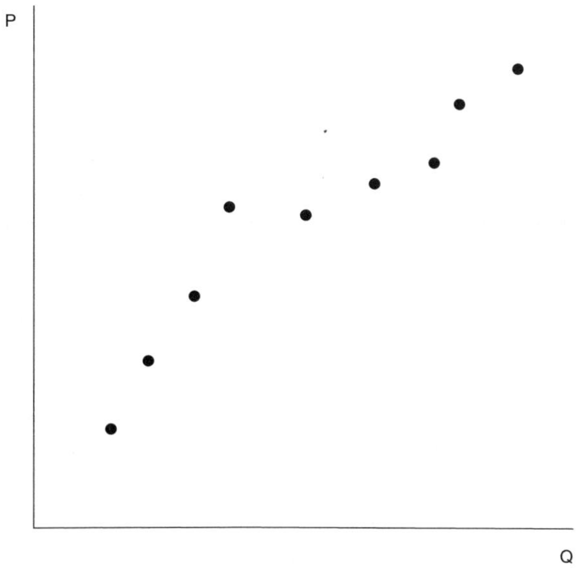

Figure 10.3 A hypothetical demand curve for pig iron.

Given Figure 10.2 represents shifts in both curves, we cannot 'identify' either curve from the ($P_{(t)}$, $Q_{(t)}$). This lack of identification provides an alternative and more plausible explanation of the data on pig iron than Henry Moore's claim that a positively sloped demand curve for pig iron in the United States was a new type of demand curve applicable to all producer goods.[16]

Dynamic adjustment processes

In general, comparative static analysis does not offer an explanation of the dynamic process of moving from one equilibrium to another, or what happens in a market if it is out of equilibrium. However, there are some models, such as the 'cobweb' model, which do set out to explain the adjustment process.[17] Here the model follows a causal chain, in which (1) the quantity supplied depends on last period's price; (2) to clear the market, the price adjusts until the quantity demanded equals the quantity supplied, and (3) this price determines the quantity supplied in the next period. This model may be written as:

Example 2 A cobweb model

(Supply equation) $$Q^S_{(t)} = \alpha^*_1 + \beta^*_1 P_{(t-1)} \quad (5)$$

(Market clearing condition) $$Q^D_{(t)} = Q^S_{(t)} \quad (6)$$

(Price determination) $$P_{(t)} = \alpha^*_2 + \beta^*_2 Q^D_{(t)} \quad (7)$$

Depending on the relative slopes of the supply and demand curves, the model may either converge to the market clearing price and stabilise or set up explosive cycles and diverge from equilibrium.[18] This is shown in Figures 10.4–5.

The problem of false trading

While the cobweb model does provide a mechanism through which the market price could converge to the equilibrium price, it still does not address the question of what is the actual process involving suppliers and demanders that brings about the adjustment. This is because of the difficulty of providing a plausible story that explains why some demanders do not buy or some suppliers do not sell at prices above or below the equilibrium price. If such 'false' trading does occur, then the mathematical solution that the quantity Q^e is traded at the price P^e does not hold, as is implied in equation (3).

16 See Morgan (1990, pp. 139–42) for further discussion of the Identification Problem in market analysis.

17 This model was developed to explain cycles in the prices of agricultural products and, for that reason, it is sometimes referred to as the hog cycle theory (see Pashigian 1987).

18 In a simple model using linear functions, there is a third possibility that if the two functions have the same slopes, though with opposite signs, the market would oscillate indefinitely between two prices and neither converge nor diverge from the equilibrium market clearing price.

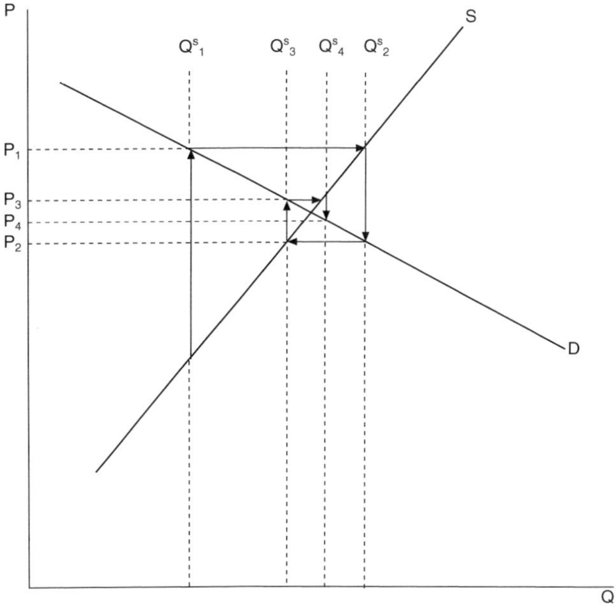

Figure 10.4 A cobweb model (stable case).

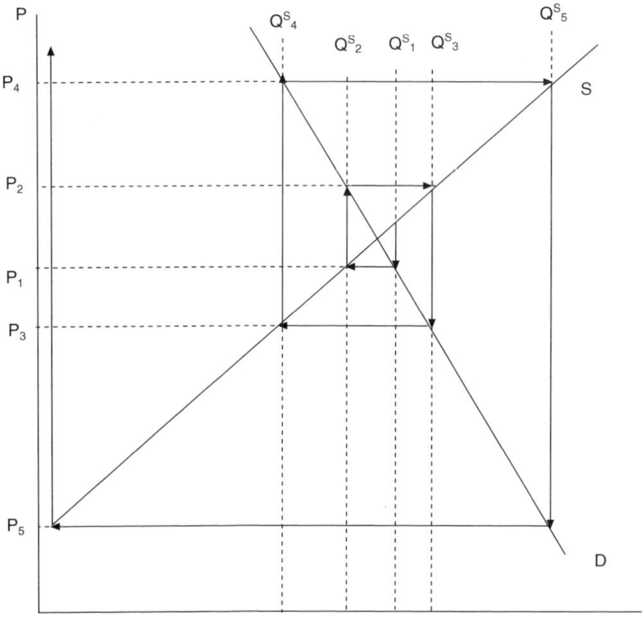

Figure 10.5 A cobweb model (unstable case).

One theoretical attempt to solve this problem was proposed by Walras in 1874 through his process of *tâtonnement*.[19] In his simplest model of exchange, there are economic agents who have endowments of *n* different goods and who are willing to supply or demand these goods depending on the relative prices. The assumption is that there is an auctioneer who offers a list of prices to all the agents and then calculates for each good whether there is excess supply or demand. He then lowers or raises the prices to remove the excess supply or demand and consults the agents again. Only when the price list he offers eliminates all excesses is trading allowed to commence, so that all the markets clear at the equilibrium prices determined by the *tâtonnement* process. While the auctioneer prevents false trading in this fairy story, the approach does not solve the problem but merely assumes it away. The actual way in which market prices and quantities are generated remains a cloudy theoretical area.

Macroeconomic models

In the aftermath of the publication of Keynes's *General Theory* (Keynes 1936), economists began to specify macroeconomic models to explain the behaviour of macroeconomic variables. A simple and widely used Keynesian model is given below.

Example 3 A simple Keynesian model

(Consumption function) $$C_{(t)} = \alpha_1 + \beta_1 Y_{(t)}\ [+u_{(t)}] \qquad (8)$$

(Income identity) $$Y_{(t)} \equiv C_{(t)} + I_{(t)} \qquad (9)$$

(Here there are two endogenous variables, $C_{(t)}$ and $Y_{(t)}$, and one exogenous variable, $I_{(t)}$. The subscript (t) indicates that data on the variables are gathered over time. The model will be explored more fully below.)

Causality versus simultaneity in econometric models

While early empirical attempts to analyse markets had shown the need to consider both supply and demand functions simultaneously, much early empirical work in economics tended to deal with individual equations and assume a causal relationship between the 'dependent' variable on the left-hand side (LHS) of the equation and the 'explanatory' variable(s) on the right-hand side (RHS). An error term was added to the right-hand side before beginning the regression analysis and the error was assumed to be random, normally distrib-

19 The word *tâtonnement* is the French word meaning 'groping', a term that possibly had fewer negative connotations in the late nineteenth century than today. For a concise discussion of the *tâtonnement* process, see Negishi (1987).

uted and independent of the variables on the right-hand side.[20] This approach to estimating parameters was challenged by the work of researchers associated with the Cowles Commission who investigated the problems of estimating the parameters in equations that formed part of a model or system of equations.

Their basic model involved a system of G equations to explain the behaviour of G endogenous variables where there were K exogenous variables in the model. They formulated the *structural form* of a model (in matrix terms) as

$$\mathbf{By} + \Gamma\mathbf{x} = \mathbf{u} \tag{10}$$

where $\mathbf{B}$ is a $(G \times G)$ matrix of coefficients on the G endogenous variables in $\mathbf{y}$ and Γ is a $(G \times K)$ matrix of the coefficients on the K exogenous variables in the model in $\mathbf{x}$. The vector $\mathbf{u}$ contains the error structure in the model. To answer the question of how to estimate the parameters in $\mathbf{B}$ and Γ the solution that the Cowles Commission proposed was to use the Method of Maximum Likelihood (ML) to define the estimators of the unknown parameters. This provided a completely general solution to the problem, in the sense that for any $\mathbf{B}$ and Γ, differential calculus provides the appropriate set of equations to be solved to find the ML estimates and, under fairly general statistical assumptions, these ML estimates have desirable statistical properties.[21]

In a properly defined model in which the G equations are independent, $\mathbf{B}$ is a non-singular matrix and we may solve the model to express the endogenous variables as a function of the exogenous variables to give the *reduced form* of the model:

$$\mathbf{y} = \mathbf{B}^{-1}\Gamma\mathbf{x} + \mathbf{B}^{-1}\mathbf{u} \tag{11}$$

$$= \Pi\mathbf{x} + \mathbf{v} \tag{12}$$

The reduced form shows clearly that (1) the endogenous variables are jointly determined by the system of simultaneous equations, rather than being causally

20 This approach to the early estimation of the macroeconomic consumption function is chronicled in Thomas (1989).

21 The Cowles Commission provided a theoretical general solution, usually referred to as Full Information Maximum Likelihood Estimation (FIML), in which all the information assumed to be known about the structures of $\mathbf{B}$, Γ and $\mathbf{u}$ is incorporated into the process of estimation. However, the set of equations to be solved to provide the ML estimates are usually non-linear, and even for small models the computational arithmetic was vastly greater than that which could be handled by the Cowles Commission in the days before powerful high-speed computers. The compromise solution proposed by the Cowles Commission was Limited Information Maximum Likelihood (LIML), in which only a sub-set of the information is used. Two-stage Least Squares (2SLS) and Three-stage Least Squares (3SLS) were other, alternative estimation procedures proposed to deal with the computational problems. The availability of powerful, high-speed computers in recent years has allowed FIML and other number-crunching methods of estimation to be applied without the need for compromise.

linked, and (2) they are stochastic, as each element in **y** is a linear combination of the elements in the error vector **u**.[22]

Example 4 For the simple Keynesian model in equations (4) and (5), the reduced form is

$$C_{(t)} = \alpha/(1-\beta) + \{\beta/(1-\beta)\}I_{(t)} + \{1/(1-\beta)\}u_{(t)} \tag{13}$$

$$Y_{(t)} = \alpha/(1-\beta) + \{1/(1-\beta)\}I_{(t)} + \{1/(1-\beta)\}u_{(t)} \tag{14}$$

The law of large numbers as the econometrician's invisible hand?

Tony Lawson has argued that

> the dependency of mathematical-deductivist methods on closed systems in turn more or less necessitates, and certainly encourages, formulations couched in terms of (i) isolated (ii) atoms. The metaphorical reference to atoms here is not intended to convey anything about size. Rather the reference is to items which exercise their own separate, independent and invariable (and so predictable) effects (relative to, or as a function of, initial conditions).[23]
>
> (Lawson 2003, p. 13)

How does this relate to the stochastic economic variables in econometric models? One answer is to see the individual economic agents as atoms, but in the sense that they are whizzing around in economic space and, even if they are travelling on predictable paths (e.g. always catching the 07.35 a.m. train from Surbiton and eating fish on a Friday), we do not have enough information in our data on quantities and prices to predict these characteristics. However, these agents respond differently to different economic phenomena, to the extent that they have different degrees of risk aversion, different expectations and aspirations, so that in aggregating their responses to what we observe in market behaviour or at the macroeconomic level, we find stable patterns across the distribution of agents' preferences.[24] The errors in econometric models sometimes

22 Herman Wold argued the case for modelling economic phenomena as causal chains and developed mathematical transformations that allowed any simultaneous equation system to be rewritten and estimated as a 'recursive system' or causal chain model. However, as the resulting parameter estimates were difficult to interpret, Wold's approach never received much support from applied econometricians. See Morgan (1990) and Hendry and Morgan (1995) for further discussion of Wold's work.

23 A more detailed account of Lawson's methodological criticisms of econometric practices may be found in Lawson (1989).

24 The variables are 'stochastic' rather than 'random' as there is usually an element of memory of things past in economic behaviour, or put less poetically, economic variables tend to be autocorrelated over time.

represent errors of measurement, but more generally are there to represent the net effect of phenomena that are not included in the model.

Lack of dynamic adjustment in early econometric models

In a typical early work estimating an equation from time series data, such as

$$Y_{(t)} = \alpha + \beta X_{(t)} + u_{(t)} \tag{15}$$

the assumption was that Y adjusted completely to changes in X within the time period being considered (usually a year in much of the early work); a one-off change in X, say ΔX, produced a one-off response from Y of $\beta\Delta X$ and then Y remained at the new level in periods $(t+1)$, $(t+2)$, etc. The assumption was also made that the error in the equation was random, but in practice the error term was frequently found to be non-random and to follow an autoregressive pattern. One stochastic model that was frequently observed was the First-Order Autoregressive AR(1) process

$$u_{(t)} = \rho u_{(t-1)} + v_{(t)} \qquad 0 \leq \rho \leq 1 \tag{16}$$

The presence of non-random errors reduces the efficiency of Ordinary Least Squares (OLS) as a method of estimation and autocorrelation was seen as a nuisance to be eliminated by applying a transformation to the data.[25] Over time, particularly with the increasing availability of quarterly, monthly or even daily data, the implicit assumption that adjustment took place within a single time period came into question. A number of dynamic models appeared to represent the dynamic adjustment process and two in particular became popular.

Adaptive Expectations

The Adaptive Expectations model was a simple, but intuitively appealing, model of expectation formation that assumed (1) expectations about some variable, $X_{(t)}$, were based on the past behaviour of X and (2) expectations were adjusted by comparing expectations with actual outcomes. If $X^e_{(t)}$ is the expected value of $X_{(t)}$, the adjustment process is

$$X^e_{(t)} = X^e_{(t-1)} + (1-\lambda)(X_{(t-1)} - X^e_{(t-1)}) \qquad 0 < \lambda < 1 \tag{17}$$

or

$$X^e_{(t)} = \lambda X^e_{(t-1)} + (1-\lambda)X_{(t-1)} \tag{18}$$

25 The transformation developed by Cochrane and Orcutt quickly became the standard procedure and was built into computer programs, such as TPS, that were developed to carry out regression analysis of economic time series.

Some algebraic manipulation yields

$$\begin{aligned} X^{e}_{(t)} &= (1-\lambda)\Sigma\lambda^{j}X_{(t-j-1)} \qquad j=0,1,\ldots\infty. \\ &= (1-\lambda)(X_{(t-1)} + \lambda X_{(t-2)} + \lambda^{2}X_{(t-3)} + \lambda^{3}X_{(t-4)} + \ldots) \end{aligned} \tag{19}$$

Suppose

$$Y_{(t)} = \alpha + \beta X^{e}_{(t)} + u_{(t)} \tag{20}$$

where, for example, $Y_{(t)}$ represents planned inventories and $X^{e}_{(t)}$ represents expected future sales of some commodity. Using equation (18) and some algebraic manipulation, equation (20) may be transformed to give

$$Y_{(t)} = \alpha(1-\lambda) + \lambda Y_{(t-1)} + \beta(1-\lambda)X_{(t)} + u_{(t)} - \lambda u_{(t-1)} \tag{21}$$ [26]

Partial Adjustment

The Partial Adjustment model was developed to explain why investment to increase the stock of capital (machinery) to some target value, $K^{*}_{(t)}$, was spread over time, rather than being carried out immediately. Let $K_{(t-1)}$ be the capital stock at the end of period $(t-1)$ and $K_{(t)}$ the capital stock achieved by the end of period t, so that the amount of investment carried out in period t is $I_t = (K_{(t)} - K_{(t-1)})$. The model assumes that the decision to invest seeks to minimise the costs of adjustment and these costs stem from two sources. The first depends on the actual amount of investment made, i.e. $(K_{(t)} - K_{(t-1)})$ and the second on any costs that arise from the failure to adjust fully to K^{*} by the end of the period, i.e. $(K_{(t)} - K^{*}_{(t)})$. It is assumed that each of the costs is different and that the cost functions are quadratic.[27] If the investor wishes to undertake the optimum amount of investment that will minimise costs, the cost function to be minimised is

$$C = \mu_1(K_{(t)} - K_{(t-1)})^2 + \mu_2(K_{(t)} - K^{*}_{(t)})^2 \tag{22}$$

Differentiating (22) and solving to find the minimum value yields the solution that the optimum amount of investment is

$$I_{(t)} = \theta(K^{*}_{(t)} - K_{(t-1)}) \tag{23}$$

where $\theta = \mu_2/(\mu_1 + \mu_2)$ and $0 < \theta < 1$. Alternatively, (23) may be written as

$$K_{(t)} = \theta K^{*}_{(t)} + (1-\theta)K_{(t-1)} \tag{24}$$

26 This result shows the importance of including the error term in the model from the outset, as one effect of the transformation applied to (20) to obtain (21) is to produce an AR(1) error term in (21).

27 This assumption allows for the possibility that costs will rise more than proportionately as the amount of adjustment or non-adjustment rises, which is plausible, and simplifies the mathematics, which is both understandable and desirable.

Suppose the optimal capital stock depends on the rate of interest, so that

$$K^*_{(t)} = \alpha + \beta r_{(t)} + u_{(t)} \tag{25}$$

Substituting (25) into (24) produces

$$K_{(t)} = \alpha\theta + \beta\theta r_{(t)} + (1 - \theta)K_{(t-1)} + \theta u_{(t)} \tag{26}$$

The point to note is that the equations to be estimated in both the Adaptive Expectations (AE) model (equation (21)) and Partial Adjustment (PA) model (equation (26)) contain the lagged dependent variable. The implication of this is that adjustment to changes in the explanatory variables on the RHS of the equation will not be completed by the end of period t, but there will be a multiplier effect that continues into the future via the lagged dependent variable. It is possible to think of short-term and long-term effects of a change in $r_{(t)}$. Suppose r increases by $\Delta r_{(t)}$ and then remains constant at the new level. Then by the end of period t, the short-term change in the capital stock will be $\Delta K_{(t)} = \beta\theta\Delta r_{(t)}$, but the lagged dependent variable continues to produce change and the multiplier process continues until we reach the long-term change, $\Delta K = \beta\Delta r$.[28]

To return to the story of early econometric studies and the problem of autocorrelation, when researchers began using the AE and PA models, they frequently found that the problem of autocorrelation that had bedevilled the early work had largely disappeared. This led to a change in attitude towards autocorrelation; rather than seeing it as a mere nuisance to be got rid of, in many, if not most, cases the autocorrelation represented an important dynamic component in economic behaviour that had been missed in the early work.

Non-stationarity and co-integration

It has been argued above that economic variables are stochastic and therefore their properties are governed by the parameters of the relevant statistical distributions. If the data are time series and they are stationary, the mean, variance and covariances of the distributions are finite and the process is easy to analyse. Unfortunately, most economic time series are trended and are non-stationary, so that the mean, variance and covariances tend to infinity as the length of the time series increases.[29]

28 The exploration of the effects of a one-off change in one of the variables in a dynamic model is a convenient exercise to illustrate the multiplier process, but is not a realistic description of the behaviour of the variables when the series are changing continuously over time. When the variables continue to change over time, there will be no equilibrium values to which they will converge.

29 It is possible to produce stationarity in a non-stationary series by differencing the terms in the series. For example, if a variable contains a linear trend, then the first differences will be stationary, the second differences of a quadratic trend will be stationary and so on for higher-order polynomials.

Until recently economists (and econometricians) ignored the non-stationarity in economic time series and the potential problems this might cause, but in the 1980s Clive Granger[30] asked a difficult question. In estimating a standard regression equation we assume the parameters are constant over time. However, if the variables are non-stationary and are increasing without limit, how do we know that they will stay in that relationship and not drift apart as they increase over time? Without going into the technical details, Granger was able to establish the conditions under which there could be a stable relationship between non-stationary variables and how to test for the presence of these conditions. Consider the relationship

$$Y_{(t)} = \alpha + \beta_1 X_{1(t)} + \beta_2 X_{2(t)} + \ldots + \beta_k X_{k(t)} + u_{(t)} \quad (27)$$

where Y and at least some of the X_k are non-stationary. Then co-integration (i.e. for the variables to be related by (27)) requires that

$$u_{(t)} = Y_{(t)} - \alpha - \beta_1 X_{1(t)} - \beta_2 X_{2(t)} - \ldots - \beta_k X_{k(t)} \quad (28)$$

should be stationary. Intuitively, if $u_{(t)}$ is stationary, deviations of Y from the values predicted by the RHS of (27) will remain finite and not drift off towards infinity.

This theoretical work has increased our understanding of the behaviour of non-stationary processes and reduced somewhat the probability of finding spurious relationships between economic time-series variables. One of the implications of this work is that the values generated by dynamic processes do not converge to fixed equilibrium values. However, it may be possible to discover stable relationships between economic variables, even when the generating processes are non-stationary and the variables are growing without limit.

Heterodox economics and econometrics

The discussion so far has concentrated on the application of econometric analysis to mainstream economics (i.e. neoclassical microeconomic and macroeconomic models), reflecting the fact that the bulk of published applied econometric work lies in this area. However, in recent years there has been some interest in the use of econometrics by some heterodox economics. One such group is the post-Keynesians,[31] a number of whom have discussed this matter.

Gerrard (2002, p. 129) notes that 'there is a long history of post-Keynesian antagonism towards econometrics. The origins of this antagonism lie in Keynes's critique of Tinbergen's early applications of econometric techniques.'[32] However, having discussed alternative methodologies of applied

30 Clive Granger was a joint winner of the Nobel Prize in Economics in 2003, along with Robert Engle. The award was largely for his work on co-integration.

31 See Harcourt (1987) for a discussion of this heterogeneous group.

32 The Keynes–Tinbergen debate is discussed in Hendry and Morgan (1995), where the original articles are reprinted.

econometric analysis, he argues that 'Econometric methods can, and should, be used more extensively within post-Keynesian economics as an essential part of a radical methodology' (Gerrard 2002, p 132).

Downward (1999, 2002) also discusses the use of econometrics in post-Keynesian economics and illustrates the possibilities in an analysis of alternative neoclassical and post-Keynesian theories of how prices are formulated. In considering the possible role of econometrics in discriminating between alternative economic theories, he suggests there are three options for post-Keynesians:

> First, one can retreat from econometric work altogether. Secondly, one can hope that eventually the traditional approach to econometrics, or even recent developments in econometric methods will, eventually *settle* debates. Finally, one can provide some modified interpretation of the role of econometrics in producing economic knowledge. It is a central contention of this chapter that the methodological emphasis on realism noted earlier permits a feasible path ahead in the third course of action by taking into account recent developments in econometrics.
>
> (Downward 2002, p. 152)

These are interesting new developments and illustrate the point made earlier that models do not have to be neoclassical or feature the concept of equilibrium to be suitable for econometric analysis.

Conclusion

Economic theory provides one of the three major components of econometrics, but in general econometricians have not developed their own models, but have tended to choose models from the body of existing economic theory rather like off-the-peg suits, accepting in the process the implicit and explicit assumptions of these theories. As was shown in the discussion of the analysis of markets, market clearing – or the existence of a market equilibrium – was taken over as part of the model. However, the experience of econometricians in analysing market data suggested the need to consider dynamic models to explain the evolution of the variables over time and it became clear that the economic processes being analysed did not converge to fixed equilibrium values. While dynamic models have been used to carry out theoretical exercises concerning short-run effects and long-run equilibria, these were conceptual exercises and bore no relation to the actual behaviour of economic time series. However, the existence of stable relationships between non-stationary variables suggests that being out of a stable, static equilibrium does not imply disequilibrium, but the need for theories that do not depend on static equilibria.

Looking back over the evolution of econometrics since the Second World War, one finds considerable lags between the development of theoretical results and their impact on the empirical researcher. Data mining has been a major problem in time series econometrics, made worse by easy access to regression software packages that reduced the burden of computation. In many cases, researchers do not begin with a well specified economic model, but rather write down a 'plausible' relationship between the variables of interest. The resulting relationship may at best be a reduced form equation that could be derived from some unspecified structural form of a model. In many cases, one suspects that the theory was developed after the empirical analysis was completed and the advice on how to publish an article in applied econometrics given in the box is not entirely cynical or inaccurate.

The current emphasis in econometric work is more concerned with the dynamic specification of models and here there has been considerable progress in treating the 'unexplained' variation in the residuals of the fitted models as containing important information about economic dynamics. One thing that has changed over time is that the early days of great confidence and hope have passed with the conspicuous failures of many model builders and growing realisation of the problems involved in analysing economic time series data. In 1950, Lawrence Klein, another winner of a Nobel Prize in Economics,[33] could write:

> Economic theory is called upon to provide the true structure of the systems of equations. The parameters of the true system may or may not be identifiable. However, if we fail to get an identified system because certain variables have been omitted from the equations or because the equations are not true, we must use economic theory to improve the equations until they do represent the truth. If the truth permits identification of the parameters, we may proceed with statistical estimation.
>
> (Klein 1950, p. 10, n. 12)

The words 'true' and 'truth' have gone from the vocabulary of most econometricians these days.

To return to the question of equilibrium, my conclusion is that, whereas the concept of equilibrium has been the source of much contention in economics, this has not been so in the case of econometrics. At best it has been paid lip service in the discussion of a number of economic models and lurked in the background of some applied work in econometrics, while the main concern in econometrics in recent years has been with dynamic issues. One explanation of this difference in emphasis was the need for econometricians to develop concepts to handle time-series data, that is, data on economic variables collected over time. Many, if not most, of these series contained trends that were difficult to explain as variations about some static equilibrium value and so the need arose to analyse dynamic situations. Thus in econometrics the focus has been on dynamics and processes of adjustment rather than on equilibrium.

33 Klein won his Nobel Prize in 1980. The quote is taken from a pioneering econometric study of the US economy in which Klein used twenty annual time series observations to estimate the parameters in a six-equation model that contained three behavioural equations and three identities.

How to publish an article in applied economics

Question Suppose you have found some economic data on a variable, *Y*, and a number of other economic variables (X_1, X_2, . . ., X_m) that might be used to 'explain' (i.e. model) the behaviour of *Y*. How do you turn these data into a publishable article in an economic journal?

Answer The process involves two stages.

Stage 1 Empirical analysis

- Run a large number of regressions, regressing *Y* on all possible subsets of the X_i, ($i = 1, \ldots, m$). Look at goodness of fit (R^2) and standard 95 per cent *t* ratios for the significant variables.
- Select the best fitting equation (denoted by equation 1) and think of a plausible economic explanation for this particular set of *X*s might 'explain' *Y*. Call this Hypothesis 1.
- Look through the badly fitting equations and select one for which there is an equally plausible, but different, economic explanation of why this alternative set of *X*s might explain the behaviour of *Y*. Call these equation 2 and Hypothesis 2 respectively.
- Destroy all the remaining regressions.

Stage 2 Writing the article An article should contain the following sections:

1. *Introduction.* This section should build up the case for why 'explaining' the behaviour of *Y* is of vital importance, probably deserving of a Nobel Prize.
2. *Theoretical discussion.* Now produce Hypotheses 1 and 2 as possible explanations and discuss them. The theoretical process involves producing a mathematical justification for the two hypotheses (i.e. models that can be used in regression analysis and which are your original equations 1 and 2). Derive some predictions concerning the expected signs of the parameters in the equations.
3. *The data.* This can be quite short and sloppy, as economists are not really interested in data. (Should some screwball contact you after your article is published and ask for your data, respond that your data were lost when your computer crashed and some person or persons unknown stole the backup disk containing the only spare copy.)
4. *Statistical analysis.* Report your regression results for equations 1 and 2. Point out that equation 1 has a high R^2 and that all the estimated parameters have the correct signs, as the theory predicted, whereas equation 2 has a low R^2 and the signs of the estimated parameters are all wrong. Clearly Hypothesis 1 is superior to Hypothesis 2.
5. *Conclusions.* Summarise the results and reiterate how earth-shaking your findings are. If you can rubbish some other economists who were foolish enough to have advocated your Hypothesis 2, so much the better, as they may then respond and you will get a second publication in your reply to their response to your original article.

Finally Submit the article and sit back to await promotion.

References

Chow, G.C. (1983), *Econometrics*, McGraw-Hill, New York.

Denton, F.T. (1985)', Data mining as an industry', *Review of Economics and Statistics*, 67, 124–7.

Downward, P. (1999), *Pricing Theory in Post Keynesian Economics. A Realist Approach*, Edward Elgar, Cheltenham.

Downward, P. (2002), 'Realism econometrics and post-Keynesian economics', in Dow, S.C. and Hillard, J. (eds) *Post-Keynesian Econometrics, Microeconomics and the Theory of the Firm*, Edward Elgar, Cheltenham.

Floud, R. (ed.) (1974), *Essays in Quantitative Economic History*, Clarendon Press, Oxford.

Friedman, M. (1957), *A Theory of the Consumption Function*, Princeton University Press, Princeton, NJ.

Frisch, R. (1933), 'Editorial', *Econometrica*, 1, 1–4.

Gerrard, B. (2002), 'The role of econometrics in a radical methodology', in Dow, S.C. and Hillard, J. (eds) *Post-Keynesian Econometrics, Microeconomics and the Theory of the Firm*, Edward Elgar, Cheltenham.

Granger, C.W.J. and Newbold, P. (1974), 'Spurious regression in econometrics', *Journal of Econometrics*, 2, 111–20.

Harcourt, G.C. (1987), 'Post-Keynesian economics', in Eatwell, J., Milgate, M. and Newman, P. (eds) *The New Palgrave. A Dictionary of Economics*, III, Macmillan, London, pp. 924–8.

Hendry, D.F. and Morgan, M.S. (eds), (1995), *The Foundations of Econometric Analysis*, Cambridge University Press, Cambridge.

Klein, L.R. (1950), *Economic Fluctuations in the United States, 1921–1941*, Wiley, New York.

Lawson, T. (1989), 'Realism and instrumentalism in the development of Econometrics', *Oxford Economic Papers*, 41 (March), 236–58.

Lawson, T. (2003), *Reorienting Economics*, Routledge, London.

Lovell, M.C. (1983), 'Data mining', *Review of Economics and Statistics*, 65, 1–12.

Malinvaud, E. (1966), *Statistical Methods of Econometrics*, North-Holland, Amsterdam.

Moore, H.L. (1914), *Economic Cycles. Their Law and Cause*, Macmillan, New York.

Morgan, M.S. (1990), *The History of Econometric Ideas*, Cambridge University Press, Cambridge.

Negishi, T. (1987), '*Tâtonnement* and recontracting', in Eatwell, J., Milgate, M. and Newman, P. (eds) *The New Palgrave. A Dictionary of Economics*, IV, Macmillan, London, pp. 589–95.

Pashigian, B.P. (1987), 'Cobweb theorem', in Eatwell, J., Milgate, M. and Newman, P. (eds) *The New Palgrave. A Dictionary of Economics*, I, Macmillan, London, pp. 463–4.

Pesaran, M.H. (1998), 'Econometrics' in Eatwell, J., Milgate, M. and Newman, P. (eds) *The New Palgrave. A Dictionary of Economics*, II, Macmillan, London, pp. 8–22.

Qin, D. and Gilbert, C.L. (2001), 'The error term in the history of time series econometrics', *Journal of Econometrics*, 101, 195–219.

Reuter, P. (1982), 'The irregular economy and the quality of macroeconomic statistics', in V. Tanzi (ed.), *The Underground Economy in the United States and Abroad*, Lexington Books, Lexington, MA.

Richter, M.K. (1987), 'Revealed preference theory', in Eatwell, J., Milgate, M. and

Newman, P. (eds) (1987b) *The New Palgrave. A Dictionary of Economics*, IV, Macmillan, London, pp. 166–70.

Thomas, J.J. (1989), 'The early econometric history of the consumption function', *Oxford Economic Papers*, 41, 131–49.

Tinbergen, J. (1939), *Statistical Testing of Business Cycle Theories*, League of Nations, Geneva.

Working, E.J. (1927), 'What do "statistical demand" curves show?', *Quarterly Journal of Economics*, 41, 212–35.

Wright, P.C. (1915), 'Review of Moore's *Economic Cycles*', *Quarterly Journal of Economics*, 29, 631–41.

11 Equilibrium in economics

Some concepts and controversies

Victoria Chick

Equilibrium has a wide variety of meanings in economics. A range of equilibrium concepts is here explained sufficiently to provide the background for a discussion of some of the controversies over its use as an organising principle for theory. Here one must be careful to distinguish between concepts of equilibrium and the equilibrium method, the latter being theory constructed to give only equilibrium solutions. I show that several controversies in economics have their roots in the application of one concept of equilibrium to work that uses another concept, and that many criticisms directed to equilibrium are really attacking some other feature of theory.

The purpose of this chapter is to introduce to a cross-disciplinary audience some of the many different concepts that economists call equilibrium and to outline some of our controversies about the use of the concept. I shall assume that it is a concept used in the construction of economic theory, not a feature ascribed to the actual economy, though I touch on that point once, briefly. Thus I hope to avoid the confusion between the ontic and theoretic interpretations, which is the main target of Lawson's chapter in this volume.

I am going to be very old-fashioned in my choice of sources, because I feel the basic lines of dissent are clearer in this literature. I am not claiming to be an expert in the history of the development of the concept in economics, nor will the discussion be organised along chronological lines. The modern interpretation of equilibrium, a solution to a mathematical model, will be given comparatively short shrift, both because it forms a large part of the discussion in the chapter by Backhouse, and because there is no controversy about a mathematical solution, only about the model to which it is the solution on grounds such as fitness for purpose. That is not my subject here, but I do address, briefly, whether it is meaningful to call a mathematical solution 'equilibrium'.

In the next section, some of the forms that the concept of equilibrium has taken in economics are outlined. Then I take up some specific examples of dissent, to do with formalism, the treatment of time, and the role of human agency, and show how conflict, misinterpretation and confusion have arisen through the application of concepts of equilibrium different from the one the author had in mind. There is a short conclusion.

Concepts of equilibrium in economics

Choice-theoretic equilibrium: a microeconomic concept

A central idea in neoclassical microeconomics is that individuals optimise some objective, subject to constraints. The consumer maximises her/his utility subject to income, the producer his/her profits subject to technology, the stock of capital, and expected prices and wages. These optimum positions are often spoken of as equilibria, for, short of that situation, the agents will act to change their consumption or production behaviour. The absence of change was for a long time one hallmark of the economists' concept of equilibrium (though this was later altered, as we shall see). This optimising concept has the implication that in equilibrium all unexploited opportunities have been exhausted. When generalised to 'markets' which involve the interaction of many agents, we have the concept about which Hicks was quite passionate: 'There is an equilibrium when all individuals are choosing the quantities, to produce and consume, which they prefer. To a conception of equilibrium that is of this type we must hold fast' (Hicks 1965, p. 23). Agents are not only choosing what they prefer, but can actually realise their choices. Thus this concept of equilibrium carries with it the implication of co-ordination of plans.

Market clearing

Utility maximising lies behind the construction of demand curves, and profit maximisation behind supply curves. It is thus an easy step to move to equality of supply and demand, or market clearing, as the criterion of equilibrium at a market, rather than individual, level. Although it comes to the same thing as Hicks's criterion, it connects with an earlier tradition, which derived from the original meaning of equilibrium: a balance of forces (from *aequus*, equal, and *libra*, balance). The actions taken by consumers and producers to achieve their optimum positions constitute the 'forces'.

A position of rest

In nineteenth and early twentieth century economics the use of the term 'equilibrium' is often non-technical and descriptive: for example, equality of (the value of) exports and imports is balance-of-payments equilibrium (the capital account was not dominant as now). When a balance of these forces was achieved, there would be no further endogenous movement until the balance was disturbed by some exogenous change. Thus equilibrium became quite generally understood as a position of rest. This position can be brought about either by a single force acting within the context of a constraint or a limit (as in the choice-theoretic concept) or (more usually in economics) by a balance of forces. Thus this concept has a dynamic story behind it, of which it is a culminating point. Famously, Marshall borrowed both biological analogies and the metaphors of the pendulum and the rest position of balls in a bowl to illustrate the concept:

> A business firm grows and attains great strength, and afterwards perhaps stagnates and decays; and at the turning point there is a balancing or equilibrium of the forces of life and decay. . . . [W]e want first to look at a simpler balancing of forces which correspond rather to the mechanical equilibrium of a stone hanging by an elastic string, or of a number of balls resting against one another in a basin.
>
> We have now to examine the general relations of demand and supply; especially those which are connected with that adjustment of price, by which they are maintained in 'equilibrium'. This term is in common use and may be used for the present without special explanation. But there are many difficulties associated with it . . .
>
> (Marshall 1948 [1920], p. 323)

Perhaps because of Marshall's very powerful use of this analogy in supply and demand analysis, the concept of a position of rest has come to be equated with market clearing in economics. I have argued (Chick 1978, 1983) that this conflation is unfortunate, and that market clearing is but a sub-set of the more general concept of position of rest. Note that this distinction points up an important hidden assumption of market clearing: that both sides of 'the market' exert equally powerful force. This assumption becomes important in the interpretation of Keynes's *General Theory*, as we shall see.

To concentrate on rest may suggest that equilibrium is a position of inertia. Verdon (1996) has argued that this is inappropriate to the study of an activity like economics and, in particular, that it ignores the propensity of living things, especially humans perhaps, to act. However, it is activity, continual production and consumption, that keeps the object of enquiry (in Marshall's case, price) constant, so in fact there is no inconsistency: the equilibrium price of a product is determined by the constant activity of agents supplying and demanding that product. The idea of a point of rest suggests a kind of permanence, assuming the equilibrium is stable. But other examples are clearly temporary – most notably the liquidity preference theory, in which the rate of interest is determined at any moment by the balance of opinion between speculators in the market for securities. Such opinion may be quite fickle.

The end of a process

A concept of equilibrium which makes more obvious the importance of activity in at least some of its manifestations is the end-point of a process, a position which is in some sense final, though there are different time horizons involved. There is overlap with the balance-of-forces idea; for example, Marshall's market equilibrium is maintained by the actions of suppliers and buyers even though the price is 'at rest'.

In economics many kinds of equilibria are end-points of processes not necessarily brought about by a balance of forces. We have the neo-Ricardian concept of a long-period equilibrium in which all capital is allocated to the most profitable activities, so that the rate of profit is equal amongst them. This too is the culmination of a process, this time of capital accumulation, and it is sustained by capital maintenance. The multiplier (understood as an adjustment to a change in autonomous spending), the multiplier–accelerator model (a dynamic model which may converge, diverge or produce cycles, depending on the parameters and initial conditions), the outcomes of games, the convergence (if there is one) to the 'true model of the economy' of rational expectations, are further examples. The attachment of the concept of end-point to equilibrium can, however, cause problems when using the *ceteris paribus* method, as we shall see later.

Although I have described the neo-Ricardian long-period equilibrium as the end-point of a process, the neo-Ricardians themselves would say that it stands as a tendency, a position toward which the economy is always moving in the here and now, not some distant state of affairs which may never come about.

Repeating pattern

A type of equilibrium in which activity is acknowledged and which is not the end of a process is the circular flow of income in the stationary state (Quesnay 1972 [1766]) and the related idea of simple and expanded reproduction (Marx 1970 [1887]). Schumpeter (1934) employed it in his *Theory of Economic Development* and, I argue, this is the main type of equilibrium used in Keynes's *General Theory* (1936). These circular flow models incorporate time: output is produced before it is sold, workers are paid before output is produced. But in equilibrium, time is immaterial: even though producers must anticipate sales, they are confident of the volume of those sales; they will be the same as last time, and the time before that. Income and production flows, wages and prices, are reproduced time after time. It is then (and only then) harmless to talk of real wages, since prices, similarly, can be projected from the past. In the stationary state there is time, but it is not material to the overall picture, only to the configuration to be found at a particular moment. Thus a system in constant motion can be described in a static way. However, these systems need not be in equilibrium: Schumpeter (1934) analysed economic development as departures from the stationary state, and in Keynes's system equilibrium is just one result among the many possible.

Limit cycles are another repeating pattern, which economists are likely to call an equilibrium but which are not included, I understand, in the scientist's notion of equilibrium. Similarly, steady-state growth or inflation, characterised by constant rates of change, are counted by economists as 'moving equilibria'.

A general definition?

Is there a general definition of equilibrium to be extracted from these examples? Machlup (1958) was unhappy with the idea of balance of forces, regarding 'forces' as 'a rather mystical concept' – and certainly these forces are often invoked in a rather incantatory way. He suggested 'a constellation of selected interrelated variables, so adjusted to one another that no inherent tendency to change prevails in the model which they constitute' (Machlup 1958, p. 9). A situation of 'peaceful coexistence' is another proposal (p. 10), similar to the criterion of co-ordination of plans. Hahn's suggestion (1984 [1974], p. 59) that in equilibrium no agent is led to modify his behaviour or his theory of how the economy works may be more general. None of these is model-dependent.

Solution to a mathematical model

The concept of equilibrium is now usually identified with the solution to economic models. This idea is detailed in Backhouse (chapter 8 in this volume). It is easy to see how this concept of equilibrium derives from the earlier ideas explained here, but it has undergone a transformation from a concept related to how economic systems work to a purely mathematical conception: a formal, syntactic property without semantic content. The conceptual content of equilibrium is thus indistinguishable from the properties of the model to which it is the solution rather than having an independent economic meaning.

With these examples we have enough background to explore, in the next section, some of the areas of dissent, disagreement and confusion surrounding the concept of equilibrium in economics.

Dissent, disagreement and confusion

Joan Robinson versus Marshall: a protest against over-formalisation?

We have seen that Marshall used the metaphor of a balance of forces in developing his idea of an equilibrium price, and that equality of supply and demand (market clearing) is central to many economists' idea of equilibrium itself. What was there in this idea, which on the face of it looks rather commonsensical, to provoke Joan Robinson to one of her most stinging attacks (1978)? The basis of her objection was that the supply-and-demand apparatus offered no way for the economy to arrive at equilibrium: one was either in it, and had to have been so since the fall of Adam, or one was not and never would be. She illustrated the latter proposition with various hypothetical adjustment mechanisms, one of which went round and round outside equilibrium and the others resembled divergent and convergent cobwebs that did not reach the equilibrium point (in the manner of Xeno's paradox). What she was really objecting to was the transformation of an account of the incentives facing buyers and sellers (or producers) reaching a point at which further trade was not advantageous into something which had become excessively formalised, where the equilibrium price and quantity were the solution to two static, simultaneous equations without the adjustment story – in other words, the move from a semantic to a syntactic understanding of equilibrium. Once that interpretation is accepted, she is perfectly right: mathematically, the model is coherent only when the variables are compatible, that is, when they take their solution values (she used to say that points on the supply and demand curves, other than the equilibrium point common to both, 'do not exist'), and Marshall's story providing a mechanism of adjustment was, at she put it, 'tear gas'. Disequilibrium makes no sense, and equilibrium becomes a purely formal property.

Equilibrium as a concept and as a method

In Chick and Caserta (1997) we called the method which delivers only solution values Equilibrium Theory. We distinguished this from theories which have some form of equilibrium but can also say something about disequilibrium and adjustment. Equilibrium Theory is a method of analysis, as distinguished from a concept of equilibrium which can be used in a variety of methods. With the development of general equilibrium theory, Equilibrium Theory, the method, has more or less taken over economics. Hicks (1981) believed that outside equilibrium, or rather, outside a mathematical solution, variables are indeterminate, and he is not alone; if equilibrium is looked at from the syntactic point of view, disequilibrium is 'unintelligible' This view ignored, or implicitly counted as indeterminate, the determination of price and sales when markets did not clear.

'Disequilibrium economics' was rediscovered in the 1970s. A textbook by that name (van Doorn 1975) treated subjects such as the proposition that the disequilibrium outcome is determined by the short side of the market, or cobweb dynamics, aspects of price theory that were an integral part of Marshall's story. The separation between the forces operating in disequilibrium from the elements that characterise the equilibrium position is a product of mathematisation. The need for a separate mechanism of adjustment is similarly reflected in the 'auctioneer' as the *deus ex machina* of general equilibrium theory or Samuelson's correspondence principle (1947).

Compare, however, Keynes in the *Treatise on Money*:

> My object has been to find a method which is useful in describing, not merely the characteristics of static equilibrium, but also those of disequilibrium, and to discover the dynamical laws governing the passage of a monetary system from one position of equilibrium to another.
>
> (Keynes 1930, p. xvii)

Here we see the difference between a theory which has an equilibrium among other results, which is what Keynes wanted to construct, and Equilibrium

Theory. In the former, disequilibrium positions can be determined.[1] The dominance of Equilibrium Theory has been enormously extended by the generalisation of supply and demand analysis to all markets in general equilibrium theory. This theory has received assiduous attention, such that probably most would agree with Hahn that it is the 'best developed' economic theory. Kornai's *Anti-equilibrium* (1971) is entirely directed against this theory, as is Kaldor's 1985 book; and Robinson's critique holds *a fortiori*. If one compares modern expressions of the theory, particularly Debreu (1959), with the original Walras (1954 [1926]), one finds the same increase in the level of abstraction, particularly the replacement of *tâtonnement* with instantaneous clearing. This substitution has given rise to a criticism, often made of general equilibrium theory, that the knowledge required to find the equilibrium is beyond human capacity: the 'auctioneer's job' is impossible.

Note that someone pushing the logic even of Marshall's model of a market to the extreme would say that every buyer and seller must know what every other agent intends, which is also too much to ask. Compare this with the comment made by Marshall (admittedly in the context of a single market): '[the agent's] knowledge of what others are doing is supposed to be generally sufficient' (Marshall 1948 [1920], p. 341). Similarly, Walras actually thought he was providing an analysis that had some correspondence with the real world. The *tâtonnement*, a 'groping', by implication somewhat in the dark on the basis of partial knowledge, was a substitute for the complete knowledge that perfect logic (or abstract formalism) demands.

What would Robinson think now, when equilibrium has come to mean only a solution! In a very important sense her critique is a protest against the possibility that economic theory might become a purely syntactic exercise – a possibility which some would say has come to pass.

Equilibrium and the competitive model

Kaldor (1972) directed his dissent to the building blocks of supply-and-demand analysis that form the basis of general equilibrium theory: the atomistic, representative agent and, particularly, the cost conditions that are supposed to obtain. The 'forces' that are supposed to bring about equilibrium are exercised by agents each of whom is too small to affect the outcome by him/herself, so no imbalance of power can arise. Systems in which there are powerful agents have been theorised, of course, and they typically have equilibria. Kaldor focused his attention on the cost conditions assumed to prevail in pure competition, namely that there should be diminishing returns to expansion of output, or equivalently, increasing costs. Since all firms start out the same size (the representative firm

1 This was the position, derived from ordinary language, which I took in commenting on Hicks in 1982. Of course I had missed Hicks's point; see Chick (1996a). The exchange is a classic conflict of understanding between one who thinks in closed systems like equilibrium theory and one who thinks in terms of open systems.

assumption sees to that) and feel the pinch of increasing costs at the same rate, no single firm or group of firms ever gains more market power than others.

The assumption of increasing costs Kaldor found to be unrealistic. It follows from the existence of increasing returns that those firms most able to take advantage of them, by developing new markets and so on, will eventually dominate the price mechanism. The system will not come to rest until increasing returns are fully exploited. He also criticised the idea of pricing to maximise profit as misplaced precision, and advocated replacing it with a mark-up over costs.

Kaldor's critique, then, was almost a polar opposite of Robinson's. It was based, not on problems of the interior logic of the system or the conflict between formal and informal systems, but on grounds of the realism of the model's assumptions. A critique on the same grounds, but for different reasons, is Davidson (e.g. 1977). For him the problems with general competitive equilibrium are its assumptions of gross substitutability (so that labour and output are substitutes, rather than complements as they are in real-world production) and instantaneous market clearing with no uncertainty (so the system cannot find a role for money). The first is not a complaint against equilibrium, either the concept or the method, but against the extension of a model of exchange to the process of production. On the second point, Davidson is a monetary theorist, so it is understandable that he finds the latter flaw intolerable – but so should any realist, and so does at least one general equilibrium theorist (Hahn 1985 [1975]). Kaldor's and Davidson's critiques, then, are examples of dissent not against the concept of equilibrium as such but against a particular model. Robinson's critique, though focused on Marshall, is of Equilibrium Theory as a method, and applies to general equilibrium theory and much theory which postdates her.

Equilibrium and the real world

A critique that crops up often in heterodox circles is that equilibrium is a useless concept because the actual economic system is never in equilibrium. It is this aspect that most sharply divides economics and the natural sciences. In the latter, equilibrium can, in most cases, be observed or measured, or inferred from concrete evidence, while this is not the case in economics. Nor do we often have proof of the existence of economic equilibrium outside our theoretical models. Does this make the concept of economic equilibrium useless? I think not, as I hope to show in later examples.

Equilibrium and time

Robinson's critique, as we have seen, was directed against the use of static analysis, though its scope is broader. Static analysis is timeless, yet there is no doubt that economic activity takes place in time and that economies evolve. The very notion of causality may require time (but see Hicks's notion of contemporaneous causality, 1979). The kind of dynamic analysis practised in economics until recently was not really 'timeful' either, as outcomes were entirely determined by initial conditions and the parameters of the model. Both Robinson and Kaldor see equilibrium as antithetical to history:

> The only truly exogenous factor is *whatever exists at a given moment of time*, as a heritage from the past. . . . [T]he heritage of all past history [determines] what can be produced of created in the immediate future. . . . The heritage of the past is the one truly exogenous factor, and its influence will determine future events to an extent which varies *inversely* with the distance of the future period from the present. . . .
>
> The very notion of equilibrium, particularly of long-run equilibrium, amounts to a *denial* of this . . .
>
> (Kaldor 1985, p. 62; original emphasis)

Robinson would scrap equilibrium theorising to restore the role of history, yet she recognised that the theory put forward in *The General Theory*, widely (but in my view not rightly) viewed as static theory, does have a role for history:

> Short-period analysis is concerned with the equilibrium of a system with a given stock of capital and with given expectations about the future. Past history is thus put into the initial conditions, so that the analysis is static in itself, and yet is part of a dynamic theory.
>
> (Robinson 1970, p. ix)

There are many ways in which economists deal with time, and they may be worth spelling out to see if equilibrium and history are totally irreconcilable or not.

Ceteris paribus

Again let me start with a Marshallian technique: 'cutting up' time by means of putting some variables 'in the pound of *ceteris paribus*'. His theory of supply and demand, for example, distinguished three 'periods': the market period, in which output had already taken place and only exchange takes place; a short period in which the capital stock available to producers is given but output remains to be decided; and, finally, the long period, in which decisions to increase the capital stock are taken. These are, or course, artificial divisions of continuous time, but they correspond to aspects of economic decision making which, though taken simultaneously, have shorter or longer time horizons.

I would describe this technique as having in mind an economy operating in continuous time, an open system, and then making suitable divisions (temporary closures), in order to suspend time and render analysis feasible (Chick and Dow 2001). When a variable is 'held constant', it is not supposed to be without influence: its influence is merely suppressed for the time being. The various equilibria found within this system are contingent on the constraints the theorist imposes, that is, are subject to the *ceteris paribus* assumption. From this point of view, an equilibrium can be 'final' in one sub-system and not final in another, a point understood by Machlup but much misunderstood in the context of Keynes's short period. In the short period, investment in new capital was only allowed to affect aggregate demand but not to affect supply conditions (costs of production). Some critics said that the equilibrium in this short period was not really equilibrium because there was positive investment, so the capital stock was increasing and there was no point of rest. The dividing line between the short and long period was more subtle in Keynes than in Marshall but the principle was the same, so this confusion is hard to understand, unless it relates to the idea that there can only be one equilibrium and that must be final. If so, it must be the one with the longest time horizon – a kind of Freudian death wish, like the attainment of thermodynamic equilibrium.[2] If that perspective is given credence, the *ceteris paribus* method of dealing with time is disallowed.

Although the theorist can adopt whatever *ceteris paribus* conditions s/he wants for as long as s/he wants, the particular choices of Keynes and Marshall are 'drawn from the life', such that there is a natural progression from one to the other. Not only that, but the equilibrium situation in the more constrained situation will lead to the breakdown of the constraints, even of the longest period. (Imagine being in long-period equilibrium or a stationary state. Surely any entrepreneur worth his salt will take – or rather make – the first opportunity to break out of this situation with a new process, product or invention.)

The classical long period

The notion of the short and long period in classical analysis, brought into present-day analysis by the neo-Ricardians, is very different from the temporary closures of Marshall and Keynes. Milgate makes the following comment on Marshall's partial equilibrium in three 'periods' (leaving aside secular change):

> The last of these categories, as Marshall makes perfectly clear in the text, corresponds to Adam Smith's 'natural conditions' (1890, p. 347).[3] The first two are to a 'greater or lesser degree more influenced by passing events, and by causes whose action is fitful and short lived' (p. 349). What is striking about Marshall's terminology is the fact that situations that from an analytical point of view would traditionally have been regarded as 'deviations' from long-period normal equilibrium (that is, disequilibria) are explicitly referred to as different cases of 'equilibrium'.
>
> (Milgate 1987, p. 181)

We see here an echo of the desire for a single, final equilibrium, as if the metaphor of balls in a bowl had no legitimacy and only when the bowl dissolves and the balls are on the floor do we have a 'true' equilibrium.

The basic idea of classical equilibrium is a centre of gravitation: 'that config-

2 I am reminded of the motto of Roskilde University: 'In tranquillo mors, in fluctu vita'.

3 In his bibliography, Milgate cites the variorum edition of the *Principles*, which was published in 1961. 1890 is the date of the first edition.

uration of values [of variables] toward which all economic magnitudes are continually tending to conform' (Milgate 1987, p. 179). Long-period equilibrium is said to be characterised by forces which are fundamental, systematic and enduring. There may be short-period fluctuations around this centre of gravitation, but they are temporary and reversible. They leave no permanent trace on the long run. Traditionally, these short-period fluctuations were monetary dislocations (too much credit, for example); equilibrium in the long period was shaped by the forces of productivity and thrift – in today's language, by investment and saving. Ricardo and the neo-Ricardians go a step further: long-period equilibrium is found only when production has 'fully adjusted to demand', that is, takes place at long-run normal capacity utilisation (minimum average cost), and all capital is allocated to the best uses, as indicated by a uniform rate of profit prevailing throughout the economy.

To the neo-Ricardians, the short period is unsuitable for economic analysis. The short period is the realm of accident, of flux. Only in the long period are the 'systematic, fundamental and enduring' forces to be found. These forces are objective; subjective elements such as uncertainty have no place there. Thus, for example, for them the combination within one theory of short-period and long-period equilibrium in Keynes's *General Theory* is impossible, for the one entails uncertainty and the other does not (Potestio 1986). The neo-Ricardian concept of equilibrium was not Keynes's and is misapplied to his analysis. (In fact, for Keynes the long period entails *more* uncertainty than the short period, as in the passage from Kaldor above.)

Although by construction the classical/neo-Ricardian long period entails far-reaching adjustment, and thus would seem to be, in calendar time, a long way off, the 'tendency towards equilibrium' is held to be present in the actual economy, and is in place 'now' and at all times. The comparison with thermodynamic equilibrium is thus not far-fetched. A comparison could equally be made with any process for which an equilibrium is the end-point which is independent of the random fluctuations which coexist with the 'fundamental forces'.

Inter-temporal equilibrium

Joan Robinson also dissented from the neo-Ricardian conception of the long period. She favoured a more historical conception, in which the long period was the outcome of a succession of short periods. We shall see that this is compatible with Keynes's conception. But it is also the basic idea behind inter-temporal equilibrium. For the neo-Ricardian Milgate, broad acceptance of this concept would lead to the end of economics as we have known it. Inter-temporal equilibrium finds market-clearing prices over a succession of time periods, each holding, say, expectations, constant. The (equilibrium) outcome of one period, which Hicks (1939) called 'temporary equilibrium', provides the basis for expectations formation in the next. The sequential character of the equilibria precludes taking equilibrium as a centre of gravitation. Subsequent concentration on different types of temporary equilibrium, 'disequilibrium cases from the point of view of full inter-temporal equilibrium', has been responsible, Milgate argues, for the acceptance of the notion of equilibrium as a solution (but see above), in which 'equilibrium has become a category with no meaning independent of the exact specification of the initial conditions for any model' (Milgate 1987, p. 182).

While I join Milgate in deploring the identification of the concept of equilibrium with a mathematical solution to any model one cares to construct, elsewhere (Chick 2002) I have made an alternative suggestion about the status of neo-Ricardian equilibrium. The 'systematic, fundamental and enduring' forces which for them characterise long-period equilibrium should instead be the basis for the selection of variables or relationships in theory construction. Surely, it is the purpose of theory to isolate those forces or relationships that are systematic, fundamental and enduring for causal analysis, whether in equilibrium or to explain the process by which equilibrium is brought about, and whether in the long, or the short, period.

Equilibrium as a recurring process

In a continuing process of interdependence of production and consumption an equilibrium circular flow, or stationary state, lays out the conditions under which a given level of production and consumption is sustainable, or will be repeated. A stationary state of this kind was brought into modern times in the schemes of reproduction in Marx. But I wish to argue, more controversially, that it is also central to Keynes's *General Theory*.

The General Theory follows Marshall's scheme of periods and is largely (but not exclusively) concerned with the short period, as defined above. It is in the short period that output and employment are determined: production always takes place with the capital on hand. The system is temporally ordered and path-dependent. I shall take as an example the simple model in which money and interest rates do not yet appear. Investment is, therefore, exogenous – indeed, consumption and investment are not really differentiated at this stage of the argument. Wages are determined, workers are hired and the level of output is determined by expectations of demand in a future (not futures) market. These expectations can turn out to be correct or not. If they are not correct for a sufficient number of observations, producers will change their expectations and, thus, their output and employment strategy. If they are correct, again for a sufficient number of observations to show that the result is not a fluke, producers will leave their decisions unchanged from one production period to the next. The latter is, *ceteris paribus*, an equilibrium circular flow or stationary state. It is not, as many commentators have averred, statics, for a time-order of decisions is preserved, as is causality. Why concentrate on an equilibrium configuration? The simple answer is that a path-dependent system must either specify exactly what producers will do if their expectations are disappointed or admit that the system can in principle go anywhere, which is hardly satisfactory – indeed, it is hardly theory.

Of course, if equilibrium is reached, it cannot last, for the reason raised earlier: positive investment means capital is being accumulated. Thus at some point long-period problems become important. In this sense the long period is brought about by a succession of short periods, even though the theorist can keep accumulation at bay for as long as s/he wants. Keynes deals with the impact of capital accumulation in only one chapter (ch. 17), because his focus is on whether that process will come to an end before or after the desire to save is satiated. If before, then the desire to save will be frustrated by a fall in income and employment, and unemployment will persist in the long run. He concluded that this was the more likely outcome.[4]

Whether applied to the long or the short period, Keynes's insistence on the possibility, even the likelihood, of unemployment equilibrium has caused enormous difficulty. (Curiously, in mainstream economics there exists the concept of equilibrium unemployment – see, for instance, Pissarides 1990 – by which is meant the level of unemployment consistent with zero inflation.) The difficulty in understanding Keynes arises from identifying equilibrium with the concept of market-clearing solutions, where such a phrase is a contradiction in terms, instead of with a state of rest, where it is not. Underlying the idea of market clearing is, as pointed out earlier, the idea that the 'forces' which bring it about are of equal power on both sides. The unusual feature of Keynes's analysis is its recognition that all the power is in the hands of producers. This is not because they occupy a monopsony position in the labour market, but arises simply from the temporal ordering of the process of producing for (uncertain, future) market sale: firms decide how much employment to offer on the basis of their expectations, and in the decentralised system of Western capitalism, if these decisions do not absorb all the labour available, that is just too bad. There is no recontracting, as in Walras, to redress the balance. Equilibrium here is not an example of a balance of equal forces: labour has not the power to change its situation. Perhaps this is rejected in mainstream economics not because it isn't true but because it is unpalatable.

Human agency

It is often remarked that taking the concept of equilibrium from science to economics was wholly inappropriate, for economics deals with conscious, thinking human beings; even in the dryest of models, where variables take the place of people, the representative agent is lurking in the background. Molecules, atoms, particles are assumed not to share the capacity for thought. The first thing to say to that point is that serious choice is reduced to mere calculation in much economics; *homo oeconomicus* in this environment is not very different from insentient beings. (And I have read scientists who speak of 'choices' made at bifurcation points, or of what photons 'know' in the two-slit experiment.) However, there is still force to the argument. We have already touched on the concept of the role of expectations in Marshall's and Keynes's work. Expecta-

4 It is something of an irony, considering the difficulty neo-Ricardians have with *The General Theory*, that a uniform rate of profit characterises Keynes's long period.

tions have found their way into the mainstream, first as workers' expectations of inflation, which allowed them to evaluate offers of money wages (e.g. Friedman), then to full-blown rational expectations, in which, in equilibrium, the agents can in principle have full knowledge (stochastically speaking) of the 'true' model of the economy. Conscious action is also at the centre of models of conjectural equilibrium, Nash equilibria and the like, where it is necessary to understand something of the strategies of others. But it is still possible to think that what is being expected or conjectured is either objective or constant. In Keynes (1936), the expedient of putting entrepreneurial flair and impatience into the pound of *ceteris paribus* along with the consequences of investment for productive efficiency will allow one to find the short-period equilibrium.

However, when we come to the idea of the crucial decision,[5] the illusion of an objective economic system must be abandoned. Crucial choices in the sense of Shackle change the economic landscape and thus cannot be repeated. Recognition of this feature of conscious life has far-reaching consequences. No longer is economic wo/man trying to fit in to her/his environment; s/he is creating it, changing behaviours, relationships, institutions, and these changes will have further repercussions. This is how the world is, but it is jolly difficult to model. So Shackle is accused of nihilism.

Another economist who is concerned with this problem is Loasby (1991). He sees equilibrium and change as complementary, rather than antagonistic. All development, he argues, requires a base of stability. This conception fits with the idea of equilibria which, rather than being final, contain within them the seeds of their own destruction, which we promoted above in the case of Keynes (see Chick and Caserta 1997).

Conclusion

There seems to me to be a sense in which equilibrium is and has been indispensable and a sense in which the concept should be used with caution. We have seen some of the uses to which equilibrium has been put, and it is difficult to imagine economic theory (including informal and verbal theory) without it. In particular, I find Keynes's use of it to make sense of a path-dependent system, in an era when simulation was not an available alternative, very valuable. I am also much taken by the sense of impermanence, of lack of finality, in Keynes's and Marshall's equilibria.

The cautions relate to ideas that have accrued to the concept, or to the confusion of concept and method, or to its ideological content. To take the last point first, equilibrium is usually seen as a desirable state of affairs, in which everyone is at their optimal position and there are no unexploited opportunities. This comfortable picture ignores power relations (explicitly ruled out in competitive equilibrium) and, most of the time, income distribution (ruled out

5 '[a decision] whose repetition is logically impossible because its very performance destroys forever the conditions in which it is undertaken' (Shackle 1970, p. 109).

by the representative agent). Equilibrium as an end point plays down that instinctive drive to action that will overturn any equilibrium in due course. I reject the proposition that equilibrium is a useless concept in economics because such a state has never been observed in an economy (at least, I think not; it is difficult to know how it would be recognised if it were to occur), because I understand and value the process of abstraction necessary to theory. I do not, however, claim that theory is impossible without equilibrium. Nor do I think that theory which gives only the equilibrium position is helpful, as it dispenses with adjustment processes and causality. When equilibrium means only a mathematical solution the concept is robbed of any but a syntactical meaning, and has no economic content. But as a concept of a configuration which will persist unless disturbed – the meaning of equilibrium in ordinary language – I believe it has a useful analytical and descriptive role to play in economics.

References

Chick, V. (1978) 'The nature of the Keynesian revolution: a reassessment', *Australian Economic Papers*, 17 (June), 1–20.

Chick, V. (1982) 'Comment on "ISLM – an explanation"' (by John Hicks), *Journal of Post Keynesian Economics*, 4 (spring), 439–44.

Chick, V. (1983) *Macroeconomics after Keynes. A Reconsideration of the General Theory*, MIT Press, Cambridge, MA.

Chick, V. (1995) 'Order out of chaos in economics? Some lessons from the philosophy of science', S.C. Dow and J. Hillard (eds), *Keynes, Knowledge and Uncertainty*, Edward Elgar, Cheltenham, 25–42.

Chick, V. (1996a) 'Equilibrium and determination in open systems', *History of Economics Review*, 25 (winter–summer), 172–83.

Chick, V. (1996b) 'A struggle to escape: equilibrium in *The General Theory*', *Ekonomska Misao i Praksa* (Dubrovnic) 5, 345–62. Reprinted in S. Sharma, *John Maynard Keynes. Keynesianism into the Twenty-first Century*, Edward Elgar, Cheltenham (1998), 40–50.

Chick, V. (2002) 'Reflections on Caravale's contributions relating to equilibrium and their relation to the interpretation of Keynes', in S. Nistico and D. Tosato, *Competing Economic Theories*, Routledge, London, 167–76.

Chick, V. and M. Caserta (1997) 'Provisional equilibrium and macroeconomic theory', in P. Arestis, G. Palma and M.C. Sawyer (eds), *Markets, Employment and Economic Policy. Essays in Honour of G.C. Harcourt*, II, Routledge, London, 223–37.

Chick, V. and S.C. Dow (2001) 'Formalism, logic and reality: a Keynesian analysis', *Cambridge Journal of Economics*, 25 (6), 705–22.

Davidson, P. (1977) 'Money and general equilibrium', *Économie appliquée*, 4. Reprinted in L. Davidson (ed.) *Money and Employment. The Collected Writings of Paul Davidson*, I, Macmillan, London, 196–217.

Debreu, G. (1959) *Theory of Value*, Wiley for the Cowles Foundation, New York.

Hahn, F.H. (1984) [1974] 'On the notion of equilibrium in economics', in F.H. Hahn, *Equilibrium and Macroeconomics*, Blackwell, Oxford. First published as an inaugural lecture, University of Cambridge.

Hahn, F.H. (1985) [1975] 'Money and general equilibrium', in Hahn (ed.), *Money, Growth and Stability*, Blackwell, Oxford. First published in *Indian Economic Journal.*

Hicks, J.R. (1939) *Value and Capital*, Oxford University Press, Oxford.

Hicks, J.R. (1965) *Capital and Growth*, Oxford University Press, Oxford.

Hicks, J.R. (1979) *Causality in Economics*, Blackwell, Oxford.

Hicks, J.R. (1981) 'ISLM – an explanation', *Journal of Post Keynesian Economics*, 3 (2), 139–54.

Kaldor, N. (1972) 'The irrelevance of equilibrium economics', *Economic Journal*, 82, 1237–55.

Kaldor, N. (1985) *Economics without Equilibrium*, Sharp, Armonk, NY.

Keynes, J.M. (1930) *A Treatise on Money*, Macmillan, London.

Keynes, J.M. (1936) *The General Theory of Employment, Interest and Money*, Macmillan, London.

Kornai, J. (1971) *Anti-equilibrium*, North-Holland, Amsterdam.

Loasby, B.J. (1991) *Equilibrium and Evolution*, Manchester University Press, Manchester.

Machlup, F. (1958) 'Equilibrium and disequilibrium: misplaced concreteness and disguised politics', *Economic Journal*, 68 (March), 1–24.

Marshall, A. (1948) [1920] *Principles of Economics*, 8th edn, Macmillan, New York. (First edition 1890.)

Marx, K. (1970) [1887] *Capital*, ed. F. Engels, Lawrence and Wishart, London.

Milgate, M. (1987) 'Equilibrium: development of the concept', in *The New Palgrave Dictionary of Economics*, II, 179–83, Macmillan, London.

Pissarides, C. (1990) *Equilibrium Unemployment Theory*, Blackwell, Oxford.

Potestio, P. (1986) 'Equilibrium and employment in *The General Theory*', *Giornale degli Economisti e Annali di Economia*, July–August, pp. 363–88.

Quesnay, F. (1972) [1766] 'Analyse de la formule arithmetique du tableau economique', in *Textes annotés*, Paris, INED (1958). Trans. M. Kucznski and R.L. Meek, *Quesnay's Tableau Économique*, Macmillan, London.

Robinson, J. (1974) 'History versus equilibrium', *Thames Papers in Political Economy*, repr. in Robinson, *Collected Papers*, V, 48–58, Blackwell, Oxford (1980).

Robinson, J. (1978) 'A lecture delivered at Oxford by a Cambridge economist', in Robinson, *Contributions to Modern Economics*, Blackwell, Oxford, 137–45.

Robinson, J. (1979) 'Introduction', in Robinson, *The Generalisation of the General Theory and other Essays*, Macmillan, London.

Samuelson, P.A. (1947) *Foundations of Economic Analysis*, Harvard University Press, Cambridge, MA.

Schumpeter, J.A. (1934) *The Theory of Economic Development. An Inquiry into Profits, Capital, Credit, Interest, and the Business Cycle*, trans. Redvers Opie, Harvard University Press, Cambridge, MA.

Shackle, G.L.S. (1970) *Expectation, Enterprise and Profit*, Allen and Unwin, London.

van Doorn, J. (1975) *Disequilibrium Economics*, Macmillan, London.

Verdon, M. (1996) *Keynes and the 'Classics'. A Study in Language, Epistemology and Mistaken Identities*, Routledge, London.

Walras, L. (1954) [1926] *Elements of Pure Economics*, trans. from the 1926 edition by W. Jaffe, Allen and Unwin, London.

12 Heavens above

What equilibrium means for economics

Alan Freeman

This chapter suggests that a mistake will be made if we suppose that the word 'equilibrium' is used by economists in the same way that a physicist uses 'energy' or a chemist uses 'molecule'. It argues that economics has not simply borrowed this idea from the natural sciences but has transformed it into something different. I show that the best way to comprehend what equilibrium means to economics is to understand that it is used in a religious, rather than a scientific, manner.

I present the formal properties of two counterposed ontological approaches in economics: the temporal and the equilibrium, or steady state, approach. Comparing the equilibrium view with the medieval concept of 'heaven' to illustrate, I show that the selection mechanisms of economic theory are dominated by esoteric or ethical-political choices rather than by exoteric or explanatory choices, and that the concept of equilibrium should be understood in this light.

> So far as hypotheses are concerned, let no one expect anything certain from astronomy, which cannot furnish it, lest he accept as the truth ideas conceived for another purpose, and depart from this study a greater fool than when he entered it.
>
> (Nicholas Copernicus, *De revolutionibus orbium coelestium*)

This chapter will suggest how a natural scientist can understand the use which economics makes of the word 'equilibrium'. I will argue that a simple concept, unexceptionable for the study of many physical phenomena, has been transformed into something completely different. If, therefore, we naively expect to find it applied in economics in the same way as 'energy' in physics or 'molecule' in chemistry, as a means of describing and explaining what an impartial observer may independently verify, we will misunderstand its real significance.

My basic thesis is that the educated public makes a mistake in accepting, at face value, the claim that economics conducts itself as a science. I will argue that, as at present practised, it conducts itself as a religion. I will argue that the concept of equilibrium[1] is the organising principle of this religion.

Testing such a controversial assertion obviously requires a definition of religion, which the Enlightenment has mythologised, portraying it as rooted in fanaticism, dogma, bigotry and the substitution of scriptural authority for evidence.

This description does fit some religionists and, the truly impartial will admit, the occasional economist. However, as a way of defining and understanding what religions really do, and how they really differ from sciences, the myth is neither accurate nor complete. It arises from a political struggle in which science and religion have been locked since the time of Galileo. It is not an objective scientific description, and has prevented both scientists and economists grasping what really distinguishes a scientific mode of enquiry from a religious one.

To try and overcome this problem, I will introduce a distinction between two functions of knowledge which, I will show, impose on our consciousness two opposed meanings for the most general abstractions which govern the way we think about our world and our society, obliging us to think as if they had only one meaning. The first function I call the *exoteric* function of knowledge. This defines a relation between society, acting as an observer, and that which society observes. In exercising the exoteric function of knowledge, the observer distinguishes herself from what is observed. To the sphere of exoteric knowledge belong most of the constructs of science – energy, gravitation, atoms, waves, and so on. Through this function of knowledge, society arranges to control nature. The second I call the *esoteric* function of knowledge, which defines a relation between society and itself. In exercising the esoteric function of knowledge, humans become collectively self-conscious and no longer maintain the distinction between the observer and that which is observed. They organise, within a rational structure, systems of law, ethics, morality and their relations to each other.

With regard to economics, my central thesis is that the esoteric function of equilibrium predominates over the exoteric and that, therefore, to understand the concept as applied in economics, one must unearth its esoteric meaning. Attempts to grasp its significance by approaching it as a purely descriptive instrument are therefore foredoomed.

To convince my readers of this point I invite them to discard two simplistic ideas. The first is the Enlightenment myth outlined above: that what distinguishes religion from science is irrationality and contempt for evidence. Writers such as Barbour (1990) have effectively demolished this idea, which we will examine further in considering the history of cosmological debate during the time of Galileo. The second such idea is that which economics has crudely

1 As will become clear later, by the word 'equilibrium' I mean the concept of general or static equilibrium. This refers to a hypothetical static state of the market in which the prices at which goods exchange, and the quantities of goods consumed, are such that there is no reason for these prices and quantities to change. Figuratively speaking, this implies that all 'forces' tending to change exactly cancel each other out, so that motion ceases.

adapted from Popper, that 'normative' or ethical judgements stand outside the realm of science. The standard formulation of this view is that:

> Normative economics involves ethical precepts and value judgements ... there are no right and wrong answers to these questions because they involve ethics and values rather than facts. These issues can be debated, but they can never be settled by science.
>
> (Samuelson and Nordhaus 1992, p. 9)

A study of the process by which economics selects its theories shows that the normative–positive distinction does not play the role proposed for it. Allegedly positive concepts such as 'market' refer not to anything actual but to an idealised, self-regulating market which does not and cannot exist. This is used, in the formulation of policy, as a standard against which actual markets are judged, so that policies are framed to modify these 'imperfect' markets by bringing them into conformity with this ideal. This notion of 'market' is not a normal abstraction, any more than the idea that a horse is an imperfect unicorn.[2] It does not describe the common properties of all species of market but is logically grounded in properties possessed by no market. It is a normative standard.

On the other hand, ethical propositions such as 'society should be more equal' are fully amenable to rational and evidence-based judgement, once one asks questions such as 'Is such a state of affairs actually possible?' 'What would we have to do, in order to bring it about?' or 'What would happen if we tried to bring it about?' Samuelson's assertion that such questions fall outside science amounts to a claim that ethics has no rational foundation, which few philosophers concede. It is an abdication of any responsibility of the scientist in the ethical sphere. In fact if a precept such as equality permits us to reorganise society, in the same way that an architect can construct a socially functional and aesthetically pleasing building, then this is a scientifically valid precept. An equal society may not now, exoterically, exist. But if, transformed into a policy, the principle of equality can be embedded in a system of laws, morals and economic relations which bring an equal society into being, then the outcome would conform to the concept, and this would confirm its validity. If on the other hand it were proposed to construct a society without agriculture, this would be dangerously utopian, because there is sound evidence that it cannot be done.

The real problem can now be restated. Experience has shown us that we may *neither* exoterically explain, *nor* esoterically organise, a market economy around theories which rest on the ideal of general, static equilibrium. There have been many attempts to do so, including the programme of financial and economic liberalisation which dominated the last part of the previous millennium and is normally referred to as 'globalisation'. They have all failed.

I therefore sustain that *in no sense* is equilibrium a valid conception, either as

2 I am indebted to John Weeks for this analogy

description or as prescription. It is not, in some deep sense, a 'possible' abstraction. There *is* no such thing as a market economy which is either governed, or governable, by its hypothetical equilibrium state. This is not the outcome of a failure of will. It is a consequence of objective properties of the market which manifest themselves in both exoteric and esoteric applications of equilibrium theory. This theory is therefore wrong absolutely, in the same simple way that flat earth theory is wrong: when we act on it, we find that what we expect to happen does not happen. We find that a state of society, which we expect to arise from our actions, does not arise.

Yet economics persists in using the abstraction of equilibrium as if it really did or can describe, in some sense, what markets actually could do, if appropriately governed. The issue is then this: why does a well paid profession organise itself around the intellectual fiction that an unattainable ideal is a practical approximation to the truth? And, given that the concept of static general equilibrium plays no actual role in describing the society we live in, what is its real meaning for economists? The purpose of this chapter is to suggest an explanation for this paradoxical fact and an answer to this difficult question.

Does heaven exist?

To illustrate the difficulties, let us suppose that a team of modern scientists set out to research what 'heaven' meant in medieval times. A first, simplistic approach would be to treat it as a protoscientific construct whose purpose is to explain how the stars, planets, moon and sun appeared to move. The pre-Copernican, Ptolemaic system of cosmology, which placed the earth at the centre of the universe and had the stars fixed in the heavens moving slowly around it, is a rather good approximation to observed reality. It tells us when stars and planets rise and set, and where to find them as the years roll on: it accurately predicts their positions, the seasons, the phases of the moon, and even eclipses. Taking this approach, our team could deconstruct works such as Sacrobosco's *Sphaera*[3] (in its day the standard reference work on cosmic motion) as a literal description of planetary, stellar and lunar movements, and would find it tolerably accurate in predicting these movements.

Our team of practical-minded scientists could easily conclude that the word 'heaven' was in its time just a medieval synonym for what we now call 'outer space' – in exactly the same way that modern scientists, when they first encounter the concept of 'equilibrium', conclude it is merely an economic synonym for an equivalent physical concept.

This judgement would be contradicted by a different use of the word 'heaven' which figures in the writings of the time – not only in Church doctrines but in the common speech of rulers, judges and ordinary people. In this use, heaven is a sacred term. It was, our team would report, the home of a non-existent prime mover of the universe: literally, God's home. It was the place that

3 See Lattis (1994: 249)

good Christians were supposed to go to when they die. Moreover this usage had real and extensive social effects. It shaped history. Millions of people went to extraordinary lengths – donating house and home, launching crusades, embarking on long and risky pilgrimages, and spending fortunes on indulgences[4] – to get into 'heaven' when dead. Heavenly origin was primary proof of secular authority, as is clear from the doctrine of the divine right of kings.

Our team would have to acknowledge that the word 'heaven' had two meanings. On the one hand it conveyed a spatial configuration: 'earth' referred to the world below: those parts of the universe which were physically at its known centre and could be reached by traversing its known surface; 'heaven' referred to the distant and inaccessible parts.

But on the other hand it was an organising principle of the social order. It was assumed, as beyond doubt, that the distant, infinite and inaccessible parts of the universe were composed of a superior substance which Aristotle called 'quintessence' or the fifth element[5] – in short, they were perfect. 'Heaven' thus defined is no more irrational than the other four elements earth, air, fire and water. On the basis of 'heaven' conceived as the realm of perfect substance, Western society constructed an ideal whose logical premise was the idea that those people and classes most qualified to own and to govern were those who could trace their origins and their policies to the eternal state of the skies above.[6]

No modern Christian promotes the idea that God and Paradise may literally and geographically be found in outer space or among the planets. That would be a blasphemous idea, since it would situate God, whose essence is perfection freed of material limitation, in an imperfect material space amidst lumps of inanimate rock and stellar dust. But in medieval times the identity of heaven and divinity was *literal*; people saw no need to make a distinction. The skies themselves were thought to be composed of the most perfect substance and there was no contradiction in placing God in them. The heavens were direct evidence of divine perfection.

We thus have a problem, which as this chapter unfolds will become the core of our approach to the concept of equilibrium in economics. The word 'heaven' in medieval thought actually had two meanings which people saw no need to distinguish. On the one hand it explained and predicted what people – more precisely, society – observed when they looked upwards. But it had another meaning which cannot simply be dismissed as superstition or ignorance. This meaning came to the fore when society had to specify, to its citizens, what was right and what was wrong: what they might and might not do, and the reasons why. 'Heaven' also signified the realm of perfection and, in this role, it was the logical foundation of the medieval system of law, morality and social relations.

4 An interesting PhD topic would be to apply modern utility theory to the demand and supply of indulgences in the early modern epoch.

5 Lattis (1994: 54)

6 Cf. Farringdon (1939) for a particularly clear exegesis of this point.

Paradigm change

In the course of time, it became necessary to make a distinction between the two meanings of heaven. By the time Galileo Galilei began constructing his controversial defence of Copernicus' revolutionary theories,[7] most writers about astronomy were fully aware that the model they had been using for many centuries was seriously wanting. They approached the decision in a way that modern science would not find altogether foreign: they considered a variety of hypotheses, considered the predictions that these hypotheses gave rise to, and assessed their likelihood in a logical manner. Nor were they unaware of Copernicus' theory or unsympathetic to Galileo's defence of it. The Pope so enjoyed Galileo's early writings that he had them read to him in his bath.

We must now grapple with a difficult point. As noted in the introduction, Enlightenment mythology has rewritten the story of Galileo as a simple battle between the forces of reason and light, represented by Copernicanism, and the forces of darkness and superstition, represented by the Catholic Church. This mythic enlightenment history was carefully constructed by Galileo's faithful student Viviano in order to marshal forces for the political battle which Protestantism successfully concluded against Catholicism and whose purpose was, in essence, to take away the Church's right to interfere in the pursuit of exoteric knowledge. This battle became a general project of rationalism and was adopted by the left wing of the workers' movement, as can be seen in Bertold Brecht's retelling of the Galileo fable. According to this mythology the Church is a simple instrument of clerical reaction. It was not scientific for the simple reason that it was uninterested in truth.

This mythology is now being carefully re-examined. Writers such as Drake (1999) and Sobel (1999) have pointed out that Galileo himself was a devout Catholic and sought not to exclude the Church from science but to protect it from adopting wrong ideas which he (rightly) believed would utterly discredit it. They and Lattis (1994) have shown that the Church in turn was far from wilfully ignorant of the key cosmological issues at stake, and was no stranger at all to rational and evidence-based discussion. It is inadequate to present the Church's opposition to Copernicanism as a simple battle between the force of informed reason and prejudiced reaction.

It is not even the case that science is universally pursued by scientists and religion by religionists – most if not all of Galileo's protagonists were themselves religionists, but of a different, Protestant, persuasion. Galileo himself was a sincere, pious man.[8] Since we find, in history, religionists pursuing a scientific mode of enquiry, we should not discount the possibility of finding scientists pursuing a religious mode of enquiry. When we understand where the distinction between the religious and the scientific mode of enquiry really does lie, we are

7 The word 'revolution' itself in modern speech derives from the title of Copernicus' major work 'On the Revolution of the Heavenly Spheres'.

8 Like Newton, guru of Enlightenment mythology and a devout if secretive follower of the Arian heresy. Cf. Fara (2002).

driven to realise that economics, as it now conducts itself, falls on the wrong side of the divide.

In a very fundamental sense the Catholic Church did get it wrong, because the heavens really do not revolve about the earth, and it forbade people to say that. It imposed a wrong mode of enquiry, as it finally admitted in 1992. It is this mode of enquiry that I believe can rightly be characterised as religious and not scientific. The question is, in precisely what sense was this so? The distinction does not lie, I would argue, where Enlightenment mythology has placed it. We are not adequately served by a crude counter-position between science, which is positivist, rational and right, and religion, which is normative, irrational and wrong.

The definition I will advance is that a mode of enquiry can be characterised as religious when it can be demonstrated that *esoteric considerations dominate over exoteric considerations in its selection of theories.*

My basic approach is to shift the focus from the nature of the knowledge and theories deployed by religious and scientific enquiry as such, to the process by which these theories are selected. In this, the ground has been prepared by Thomas Kuhn's (1962) pathbreaking account of 'paradigm change', of which no scientist can fail to be aware.

Kuhn's fundamental insight is that scientists themselves do not behave as simple Popperian positivists. They do not in fact simply drop one explanation as soon as the facts refute it and pick up another, superior explanation. Science, as an organised social body, passes through periods of intense competition between rival explanations, at the end of which the new explanation triumphs over the old.

But Kuhn himself goes to the opposite extreme of Enlightenment mythology. He presents the Copernican revolution merely as one instance of a scientific paradigm change. Why didn't scientists simply abandon the Ptolemaic view immediately? Because, according to Kuhn, that is what scientists do. This is how science progresses.

There are two problems. First, Kuhn never considers the social sciences, which means the evidence is somewhat incomplete. Second, the transition to Copernicanism, which he presents almost as an archetype in his study of science, does not conform to the pattern of the other scientific revolutions which he studies. The Galilean heresy was not adopted in the same way as the wave theory of light, or oxygen, or relativity, or any other more modern scientific doctrine. Both the process of change, and the factors that governed it, were quite different.

The debate on relativity was over in less than a generation. Michelson first asserted that the velocity of light was constant in 1880, and proved it with Morley in 1887. Poincaré more or less correctly formulated modern doctrine in 1898. Einstein published the special theory in 1905. By 1920 the new theories were more or less universally accepted in the scientific world.[9] The transition thus lasted, at an absolute maximum, fifty years. But Copernicus' work pre-dates the victory of Galileo's version of it by 200 years, and was moreover originally

9 Cf. www-groups.dcs.st-and.ac.uk/~history/HistTopics/Special_relativity.html.

available 2,000 years earlier, when it was first advanced by Aristarchus of Samos,[10] only to be suppressed at the instigation of the Greek oligarchs. The transition was the longest in scientific history.

Moreover Copernicanism, which was fully known and understood by pre-Galilean scholars, was not 'rejected' through some process of natural selection. It was suppressed. The Holy Office in 1616:

> Judged formally heretical the proposition that the sun is the center of the world and completely immovable by local motion. At the same time they judged erroneous in faith the proposition that the earth is neither the center of the cosmos nor immovable but moves as a whole and with a diurnal motion.
>
> (Lattis 1994: 139)

The Congregation of the Index in the same year condemned Foscarini's pro-Copernican book and suspended 'until corrected' Copernicus's own *De revolutionibus*. Galileo was not simply rejected for publication or passed over for promotion: he was instructed to recant, placed under house arrest and solemnly forbidden to disseminate his ideas. Copernicus's works were condemned as heresy and their promulgation was prohibited for centuries.

The decisive question is: by what actual process were Galileo's views rejected? How did the Church and its scholars actually arrive at these decisions? The purely intellectual, exoteric debate cannot be ripped out of this social, political and esoteric context. When this question is asked, we can begin to grasp why, despite its scholarly and logical approach, medieval cosmology cannot be treated as a simple body of scientific knowledge.

Scientific and religious processes of paradigm change

Resistance to heliocentrism did not centre on observational accuracy at all. It centred on the esoteric significance of the substance of heaven. Faced with alternative hypotheses about reality, both of them logical and both containing an explanation of what could be observed, the choice made by the Church was determined by what these hypotheses conveyed about the social order. If the very heavens are corrupt, then mere human imperfection requires neither king nor cardinal, emperor nor pope, to right it. Ptolemaic cosmology was defended because it conferred on the papacy authority as lawgiver and arbitrator in the never-ending disputes between the kings, queens, emperors, knights and other temporal rulers of the imperfect earth.

Moreover this approach to heaven was not simply 'arrived at by observation'. It was consciously introduced by Plato, who requires that the gods should reside in the heavens precisely in order to make them inaccessible to the common people:

10 See for example, Sambursky (1987).

> When you and I try to prove the existence of the gods by pointing to these very objects – sun, moon, stars and earth – as instances of deity and divinity, people who have been converted by these scientists [Anaxagoras] will assert that these things are simply earth and stone, incapable of paying any heed to human affairs.
>
> (*Laws* 10:886D, cited in Sambursky 1987: 54)

Plato's answer makes clear his concern. Greek heliocentric cosmology, adopted with scant modification by early Christianity, was never merely a theory of nature. It was simultaneously a theory of society. It was an account of human conduct, of the social order. Plato is cynically explicit: people must believe that the heavens are perfect, because otherwise they will not accept them as the abode of astral gods.

As such it was the foundation of a rational and law-governed system. When deciding on such questions as the legitimacy of succession or the punishment of crime, the Pope and his agents referred not to arbitrary tyrannical whim but to scripture, precedent and scholarly interpretation – in short, law. It is of course true that the Church was notorious for its blatant disregard of its own laws.[11] Nevertheless, if what was involved was a simple fraud, we cannot explain why, when Church decisions appeared wrong, they were challenged and opposed on the precise grounds that they contradicted divine law. Most struggles both against and within the Church, until very late in history, took the form of disputes not about its right to legislate but about the way it chose to interpret the law – that is, they accepted the logical premise and even the manner of reasoning, disputing only its application.

Does this imply that in the 2,000 intervening years science was set aside for political expediency? The evidence does not support this. One has only to read the debates among the Ptolemaic astronomers to realise that they passionately believed their theories. The point is, however, that they simultaneously understood these theories as an exoteric account of what the heavens really consisted of, and as an esoteric account of their own status on earth as observers of these same heavens.

To displace the earth from the centre of the universe did not just deprive Plato's successors and Galileo's peers of an explanation of material movement; it deprived them of an explanation of why they were there to observe it. Political expediency then intersected this theoretical dilemma, not as in Enlightenment mythology as the crude suppression of obvious truth, but as the determinant of the selection mechanism. It was simply *easier*, and more likely to lead to a productive career, for an astronomer of the day to skirt round and avoid theories and ideas which might well deprive him of office, income and, possibly, his life. As Lattis notes:

> Before the condemnation [of 1616, see above] they [the Jesuit astronomers] would have had to be somewhat cautious about expressing Copernican

11 See for example, Chamberlain (2003).

> sympathies in part so as not to offend collegial sensibilities in the Collegio Romano. But the automatic and obligatory anti-Copernican prejudice after the condemnation effectively forced them not to consider that alternative at all.
>
> (Lattis 1994: 202)

In just the same way today it is simply *easier* for a promising young economist discreetly to steer clear of the heretical ideas of Marx, the radical readings of Keynes or the uncomfortable conclusions of the Austrians. What leads to publication, promotion and funding are theories which do not provoke existential angst among politicians and bankers. But these career-determinate selection mechanisms constitute the actual social and political process by means of which an economic theory is arrived at.

The economist of today, like the astronomer of yesterday, perceives she has a choice between alternative theories. Yet a selection mechanism exists, then as now, which operates by determining the range of alternatives which the profession considers it legitimate to consider and, not least, for which it can secure admission, funding, fame and promotion. When one steps back and views the process as a whole, the outcome of the selection process is to favour those theories whose esoteric functions perpetuate the existing order and its interests. Just as the Ptolemaic system was a theology and not a science, not because it was observationally inferior but because in the social process which preserved it, its esoteric properties dominated its exoteric properties, in the same manner, I will argue, the concept of equilibrium is, as currently defended and applied within economics, selected in a theological and not a scientific manner and is, therefore, to be understood only by unearthing its significance for the social order.

Equilibrium and temporal paradigms stated and compared

This second part of this chapter aims to demonstrate that the concept of 'equilibrium' has played the same role in economics as the idea of 'heaven' in medieval cosmology.

I set aside an innocent use of the concept which borrows from the natural sciences, and which involves the idea of equal but opposed forces operating at a particular point – for example in fixing the price of one good. Sometimes known as 'partial equilibrium', this idea has no necessary ideological implications. In modern economics, however, the idea developed under the influence of Walras and Marshall into a more general conception which has transformed it into something altogether different. This is the idea of 'general equilibrium', sometimes known as comparative statics. Its earliest form was the doctrine against which Marx and Keynes alike railed at great length, and was originally known as Say's law, widely regarded as a prototype of all later theories of general static equilibrium.[12]

12 See Sowell (1972).

In the physical sciences the idea is associated with a relation between force and movement. But economics has stripped away this meaning to reveal an absolute logical core, namely the *absence of movement.* The basic idea of general equilibrium is that we should abstract from movement by means of a particular device, which is to suppose that this movement has stopped. General equilibrium then solves a set of simultaneous equations expressing this condition by supposing that the prices charged and the quantities sold – including the jobs performed – are the same at the end of a given period of time as they were at the beginning. It then solves for those prices and quantities which would allow such an economy to exist.

An analogy might be the following: if we want to know in the most general sense how a body of water behaves (for example to decide how much concrete to put in a dam) then we do not want to be preoccupied with random disturbances such as waves; we should therefore treat the body of water as if it was a still and flat lake.

This is not to say that the equilibrium economist does not wish to study change. She studies it, however, as the difference between two static states. Continuing the analogy of the lake, one may wish to know, for example, whether it will be necessary to build a stronger dam if the lake is made six feet deeper. One is not interested in what happens while the lake is filling up; only in what will happen to the dam when the extra six feet of water have been added. In the same way, an economist does not interest herself in the way prices will 'adjust' if the government increases tax from 20 per cent to 23 per cent. She asks only what difference exists between two ideal models of the economy; in one of these models, tax is 20 per cent. All prices, job levels and quantities consumed are supposed static. In the second model, tax is 23 per cent. All prices and quantities are again static, but at a different level.

The idea introduces a key ideological presupposition by the back door, in assuming that a static state may ever be arrived at. It supposes in advance, in effect, that the market works. It thus introduces a *petitio principii*: it assumes the market is perfect in order to study the cause of imperfection. This is the key to the esoteric properties of the equilibrium paradigm. I draw attention to three of its key properties.

1 Some variables are in fact allowed to change – in the above example, the tax rate. In other models it might be technology, or consumer preferences, or entrepreneurial behaviour. Thus the economist separates her or his variables into two broad groups: the *exogenous* variables, which are determined from outside the economy by politics, culture or psychology, and the *endogenous* variables – usually prices and quantities – which respond to these exogenous changes by adjusting their levels. Thus we can be more precise about the elimination of dynamics: such models assume away all dynamic effects of the endogenous variables.
2 The movement of prices, jobs and quantities is not just unimportant – it is eliminated. In reality, changing the tax rate will provoke a more or less dis-

ruptive shift in prices and employment, launching it on a path different at all points from either hypothetical static state. These disruptions may or may not produce lasting effects. There exist, however, decisive phenomena – long-term unemployment, business cycles, world inequality, the prolonged phases of declining profit rates sometimes identified with Kondratieff waves, and so on – which cannot be explained in any other way except to recognise that dynamic or 'path-dependent' effects, as they are known, do indeed produce lasting effects of enormous importance to the world we live in. In an equilibrium theory, these effects do not and cannot exist. The theory simply cannot express them. All dynamic effects are assumed away *a priori* and cannot subsequently be reintroduced. To pursue the analogy of the lake, therefore, the theory cannot explain the phenomenon of a waterfall or a river.

3 In consequence, all such theories must necessarily attribute to an external cause any deviation of the market from the equilibrium ideal. In them, the exogenous variables are the only possible source of motion, so that they bear the entire weight of explaining what really goes on. To pursue the analogy to its conclusion, the economist would have to explain curved water, as seen in waterfalls, by arguing that somebody bent it. Economic theory and policy are a litany of non-market causes for the market's problems – bad governance, poor monetary regulation, terrorism, oil shocks, trade unions, regulatory regime – everything but the market itself.

It is useful to summarise this system mathematically. A mathematical formulation, properly applied, encompasses the most general properties of all equilibrium systems. It therefore exposes what is necessarily and logically common to all such systems. It is then incumbent on any economist that disputes the conclusions, or wishes to claim that they do not apply to a particular model or branch of economic theory, either to demonstrate a flaw in the mathematical logic or to demonstrate that the particular model which she or he wishes to defend against my conclusions is not a system of this type.

This extends to systems such as rational expectations which do not explicitly declare themselves as equilibrium systems. Rational expectations suppose that agents act in such a way that their actions result in a future state of affairs which confirm these actions, generating demands and supplies which do not lead to any general excess of either. A society that conforms to this supposition is defined by a set of simultaneous equations which express the condition that demand and supply balance in all sectors and is hence covered by the mathematical formulation given below. Whether or not such a system is etymologically described by its proponents as a general equilibrium system, it is mathematically and logically identical to one.

By providing a mathematical statement of an equilibrium system I offer a definition of the conception of equilibrium to which this chapter refers. Other scholars are at liberty to advance theses about the alternative concepts of equilibrium in economics which depart from this definition, and, if adopted, such ideas may even free economics of its esoteric prejudices. However, this chapter concerns the actual role that the concept of equilibrium has played in the evolution of economic thought. Moreover my formalisation conforms to the version advanced by equilibrium's foremost advocates, notably Walras and the school of Arrow and Debreu,[13] which are widely accepted by economists as the 'standard' version of the theory.[14]

I will then show, in support of the claim that economics makes its choices esoterically and not exoterically, that in a series of major debates where the profession has been obliged to choose between a general equilibrium system (as mathematically defined below and regardless of the terminology introduced to describe it) and an alternative not subject to any of its limitations, it has in every case opted to choose the equilibrium variant. This is a general pattern. It establishes that, faced with two generic alternative approaches, economics almost invariably opts for one of them. I will argue that the basis of this choice is not the exoteric properties of the variant adopted, but its esoteric properties, that is, the account of the social order which is concealed within it.[15]

I will specify two generic types of system: an *equilibrium* or *simultaneous* system and a *temporal* system. These two systems, applied to more or less any body of economic ideas, provide different predictive paradigms yielding alternative quantitative predictions of reality.

Suppose some general dynamic system contains variables of two types: exogenous and endogenous. The endogenous variables are all those that the economist thinks of as intrinsic to the market – prices, quantities produced, labour inputs, profits, the interest rate, wages, and so on. Let the state vector of all these variables at time t be x_t.[16]

The exogenous variables are all the rest. In a marginalist or Walrasian framework these consist of consumer preferences and production functions. In a physicalist or Sraffian framework they consist of physical quantities of inputs and outputs. In a rational expectations framework they consist of agent predictions of the supply and demand for products. In general there is no specific limitation on what may be included. The critical mathematical property of an exogenous

13 See Debreu (1959).

14 See for example, Eatwell *et al.* (1989).

15 It has been argued that modern economics no longer uses the concept of equilibrium and that, therefore, the conclusions of this chapter regarding economics no longer hold. This is first of all disputable. We are concerned not just with systems that adopt the self-description 'equilibrium' but with all formally analogous systems, such as rational expectations theory, which adopt the method outlined in our mathematical formalisation. Second, economists do in fact repeatedly, in popular and pathbreaking modern works, very explicitly apply equilibrium theories as, for example, in New Trade Theory (see Fujita *et al.* 1999) and in monopsony theories of wage determination (see Manning 2003). Third, we are concerned with the history of economics. If its practice has changed in the last five years this is excellent if unexpected news, but this does not in any way offset the evidence of 200 years of previous evolution. Fourth, the topic of this book is to assess the concept of equilibrium. If this concept has vanished from the present, it is hard to see what choice we have but to seek it in the past.

16 x_t may contain differences or derivatives of its other components for example $x_t = \{p_t, p_{t-1}\}$ or $\{p_t', p\}$. This convention makes it easier to express dynamic relationships of order greater than 1.

variable is simply that, in distinction from an endogenous variable, its value at one time is permitted to be dependent on its value at another time.

Let the state vector of all these variables at time t be a_t. Now write down a general dynamic equation for the system:

$$x_t = f(a_t; x_{t-1}) \tag{1}$$

The function f constitutes the economists' theory: that is, it tells us in what state the economy will be at any given time, as a function of the present value of the exogenous variables, the past value of the endogenous variables. This is perfectly determinate for any f and a, given an initial condition at some time $t = 0$. Such a system provides a *temporal* determination of the endogenous variables x_t given by the parameters a and the initial state of x.

There is a different approach which is, in fact, a special case of the temporal view. If we abstract from all effects resulting from changes in x_t we can assume that

$$x_t = x_{t-1}$$

This gives us a *fixed-point* equation

$$x_t^* = f(a_t; x_t^*) \tag{2}$$

A very general theorem in mathematical topology tells us that for all parameters a and a very general variety of functions f,[17] a solution x_t^* exists to this equation.[18] Thus it solves the 'quantitative' problem – it allows us to calculate the variables. It gives a prediction. This prediction is of course false, but can be treated like any prediction as an 'approximation' – as something to which reality is close, but from which for various reasons reality departs. This is in formal mathematical terms what economics really means when it uses the word 'equilibrium'.

In Galileo's terms the temporal and the equilibrium approaches are two different 'world systems'. This is the most important thing for any natural scientist to grasp when grappling with what equilibrium in economics is really about. They produce different ways of thinking about the world, different ontological systems, both exoterically and esoterically. However, the differences are not

17 Specifically, f should be a convex mapping whose domain has an Euler number of zero. This is wide-ranging but it should be noted is more restrictive than the condition for a temporal solution to exist.

18 The theorem is colloquially known as the hairy ball theorem, because it proves that you cannot comb a ball covered in hair without leaving at least one hair sticking up. There may be more than one fixed point (many hairs may stand up); the equilibria may be stable (the hairs come to a point) or unstable (the hairs sprout) but at least one hair must stand straight up. See tinyurl.com/qxm79 (accessed 23 March 2006) or a more light-hearted version on tinyurl.com/8jb8k (accessed 23 March 2006).

confined to meaning. They produce different and verifiable predictions; in excluding temporal approaches from consideration, therefore, economics ceases to be a science even in the narrow Popperian sense, because it excludes the possibility that the equilibrium prediction may be falsified by comparing it with the temporal prediction.

In the actual translation of these two systems into practical economic paradigms, as noted above, it is accepted that reality will deviate from the predictions of the model. Disputes between the two paradigms thus reduce to the meaning which is assigned to the deviation. For the temporal system, the model is generally considered to predict the *average* in some sense of the observed variable, so that observed reality can be modelled as:

$$\bar{x}_t = f(a_t; \bar{x}_{t-1})$$
$$x = \bar{x}_t + \epsilon_t \qquad (1a)$$

for the equilibrium system, reality is modelled by

$$x_t^* = f(a_t; x_t^*)$$
$$x = x^* + \epsilon_t^*$$

$\bar{x}_t$ is an exoteric observable, so all elements of any temporal paradigm are directly accessible to observation and measurement. x^* is an esoteric ideal, by definition not observable, since it represents a state that the system never occupies.

In equilibrium systems, this esoteric ideal is conceptually thought of as being the same as the centre of gravity or time average and, indeed, it is generally not accepted that the two may diverge. In fact they do, as it is mathematically easy to demonstrate. To be precise, the fixed point coincides with the time average only for a limited range of functions f and time paths of the parameters a, and above all not when these show secular, that is, monotonic, variation. If such cases – as when, for example, a stands for technical productivity, which generally rises throughout the history of capitalism – the predictions of the two systems, for example their prediction of the average profit rate, simply diverge.

The major qualitative predictions of equilibrium systems definitely are therefore directly falsifiable in the Popperian sense: in particular they do not predict self-sustaining economic periodicity (crisis), secular growth in income polarisation, or prolonged periods of stagnation or high unemployment. Equilibrium theory, however, deals with this contradiction through the meaning assigned to the error term ϵ_t which is, in effect, treated as a measure of deviation from perfection, as a consequence of non-market and external effects.

Thus in summary the temporal and equilibrium determination of quantitative results are not the same; they give rise to different predictions and are hence testable hypotheses, in the Popperian sense. Nevertheless, they give rise to two sets of meanings for all those variables which are endogenous to the system.

x_t and x_t^* are not merely different numbers, they provide different ways of thinking about the objects to which they refer.

Exoteric properties of the equilibrium paradigm

The exoteric failures of economics are part of everyday life. In the words of Paul Ormerod (1994):

> Economists from the International Monetary Fund and the World Bank preach salvation through the market to the Third World . . . Yet economic forecasts are the subject of open derision. Throughout the Western world, their accuracy is appalling. Within the past twelve months alone, as this book is being written, forecasters have failed to predict the Japanese recession, the strength of the American recovery, the depth of the collapse in the German economy, and the turmoil in the European ERM.

Everyone makes mistakes. Thomas Watson, IBM's founder, is alleged to have said that the best way to double your rate of success is to double your rate of failure, a nostrum which appears to be the guiding principle of much international economic policy. What distinguishes science from dogma, however, is the mechanism – above all but not only when confronted with failure – which leads to changes in theory. What does economics actually do? I submit that, in virtually every school and every subject, faced with the choice between temporal and equilibrium paradigmatic variants, it either adopts the equilibrium variant immediately or gravitates rapidly towards it without testing the temporal variant; or, even worse, having tested this variant it nevertheless excludes it from consideration. To take a few examples:[19]

1 *The debate around Say's law.* Keynes's well known demolition of this law is accompanied by a mini-history which clearly shows how opposition to this absurd thesis was confined to a tiny minority of economists. Today few explicitly defend Say's law as such following the experience of the Great Depression. Yet Say's fundamental conclusion is more or less standard orthodoxy and is expressed in the view that the cause of every crisis is, ultimately, governance. That is, it is an almost universal tenet of economic faith that a market economy cannot and does not produce either a general glut of products, nor a general shortage of jobs, from within itself.

2 *Marginalism.* The founders of marginalism themselves, such as Böhm-Bawerk, were temporalists. Böhm-Bawerk considered simultaneous (equilibrium) analysis 'a mortal sin against logic'. Yet today temporal marginalism – Austrian economics – is confined to the work of an isolated minority.[20]

19 A comprehensive list is provided in Freeman (2004).

20 For a clear account of the difference between the Austrian and General Equilibrium view, together with an excellent account of the practical exoteric predictive differences between the two systems, see O'Driscoll and Rizzo (1996).

3 *Marx's determination of value* is temporal through and through. In 1905 von Bortkiewicz first published a 'correction', replacing it by a system of simultaneous equations. Although this determination contains insoluble contradictions not present in Marx's own theory, and fails (unlike Marx's theory) to yield an explanation of the clearly observable phenomenon of long-term declines in the profit rate, economists – not least, Marxist economists – have since Sweezy's (1942) endorsement of the Bortkiewicz interpretation almost universally accepted it as Marx's own view.[21]

4 *Keynes.* It is only within a non-equilibrium interpretation that it is possible unequivocally to explain the phenomenon of long-term and large-scale involuntary unemployment.[22] Indeed, the whole point is that the assumption of full employment is itself an equilibrium condition. Yet within a few years of the publication of the *General Theory* Hicks had already re-theorised it as a general equilibrium model, and since then every generation of students is basically told that Keynes 'is' the ISLM interpretation proposed by Hicks.[23]

5 *Real Business Cycle models.* The field of economic dynamics is one of the few where it remains possible to test and compare the predictions of endogenous non-equilibrium models with those for which all cyclic phenomena are essentially the result of external shocks. Yet despite the generally very poor and limited practical validity of RBC models, which assume that cyclic behaviour is a disturbance of equilibrium propagated through time, they remain the dominant paradigm in the field.

6 *Rational expectations.* One of the principal instruments for inserting non-equilibrium analysis into Keynes's framework is the uncertainty of the future. Rational expectations put this genie back in the bottle, by supposing that whatever agents believe about the future is in fact what will actually happen.[24] Uncertainty, thereby, is eliminated by supposing it does not exist – a novel take on a hundred years of quantum mechanics. Equally startling is the evolution of 'non-equilibrium Walrasian' approaches, which had a promising beginning and have virtually vanished from the intellectual scene. Five years ago I asked one of the founders why nothing more is being published in this school. 'Because unless the words "Rational Expectations" are in the title no one will publish it' came the answer.

7 Perhaps the only promising recent development has come in econometrics with a real recognition that time-series analysis on simultaneous equation lines introduced insurmountable problems of serial correlation. But this was known eighty years ago. 'Process theory' gave way to Haavelmo's simultaneous equation approach, which was standard until very recently.[25]

21 See Freeman and Carchedi (1995) and Freeman *et al.* (2004), as well as the extensive papers to be found at www.iwgvt.org (accessed 22 February 2006) and akliman.squarespace.com (accessed 22 February 2006).

22 Cf. Patinkin (1965) for a clear statement of this point.

23 See Davidson (1991).

24 See O'Driscoll and Rizzo (1996: 213–20) for a clear discussion of this.

25 See Ekeland (2006).

These 'choices' may be wrong, or they may be right. The point is that they were not dictated by observation or evidence. The triumph of the equilibrium paradigm is entirely due to its esoteric, and not its exoteric, properties. We may view the history of economics as, in essence, a succession of 'large choices' of the Kuhnian type between broad paradigms in which, empirically, the choice made is always the equilibrium variant. Having made a large choice, economics may conduct a great deal of very practical work to explain ϵ, the deviation from prediction. This is scientifically objective and collects data, produces many regressions, tests many hypotheses and turns out useful results. But it never returns to the basic theoretical question: does the esoteric ideal in fact correspond even mathematically to the exoteric average?

The critical point is the manner in which this question is avoided: by not even posing it. The temporal alternative is in every case excluded *a priori* on the basis not of evidence but of 'logic'. Just as the Catholic Church banned the very admissibility of a Copernican solution, economics in practice rules out, and refuses to consider, the possibility of a temporal alternative. The exoteric significance and predictions of equilibrium economic theories do not determine whether or not the equilibrium paradigm is adopted. If, therefore, we wish to understand the true meaning of equilibrium we have to turn to a different logic, a logic which is not stated but in fact drives the process of theoretical selection – the esoteric significance of the concepts that it produces, and the system of logic concerning the social order to which this gives rise.

Religion without gods

It will not have escaped the reader that economics lacks one rather essential requirement for a religion: namely, a god. Are gods a necessary feature of religion?

We can get a handle on this by considering a much more modern example: the history of the theory of evolution. Why did this eventually catch on? Because it provided the essential missing element which the new contesting cosmology – economics – required to explain an altogether different social order, namely the survival of the fittest.

Darwinism facilitated a new unity between the world of nature and the world of humans. Without any divine intervention at all, competition between humans could be hypostasised as an expression of the natural order. Concepts such as 'competition', 'evolution' or 'natural' in economics carry an unacknowledged ideological load. Their exoteric meaning is a simple description of economic process. But the weight they carry, within the minds of the policy makers and the people alike, arises from the simple unity of thought that results: we compete because we are animals; we can understand why firms live and die because it is in their nature; unemployment and poverty are not the simple consequences of human decisions but the expression of a universal natural order.

From antiquity until the ownership of land and labour became generally alienable and hence monetised, aristocratic social power was rooted in the person of the aristocrat. This personal power is what had to be explained. This essential intellectual function was played by cosmology, because it explained why monarchs and aristocrats existed, and why they had power over others. With the rise of money and the commodity form, personal power fades and power arising from abstract wealth rises. Hence it is the power of the owners of commodities, and above all money, that requires justification. It is no longer the monarch who obstructs the course of history but the financier, and the place of cosmological religion is taken by monetary religion, which provides just as absolute a justification for the actions of financiers as pre-Copernican cosmology did for the monarchy.

The esoteric core of the equilibrium paradigm is that it makes it impossible for the market to produce failure from within itself. Where, then, does failure come from? In medieval times, human misery was treated as an act of God. Humble nature was unacceptable as causal agency because that would remove the justification for feudal authority. Economics has reversed this concept of agency. The market itself – actually a uniquely human product – is explained as a product of exogenous forces. Its plagues and famines are still the outcome of exogenous forces but these are no longer divine. The new gods are the technical relations of production and the innate biological drives of agents, and the new sin is to stop them having their way with our markets.

This removes purely human agency from the field just as effectively as divine intervention. Interference with the market becomes a crime against Nature, a distortion of its innate perfection. Consequently all private benefit received from the market is the outcome of natural forces: capitalists are rich because nature intended them to be. Take their riches from them, and things can only get worse. Poverty, destitution, famine: these are sad but inevitable consequences of nature. Any policy designed to offset or overcome them is misguided. Nature, in a word, has been enthroned as a God, by excluding humans from Nature.

If it were to be accepted that the market is merely a dynamic system, which may or may not succeed, it would also be accepted that the market is merely one among many possible human creations. We may choose to allow prices and the movement of capital to allocate each human being her or his 'allotted' share of society's products, or we may decide that we don't like what the market gives us and seek to change it, overriding those laws of property and exchange which permit the market to work. In so doing, however, we override the distribution of products and social functions to which the market gives rise. We transfer incomes and wealth from one class to another. In particular, we are likely to take both power and wealth away from social classes, such as those that own capital or those that dominate the wealthier countries, and give it to others. That is a threat to them. It undermines their status and in extreme circumstances their existence.

The most important formal property of the equilibrium system is thus that it eliminates the ideological and social threat posed by accepting the market as a mere system of organisation among others. Finally, however, it possesses a further formal property, which explains its selection mechanism. Equilibrium theory sustains, justifies and codifies a private interest – classes with money. It expresses, as if it were a law of nature, the reasoning behind measures which, were they put directly and explicitly to people, would be rejected because of their partisan and hence unjust consequences.

The exoteric language of economics has immense social power. At the time when Argentina's currency collapsed, when almost no politician retained anything approaching sufficient support to govern, the economist Rudiger Dornbusch proposed that Argentina's economy should be handed over to a committee of economists – a proposal not far from handing over the fire brigade to the arsonists. Nevertheless, the very same people who refused to allow three successive Presidents to assume their functions were shown by opinion polls to support the Dornbusch proposal by between 50 per cent and 60 per cent.

This is characteristic of a relation between society and the esoteric classes which is remarkably similar to that between society and the clerical and monastic classes in feudal times. Notwithstanding the substantial and transparent grievances of many of the common people, often arising from private abuse by clerics and monarchs alike,[26] people considered the *system* of monarchic rule and canon law to be entirely right. In purely material terms this reflected the insufficiently developed state of a realistic alternative. But in ideological terms what is striking is the immense symbolic and ideological power, in the minds of men and women, of the primary concepts of divine authority.

This spells out the conditions for reform. It is at the precise point when ordinary people begin to doubt the social order that a thirst arises for different economic explanations. The ethical economist, therefore, has a duty not to offer a new 'authority' – a new heterodox orthodoxy – but genuine pluralism, genuine access to the full range of options. What is required from equilibrium theory – which it almost never concedes – is a statute of toleration, an acceptance that the public have the right of access to the full range of alternatives: in short, genuine pluralism.

References

Barbour, I.G. (1990), *Religion in an Age of Science*, SCM, London.

Brenner, R. (1998), 'The Economics of Global Turbulence', *New Left Review*, 229, 1–264.

Chamberlain, R. (2003) *The Bad Popes*, Sutton, Stroud.

Copernicus, N. (1543) *De revolutionibus orbium coelestium*, published in English translation at webexhibits.org/calendars/year-text-Copernicus.html (accessed 23 February 2006).

Davidson, P. (1991), *Controversies in Post-Keynesian Economics*, Edward Elgar, Aldershot and Brookfield, VT.

Debreu, G. (1959), *Theory of Value. An Axiomatic Analysis of Economic Equilibrium*, Yale University Press, New Haven, CT.

Drake, S. (1999), *Galileo*, Oxford University Press, Oxford and New York.

26 See for example, Chamberlain (2003).

Eatwell, J., Milgate, Murray and Newman, Peter (1989), *General Equilibrium*, Macmillan, London and Basingstoke.

Ekeland, A. (2006), 'Haavelmo – a Low-key Heterodox?', paper submitted to the sixth annual conference of the Association for Heterodox Economics.

Fara, P. (2002), *Newton. The Making of Genius*, Macmillan, Basingstoke and Oxford.

Farringdon, B. (1939), *Science and Politics in the Ancient World*, Allen and Unwin, London.

Freeman, A. (2004), 'Science, Religion and the Reform of Economics', presented to the fourth annual conference of the Association of Heterodox Economists, Nottingham, July.

Freeman, A. and Carchedi, Guglielmo (1995), *Marx and Non-equilibrium Economics*, Edward Elgar, Aldershot and Brookfield, VT.

Freeman, A., Kliman, Andrew and Wells, Julian (2004), *The New Value Theory Controversy in Economics*, Edward Elgar, Aldershot and Brookfield, VT.

Fujita, M., Krugman, Paul and Venables, A.J. (1999), *The Spatial Economy*, MIT Press, London and Cambridge, MA.

Jaffé, W. (ed.) (1965), *Correspondence of Léon Walras and Related Papers*, North-Holland, Amsterdam.

Kliman, A. and Freeman, Alan (2000), 'Two Concepts of Value, Two Rates of Profit, Two Laws of Motion', in *Research in Political Economy*, 18, 243–67.

Kuhn, T.S. (1962), *The Structure of Scientific Revolutions*, University of Chicago Press, Chicago and London.

Laibman, D. (2004), 'Rhetoric and Substance in Value Theory: an Appraisal of the New Orthodox Marxism', in Freeman, Kliman and Wells (eds), *The New Value Controversy in Economics*, 19–36, Edward Elgar, Aldershot and Brookfield, VT.

Lattis, J. (1994), *Between Copernicus and Galileo. Christopher Clavius and the Collapse of Ptolemaic Cosmology*, University of Chicago Press, Chicago.

Manning, A. (2003), *Monopsony in Motion*, Princeton University Press, Princeton, NJ.

O'Driscoll, P. and Rizzo, Mario J. (1996), *The Economics of Time and Ignorance*, Routledge, London and New York.

Okishio, N. (1961), 'Technical Changes and the Rate of Profit', *Kobe University Economic Review* 7, 86–99.

Ormerod, P. (1994), *The Death of Economics*, Faber and Faber, London.

Patinkin, D. (1965), *Money, Interest and Prices*, Harper and Row, New York.

Sambursky, P. (1987), *The Physical World of the Greeks*, Princeton University Press, Princeton, NJ.

Samuelson, P. and Nordhaus, William D. (1992), *Economics*, McGraw-Hill, New York.

Sobel, D. (1999). *Galileo's Daughter*, Penguin Books, London and New York.

Sowell, T. (1972) *Say's Law. An Historical Analysis*, Princeton University Press, Princeton, NJ.

Sweezy, P.M. (1970), *The Theory of Capitalist Development. Principles of Marxian Political Economy*, Modern Reader Paperbacks, New York.

Townshend, H. (1936) 'Liquidity-premium and the theory of value', *Economic Journal*, 47 (185), 157–69.

13 The hypostatisation of the concept of equilibrium in neoclassical economics

Andy Denis

This chapter explores the meanings of 'equilibrium' in economics, distinguishing salient appropriate and inappropriate modes of deployment of the concept. I examine a specific instance of the deployment of the concept of equilibrium by a neoclassical writer – Robert Lucas – and conclude that the concept has been hypostatised, substituting an aspect for the whole. The temporary is made permanent, and process subordinated to stasis, with apologetic results. Under far-from-equilibrium conditions, equilibrium is not even an approximate description of the condition of the system, but an abstraction – something which might obtain should a process under consideration run to its conclusion. The order of the system is not an equilibrium, but an ephemeral balance of forces, destined to be disturbed by the passage of time. I suggest that the hypostatisation of equilibrium exemplifies the contrast between formal and dialectical modes of thought, and that the heterodoxy can make its most telling contribution by applying a dialectical notion of equilibrium.

The notion of equilibrium is a focus of controversy in economics, in particular between orthodox and heterodox approaches, yet what is wrong with the concept is not necessarily immediately obvious. How could we begin to understand economic phenomena without the concept? People have interests. They therefore have a motive to change their behaviour if they find they're not doing the best they can to fulfil those interests, and to maintain their behaviour if they are. How can we even begin to understand the economic behaviour of individual agents without such a notion of individual optimising equilibrium? Without it, it seems, what we do becomes indeterminate, arbitrary, inexplicable. At the macro level, too, the pattern of activity – all too often pathological: turbulence, traffic jams, unemployment – must have some structure, some stability. The pattern must endure at least long enough to matter to us. For such stability to be intellectually comprehensible, it must occur for a reason, otherwise it is arbitrary and mysterious. Again, some notion of equilibrium, of at least a temporary balance of forces, seems a *sine qua non* of rational enquiry.

So the problem cannot be the use of a concept of equilibrium, full stop. But clearly there *is* a problem. If not in the existence *per se* of equilibrium in economics, then perhaps it lies in the way equilibrium is used, in its *mode of deployment* in economics. It is well known that the use of the equilibrium concept is characteristic of the neoclassical school – indeed, orthodox mainstream economics has been criticised from all points on the heterodox compass for its reliance on equilibrium thinking. The point of this chapter will be to elucidate the differences between orthodox and heterodox modes of deployment of the notion of equilibrium. In particular, I will argue that the concept of equilibrium in neoclassical economics is a hypostatisation. I start by considering a specific instance of equilibrium theorising – the case of the new-classical school of thought in macroeconomics – in some detail. I then make some more general comments on the deployment of equilibrium concepts in orthodox and heterodox economics. On the basis of this discussion, I then tease out some salient appropriate and inappropriate modes of deployment of the notion in science and, in particular, economics. A final section concludes by suggesting that heterodox currents in economics may be well placed to contribute by articulating a more dialectical conception of equilibrium.

An instance of neoclassical equilibrium theorising: the new-classical school

The first thing to note about Robert Lucas's *Models of Business Cycles* (1987) is its claim to be dynamic. It is at the heart of the heterodox critique of orthodox equilibrium theorising that the latter is essentially static, so the claim is significant.

Lucas starts his book – the text of a series of lectures given in Helsinki in 1985 – by setting out the subject matter, the 'process of dynamicisation' of macroeconomics (Lucas 1987, p. 3). He insists on his interest in 'the law of motion' of the system, 'the law of motion . . . of the system as a whole' (Lucas 1987, pp. 7, 14).

> Dynamic economic theory . . . has simply been reinvented in the last 40 years . . . While Keynes and the other founders of what we now call macroeconomics were obliged to rely on Marshallian ingenuity to tease some useful dynamics out of purely static theory, the modern theorist is much better equipped.
>
> (Lucas 1987, p. 2)

It all sounds very encouraging: whereas in the past we had to 'tease useful dynamics out of a purely static theory', nowadays we are 'much better equipped'. The reader might be forgiven for thinking that our theory is no longer essentially static. However, that is not I think what Lucas is saying at all. It does no violence to his argument to read him as saying that 'the modern theorist is much better equipped' than the Keynesians were 'to tease useful dynamics out of a purely static theory' because while the Keynesians were 'obliged to rely on Marshallian ingenuity' for this purpose, we have something much better, namely 'the general formalism of dynamic games'. It is this formalism which constitutes the critical difference between his own standpoint and Keynesianism: 'the main criticisms of Keynesian models and their use in formulating policies . . . are all straightforward consequences of the acceptance of the general formalism of dynamic games that I am using here' (Lucas 1987, p. 16). So we can see that Lucas's references to the 'dynamicisation' of macroeconomics cannot be interpreted as a claim that the 'purely static theory' has been *replaced* by a dynamic one. Rather the purely static theory is retained, but we now are much better equipped to tease useful dynamics out of it. As we shall see, any claim that the purely static theory had indeed been replaced would in any case be a misrepresentation of the neoclassical theoretical standpoints discussed in his book.

At the heart of the models of business cycles to which the title of Lucas's book refers is something called a Bellman equation (Lucas 1987, p. 14, equation 2), in which

> Optimal behaviour means maximising the sum of immediate and long-term pay-offs . . . the system (2) is in *equilibrium* when each agent i chooses the action a_i which [optimises at the individual level] given the actions . . . chosen by all the other agents.
>
> (Lucas 1987, p. 14)

The individual agent is in equilibrium when he adopts the action which maximises his present and expected future payoffs, given the actions chosen by the other agents – and we have a social equilibrium, a Nash equilibrium, when this is true for everyone:

> I have described the actions a_i simultaneously chosen by agents as a (Nash) *equilibrium*, but the term equilibrium in this (now entirely standard) context obviously does not refer to a system 'at rest', nor does it necessarily mean 'competitive' equilibrium in the sense of price taking agents, nor does it have in general any connection with social optimality properties of any kind.
>
> (Lucas 1987, pp. 15–16)

The important claim here is that the Nash equilibrium is not 'at rest'.[1] It is important to understand the sense in which the system is not at rest. The reason is simple, and set out early in the first chapter after the introduction:

> A useful model . . . is going to take the form of an explicit description of the way the economy evolves through time. We will want to consider

1 The claim that the equilibrium implies nothing for social welfare is also interesting and I have dealt elsewhere (Denis 2004) with the issue of the relationship between individual optimisation and social optimality, with particular reference to Lucas.

> stochastically disturbed systems, so let e_t denote independent drawings of an exogenous shock from some fixed distribution $G(e)$, and let the law of motion of s_t, a complete description of the 'state of the system' at date t, be denoted $s_{t+1} = F(s_t, e_t)$.
>
> (Lucas 1987, p. 7)

The system is thus not at rest because it is being continually shocked away from the equilibrium it would have if there were no such shocks. But those shocks are entirely exogenous: nothing in the model affects the magnitude or sign of the shock in each period – other than the statistical properties of the distribution $G(e)$, which themselves are a timeless given. Hence the equilibrium which actually obtains at one moment in time is different – not only from the equilibrium at any other point in time but also from the equilibrium if applied again to *the same point in time*, since the drawing from the distribution $G(e)$ of exogenous shocks will be different. A simulation based on the Bellman system of equations will therefore appear to show change over time. But this is an impoverished notion of change, as we will see below. It is, in Lucas's own phrase, dynamics teased out of a purely static model, a very long way indeed from a truly dynamic conception of the economy.

So in what sense is this an equilibrium approach? It is an equilibrium approach because the Bellman equation is timeless. Given the tastes and preferences of individuals, technology and government policy, the outcomes will always be the same for the same shocks: none of these things is itself endogenised. Each *individual* is in permanent equilibrium, as each is assumed to optimise subject to the actions of all other agents; the *society* is in continuous equilibrium as all individuals continuously optimise. With the addition of the shocks, change takes place but not development; it is just the same distribution of events being randomly selected from. The system has been 'dynamicised' – time has been impounded. But the time involved is fake time, fictitious time: it is logical time, not historical time. What comes first is equilibrium, and process is secondary. We move between one equilibrium position of the economy and another. But there is no rhyme or reason to the transition, and no arrow of time. Any actual simulation would be just as good in reverse.

Without examining the subsequent models which Lucas discusses, at a level of detail which would rapidly become tedious, we can say that these features, and, in particular, this use of the concept of equilibrium, remain for the duration. For Lucas, change is *equilibrium change* throughout, as he himself indicates later on with reference to the Kydland and Prescott Real Business Cycle model (Lucas 1987, p. 38, equation 10):

> The study of (10) thus provides an indirect method for . . . describing the competitive equilibrium motion of the endogenous state variables . . . the equilibrium behavior of the capital stock can be simulated by drawing shocks $\{x_t\}$ from the assumed distribution $G(x', x)$ . . . the model generates

> time series for these variables [sc consumption, employment and factor prices] as well.
>
> (Lucas 1987, pp. 38–9)

In the conclusion of the book, Lucas returns to the purpose of the series of lectures which it records, that is, to consider, particularly in relation to policy, 'the incorporation into macroeconomics of economic dynamics' (Lucas 1987, p. 103). So again, in Lucas's view we have a macroeconomics which is still 'purely static', but into which it is possible to 'incorporate' some dynamics – that is, 'dynamicising' it does not overthrow it completely or change it beyond recognition, but adds something to make the static equilibrium account a better approximation to the world. So the static equilibrium concept is still primary, and dynamics, however favoured by Lucas, a secondary add-on. The whole fails to become truly dynamic: the 'dynamics' are too leaden, too tied to the statics.

To take what is perhaps the most important example of what is being left out here, it is highly significant that there is no systematic capital accumulation leading to a declining marginal efficiency of capital, or rate of profit, as suggested by Keynes and Marx. Much of chapter V of Lucas (1987) is taken up with a discussion of a model due to John McCall, which he reviews very favourably. There is *no capital* in this model:

> The general equilibrium in this McCall economy is one of autarchy: workers do not have to deal with capitalists, since capital (trees) is so abundant that it is not worth while to establish property rights in it; neither do they trade with each other, since all any of them obtain from their labor is a single good: apples.
>
> (Lucas 1987, pp. 59–60)[2]

Later on Lucas (1987, pp. 98–100) discusses his own 1972 paper 'Expectations and the neutrality of money', in which 'capital in all its forms was excluded from the model' (Lucas 1987, p. 100). Of course, any model has to make simplifying assumptions and leave things out, but to imagine that one can have a whole economic research programme in which the 'elephant in the living room' of self-augmenting capital is systematically ignored must surely lead to utter sterility of thought.

This section has looked at a specific instance of neoclassical deployment of the equilibrium concept and suggested that Lucas's notion of equilibrium change

2 While in this model there is no capital, McCall goes to the opposite extreme and beyond with labour: the model also supposes there is a *continuum* of workers (Lucas 1987, p. 60) – that is, between every two workers there is another worker: not just an infinity of workers, but a higher infinity. Neither of these assumptions is particularly uncommon in neoclassical macro models.

Notice that Lucas tacitly concedes here that a useful concept of capital will address social relations, not things: there is no capital, not because the means of production, apple trees, do not exist, but because no one wants property in them, that is, to exclude anyone else from using them.

represents an impoverished notion of process and time, in which equilibrium and stasis dominate process and motion, change is without development, and time without history. The next section looks at the use of *equilibrium* in neoclassical economics more generally.

Equilibrium in neoclassical economic thought in general

Giocoli, in a history of mid-twentieth century neoclassical economics (2003), distinguishes between two self-images of the neoclassical school – the *systems of forces* (SOF) and the *systems of relations* (SOR) views. Giocoli's thesis is that over, very roughly, the century from the 1890s to the 1980s, a transformation took place in the self-image of neoclassical economics, from SOF to SOR views of what economics is about. The SOF image is the traditional view of the discipline as investigating economic processes, including equilibrating processes, generated by market and non-market forces. The SOR image presents economics as a discipline investigating the existence and properties of economic equilibria in terms of the mutual consistency of the given formal conditions, and ignoring the processes required to generate and underpin it. Both embody equilibrium theories, but in the SOF image the focus is on 'the explanation of *how and why* a certain equilibrium has been reached', while in the SOR image the focus is on 'the demonstration of the existence of an equilibrium' though, Giocoli immediately adds, citing Hutchison, not its actual, empirical existence but its conceivable, logically or mathematically non-contradictory 'existence' (Giocoli 2003, p. 5).

Giocoli identifies the principal theme of the development of economics in the 1930s as

> the last important attempt to preserve, if not enhance, the traditional image of economics as a discipline dealing with systems of forces, that is, as a discipline which investigates the actual working of the economic system and, in particular, its equilibrating processes. In a nutshell, the attempt consisted of a reformulation and extension of the notion of economic equilibrium to a multi-period, multi-agent setup . . . as well as an explicit appraisal of the out-of-equilibrium functioning of the economic system. Hence the key theoretical issues became the modeling of the disequilibrium processes . . . The program developed inside a more general theme, that of turning the static neoclassical equilibrium theory into a dynamic one.
>
> (Giocoli 2003, pp. 135–6)

Giocoli argues that this attempt was unsuccessful, partly because of 'unavoidable inconsistencies between the willingness to investigate the disequilibrium behavior of the economic system and the desire to preserve the notion of equilibrium as the central category of the analysis' (Giocoli 2003, p. 137). Unsurprisingly, perhaps, it was the preservation of equilibrium which triumphed:

> What remained of the original program was, on the one side, the reduced version of dynamics developed in Samuelson's *Foundations*, namely, the analysis of the system's local stability around an equilibrium whose actual emergence was no longer an issue to be dealt with, and, on the other, the general equilibrium model of Arrow and Debreu, which did embrace a multi-period approach but compressed all the dynamics into a time-zero instantaneous equilibrating process. Even when the latter model provided in the late 1950s the benchmark for the analysis of global stability, no actual theory of the out-of-equilibrium functioning of the system could be offered as this was simply impossible in an Arrow and Debreu world.
>
> (Giocoli 2003, p. 137)

Giocoli touches here on some of the key issues concerning the way the equilibrium concept has been deployed in the neoclassical mainstream. Two things are clear from his account. First, even the SOF version implies that the economic system can be understood as an equilibrium: the image of the economy as a whole is one of a static equilibrium, the maintenance of which is explained by the operation of equilibrating forces, forces which only operate once the equilibrium has been disturbed by exogenous forces. This leaves us with a profoundly static and ahistorical image of society: there is no theoretical basis here for immanent development or novelty. The recognition that the model might not be entirely adequate is addressed not by replacing it with some more essentially dynamic concept, but by adding dynamics on to the static core, notably by relaxing the perfect information assumption and introducing various models of learning and expectations adjustment. Second, the SOR version is clearly significantly worse, focusing the entire attention of the researchers involved on the study of theoretically conceivable equilibrium states, divorced from any possibility of learning about the equilibrating processes which might lead to and sustain such states. This, I submit, cuts us off from all possibility of learning about the forces which actually underpin and shape our society.

In this section I have suggested that there has been a degeneration in the use of the equilibrium concept by the neoclassical school, that the concept has become more divorced from reality and has tended to take on a life of its own. In the next section attention turns to the way the concept of equilibrium has been used by two heterodox writers, Marx and Keynes.

Equilibrium in heterodox economic thought

To support the contention that I am building up to, namely that it is not the concept of equilibrium itself which is faulty in neoclassical economics, but the way it is used, this section will identify legitimate uses of the notion in two heterodox thinkers – Karl Marx and Maynard Keynes.

Keynes, for example, asserts his agreement with the first 'fundamental postulate' of the classical system that 'the wage is equal to the marginal product of labour' (Keynes 1973, pp. 5, 17). The implication is that demanders of labour are always in equilibrium: at each given level of the wage, firms employ just that quantity of labour which maximises profits. Should the wage exceed the marginal product of labour, each firm would have an interest in reducing employment, and vice versa if the opposite should hold. In equilibrium agents have an incentive to continue their current behaviour; out of equilibrium they have an incentive to change their behaviour so that the equilibrium is restored. In exactly this vein, Victoria Chick gives us a further instance of Keynes making use of the equilibrium concept:

> A producer decides how much to produce, and possibly how to price the product, then waits for the market's response. If his expectations are falsified, he might change the level of output ('might' because one observation is not enough to know with any confidence that the 'error' was not random). If he was (roughly) right, and no new information from other sources changed his expectations, he would continue as before. The same outcome for all producers, on average, would produce an equilibrium of output and employment.
>
> (Chick 2002, p. 4)

Marx, too, adopts this approach at many points in his analysis. The exchange of commodities in what Marx calls 'simple circulation of commodities' (Marx 1954, p. 154) takes place at their values, their incorporated social labour. But this is only so on average, in equilibrium: 'The exchange . . . of commodities at their value is . . . the natural law of their equilibrium' (Marx 1959, p. 188). Specific prices will deviate from values because of all sorts of extraneous circumstances – errors and frauds, the exertion of force, temporary over- and under-supply, and so on.

Exactly the same goes for Marx's account of the relation between market prices and prices of production in the circulation of capital:

> if the commodities are sold at their values . . . very different rates of profit arise in the various spheres of production . . . But capital withdraws from a sphere with a low rate of profit and invades others which yield a higher profit. Through this incessant outflow and influx . . . it creates such a ratio of supply to demand that the average profit in the various spheres of production becomes the same, and values are, therefore, converted into prices of production. Capital succeeds in this equalisation, to a greater or lesser degree, depending on the extent of capitalist development . . . The incessant equilibration of constant divergences is accomplished so much more quickly, (1) the more mobile the capital. . .; (2) the more [mobile the] labour-power. . .
>
> (Marx 1959, pp. 195–6)

Thus equilibration depends on the flow of capital and labour between industries to bring about an equal rate of profit in every industry, an equalisation which cannot be expected to be either instantaneous or perfect. Price will equal value in simple commodity circulation, or price of production in capitalist circulation – the equilibrium price in each case – only by coincidence, as it were, in the process of the higgling of the market. The resulting equilibrium is a temporary and ephemeral balance of forces, destined to be disturbed by the passage of time – exactly as Keynes's equilibrium levels of output and employment in the passage from Chick cited above.

It would be mistaken, however, to see this as fundamentally in conflict with the notion of equilibrium deployed in much of neoclassical economics. The price of production is the long-run equilibrium price in the sense that it is the centre of gravity which continually attracts the commodity's price. Deviations of price from price of production are due to exogenous factors, such as fluctuations in supply and demand, whose effects are eliminated over time by movements of capital between firms and industries. It would be mistaken to claim here that equilibrium characterises the short run and disequilibrium the long run. It is indeed the case that the higgling of the market will bring about the accidental equality of price and price of production from time to time. That is an accidental and ephemeral instantaneous equilibrium. But the reason for the deviation from equilibrium which then ensues is the intervention of exogenous factors, not the continuation of any endogenous processes. Were exogenous shocks no longer forthcoming, the system would settle down to a long-run equilibrium. The magnitude and frequency of such shocks are a matter of the volatility of the exogenous variables and raises no difference of principle between a system which is normally very close to equilibrium and one which is frequently shocked further away. Even with the continuation of such shocks in the longer run the equilibrium acts as an anchor for the system and continues to determine long-run values of the key variables.

In both the examples from Keynes and Marx, use has been made of the same equilibrium concept which characterises neoclassical economics, a use which is appropriate in context. No social science can do without this concept of equilibrium. But the approach of writers such as Marx and Keynes (Denis 2002) is, in different ways indeed, profoundly historical: the economic system – population, technology, accumulated wealth and the systems of social relations within which economic activity takes place – are all conceived of as evolving and developing, not in response to the impact of exogenous factors, but from their own inner nature.

A critical example for both concerns the accumulation of capital. Both writers regard capital accumulation – the subordination of consumption to production – as a critical component of the economic system. Both draw the conclusion of a long-term decline in the rate of profit, with periodic crises of realisation due to the overproduction of capital. For them, a static situation with a given capital stock can be imagined and studied, but the mere passage of time must disturb the imagined peace – it is in the nature of the capital stock to grow, to self-augment, without the need for any prompting by exogenous variables.

The main purpose of this chapter is to sketch a fundamentally dynamic concept of equilibrium which is legitimate and productive in economics, and to present a *prima facie* case that, instead of that concept, neoclassical thought deploys a fundamentally static concept of equilibrium: a substitution which I argue hypostatises *equilibrium*. The purpose of this section has been to underline that the static notion is not in itself flawed – indeed, heterodox writers such as Marx and Keynes make free use of it – but inappropriately deployed in neoclassical macroeconomics. The next section spells out appropriate and inappropriate modes of deployment of the equilibrium concept in greater detail.

Ways of deploying the equilibrium concept

I want here to sketch very briefly what I regard as an appropriate mode of deployment of the equilibrium concept in science.[3] I will first identify two possible valid uses of *equilibrium*, one static and one dynamic, and the one invalid use of the concept with which, I think, neoclassicism can fairly be charged. Then I want to explore in a little more detail the dynamic version, which, though both valid and important, is not employed in neoclassical economics.

I think we can identify three salient uses of the concept of equilibrium.

1 The system is at or near a normal state or condition such that small moves away from it set in motion forces returning the system to the attractor state. The system can be modelled as an equilibrium state. For some purposes, the equilibrium can simply be assumed to hold. If greater detail is required, a distinction can be made between a short and long run: in the long run, the system may be considered as, at least approximately, or for practical purposes, in the attractor state; in the short run, (a) changes in exogenous variables shock the system away from the attractor state, and (b) divergence of the system from the attractor state itself sets in motion forces returning it to its normal condition.

   Note that the degree of volatility does not in itself make a profound difference of principle: one system may actually be in the equilibrium condition for lengthy periods, and only occasionally moved away from it by relatively small shocks. The forces returning the system to equilibrium following a shock may be sufficiently damped to avoid overshooting. Or the opposite may be true – the system is highly volatile, frequently shocked away from equilibrium, with strong endogenous forces leading to overshooting. Both cases may be modelled as equilibrium systems, with average levels of key variables of the system determined by their equilibrium values, the difference being only that the short-run dynamics are empirically more important, and complex, in the second case. As Weintraub says, encompassing respectively the long-run and short-run perspectives just mentioned, equilibrium in a stable dynamic system can be viewed 'as a state of no

3 I will ignore here the concept of an unstable equilibrium, which, though an important theoretical concept, is not, I think, of practical relevance in the present context. All references to equilibrium here are to be understood as at least locally stable.

motion, and as an attractor of arbitrary motions of the underlying dynamic process' (cited in Giocoli 2003, p. 138).

This is nevertheless an essentially static concept of equilibrium, in the sense that stasis is primary, and any dynamics in the model are entirely secondary and subordinate. In appropriate contexts this mode of deployment of *equilibrium* is unexceptionable: indeed, I have suggested that it is to be found frequently in heterodox writers such as Marx and Keynes.

2 For a system operating in a far-from-equilibrium context, in the sense described by Prigogine and Stengers (1984),[4] the processes underpinning the continuity of the system as a whole may be conceived as equilibrating processes; however, the equilibrium towards which they are moving is *never* even approximately attained, as other processes intervene and prevent them from running to their conclusion. The persistence of the system as a whole depends on the maintenance of these equilibrating processes, and the disequilibria giving rise to them. The equilibrium which constitutes the logical terminus of each of these processes, were it ever attained, would also spell the dissolution of the system itself. 'Living systems are never in equilibrium. If they were, they would be dead!' (Ferdinand 1976, p. 224).[5] In this use of the term, the *equilibrium* of the equilibrating processes is not how they *are*, but how they *would be*, were those reactions to continue in isolation. *Equilibrium* is an abstraction, a helpful one perhaps, but not one which describes anything that exists.

This is an *essentially* dynamic use of the equilibrium concept: the dynamics of the processes underpinning the system are primary, and any possible, conceivable state of rest is secondary, an extrapolation. The difference between the two valid deployments of the concept of equilibrium can be put thus: in an at-or-near-to-equilibrium system only changes in exogenous variables can move the system as a whole away from its equilibrium. In the far-from-equilibrium case, the system exhibits regularity and orderliness, a homeostasis in living organisms, but these do not themselves constitute an equilibrium: the mere passage of time brings about changes in the system as endogenous changes in the processes on which the system depends bring about the growth and decay of the whole. A notable feature of both the static and dynamic concepts is that, to be meaningful, the theory has to articulate the equilibrating processes, that is, to give an account of the operation of those forces when the system is out of equilibrium, regardless of whether its normal condition can be characterised as an equilibrium.

4 Prigogine and Stengers argue that 'social evolution' has usually involved an unfortunate importation into the social sciences of concepts such as optimisation and equilibrium which had only a restricted validity even in their native domain of physics. Ignoring the *openness* of systems, we also ignore 'inertial constraints' (i.e. path-dependence, hysteresis), the possibility of surprises, the incorporation of time and history, and 'fundamental uncertainty' (Prigogine and Stengers 1984, p. 207).

5 The title of this section in Ferdinand (1976: 224) is 'Near-equilibrium and non-equilibrium reactions in metabolic pathways'. I am indebted to Harold Jefferies for pointing this citation out to me.

3 The attempt to apply the equilibrium concept, valid in the first kind of system indicated above, to the second, where it is not, constitutes a hypostatisation. It substitutes something which is merely an aspect, moment or tendency implicit in the system for the system itself. The argument of this chapter is that although valid applications of the first kind of equilibrium abound in neoclassical economics, as in other schools of thought in political economy, not only is the second kind absent in mainstream economics, a critical shortcoming in itself, but it is systematically replaced by the third kind, the illegitimate use of an equilibrium concept to describe a system which is dependent on the continuation of disequilibria. Earlier sections of this chapter, on Lucas and the neoclassical school, indicated some examples of this misuse.

I want now to sketch very briefly what I regard as an appropriate mode of deployment of the equilibrium concept in science ignored by neoclassical economics, the dynamic equilibrium concept identified at 2 above. For my main example (for which I am indebted to Pask 1998, pp. 75–7), I will look at the equation for the formation and dissolution of oxyhaemoglobin in the process of respiration:

$$\text{oxygen} + \text{deoxyhaemoglobin} = \text{acid} + \text{oxyhaemoglobin}$$

The equation above can be understood as expressing an equilibrium in which all four reagents exist together in stable proportions. Our theoretical understanding of the structure and properties of the molecules of each of the four reagents, and practical experiment and observation, can tell us what those proportions are, and what can be expected to happen if we exogenously change the quantity of any of the four in a closed system. This knowledge makes an essential contribution to our understanding of respiration. But we don't model respiration as an equilibrium, a state of rest to which internal forces will return us if we should be shocked away from it. On the contrary, we model respiration as a system of interacting processes: in the lungs the concentration of oxygen is high, pushing the equation from left to right. In the tissues of the body the opposite is the case and the equation proceeds from right to left. In each case the oxyhaemoglobin or, respectively, deoxyhaemoglobin, produced by these reactions, is swept away by the bloodstream: at each locus the disequilibrium is maintained and continues indefinitely. So the equilibrium relationship is understood as embedded in a process. It is understood as an attractor towards which one set of forces is bringing the system, at the same time as another set is pushing it away. Yet knowledge of the equilibrium, which in reality could occur only with the death of the organism, is essential to understanding life.

The story told is an *essentially* dynamic one, in which equilibrium is an abstraction, a moment, a tendency. The notion of equilibrium points beyond itself: equilibrium in the cell to equilibrium in the lung, removal of oxygen from oxyhaemoglobin to oxidation of glucose, the transport of oxygen in the form of oxyhaemoglobin to the transport of the carbon dioxide generated in cellular respiration, the process of respiration to the processes of nutrition in this, and photosynthesis in other, organisms, and so on.

Neoclassical economics, by contrast, assumes that the economic system as a whole is always in or near an equilibrium and hence can be understood in equilibrium terms. Equilibrium is not understood as an abstract moment or aspect of a living system, but as an approximate description of the way things are. Movement and change can then be regarded as secondary, as the recovery of the underlying state of rest by adjustment to exogenous shocks. Hence, equilibrium as a valid aspect or moment of the real economic process is abstracted and turned into something lifeless and static. Any thing or process in the world is a unity of stasis and change, of continuity and discontinuity: to abstract a real part of that unity, and one-sidedly make it primary, is to hypostatise[6] or reify it. To do so denies the real process and presents the present, the *status quo*, as permanent.

Although characteristic of living systems, what has been said above applies much more generally. A further instance concerns the hydrological cycle of evaporation and condensation by means of which water vapour from the seas falls on land as precipitation and is returned to the sea by the drainage system. Both condensation and evaporation are disequilibrium phenomena – they are phase changes in opposite directions between the liquid and gaseous states of water, and occur under opposite conditions. Evaporation occurs in the presence of relatively dry air and a source of energy. Just as in the case of the formation of oxyhaemoglobin, the process would rapidly run to equilibrium – and hence cease – in a closed system. The process can continue only to the extent that the now relatively humid air is removed and replaced by dryer air, by the action of air currents, themselves brought about by convection currents in the atmosphere as the planet exchanges heat with its environment.

In these cases we *cannot* model the condition of the system in question as an equilibrium. What is required is a dynamic model of each of the relevant processes underpinning the system, and their interaction. These processes can – and, indeed, should – be seen as equilibrating forces, forces brought into existence by the disequilibrium of the system, forces which in a closed system would lead to an equilibrium and the end of the system which they underpin. If the formation or dissolution of oxyhaemoglobin, or the evaporation or condensation of water, were to be in equilibrium, were to have run to completion, then there would be no respiration or hydrological cycle. To describe such equilibria may be helpful and add to our knowledge of the process at work. But what is being described is not a state or condition of the world, or even an approximation to it, but a hypothetical condition – the logical terminus of a process taken in isolation.

6 'The worst enemy of clear thinking is the propensity to hypostatise, i.e., to ascribe substance or real existence to mental constructs or concepts' (Mises 1978). Kant says of the dogmatists that 'they hypostatise what exists merely in thought, and take it as a real object existing . . . outside the thinking subject' (Kant, cited in Sorensen 2003, pp. 299–300).

Equilibrium and stability

Up to this point I have exclusively used the term *equilibrium* in the more formal, demanding and precise sense normally adopted by economists. In this sense, an equilibrium, once achieved, will endure for ever, barring exogenous shocks. However, the term is also used also in a looser, more commonsense way to indicate an equal balance between opposing forces, without any assumption of persistence or permanence. The appendix to this chapter sets out the dictionary definitions of the term – starting with this commonsense meaning. In this usage, an initially weak army which is gaining strength and a stronger one which is becoming weaker will at some point find themselves in equilibrium. This is clearly not a formal equilibrium in the sense that only exogenous shocks will disturb it and endogenous forces will then restore it. I take no exception to this looser usage. Where there is indeed persistence it is often better to use the term *homeostasis*, but the two are often used interchangeably. On the first page of Gordon Pask's introduction to cybernetics, he explains that the theme of cybernetics is

> how systems regulate themselves, reproduce themselves, evolve and learn. Its high spot is the question of how they organize themselves . . . The crux of organization is stability . . . equilibrium . . . is always implied by the word stability . . . A great deal of cybernetics is concerned with how stability is maintained with 'control mechanisms'.
>
> (Pask 1968, p. 11)

So, according to Pask, much of cybernetics is concerned with the study of mechanisms which maintain equilibrium. But this is emphatically not the formal notion of equilibrium employed in neoclassical economics. We can see this when he discusses biological instances of control:

> The overall homeostatis,[7] preserving the organism, can be expressed as the conjoint action of many homeostatic systems, each preserving a structure or condition needed for the functioning of the others . . . The mechanism of breathing . . . maintains several homeostatic equilibria . . . [while] many mechanisms co-operate to maintain one equilibrium.
>
> (Pask 1968, p. 73)

This, I submit, is how economics should be.

Conclusion: from equilibrium to dialectics?

The neoclassical use of the concept of equilibrium has been criticised by post-Keynesians, Marxists, Austrians, institutionalists and other heterodox currents. This chapter has argued that there are two possible valid applications of the

7 This should read: homeostasis.

concept of equilibrium in economics. Any model of the economy will contain variables in a static equilibrium relationship: disturbances which move the variables from that relationship set in train equilibrating forces. On the other hand, any worthwhile model of the economy as a whole will impound its far-from-equilibrium status, and treat the processes on which it depends as equilibrating forces which can never reach equilibrium while the system as a whole persists. In line with its reductionist ontology, which denies the micro–macro dichotomy and attempts to reduce all economics to microeconomics, neoclassical economics ignores this distinction, and stretches the static equilibrium concept to circumstances where only the dynamic version is appropriate. The result is a hypostatisation: equilibrium, which is only an abstraction and extrapolation, the logical terminus of a component process taken in isolation, is extracted and one-sidedly substituted for the whole. The temporary is made permanent, and process subordinated to stasis, with clearly apologetic results.

I would like to conclude by suggesting that this hypostatisation exemplifies the contrast between formal and dialectical modes of thought, and that it is in the application of a dialectical notion of equilibrium that the heterodoxy can make its most telling contribution. Sciabarra (2000) argues that making process primary, which we might expect of Austrian economists, is the essence of dialectics, which we might (wrongly, in his view) identify with Marxism:

> One of the principles of dialectics is that in any analysis of any object of inquiry . . . our understanding of the object must include a focus on dynamics. How an object comes to be what it is, which forms it currently takes, and where it might be tending are all a part of its identity.
>
> (Sciabarra 2000, p. 141)

And:

> This view has ramifications for relations . . . conceived dynamically . . . Norman . . . argues correctly that 'we cannot construct change and motion out of static elements'. Our analysis must begin with the fact of change, from which we can abstract and inquire into particular moments . . . some economists in the Austrian tradition hold that process is one of the most important aspects of any analysis. Rizzo . . . argues, for example, that in the neoclassical 'static conception of time, the present is a virtual stop – the very negation of passage or flow'.
>
> (Sciabarra 2000, pp. 183–4)

If this view is, as I believe, fundamentally correct, the question 'What is wrong with equilibrium analysis in neoclassical economics?' can be fully answered only by contrasting it with a dialectical approach. Hegel, at the beginning of the *Science of Logic* (Hegel 1929, ch. 1), shows the inadequacy of a static concept of *being*: being consists of the two dynamic categories of coming-to-be and ceasing-to-be, of origin and decease. Hence, in reality, anything which *is*, can only be understood as in *transition*, and, as Keynes says, 'it is in the transition that we actually have our being' (Keynes 1973, p. 343 n. 3). Perhaps it is here that the heterodoxy can make its most telling contribution.

Appendix

The meanings of equilibrium

The *OED Online* (Simpson and Weiner 2000) entry under the catchword *equilibrium* starts with an etymology, according to which the word is derived from the Latin *aequus* equal and *libra* balance. In a physical sense *equilibrium* is, in the words of the first definition given,

> The condition of equal balance between opposing forces; that state of a material system in which the forces acting upon the system, or those of them which are taken into consideration, are so arranged that their resultant at every point is zero.
>
> (Simpson and Weiner 2000, 'equilibrium')

A *resultant* in turn is: the total or sum, material – or, metaphorically, other than material – force which is the equivalent of two or more forces acting from different directions at one point, or, more generally, the composite or final effect of any two or more physical or non-physical forces, the product or outcome of something (Simpson and Weiner 2000, 'resultant').

As an extension of this meaning of equilibrium, the *OED* introduces an 'equilibrium of temperature', where two bodies having the same temperature are said to be in such an equilibrium, since there is now no force causing either to change its temperature when the two are brought together. The implication is that a temperature differential or gradient introduces a force for change and hence constitutes a state of disequilibrium.

Extending the idea again, in a similar way but more systematically, the dictionary introduces the second definition of equilibrium, 'The state of equal balance between powers of any kind; equality of importance or effect among the various parts of any complex unity.' This implies that a state of formal disequilibrium, where the forces in some system were unequal and therefore there was a tendency to some change in that system, might still be considered an equilibrium, since the powers bringing about that change are equally balanced, and hence there is no tendency to change the rate of change itself: there is a steady state of change. Having subsumed not merely the *state*, but also the *rate of change* of a system, in a concept of equilibrium, there is little to stop one going further and assuming not a *constant* rate of change but one itself subject to steady change – a steady state of acceleration. And so on.

To illustrate:

1. An object which has fallen from a height is in equilibrium on the ground, as the acceleration towards the earth's core due to gravity is exactly offset by the acceleration away from it due to the reaction of the ground the body is resting on. The body is stationary: we have an equilibrium of forces in which the body is at rest.
2. Before impact, the body is moving, but can be considered, if it has reached terminal velocity, to be in equilibrium, since the force of gravity is, again, exactly matched by the resistance of the air, such that the body is subject to no new net acceleration and tends merely to continue its uniform motion, to continue its descent at the same speed.
3. Before reaching terminal velocity, the body is accelerating, but if it is accelerating at a constant rate, such as $9.8\,ms^{-2}$, then again it can be said to be in an equilibrium by a similar argument.
4. But if the rate of acceleration is declining, as indeed it must be if it is to reach a terminal velocity, then if the rate of decrease of the rate of acceleration is constant, it can still be said to be in equilibrium.

The implication is that the concept of equilibrium seems to be indefinitely extensible, via an infinite regress, to mirror the changing nature of the real world. We will return to this point.

Thus far we have considered only the general notion of equilibrium, not the specific use of the term in economics. In the 1993 Additions to the Second Edition, the *OED Online* dictionary notes a specific instance of the meaning in economics: 'A situation in which supply and demand are matched and prices stable.' Examples are cited from Jevons, the *Encyclopaedia Britannica*, Keynes's *General Theory* – 'Effective demand, instead of having a unique equilibrium value, is an infinite range of values' – Hanson, *The Economist* and Frank Hahn. By the argument above, however, *equilibrium* in economics could refer, much more widely than merely to the equality of the forces of supply and demand, to any situation of stasis, of constant change, of constantly changing rate of change, or any regularly occurring changing situation. So we have stock and flow equilibria, equilibrium prices and rates of inflation, and so on. In sum, it seems, *equilibrium* – in economics as well as in natural science domains – need not imply stasis, but the forces involved in the system under consideration are lawful and regular rather than arbitrary.

This is significant for our enquiry, since it creates the impression that, taking the argument to its logical conclusion, we can understand *any* situation whatever as in some sense an equilibrium: all we need to understand the situation is to know what the powers are which are involved, and the magnitudes and rates of change of the variables resulting from the interaction of those powers. It is clear that neoclassical economics makes this implication. To take the example of economic growth, considered in a well known textbook:

> Usually, equilibrium means that things are not changing. Now we apply equilibrium not to levels but to growth rates and ratios. The steady state is

> the long-run equilibrium in growth theory. Along the *steady-state path*, output, capital, and labour grow at the same rate. Hence output per worker and capital per worker are constant.
>
> (Begg *et al.* 2003, p. 428)

But this approach is an illusion: in this vision we approach reality only by an infinite regress. To assume that we know all the powers involved, their magnitudes and rates of change of variables caused by the interaction of the powers is to assume that we already know the system, that the infinite regress has been completed. Note, also, that as we go from rest to constant motion, and from constant motion to constantly varying motion (constant acceleration), and from that to constantly varying acceleration, we still retain the unwanted baggage of smoothness and constancy at each stage. However far we may proceed along this infinite regress, we never reach the concrete, we never apprehend time, novelty or the intrinsic lumpiness of the world.

References

Begg, D., Fischer, S. and Dornbusch, R. (2003) *Economics*, 7th edn, London: McGraw-Hill.

Chick, V. (2002) 'Theory, Method and Mode of Thought in Keynes's *General Theory*', paper presented at conference of the International Network for Economic Method, University of Stirling, September.

Denis, A. (2002) 'Collective and individual rationality: Maynard Keynes's methodological standpoint and policy prescription', *Research in Political Economy*, 20, 187–215.

Denis, A. (2004) 'Two rhetorical strategies of *laissez-faire*', *Journal of Economic Methodology*, 11 (3), 341–57.

Ferdinand, W. (1976) *The Enzyme Molecule*, Chichester: Wiley.

Giocoli, N. (2003) *Modeling Rational Agents. From Interwar Economics to early modern Game Theory*, Cheltenham: Edward Elgar.

Hegel, G.W.F. (1929) *The Science of Logic*, trans. W.H. Johnston and L.G. Struthers, 2 vols, London: Allen & Unwin.

Keynes, J.M. (1973) [1936] *The General Theory of Employment, Interest and Money*, vol. VII of *The Collected Writings of John Maynard Keynes*, eds Austin Robinson, Elizabeth Johnson and Donald Moggridge, London: Macmillan/RES.

Lucas, R.E., Jr (1987) *Models of Business Cycles*, Oxford: Blackwell.

Marx, K. (1954) [1887] *Capital. A Critique of Political Economy*, I, London: Lawrence & Wishart.

Marx, K. (1959) [1894] *Capital. A Critique of Political Economy*, III, London: Lawrence & Wishart.

von Mises, L. (1978) *The Ultimate Foundation of Economic Science*, Kansas City: Sheed Andrews and McMeel. Online: Ludwig von Mises Institute www.mises.org/ufofes/ch5~4.asp (accessed 27 May 2005).

Pask, G. (1968) [1961] *An Approach to Cybernetics*, London: Radius Books/Hutchinson.

Prigogine, I. and Stengers, I. (1984) *Order out of Chaos. Man's new Dialogue with Nature*, London: Random House.

Sciabarra, C.M. (2000) *Total Freedom. Towards a Dialectical Libertarianism*, University Park PA: Pennsylvania State University Press.
Simpson, J.A. and Weiner, E.S.C., eds (2000) 'Equilibrium', *OED Online*, Oxford University Press. (*Oxford English Dictionary* 2nd edn, Oxford: Clarendon Press, 1989) dictionary.oed.com/cgi/entry/00077256 (accessed 5 December 2003).
Simpson, J.A. and Weiner, E.S.C., eds (2000) 'Resultant', *OED Online*, Oxford University Press. (*Oxford English Dictionary* 2nd edn, Oxford: Clarendon Press, 1989) dictionary.oed.com/cgi/entry/00204541 (accessed 5 December 2003).
Sorensen, R. (2003) *A Brief History of the Paradox. Philosophy and the Labyrinths of the Mind*, Oxford: Oxford University Press.

Name index

Subject index